Helen C Black

Pen, Pencil, Baton and Mask

Biographical Sketches

Helen C Black

Pen, Pencil, Baton and Mask
Biographical Sketches

ISBN/EAN: 9783337028947

Printed in Europe, USA, Canada, Australia, Japan

Cover: Foto ©Thomas Meinert / pixelio.de

More available books at **www.hansebooks.com**

BIOGRAPHICAL SKETCHES

MRS. BLACK

Ex Libris
C. K. OGDEN

PEN, PENCIL, BATON AND MASK

BIOGRAPHICAL SKETCHES

BY

HELEN C. BLACK

AUTHOR OF 'NOTABLE WOMEN AUTHORS OF THE DAY'
'TWO WOMEN'S TRAMP IN SOUTH AFRICA' ETC.

WITH SIX PORTRAITS

LONDON
SPOTTISWOODE & CO., NEW-STREET SQUARE, E.C.
AND 54 GRACECHURCH STREET
1896

All rights reserved

TO
LADY BARNBY
WITH MUCH AFFECTION

NOTE

EIGHTEEN of the following biographical sketches have not hitherto been published. Of the remainder, many ran as a series in 'Lloyd's Weekly' under the title of 'Half Hours with Celebrities'; some few have appeared in 'The World'; portions of two, respectively, in 'Black and White' and in 'The Sketch'; 'The Queen,' 'St. Paul's'; while two were written for 'The National Press Agency.' These are now republished, with the respective Editors' kind permission, and are revised, corrected, and brought up to date.

HELEN C. BLACK.

CONTENTS

	PAGE
SIR JOSEPH BARNBY	1
MARIE CORELLI	6
SIR EDWIN ARNOLD, K.C.I.E., C.S.I.	12
ELLEN TERRY	18
W. E. NORRIS	28
CARLOTTA ADDISON (MRS. LA TROBE)	34
SIR HENRY IRVING	41
MADAME ALBANI-GYE	46
GEORGE ALEXANDER	50
MRS. PARR	57
SIR AUGUSTUS HARRIS	64
SARAH GRAND	70
HENRY ARTHUR JONES	77
MRS. CROKER	83
GEORGE R. SIMS	92
KATE TERRY (MRS. ARTHUR LEWIS)	98
JOHNSTON FORBES-ROBERTSON	105
MRS. AMYOT	115
F. C. PHILIPS	127
SOPHIE LARKIN	134
FREDERIC COWEN	139
EMILY GERARD (MADAME DE LASZOWSKA) AND DOROTHEA GERARD (MADAME LONGARD DE LONGARDE)	144
WILLIAM TERRISS	162
MARION TERRY	166
THE REV. PROF. MOMERIE, M.A., D.Sc., LL.D.	170
GENEVIEVE WARD (MADAME LA COMTESSE DE GUERBEL)	178
G. A. STOREY, A.R.A.	182

CONTENTS

	PAGE
DORA RUSSELL	188
GEORGE GROSSMITH	194
KATE PHILLIPS (MRS. H. B. CONWAY)	199
THE VERY REV. R. HERBERT STORY, D.D., LATE MODERATOR OF THE GENERAL ASSEMBLY.	205
MRS. PATRICK CAMPBELL	213
HENRY BLACKBURN	216
MRS. L. T. MEADE	222
FRED TERRY AND MRS. FRED TERRY (JULIA NEILSON)	229
KATE RORKE (MRS. GARDINER)	234
EDWARD TERRY	238
MARY MOORE (MRS. JAMES ALBERY)	243
CLIFFORD HARRISON	248
MISS LE THIÈRE	254
W. H. PREECE, C.B., F.R.S.	260
OLGA NETHERSOLE	268
JOSEPH HATTON	273
PHYLLIS BROUGHTON	283
FITZGERALD MOLLOY	287
GERTRUDE KINGSTON (MRS. SILVER)	294
THE REV. PROF. SHUTTLEWORTH	299
MISS FORTESCUE	306
TIVADAR NACHÈZ	311
BEATRICE WHITBY (MRS. PHILIP HICKS)	316
ARTHUR à BECKETT	320
LOUISE JOPLING-ROWE	327
CICELY RICHARDS	333
ANNIE S. SWAN (MRS. BURNETT SMITH)	338
TRISTRAM ELLIS	345
MRS. KENT SPENDER	351
VIOLET VANBRUGH (MRS. ARTHUR BOURCHIER)	357
EVELYN MILLARD	361
FANNY BROUGH	366

LIST OF PORTRAITS

MRS. BLACK . . . *Frontispiece*

SIR JOSEPH BARNBY . . . . . *To face p.* 1

MADAME SARAH GRAND . ,, 70

REV. PROFESSOR MOMERIE, LL.D. . . ,, 170

MR. CLIFFORD HARRISON ,, 248

MR. ARTHUR À BECKETT . ,, 320

SIR JOSEPH BARNBY

SIR JOSEPH BARNBY[1]

IF there be one thing more remarkable than another—outside the musical gifts—of the distinguished oratorio-leader and composer, Sir Joseph Barnby, it is his absolute hatred of humbug, his gentle, genuine nature, and his simplicity of character. The same atmosphere is observable throughout the family, from your gracious hostess herself to the three children of the house—a bright, friendly pair of Westminster scholars, and a sweet young maiden just at the age where 'the brook and river meet.' The air is full of winning cordiality and kindness in this home of harmony and of love, for Lady Barnby has the happy knack of bringing people together, and of impressing her charming and vivid personality on them, and the young people have imbibed the unconscious influence of their parents, and are natural and unaffected as heart could wish.

Sir Joseph Barnby was born at York, and is the youngest of fifteen children—a circumstance which naturally caused his father to be a poor man. 'But remarkable in his way and a perfect dear,' says his gifted son. From both sides he inherited musical talents, and it is on record that the Sheriff of York's sister well remembered the infant Joseph standing on her knee and at the early age of two years singing, in true if lisping accents, the anthem 'Lord of all power and might,' though Sir Joseph laughingly declares that, with six elder brothers choristers at the Minster, he was so steeped in music that the achievement was not half so wonderful as

[1] Since the serial publication of this sketch, the death of the much-beloved musician has taken place.

it looks. At the age of eight he too took his place in the choir, and before he was fifteen he held an organ in a church, while during his holidays every spare moment was spent in reading. 'I was an omnivorous reader,' he remarks, 'and was so wrapped up in my books that I used to forget meals. Architecture ran music close, and has ever been a passion with me.' When the young chorister's voice was no longer suitable he gave lessons for a year, and then in family council it was decided that he should be sent to the Royal Academy of Music, where, being saturated with the compositions of old Church masters, he got to the head of the class in his first term. He remained a few years at the Academy, and the end of his career there was marked by what he calls 'a failure,' though it was one that tended to his own credit. It was the first time the Mendelssohn scholarship, founded by Jenny Lind, who collected between two and three thousand pounds for the purpose, was put up for competition. Among the thirty-nine candidates were Arthur Sullivan and himself. These two came out at the top, and ran a dead heat, so it had to be tried for again. 'Sullivan got it,' says Sir Joseph, 'and very justly. I do not know any composer whose works have given me more pleasure. I look on him as the greatest that England has ever produced, and she may well be proud of him.' About this time the young musician was summoned to York to relieve his brother, who was doing a large musical practice in his native town, but a few weeks' experience were sufficient to show him that his thirst for knowledge could never be satisfied in that city, or obtained in the volume that he desired. Curbing his ambition, however, for a time, he made a home for his father and sister, which had a steadying effect, and when the beloved and honoured father passed away suddenly and, a year later, his sister married, he felt free to soar. 'I wrote to my brother,' says Sir Joseph, reflectively, 'and said I would go to London if he could find me a post at 30*l.* a year. He found one at the exact sum as organist of St. Michael's, Queenhithe. I had not enjoyed that princely income more than three months before I was offered a new appointment with an additional 10*l*. at St. James the Less, which you can almost see from this window. I had never contemplated much success, but,' he adds softly, after a pause, ' in going through life I have been uniformly lucky.' After a period of ten months the first great opening came. The young musician was appointed organist and director of the choir at St. Andrew's, Wells Street, where he worked a complete reformation. Hitherto the music in churches had been of the antiquarian type, while its performance was often discreditable; indeed, Sir Joseph remembers on his first visit to St. Paul's Cathedral only two choirmen were present, both altos, and one of these was an old man who evidently thought himself one too many, as he sat down and took no part in the service. But another state of things was speedily brought about. Gathering around him good men, among whom was Edward Lloyd, who remained with him for four years, the new organist and director introduced Gounod's sacred music for the first time with orchestral instruments. Just about that time he received an offer from Messrs. Novello to act as their musical adviser, and these two events enabled him to begin the development of modern cathedral music, for which the world owes him a deep debt of gratitude. In a year or two, at the suggestion of the Novellos, and with their assistance, he organised the famous Barnby choir, and began a series of concerts every year at St. James's Hall. Sims Reeves, who had sung at some of them, pressed the idea of turning it into an oratorio choir, and so began that wonderful series of oratorio concerts that became known all over the country. In one evening alone Beethoven's ninth Choral Symphony and the great ' Mass in D ' were given, and in the same series Sir Joseph Barnby resuscitated the ' Great Passion ' of Bach, together with innumerable other works. As time went on the indefatigable leader found that his engagements were considerably interfered with by three heavy services on Sundays and two on week-days, and he exchanged St. Andrew's for St. Anne's, Soho.

It was at Westminster Abbey that Sir Joseph Barnby first started the series of Passion services that, later, he inaugurated with full orchestra every Friday during Lent at St. Anne's, the fame of which spread all over the land. Going to Dean Stanley, he obtained his sanction for special services on Tuesday in Holy Week, whereat the 'Great Passion' of Bach should form a meditative service. Those who were present can never forget the impressive and thrilling nature of that performance. Sir Joseph got together a surpliced orchestra and chorus of five hundred people, who assembled in the semi-darkness of the transepts. As soon as the great organ pealed out, the procession moved along, carrying their instruments, and appeared to the crowded congregation who were assembled in the nave, in the broad glare of gaslight under the organ screen. Jenny Lind, who was present, remarked to Sir Joseph that she had never been more affected in all her life. His whole soul is in the orchestra. Unlike the organ, where each stop is of wood or metal, he regards each stop as an immortal soul in orchestra, and with his great choir, composed chiefly of persons of strong individuality, he welds them into one harmonious whole with the utmost subtlety of mind and sympathy. 'It is not,' he explains, 'like a general who orders his men in a certain direction. You make them think with you—identify themselves with you.'

In 1870 the Franco-Prussian war sent Gounod to these shores, just about the time the Albert Hall was completed. The opportunity was hailed to raise a great choir, of which Gounod was conductor for eighteen months. When he returned to Paris, and it became necessary to seek for a successor, Sir Joseph Barnby was unanimously elected to the conductorship of the Albert Hall Choral Society.

After two or three years of successful work in conjunction with this society, he was offered the exceedingly lucrative post of Precentor and Director of Musical Education at Eton, and as this was not to interfere with his work at St. Anne's, or with the conductorship at the Albert Hall—where he has introduced more new works of a large calibre to London audiences than any man living—he found it possible to accept the offer, and carried on his Eton work for seventeen years. In addition to these duties he has conducted at most of the State receptions—of the Shah twice, after an interval of eighteen years—of the Czar, of the Emperor of Germany, and also at the opening of the Fisheries and Colonial Exhibitions, &c. In 1892 a vacancy occurred in the principalship of the Guildhall School of Music, and Sir Joseph, feeling a strong desire to enter once more into the fierce fight of metropolitan life, accepted the appointment, although it entailed the serious loss of half his income. It is characteristic of the unselfish nature of the man, who had done all that he could do, and who felt that the power of doing good in such a position would be gigantic, to let no such mundane considerations stand in the way. He had scarcely accepted the post when he received an intimation from Lord Salisbury that the Queen had notified her desire that he should receive the well-merited reward of knighthood. As a composer Sir Joseph Barnby has contributed largely to the world of music. Among many works are his oratorio 'Rebekah,' his motett 'King all Glorious,' the cantata 'Psalm xcvii.' composed for the Leeds Festival, together with hundreds of anthems, part-songs, services, trios and chants. Indeed, hard work, 'the genius of industry,' may be said to be the keynote of his existence.

Alike in private life and as a conductor, Sir Joseph Barnby possesses a personal magnetism that draws all hearts towards him. Souvenirs of the esteem and affection in which he is held abound on all sides of Lady Barnby's drawing-rooms. Albums in handsome Russia leather bindings, with inscriptions and autographs illuminated by hand in gold, red, and blue—one from his 'German admirers in London, in grateful remembrance of his "Parsifal" concerts at the Royal Albert Hall'; another from the E.C.R.V. band at Eton, with a silver salver, a gift of the Musical Society; a massive silver tray from the entire staff of the Professors of the Guildhall School; a silver casket from the Cardiff Musical Festival committee, and innumerable other offerings. Lady Barnby mentions, with tender pride, the marriage gift presented to Sir Joseph, a dessert-service of gold dishes and silver candelabra and candlesticks from the Royal Choral Society, Albert Hall, to which they added a tea and coffee service 'for his wife,' which she has used every day since. Then there are a great four-handled Eton loving cup, a silver-gilt rosewater dish from the choir of St. Anne's; the beautiful old punch bowls, gifts from Sir Arthur Sullivan and the students of the Royal Academy of Music, and silver cigar and cigarette cases galore.

But amidst all these outward tokens of affectionate appreciation the noble-hearted wife and devoted children have a deeper joy and pride in the knowledge of what Sir Joseph Barnby has done for the world in elevating and refining the soul of the public by work that will never die.

MARIE CORELLI

It is an open secret that Miss Marie Corelli has the strongest objection to being 'interviewed,' and has never even availed herself of the oft-repeated invitation to 'sit for her photograph.' In the circumstances, therefore, the reminiscences of sundry hours spent in her company, together with a subsequent conversation during a journey with a group of people who as yet know her not, save through her writings, may convey some idea, not only of the personality, but also of the character of the gifted young author.

Reminiscences first. A chance meeting and a graceful act of courtesy on her part began what has since developed into a firm friendship. Some few years ago, there happened to be a particularly brilliant meeting of the popular Salon of Science, Literature, and Art. The rooms were filling fast, and the whole assembly thronged in to listen to a recitation by a clever American humourist. Gently urged on by the stream, I found myself standing near a large divan, already well filled by guests. Among them sat a little fair girl, robed in white silk, with a ribbon of the same colour round her abundant golden-brown hair. She looked so youthful as almost to suggest the idea that she could hardly yet be 'out.' Catching her eye, she smiled, and with a baby hand made a gesture to indicate that space could be made for me. No word was spoken until the recitation was concluded, and then, on thanking her cordially, a brief conversation on music ensued, which at once convinced me that here was no ordinary individual. Gliding on from one subject to another, the talk presently turned on the people around, and, having previously heard that Miss Corelli was expected to be present, I asked my companion if she knew her by sight. 'Yes,' said the young lady, demurely, 'I may say that I know her fairly well, and ——' But before the sentence was finished, a friend had claimed her attention and pronounced her name. Then, giving me a little mischievous bow and an arch smile, she was borne away to the refreshment room. And as time went on, many more meetings came about, and, bit by bit, the young author's personality, surroundings, and writings became more and more familiar, and enabled me, without betraying any confidence, to enlighten the group of people aforementioned upon many points.

But a few days ago a journey had to be made to Hants on business. Arriving somewhat late at Waterloo, the carriages were nearly all full, and while I was hurriedly seeking for a place, a head was popped out at the window of a compartment, and I was bidden by a friendly voice to take a vacant seat therein. The voice proceeded from a bride, who, with her husband, was returning from a three months' honeymoon tour. Glancing round, it was pleasant to note that the two remaining passengers were also not strangers. One was an eminent divine, distinguished no less for his eloquence in the pulpit than for his genial nature. The other was Sister ——, a lady of renowned goodness and of ancient lineage. Amid cordial greetings and desired introductions the train sped on its way, and conversation soon became general.

'I see you have our favourite book in your hand,' said the bride; 'we bought it in Paris, and all Marie Corelli's other works in the Tauchnitz edition, and I am ashamed to say we smuggled them over, and are having them bound in morocco. Have you ever seen her? and is it true that she is very tall and stout, with prominent eyes, and an incipient moustache?' But ere I could reply for inward mirth, the clergyman remarked, in all good faith: 'I can tell you. She was pointed out to me in Rome, on the Prado, two years ago. She is a majestic and massive woman, with black hair, bound tightly round her head, dark eyes, a deep, contralto voice, and commanding presence. I was discussing her once with our mutual friend'—turning to me—'the late Edmund Yates, and I remember that he said he always pictured her to himself in classic draperies, with Greek symbols about her, and sandals.'

But at this juncture the situation became too much for my gravity, and a laugh was irresistible. 'For you are all so wrong,' I exclaimed, 'so funnily and entirely wrong. *I* know her personally—have known her for years. She is *petite*, and extremely fair, and her eyes are grey, and deeply set, and her hair is soft and fluffy, and curls round her head. Her voice, too, is sweet and silvery; she is so bright and joyous in manner, and, besides, she was not in Rome at all that year!' After various exclamations of surprise from my fellow-travellers, the Sister observed, with a smile: 'Well, as there is still nearly an hour before we arrive, and we are all admirers of her books, pray tell us all you can about her.' Musing awhile to collect my thoughts, I began with the mention of the meeting at the Salon, and continued thus: 'The *motif* of this work, "Barabbas," now in its sixteenth edition, was actually conceived when Marie Corelli was at her studies in a convent. By nature mystical and profoundly religious, she was even then vividly impressed by the beauty and the reality of the services at the chapel, and used to long to write down these impressions. The idea grew and strengthened until it finally resulted in this impassioned and intellectual work, which none can carefully read without being struck by the powerful style of the young author, the conscientious and earnest feeling, the reverence for the subject, and the deeply poetic vein displayed throughout.'

'Quite true,' said the clergyman, 'I entirely agree with you. Opinions may differ, always will differ, on every subject under the sun, but, as Clement Scott lately observed, the public taste is healthy—not morbid, and that public taste has given a verdict for Marie Corelli of which she has every reason to be proud, but, pardon me, I interrupt you.'

'Her works,' I resumed, 'have been more widely translated than those of any living author, into Dutch, Swedish, Russian, German, French, Modern Greek, and Spanish. "Barabbas," indeed, can be found in Gujurathi, and both that and "A Romance of Two Worlds" in Hindustani. This of itself is sufficient to indicate the popularity of her books, abroad as well as at home, where they have all passed into many editions, and are as extensively circulated now as when they were originally brought out. Her letter-boxes and autograph-albums are treasures that would tempt a collector to make raids on them, so numerous are the letters from all parts of the world—from crowned heads, from distinguished statesmen, and so forth, down to the working miners in Australia and in California, who, reading her books, seem mysteriously constrained to write to her with the plain address of "London, England," simply to express their gratitude and admiration.'

'From her writings,' remarked the bridegroom, himself a 'double first' Oxford man, 'it is manifest that Miss Corelli must be well versed in all the classical authors, living and dead, and is likewise a good linguist.' 'That is so,' I replied, 'and her library is remarkable. The books are so well worn, too. She delights in Plato, nearly knows her Shakespeare by heart, and studies Dante and Goethe in the original.'

'"Thelma," "A Romance of Two Worlds," and "Ardath,"' observed the bride, 'were first favourites for a long time. My husband used to prefer "Vendetta" and "Wormwood." But now we think that her latest book, "The Sorrows of Satan," bids fair to run "Barabbas" close in public favour. It is so vivid and realistic, and so powerfully descriptive.' The Sister put in a word for 'The Soul of Lilith,' but confessed that she 'could hardly make a choice,' and added, after a pause, as she touched the crucifix at her side, 'But she is of our faith, and evidently a great student of the Bible, for she is so correct in all her details.'

'Yes; that is absolutely true,' I answered, 'which makes it the more remarkable that, quite lately, she was accused of making a "Gospel according to Corelli," and of inventing the two angels at the sepulchre on the Resurrection morn!'

'Ah!' said the clergyman, quickly, with a smile, 'then her accuser had not read *his* Gospel according to St. John'; and, taking a little volume of Holy Writ from his pocket, he read aloud the 20th chapter to the end of the 12th verse, emphasising the words, 'Two angels in white!'

A silence followed, and then a question—essentially feminine—was hesitatingly asked by the bride. 'And her dress? the Greek fillet, the sandals, the classical draperies?'

'All purely imaginary,' I said, 'as poor Mr. Yates found out for himself during his last visit to Cannes, where Miss Corelli and her party were staying at the same hotel. They all became devoted friends, and enjoyed many a laugh over his preconceived notions of her. She dresses after the manner of ordinary mortals—with a difference. Possessed of highly cultivated artistic tastes, alike observable in her surroundings and costumes, she wears suitable as well as pretty clothes. The last time I went to see her, she was clad in a tea-gown composed of old gold-coloured silk, beautifully embroidered, and a darker shade of golden-hued velvet made the train, which became well the childish figure and fair young face. She showed me, on her wrist, a unique bangle, a much-prized birthday gift from two friends, on which was mounted in classical design, according to an old drawing of the ancient Egyptian era, a specially rare green scarabæus, six thousand years old, purposely procured from the museum of royal scarabæi in Cairo. At my request she played to me on a peculiarly sweet-toned mandolin with much skill and expression. There were flowers grouped here and there, and on the grand pianoforte stood a large autograph picture of the Prince of Wales, his recent gift at Homburg.'

Time was speeding, and but five minutes remained ere the train was to arrive at the station. Turning to the Sister, who had been listening with rapt attention, I remarked: 'There is a touching incident to relate, which is not only interesting in itself but is highly indicative of the deep feeling of reverence with which Marie Corelli approached the task of writing "Barabbas: a Dream of the World's Tragedy." Her desk was placed opposite a picture after Guido's "Ecce Homo," under which a red lamp burned continuously. A friend presented her with a gold penholder, set with a single pearl at the top. With this pen alone, consecrated to the work, Marie Corelli wrote, from the first word to the last, the book which is now so famous.'

'It is deeply interesting,' said the ecclesiastic, with a hearty handshake, as the train glided in and the party prepared to disperse. 'I, for one, can assure you I never had a pleasanter journey in my life, and I shall look forward to the honour of being introduced some day to the scholarly and gifted young writer.'

SIR EDWIN ARNOLD, K.C.I.E., C.S.I.

POET, *littérateur,* journalist, traveller though he be, the handsome flat wherein Sir Edwin Arnold finds a *pied-à-terre* bears few indications of his eventful life or of his long residence in India and wanderings over the Land of the Rising Sun, whose people he learned to love so well. A large square anteroom leads into what is naturally the most interesting portion of his home—the bright, cheerful study so characteristic of the man. A tiny despatch-box —the companion of many journeys—stands on a small table, and is quite large enough for one who, with such orderly, methodical habits, knows where to put his hand on any paper required, and 'can write on the top of a hat as well as anywhere else.' The bookcases contain only a few relics of a once vast library, for Sir Edwin dislikes accumulations, and considers that portable property is a great nuisance. Wherefore he has twice dispersed his books and household gods among his children, so as to be free of effects; nevertheless, there are some little possessions of interest which he retains, 'only for the present,' he remarks significantly. 'Those who see my flat know I live elsewhere; and though I make books I never keep them.' Among the pictures on the walls there is one of the Emperor of Japan on horseback, another of Prince Siddartha drawing the curtain over the couch of his sleeping wife before he went forth on his act of renunciation, and a fine proof-before-letters engraving of Noel Paton's 'Oberon and Titania.' There are plenty of deep, comfortable lounging-chairs, presumably for the use of his friends; for Sir Edwin himself, with perfect physical health, never knows what it is to be tired or to have had even one headache, and attributes it to the fact that he never frets, never hurries, and looks upon life as a fine art, and that it is as reasonable to study to preserve a healthy body for the soul as it is for a good soldier to keep his scabbard in order for the useful blade. And yet in a career so chequered, so full of incident, adventure, and unceasing work, it can only be the bright, optimistic spirit within that enables Sir Edwin Arnold to declare that, having done everything, seen everything, known most people, and had a vast experience of the world, he has a contented mind, and that to him to-morrow is always better than to-day. If asked when he is happiest, he would say on the present occasion, and he works simply because he loves work. Hence it is that his *entourage* is of slight importance; and though he laughingly assures you that he feels somewhat as Dr. Johnson felt when Boswell told him he was going to write his life, and could almost answer in the same words, 'I will take your life if you do,' he yields to your request for a few particulars of his career, 'for auld acquaintance sake and a wish to please.'

A born poet and a student from childhood, Edwin Arnold simply was weaned on books, and remembers well, when he was five years old, his father, who always did things on a large scale, sending up to his room a washing-basket full of quartos and folios, among which those of Dampier and La Perouse first fired his imagination with a love of history, of geography, and of travel; while Pope's 'Iliad' he would devour in bed, turning his shoulder to the window to catch the last glimpses of the waning light.

His schooldays were passed at King's School, Rochester, and King's College, London; after which he was elected to a scholarship at University College, Oxford, where he won the Newdigate prize for his English poem on 'The Feast of Belshazzar,' and the following year was chosen to give the Address to the Prime Minister, Lord Derby, on the occasion of his being installed Chancellor of the University. Leaving Oxford with high honours, he was elected Second Master in the English Division of King Edward VI.'s School at Birmingham, and later, turning his footsteps towards the East, he was appointed Principal of the Government Sanskrit College at Poona, and Fellow of the Bombay University. The young Principal's quick mastery of Oriental languages and keen insight into the complex Oriental character, together with an innate tact in dealing alike with the native princes, the heads of departments, and the students, enabled him to be of considerable use in educational affairs, and he was twice thanked by the Governor in Council for his services. Nor was he distinguished in official and social life only. With the physical vigour and activity which do not generally go with powerful intellects, he was an ardent sportsman, and had many thrilling adventures while in pursuit of 'big game' and out pig-sticking. Neither was his pen idle during those years. He contributed constantly on subjects of natural history to various journals, and poetry, as well as more abstruse subjects, also occupied his attention. An early work of his was 'Education in India'—a question in which he was deeply interested—followed by 'Griselda: a Drama,' and 'Poems, Narrative and Lyrical'; after which followed 'The Euterpe of Herodotus' (which he translated from the Greek text, with vocabulary in English, Sanskrit, and Marathi) and 'The Book of Good Counsel'—a metrical translation of a celebrated Sanskrit classical work. Following these came a history of the Administration of India under the late Lord Dalhousie. Among other productions were 'The

Poets of Greece,' 'Hero and Leander,' and 'The Indian Song of Songs'; by-and-by the famous and delightful epic poem upon the life and teaching of Buddha, 'The Light of Asia,' charmed all the world, and passed through more than sixty editions in England and eighty in America.

Among some of Sir Edwin Arnold's earlier works, which are as widely read to-day as when they were first issued, are volumes respectively entitled 'Indian Poetry,' 'In an Indian Temple,' 'The Song Celestial,' 'Poems National and Non-Oriental,' 'The Secret of Death,' 'Death—and Afterwards,' and 'Pearls of the Faith, or Islam's Rosary,' the 'Pearls' being the ninety-nine beautiful names of Allah (Asmá-el-Husná), with comments in verse from various Oriental sources. In later years he has published 'Indian Idylls,' 'In My Lady's Praise,' 'Lotus and Jewel,' 'Potiphar's Wife and other Poems,' 'Japonica,' &c. With 'The Light of Asia,' and 'With Sadi in the Garden,' must be bracketed one of his most successful works, 'The Light of the World,' which has lately been reissued in an *édition de luxe*, profusely illustrated with special designs by Mr. Holman Hunt, and which is dedicated to the Queen. A late volume of poetry is entitled 'The Tenth Muse,' which is 'Ephemera, the Muse of Journalism,' and is dedicated by invitation to the Duchess of York. In prose, two deeply interesting books have a fascination of their own, called 'Seas and Lands' and 'India Revisited.' He has also written a play in four acts, entitled 'Adzuma, or the Japanese Wife,' and a prose work, 'East and West.'

Sir Edwin Arnold's foreign Orders alone are a collection of curiosities. 'The Light of Asia' brought him the decoration of the White Elephant from the King of Siam; the Order of the Lion and the Sun came from the Shah of Persia on the production of another fascinating volume, 'With Sadi in the Garden; or, the Book of Love,' a poem founded on a single chapter of the work of the Persian poet, Sadi. In later years, during his visit to Japan, the Emperor conferred on him the Order of the Rising Sun, which carries with it the dignity of *Chokunin* of the Empire; not to speak of the Imperial Order of the Medjidieh from the Sultan, and the Imperial Order of Osmanieh. The decoration of Companion of the Star of India he received on the occasion of the proclamation of the Queen as Empress of India; and eleven years after he was created Knight Commander of the Indian Empire. He is likewise a Fellow of the Royal Asiatic and other societies, and Honorary Correspondent of the Geographical Society of Marseilles.

In 1861, when peace was restored, Sir Edwin Arnold quitted India for a brief rest after the harassing fatigues and anxieties of the Mutiny, and returned to England. It was then that his long and close connection with the 'Daily Telegraph' began, almost, it may be said, by accident. He paints in vivid word pictures how he was sitting alone in a punt in one of the most picturesque nooks of the river Dart, with fishing-rod in hand, basking in the quiet sunshine, with a copy of the paper beside him. His eye lighted on an advertisement in the journal for a leader-writer, and in a moment the current of his thoughts was changed. Should he or should he not answer it? On the one hand, he must resign the freedom of his official position, and give up his beloved India; on the other, a residence in London, but the companionship of his children. It was a momentous question. Slowly and deliberately Edwin Arnold weighed the merits of each course, with the result that he decided to apply for the post, to resign his appointments abroad, and to cast in his lot with the new mission of the popular press. It was a great change to one who had been practically his own master in the luxurious Eastern world, whether in the bustle of official position or in the solitude of the jungle, to consign himself to a town life and to the directorship of others. The brilliant young leader-writer soon found himself at home and happy in Fleet Street with congenial spirits, and ran up the scale so rapidly that it was not long before he joined the editorial staff. From that never-to-be-forgotten summer day in the punt to the present, he has contributed between nine and ten thousand leading articles to the columns of the 'Daily Telegraph,' besides a long series of letters written during his residence in Japan, and when India was 'revisited.' He describes in characteristic words the fascination the Japanese people have for him. 'They are so polite, cheerful, and clean,' he says, 'so simple in mode of life. They love old people, they respect their fathers and mothers, and are free from avarice.'

It was Sir Edwin Arnold who suggested to the proprietors of the 'Daily Telegraph' and who organised the first expedition of Mr. George Smith to Assyria; he was also largely associated with the arrangements made on both occasions for sending out Mr. H. M. Stanley by that journal, in connection with the 'New York Herald,' to follow up the work of David Livingstone, and he relates an anecdote à propos of these expeditions. When Mr. Stanley was consulting him about a code of laws to be drawn up in dealing with the people, Sir Edwin suggested that it should contain 'death to any man who killed an elephant—noble, useful animal—for the sake of getting a paper-knife made out of its tusks,' and, jokingly, death to any one who called his own river and mountain in Africa (the Edwin Arnold river, which runs up into the Congo, and Mount Edwin Arnold, between Victoria and Albert Nyanza) by any other names. That geographical immortality has to be strictly defended is proved by the recent conduct of the Intelligence Department of the War Office, for in one of its late maps the name of Mount Edwin Arnold had been omitted, and that of Lobaba substituted—an error that has since been corrected.

With a mind attuned to all that is lofty alike in ideas and in aims and full of the imagery of poetry, Sir Edwin Arnold possesses a peculiar simplicity of character, together with a magnetic power of sympathy, and a detestation of all uncharitableness. His conversation is full, now of sparkling anecdote, anon of thrilling pathos, as may suit the subject, while the gentle, courteous manner has a charm all its own. His brightness is infectious; it seems to brace and invigorate even the most depressed of those with whom he comes in contact, and to cause them to look upon life through his own rose-coloured glasses, as he quotes, in low, earnest tones, from 'The Light of the World':

> 'Our worst of woes
> Is like the foolish anguish of the babe,
> Whereat the mother, loving most, smiles most.'

ELLEN TERRY

In her long white embroidered robes as Guinevere, Miss Ellen Terry might pass for a girl of nineteen. Time deals tenderly with the gifted artist. Would that it could be made to stand still altogether with her as far as the public is concerned, for there can never be a second Ellen Terry, and her name, shining alone in its lustre, will be handed down to generations of posterity.

But a little while ago you were at Mr. Johnston Forbes Robertson's (the Sir Lancelot of 'King Arthur'), and gazed for long at a lovely portrait of her on the wall. She seemed to look down from her frame with a witching smile as you and the actor conversed about her, and recalled one after another of her great histrionic triumphs. Can it be possible that it was painted nearly twenty years ago? It might have been taken only the other day; but it is a fact that it was about that date exhibited at the Royal Academy, and was executed by the painter-actor while in his teens.

And her voice! The 'Terry' voice! It follows you home through the fog and the frost, with its rich, musical cadence, its perfect and harmonious utterance, its clear, bell-like notes, its tones of pathos and unutterable feeling. And the tears that tremble unshed in the blue eyes in the strongly emotional scenes—anon a happy, girlish laugh! Who does not know it all, and love her for it? There is something so delicious, too, in her underlying sense of humour and her keen appreciation of fun. Quite lately a most comical little incident occurred, which, though simple in itself, was strongly provocative of mirth. She had driven herself in her pony cart to her cottage in the country for a brief 'Saturday to Monday' rest, as is her wont when engaged in particularly hard work. On her return journey, wishing to be entirely alone and uninterrupted, and in open air among the beautiful surroundings of Nature to study and think out the play, her only companion was a kitten in a basket at the back of the cart. But the kitten mewed and cried, and sadly disturbed the current of her thoughts. She took it out of the basket and placed it by her side, where it sat contentedly enough, gazing at her as she declaimed her words aloud, the only other witness—the pony! By-and-by she reached the village inn at Sevenoaks, one of her halting-places during the two days' drive. Going up to her dressing-room, Miss Terry prepared for a private rehearsal, and arranged a row of candles, for footlights, before a large swinging cheval-glass. The kitten, who seemed to know what it was all about, surveyed her quietly from a chair. She was presently 'spouting away,' with arm uplifted in tragic gesture in a most telling scene. It was a supreme moment. Suddenly 'click' went the spring—the looking-glass executed a hasty somersault! It seemed to jump at her as though it would topple her over. The kitten, much astonished, leaped high in the air; then, as the mirror righted itself, caught the reflection of its own little person therein, and made a succession of such ridiculous antics and absurd contortions, after the graceful fashion of kittenhood, that Queen Guinevere almost rolled on the floor in paroxysms of merriment. If the good people below heard the rippling peals of laughter they must have thought that there was something exceedingly funny to come off in at least one scene of 'King Arthur.'

But to be serious. Looking back through a vista of years, it appears as if your first vivid remembrance of the great actress dates from an early representation of 'The Merchant of Venice,' at the old Prince of Wales's theatre, when, as Portia, she sent the public into ecstasies over the celebrated speech, 'The quality of mercy is not strained,' and the delightful badinage of the scene that followed. Not only remarkable genius was displayed there, but the finished training, the cultivation and unceasing study that she brought to bear upon it. In her childish days she had shown such an extraordinary depth of pathos and skill in juvenile Shakespearean characters that it was even then confidently predicted that she had 'a great future in store'—a prophecy that her subsequent brilliant career has abundantly realised.

Turning over at random a multitude of cherished old playbills of later years, in which her name appears, picture after picture of her rises distinctly in the mind. Her Mabel Vane in 'Masks and Faces,' Lilian Vavasour in 'New Men and Old Acres,' Olivia, Juliet, Ophelia, Desdemona, Beatrice, Viola, Cordelia, Lady Macbeth, and many others. But it is idle to meditate in which part she is best. There is but one reply to such mental queries. She is best in each. And now it has come to her latest *rôle*, and each can form his or her own judgment of her absolutely perfect Queen Guinevere.

Now it is a fact that, since the production of 'King Arthur,' countless letters have poured in from 'country cousins,' and the like, couched in more or less affectionate terms: 'Do write us a long account of Ellen Terry as Queen Guinevere. What does she say in such and such a scene? How does she look when she says it? Describe her dresses accurately. Go into graphic details and tell us everything,' and so forth. This is a 'large order.' You could no more 'describe' her wonderfully artistic apparel than you could the inner appearance of the planet Jupiter! And as to 'how she looks,' and 'says,' and 'does it,' it would need the entire pages of a newspaper, and the pen of a Clement Scott, to give any adequate idea. Besides, there is a covert hint in the queries. In a moment of weakness you somewhat meanly struggle out of the difficulty through the medium of sixpenny wires : 'Description impossible ; come, see for self.' While on the subject, it may be recorded that there is a perfect passion in the minds of many people to obtain her autograph, for which many cunning little subterfuges are devised, often through friends. Enjoying the privilege of a much-valued friendship with the great artist, it has not infrequently been your own lot to receive fat little albums or 'birthday books' (stamps for return omitted), with gushing letters enclosed, running thus : 'Do pray try to coax Miss Ellen Terry to write her name in my book, or a verse, or something she has said on the stage, or a proverb—anything. I should value it for ever after.' Not for worlds would you take such a liberty! You get out of this by a post card curtly saying 'cannot,' which often evokes an indignant reply card, 'Say, rather, *will* not.—X.Y.Z.' Miss Terry is simply pestered with such requests ; but, in her goodness of heart and tender charity, she, too, devised a little scheme, and requested a small fee for consenting, the which formed a goodly sum for a child's cot at some hospital.

But little do the 'butterflies' and idlers know of the vast demands on her time and strength, in the art for which she lives and in which genius and ever-constant work exhaust alike body and mind. Her best friends are those who recognise this and leave her most in the quiet and peace that she so greatly needs. But there is one question on which you are able to gratify the longing of those, who, knowing her not save before the footlights, often express curiosity as to her immediate surroundings. 'Though you need not exactly localise the spot,' she whispers, with an arch smile. Wild horses should not extract the information ! Those horrid little albums ! They would soon make their way to her private abode ! Well, then, it is not a hundred miles from Kensington, and is one of a certain set of red-brick buildings with a big garden in front. Directly you enter you feel that it is not, somehow, as other houses. The staircase is hung with original engravings, each of whch is full of interest. A litter of music lies near the open grand piano in the square, yellow drawing-room, with its amber-coloured hangings ; a big, restful couch—a comfortable lounge for a weary player—is pushed near the fire, with little table, loaded with books, at hand, and a bouquet of white hothouse lilac, while other white flowers, hyacinths, and pale Gloire de Dijon rosebuds are carelessly yet artistically grouped here and there and fill the air with fragrant perfume. The numerous pictures and photographs would take hours to inspect thoroughly. Here are Adelina Patti, Sarah Bernhardt, Eleanora Duse, and many of the Terry family. Two lately added are particularly interesting just now—one is of her niece, Mabel Terry Lewis (youngest child of the celebrated Kate Terry, Mrs. Arthur Lewis), who made such a promising *début* in 'A Pair of Spectacles,' and showed that she inherits not only the voice but other charming attributes of this beloved family ; the other is a fair little nephew, Horace, aged seven (the son of Mr. Charles Terry), who, on the same evening, and at the same theatre, made his first bow to the public in Mr. Arthur à Beckett's pretty play 'Faded Flowers.'

By the way, his little part was too soon cut out, owing to the stern decrees of the L.C.C., simply from the accidental omission to procure the necessary ten days' previous licence. As the play was only produced at five days' notice it was obviously impossible to cut each of those days in two. One evening two myrmidons of the law called at the theatre and took the clever child in charge, whereat the baby actor up and spake boldly, with threat of future vengeance, 'Well, never mind, when I'm a man I'll pay them out,' the which terrible menace must have alarmed his captors overmuch. Meantime the bread was taken unnecessarily out of the child's mouth.

And there is one who sits in a great armchair, knitting, and with the identical kitten curled up peacefully on her lap, whom all love and delight to honour, and this is an elderly lady, with serene and beautiful face and silver hair, who has made her home with Miss Ellen Terry for over thirty years, and who is the great player's most beloved and devoted friend.

W. E. NORRIS

UNQUESTIONABLY it may be said of Torquay that it is one of the fairest, nay, quite the fairest spot on the south coast of England. Situated high above the rivers Exe and Teign on the one side and the Dart on the other, the thickly wooded cliffs and picturesque buildings, the luxuriant foliage and ever-turning, twisting roads—from each point of which fresh beauties are discovered—conspire to make what was described by Tennyson in his youth as 'the most lovely sea-village in England.' It is said that Napoleon Bonaparte, on landing when Torquay was yet in its infancy, exclaimed enthusiastically, 'What a lovely country! How much it resembles Porto Ferrajo in Elba!' Now, in these latter days, when the hand of time has mellowed the work of man, and, with the utmost artistic judgment, every natural advantage has been fully developed, there is, indeed, nothing left to be desired to render the beautiful town an ideal residence in all seasons of the year. It is little wonder, therefore, that the residents regard it with peculiar affection and point out with pride that whilst in winter the climate is deliciously mild, being sheltered from the rough east and north-east winds, in the hottest summer it registers twenty degrees cooler than in London. This fact entirely disposes of the erroneous impression that prevails abroad and is so often quoted, 'If you go to Torquay in summer you will be roasted alive!'

It generally happens in life that results gained are by no means in proportion to the amount of physical labour and trouble expended to procure them. The present instance, however, is the proverbial exception that proves the rule. Having firmly resolved on one of the brightest days of an abnormally fine season that you will climb to the highest pinnacle of Torquay or perish in the attempt, to see the well-known and popular writer, Mr. W. E. Norris, it is delightful to find on reaching the summit that a strong and cooling sea breeze has arisen, while the glorious scenery around, and presently the hearty welcome of the genial author, more than repay you for the fatigue incurred. To the jaded Londoner, whose steepest ascent is generally Piccadilly, the circuitous and tortuous hills of Devon are at first somewhat appalling, for Nature has indeed been lavish in these gifts to this highly favoured county.

It is perhaps the extremely cheerful aspect of Torquay that is so striking on first sight. The diversified and charming scenery, the artistically built residences, each standing in its own garden, the distances that you see around, all give the place a beauty unsurpassed by any other health resort.

A sharp decline of a few yards from the iron gates of a carriage drive on the right side of the road, leads to the open hall door of a large, stone-coloured, substantial but rather rambling house, built literally on the side of a cliff. Running all along the front and sides is a wide, shaded asphalte verandah, whereof the supports are covered with clustering jasmine and clematis. Entering the hall, the first room on the right into which you are shown is manifestly the room where Mr. Norris composes his fascinating novels; while resting for a few moments you have leisure to glance around, and naturally your first attraction is the beauteous prospect from the open French windows. A light haze softens every outline, also the horizon where the deep blue of sky and sea merges into each other, varied only by the shadows of a few passing clouds which are reflected in darker tints on the water. As if to heighten the effect of the scene and to complete the picture, a fleet of Brixham trawlers opposite is just sailing out of the port where William of Orange landed in 1688, a glint of sunshine catching every sail in succession. Far away on the right, Paignton is visible, and dotted here and there in the foreground handsome villas of varied build peep out between the trees, no two houses apparently standing on the same degree of altitude.

The study window faces a slope leading to the yet further sloping lawn by a flight of narrow steps cut into the ground, flanked on both sides by a thick, low hedge of cotoneaster with its green leaves and crimson berries. The kitchen garden much further down is half hidden behind the golden yews, Portugal laurels, deodaras and araucarias that stud the lawn. All this is seen from the small but neatly arranged writing-table, where, however, no particular trace of its owner's craft is to be discovered, though a high cabinet near with narrow drawers looks as if it contained MS. The delicate yellow wall-paper makes a good background for many choice etchings and original engravings. A large Oriental curtain drapes the west wall and harmonises perfectly with the subdued tints of the window curtains and the rich hues of the thick Persian carpet on which no footfall can be heard. Bookcases of every description and shape, revolving and dwarf, narrow and broad, are tightly filled with well-selected and well-bound volumes, for Mr. Norris is as fond of reading as he is expert at writing, and, being a good linguist, his foreign collection is extensive. His favourite writers of fiction are Blackmore, Thomas Hardy, and Henry James, for whom he has the strongest admiration. 'The latter is a personal friend,' said Mr. Norris, 'for whom I have the greatest regard. His work, I think, is as true and attractive as he is himself, which is saying a good deal.'

It is the room of a student, but not too grave a student; it is luxurious, but not enervating; and on all sides it is indicative of the simple good taste, combined with an innate love and appreciation of all that is beautiful in nature and in art, that is among Mr. Norris's strongest characteristics.

There is a sense of rest and refinement in this peaceful and lovely home with its grand environments of sea and land that seems to match with the author's appearance. He is above the middle height, slight and graceful in build, fine dark-grey eyes that sparkle below a broad, clever-looking and thoughtful brow, while the high-bred, courteous manner has a charm all its own, and his conversation, which it is most difficult to get centred at all on himself, is full of brightness and interest.

So much is indicated by a man's surroundings that it is often easier to arrive at a correct conclusion of his habits and disposition by silent observation than by direct inquiry. The open piano yonder and vast heap of music, the splendid pink begonia in full bloom on a high stand beside the writing-table, alike imply that Mr. Norris is an ardent lover of music and has a passion for flowers. Both suspicions are correct. Meeting your inquiring glance on these subjects, before the question escapes you, he remarks, smiling, 'Yes, I care more for music and gardening than anything else. As to music,' he continues, the while turning over the pages of a volume of Bach, 'I have always loved it. I used to play the piano as a small boy, but being most incorrigibly idle, I declined —and much regret it now—out of school to take lessons, and I gradually neglected it again until I was grown up and had got rather too stiff in the fingers to do much good.

Of the technical side of music and composition I know just enough to be conscious of my own ignorance, therefore I am most unwilling to dilate on the subject. However, everybody has a right to his more or less ignorant preferences, and I may safely say that the older I grow the more I appreciate Bach. Among living composers I should venture to place Brahms first, but really I have no right to speak didactically upon such a matter. Now-a-days most people seem to think it necessary that they should choose between Schumann and Chopin. If that must be done—and I don't see why it should—I should have to class myself amongst the humble admirers of the former, much as I delight in the latter.' Hearing this you would fain coax him to the piano, but in vain. He smiles, shakes his head, and says he now plays only for his own amusement.

William Edward Norris was born in Cavendish Square, London, and is the younger, now the only surviving, son of the late Sir William Norris, formerly Chief Justice of Ceylon. The great house of his birthplace saw but little of his childhood, as all his earlier years were spent at Burrow Green House, a large, old-fashioned homestead taken by his father, near Godstone, where among the beautiful and extensive views of the Surrey Hills his inborn love of fine scenery was fostered and encouraged. He was first sent to school at Twyford, near Winchester, where the Rev. G. W. Kitchin, now Dean of Durham, was head-master. His next move was to Eton, where he spent four years, which he describes as 'four absolutely happy years,' living in the house of the Rev. J. J. Joynes, where he made many friends.

'I had a good time during those few years,' Mr. Norris remarks, as he tranquilly smokes a cigarette, and between the puffs seems to be thoughtfully recalling reminiscences of the past. 'I was sorry to leave, though I cannot pretend to have distinguished myself in any respect. I had a certain facility for the composition of

Latin verse, in those days considered an important branch of study at Eton, and this probably saved me from getting into any very serious trouble. Otherwise I was a decidedly lazy boy, and got on as comfortably as lazy boys used to do in the good old times when it was not thought essential to teach everything badly and nothing thoroughly.'

On leaving Eton, young Edward Norris went abroad to study modern languages, with the intention of entering the Diplomatic Service, but subsequently gave up this idea and was called to the Bar at the Inner Temple, although he never practised. It was then that he turned his attention to literature, contributing a short story, entitled 'M. Bédeau,' to the 'Cornhill Magazine.' This story showed so much originality and distinct talent that it was at once accepted. (Mr. Norris's own modest version of the transaction is: 'Much to my surprise it was published!') Being encouraged by Leslie Stephen, who was at that time the editor, the young writer soon sent in some more stories, and began his first novel called 'Heaps of Money,' in which the character of Mainwairing is one never to be forgotten.

'Very probably,' remarks Mr. Norris, 'without Leslie Stephen's kind encouragement I should never have written any novels at all. I must just say a word of the sincere respect and gratitude that I feel for him. He was by far the most conscientious and exacting editor with whom I have ever had to deal; but his criticisms were always right, and were expressed with the utmost consideration for the feelings of his contributors.' The first book was speedily followed by 'Mademoiselle de Mersac,' a truly interesting work, in which he guides us through three generations 'as gracefully,' to quote a sapient critic of that time, 'as a well-bred man might point out the portraits of his ancestors in the family picture gallery.' This popular book ran through the same magazine as a serial, and caused so much favourable criticism that the

first edition was immediately exhausted. Like all Mr.
Norris's works, it will bear more than one reading; with no
particularly strong plot, the interest is sustained by the vivid
delineation of character and the naturalness of incident.
It has now passed through many editions, and with many
of his works has wittily been described as having attained
that measure of popularity 'of which the outward and
visible sign is generally bad print and the superscription
" Fscap. 8vo. picture boards, 2s." '

'Matrimony,' 'No New Thing,' and 'Thirlby Hall'
followed during the next three years. The first of these
is distinguished by its clever character sketches, the
second is more conspicuous for the true pathos displayed
in many of the scenes, combined with the underlying
sense of humour prevailing in its pages, while the third
forcibly attracts the attention of the reader by the simplicity, power of style, and facility of expression which bring
every description of its scenes so truthfully before him.

It was after the publication of 'Thirlby Hall' that
people began to say freely that a second Thackeray had
arisen in these later days, not only with regard to Mr.
Norris's method and manner of writing, but in the brilliant finish of his literary style and in the quiet, good-
humoured cynicism combined with the pathos which
distinguished the great bygone writer.

'Adrian Vidal' was the next book, and this history of
an author is interesting as giving Mr. Norris's own views
on the profession of a novelist. 'The Man of his Word
and other Stories,' 'The Bachelor's Blunder'—out of
which surely a good play might be made—and 'My Friend
Jim,' all came out in the same year. No signs, however,
of any undue haste are visible in any of Mr. Norris's
writings. Each is characterised by minuteness of observation, quiet humour and conscientious study, and, crowning joy to the inveterate novel-reader, not a dull page is to
be found anywhere.

'Chris,' a charming story, 'Major and Minor,' and

'The Rogue,' 'Misadventure,' 'The Baffled Conspirators,' and 'Mrs. Fenton,' are the titles of other of the author's books. All his novels have previously run through different magazines or the principal weekly illustrated papers before being issued in the orthodox two- or three-volume form. 'The Rogue' has little or no plot, but a most interesting story is made of it by the ingenuity with which a series of episodes and incidents are woven together.

Although want of space prevents allusion to the whole of this valuable addition to the world of fiction, mention must just be made of a few other of Mr. Norris's books, as they are too good to be left out. 'Marcia,' 'Mr. Chaine's Sons,' 'Miss Wentworth's Idea,' 'A Deplorable Affair,' 'His Grace,' 'A Victim of Good Luck,' and 'Countess Radna,' a cleverly told tale of 'a marriage which is disappointed and a wooing thwarted,' all these suggest themselves at random as books to be recommended. His latest are 'Matthew Austin,' 'A Despotic Lady,' and 'The Dancer in Yellow.' The charm of Mr. Norris's works undoubtedly lies in the fact that, if somewhat slight in plot as before hinted, there is so much interesting incident, such bright conversation, and the stories are so well told that they carry away the reader to instructive as well as to amusing worlds of romance. Many of their characters awaken lofty and noble ideas in the imagination as well as a sense of admiration of their lovableness. They are never priggish, never conventional, never too exciting nor sensational, yet are they living, breathing, everyday persons that you can almost hear speak, and when all this is clothed in pure diction, in the elegant and fluent phraseology of a refined and scholarly writer, it is easy to imagine the cause of their fascination.

His working hours are from three to six every afternoon. He plays golf most mornings in the week, and is secretary to the Golf Club. His method in writing he explains as follows: 'I always think a thing out in the

rough, draw up a skeleton of the whole, make a sort of
scheme with some central figure round which I build,
then I divide it into chapters, place the contents of each
chapter and never start until all that is done. Then I go
ahead, and seldom make any alterations or corrections.
My secretary copies each day's work when finished. I
never make out much of a plot, and,' he adds quaintly, 'it
is always a matter of surprise to me that people should
like my books. They never turn out what I mean them
to be. I have no personal liking for what is called the
modern realistic school of fiction, because I don't see the
good of it. One does not go to a novel for information as
to the uglier facts of existence.'

In politics Mr. Norris is a strong Conservative, but
declares himself in this respect to be 'very old-fashioned,
indeed the only old Tory left.'

For a good many years he spent all his winters abroad
—in Algeria, Greece, and the Riviera, &c., traces of which
journeyings are to be found in many of his writings,
notably in 'Mademoiselle de Mersac.' He has now fallen
out of that habit, and, although quite in the prime of life,
he lives chiefly in Torquay, seldom staying long in London,
and only occasionally visiting friends. By no means
robust in constitution, he yet enjoys fairly good health in
the equable climate and in the quiet life of his adopted
county, save for periodical attacks of gout which, he
laughingly declares, he is 'very far from having deserved.'

At this juncture a summons to luncheon arrives.
Rising, Mr. Norris takes you into a bright and cheerful
dining-room. On the pale tinted walls hang masterly
portraits in crayons, by Richmond, of his parents and only
sister, who is married to Sir Arthur Havelock, Governor
of Ceylon. These pictures immediately suggest the idea
that there is yet one more tour that Mr. Norris may be
induced to take, and this is a visit to Ceylon. The interests of the novel-reading public, indeed, almost require

him to make the expedition and to let his facile pen revel amongst the gorgeous scenery between Colombo and Kandy, and the grand mountains, 'draped with forests of perennial green,' of beautiful Neuera Ellia.

Nearly the same view as obtained before, but rather more expansive, is seen from the windows. Your host looks too youthful for you readily to credit that he is the father of the fair girl who graces the head of the table and who receives you so pleasantly. They are 'always taken for brother and sister,' she remarks, but it is easy to see in every look how proud she is of her distinguished father. The small hands and slight physique of your young hostess would scarcely lead you to imagine that one of her keenest enjoyments is the chase, but such is the fact, and she can hold her own over a not too easy country, and is generally to be found in first flight, as many a brush and pad in her rooms can testify.

After luncheon a stroll round the garden is proposed, and this time it is all upward climbing by the back of the house. On the left side of the verandah there is a high hedge of the evergreen escallonia, with its glossy foliage and crimson blossoms, leading to the flower-beds and hothouses, where several varieties of ferns and sundry tropical plants abound, together with a wealth of bloom; these houses are a great delight to Mr. Norris, although he asserts that ' my own special gardening now-a-days chiefly consists in growling at the gardener, who meets my reproaches with a benign, superior smile. I haven't time to superintend his so-called duties, and the consequence is that I don't get half the flowers I ought to get, except when a show is imminent, and then he won't let me cut them!'

The next path leads to the kennels, and on entering the yard you are surrounded and noisily greeted by several thoroughbred Irish terriers, big and little, and a great solemn-looking Scotch deerhound, who are all perfectly friendly and escort you to the stable, where a loose box is inhabited by 'All Fours,' a handsome, thoroughbred black mare, standing nearly sixteen hands, with powerful quarters, glossy coat and small lean head. The beautiful Irish hunter is on the best of terms with her young mistress, and carries her 'like a bird,' through many a long morning's cubbing or run with the South Devon Hounds.

Another turn leads to the outer gates, and here you take leave of the talented and scholarly author, of whom it has been often said that he 'always writes like a gentleman, often as a wit,' and that he 'could not if he would write anything that is not worth reading.'

But, to your great satisfaction, you find that the pleasant day is not to conclude without an excursion. A friend's welcome voice from a carriage that pulls up close by, bids you jump in and accompany her through the New Cut, the Lincombe and Ilsham Drives. The light haze of the morning having lifted, every object is clear; peeps of Dartmoor can be seen in the distance, far-stretching views of the red-soiled coast from the Teign and the Exe; anon the Dart, glistening like silver in and out, the great rocky sea-caves at Livermead, in bold relief against the horizon, flooded with sunshine—all make a perfect panorama on which one might long linger. Here, just at the best point, the carriage pauses. 'One can scarcely believe,' says your companion in a low, meditative tone, as she gazes dreamily across the distant sea, 'that this was once an obscure fishing village. Torquay first began to gain repute in the Napoleonic war of 1815. Man has done much for it and Nature much more. The geology of the place is also most interesting. At the far-famed Kent's Cavern, which we shall see on the road home, prehistoric remains have often been discovered in layers of different depth. A story is told of a schoolmaster and all his pupils descending to inspect the cavern and never afterwards being heard of, but,' she adds with a laugh, 'that must be taken with a grain of salt.' Not the least of the many attractions of the fair city is the raised Terrace running parallel with the Torbay Road at the foot of Waldron Hill, where even in mid-winter such plants as orange trees, geraniums, almonds, hydrangeas are always in bloom, and just now you have the good luck to see an aloe in full blossom, an event that popular tradition attributes to it only once in a hundred years!

Anstis Cove, with its cottage by the sea, is also passed on the road back, which gradually descending, you soon reach the Strand, and after a walk round some open grounds to view the garden of sub-tropical plants, where great feathery palms and broad-leaved shrubs lead you back in imagination to India and Singapore, you finally alight at the Club and reading-rooms facing the pier. This club, founded and organised by the public-spirited and enterprising townsman, Mr. Iredale, is well worth a visit. Thousands, nay, tens of thousands, of volumes, new and old, comprising almost every known work of reference, are to be found in the libraries. The reading-rooms are stocked with copies of the best fiction, of standard works, tomes ancient and modern, and magazines and newspapers up to date. Finally, the secluded writing-room contains temptations not to be resisted, and affords an excellent opportunity of recording the impressions of a most enjoyable day whilst yet fresh in the memory.

CARLOTTA ADDISON

(MRS. LA TROBE)

ONE of her first ventures on the boards whilst yet a child was well calculated to give any little novice the feeling known as 'stage fright.' She had to come up through a trap as an apparition in the ghost scene of 'Macbeth' at the Liverpool Theatre. The house was full, the lights were low, there was a hush of expectancy amongst the audience. She had just given the Thane the admonition to 'be bloody, bold, and resolute.' As the trap was about to descend with its feather-weight burden clad in ghostly drapery, some slight disarrangement below caused it to sway ominously, which so terrified the child that, forgetting where she was, in an agony of fear she whispered audibly, 'Let me down, let me down!' and down she went rapidly. The *contretemps*, happily, was unobserved in front, and the hasty mutter passed as part of the performance; but it by no means escaped the Argus eye of the stage-manager, who, at the conclusion of the scene, severely reprimanded the little girl, and told her that if she gave way to such fears she would never 'rise in her profession.' While meekly accepting the rebuke, even at that early age her keen sense suggested the hope—to which she of course gave no utterance—that the exigencies of her profession might never again require her to 'rise' in such a dangerous manner.

It was during a temporary residence of the family at Liverpool that Carlotta Addison, the youngest of three children, first saw the light. Her father, Mr. Edward Addison, who was a well-known actor chiefly associated with Charles Kean's management at the Princess's Theatre, London, happened just then to be fulfilling a short engagement at Liverpool. A good all-round actor, his speciality was in impersonating 'old men's' parts, from the time he was eighteen. 'The talent originated in himself,' remarks his daughter; 'no member of his family had previously gone on the stage, and, indeed, he gave great offence to his relations by so doing, for they belonged to the stricter sort of those days, and held the calling of a professional actor to be *infra dig*. Mrs. Addison died when the little 'Lottie' was an infant, and, with almost her last breath, she exacted a promise from her husband that the two sisters should never be separated during girlhood. This promise was faithfully kept, and they attended the same schools, first in England and then in Paris. Inheriting much of her father's love of study and of music, the young girl devoted herself to her books and piano, in which she soon became a proficient. She was looked upon as 'very old, very steady, and very quiet in her habits,' but such good use did she make of her time that, when her elder sister was considered sufficiently advanced in her education to leave school, Carlotta, at the age of thirteen, was allowed to leave also. On their return home she suddenly announced her intention of 'going on the stage,' and her sister having the same idea, the girls, with the consent of their father, at once entered upon the requisite course of study.

'Never,' says Carlotta Addison with much feeling, 'was there such a parent! He was father, mother, friend—everything to us. He was a man of singular sweetness of disposition, and while from our childhood he was firm in exacting implicit obedience, he had a happy talent for inspiring us with such perfect confidence that we never had a thought apart from him. We showed him all our letters and poured out all our hopes and wishes to him. He was highly intellectual and cultivated, and held strong opinions on the training of the character as well as of the cultivation of the mind. He was most particular where we went, and took us chiefly to houses such as Dr. Westland Marston's, where we met literary and artistic society, and, young as we were, we used to sit spell-bound while listening to all the clever and interesting conversation that we heard—an education in itself. To his wise and tender training,' she adds after a pause, the while tears tremble in her blue eyes, 'I owe all—everything!'

A severe course of study in the provinces ensued under the management of Mr. Copeland, of Liverpool, whose discipline, though strict, was always tempered with justice. Afterwards she and her sister were transferred to Mr. Chute's company at Bristol, and Miss Carlotta Addison speaks of this period of her work with enthusiasm, and of the great kindness and encouragement that they received from him. Here the young actress worked with all her will, playing at first children's parts, later, anything and everything, from 'carrying on a message' to pantomime and Shakespearean characters; consequently, when she returned to London at the age of sixteen, she had become thoroughly at home in the 'business' of her profession. Her first engagement in town was at St. James's Theatre (under the management of Miss Herbert) as Lady Frances Touchwood in 'The Belle's Stratagem,' with Mr. Irving as Doricourt, followed by the part of the Little Duck, in Mr. W. S. Gilbert's first burlesque, 'Dulcamara, or, The Little Duck and the Great Quack.' A few weeks after came a great opportunity. The play was 'She Stoops to Conquer,' one of the many old comedies which she had well studied by her father's advice. At the conclusion of the performance, on one eventful night Miss Herbert was taken suddenly ill and as she had no understudy, Carlotta Addison was asked to take her part of Miss Hardcastle on the ensuing evening, with strict injunctions to 'take the book in her hand and read it.' No such precaution, however, was necessary. She was letter-perfect in the whole, and without even a single rehearsal she impersonated the character with so much grace and *aplomb*, that she won rounds of applause and was repeatedly called before the curtain.

After the run of this piece the young player 'rested' for a brief period; but, being always willing to take any insignificant *rôle* rather than remain idle, she accepted a small engagement with the late Miss Patty Oliver, an actress whose large-hearted and unselfish disposition always prompted her to encourage and push on a promising *débutante*. Miss Oliver was then playing in 'Meg's Diversion,' and subsequently in the popular burlesque of 'Black-eyed Susan.' She gave the girl her Meg to understudy, and coached her in the business, and very soon handed over that part to her.

Then came what Carlotta Addison describes as 'the

happiest time of her life.' It was at the old Prince of Wales's Theatre, Tottenham Court Road, under the management of Mr. and Mrs. Bancroft, in the delightful Robertson comedies, when she was brought well to the front in the original parts of Ruth in 'M.P.,' and Bella in 'School'—*rôles* that will always be associated with her name. Here she struck out for herself an entirely individual line in the natural, spontaneous delicacy and simplicity with which she represented the refined and unaffected girlhood that Mr. Robertson was so happy in depicting.

'No words can describe,' says Miss Addison enthusiastically, 'what a perfect time that was! We were like a happy family. It was not only one person's success, but every one's. Mr. and Mrs. Bancroft were always so kind and encouraging, and so delightful to work with. There was no discordant element, and each did his or her best with hearty good-will. The memory of those days will ever be dear to me.'

Slowly but surely wending her way to the front ranks, each year scored further successes. The admirable and thorough training of her girlhood stood her in good stead, and each step was one in advance. She played in many notable productions at the Globe (with the late Mr. Montague), such as 'Partners for Life,' and 'Cyril's Success' (H. J. Byron), and the lame fairy, Peep, in Albery's delightful fairy drama 'Oreana'; afterwards Nerissa in the 'Merchant of Venice' at the Prince of Wales's with Ellen Terry as Portia. But it was later at the Haymarket, in 'Married in Haste,' that she bounded many steps up the ladder of fame; and none who saw her as Ethel Grainger will forget the sympathetic tenderness and womanly grace—so full of poetic sentiment—with which she impersonated the modest, shy, yet impulsive and passionate heroine.

'I remember,' says Miss Addison, laughing, 'an incident connected with the play of "Virginius," in which I was Virginia, that even now causes me a shudder. The Roman father (Virginius) was acted by the celebrated tragedian, G. V. Brooke. A sharp, real butcher's knife, instead of the usual "property" harmless weapon, was accidentally placed on the stage. Fortunately Mr. Brooke happened to notice it before the curtain rose. Imagine my horror when he told me that had he not discovered the mistake that had been made, he must have killed me in real earnest in the scene where he had to "kill" Virginia!'

Behind the glass doors of a handsome Chippendale corner cupboard—a treasured gift from a valued American friend, Mrs. Prescott—among a litter of pretty Venetian glass and Oriental china—stands a common earthenware jug in a prominent position. At first sight it looks as if its more appropriate place might be on the kitchen dresser; but no, it has a story, something like that of the luck of Eden Hall. Miss Addison has a superstition connected with that homely piece of pottery. It is the jug that she used for over four hundred nights, as Bella in 'School,' to fetch the milk. It was originally white, but after the first performance an artist remarked the dead white was too *voyante* among the surroundings. A yellow one was ordered, but somehow forgotten, and the property man hastily laid a brush of colour over it for the evening's use, offering to get a new one for the next day; but the young actress had become attached to her jug, and declared it had brought her luck. Everyone laughed at her, and prophesied it would be broken and replaced many times, but she kept it intact throughout the run of the piece and at its conclusion Mr. Bancroft presented it to her before the entire company. There are other memories of her early stage life, notably a handsome silver clock and barometer, a gift from the same kindly manager and his wife; but this was after her marriage, when she had returned to what she calls her 'old home' at the Prince of Wales's Theatre, on the conclusion of a revival of

'London Assurance,' in which she played Grace Harkaway in that memorable and distinguished cast composed of the Bancrofts, the Kendals, Arthur Cecil, Kemble, and poor George Honey. The great old-fashioned velvet bag with massive silver mounting that hangs by the side of the pale yellow-tinted tiled hearth was given to her by the 'Old Stagers'—the Zingari Cricket Club, with whom Miss Addison played regularly for many years during the Canterbury cricket week. The dainty little silver Queen Anne tea service on yonder small table laid out with appetising cakes and muffins, was also a gift from the Club in commemoration of their jubilee. A picture with a fine sea effect over the mantelpiece was painted by Mr. La Trobe, and the one opposite was the last executed by his father, the late Governor of Victoria, before he went blind. The bright rays of the setting sun cast opal-hued and golden colours on two exquisite Watteau fans, with mother-of-pearl handles, framed and hung on the opposite walls. Mr. La Trobe, his wife says, is responsible for the artistic decoration and originality of the furniture, for he has among many talents a genius for designing and inventing, and he has exercised it to much purpose in the charming little house.

'The family,' she remarks with a smile, 'really consists of five, for Prince (a handsome, intelligent Dachshund that she is caressing) would be hurt if he were left out; he is quite a "person," and so lovable and faithful!'

After her marriage Mrs. La Trobe's domestic duties caused her to retire for a while into private life, but it was always her intention to return to her beloved art; and as soon as her two children were of an age to be left, she resumed her career and joined Mr. Clayton's company at the Court, where she played a succession of *rôles*. Inheriting her father's predilection for impersonating middle-aged and elderly parts, she created that of Lady Dolly in 'Moths'; but when Pinero's charming play, 'Sweet Lavender,' was produced at Terry's, she scored her biggest triumph of all, as the patient, reserved, and long-suffering Ruth Rolt, and showed herself the true artist. The tender womanliness and sympathetic grace of her own nature were here displayed to the fullest advantage, while the style and brilliant finish of her performance made it the perfection of histrionic art.

'It was my most favourite part,' she remarks in subdued tones; 'the sorrows and troubles of poor Ruth were so real to me for those few hours nightly, and though the piece ran for over two years I never wearied of it. I could have gone on playing it until now, and when it was over I felt as if I missed something out of my life.'

Her latest *rôle* is Lady Bletchley in F. C. Philips and C. Brookfield's delightful play 'A Woman's Reason.'

It is only natural that with such a sweet, lovable nature this accomplished actress is a universal favourite, alike in her own profession as in society. Indeed, it may be said that she never made an enemy or lost a friend. It is proverbial amongst those who have the pleasure of knowing her intimately that in Mrs. La Trobe's house one never hears an unkind word nor breath of scandal about anybody, while her well-known and gentle sympathy is extended to each and all, either in trouble or in joy.

SIR HENRY IRVING

THERE is always a peculiar glamour and fascination inseparably connected with histrionic life that commends itself more or less forcibly to the imaginative, non-professional mind. Brilliant vistas of intoxicating triumphs, of applauding audiences, of success easily won, are the enchanting visions of many a young would-be actor, who little dreams of the hard practical work, of the days and nights of unremitting toil, that, even when there is real genius, constitute the life of the true artist. There is no royal road to this more than to any other profession; and, as Henry Irving is always the first to proclaim, he who would ascend the heights must climb step by step from the lowest rung of the ladder with patience and with courage; happy, indeed, if he can also bring to bear the equable temperament and the strength of will that can neither be unduly cast down by failure nor injured by success.

With considerable trepidation—nay, with a feeling that it is almost a presumption—do you modestly approach the pleasant task of chronicling a slight sketch of the career of the illustrious actor, whose name, when this brief span is over, will go on for ever—aye, in future historic records. The mind involuntarily travels forward, and pictures—say, in Anno Domini 1995—some such conversation as the following :—' Grandfather,' will say a lad, who has just seen and grumbled over his first play, and is poring over a well-worn memoir of the great artist, ' saw you ever Henry Irving?' (By the way, will the generation of that date revert to the stilted and high-flown phraseology of past centuries, or will they adopt, with the march of civilisation, a still more free and easy style than that of the present epoch?) ' Nay, my boy,' will be the reply of his aged grandsire, in piping voice; ' but your great-grandfather did, and I mind me well the tales he told me, and how he was present on the opening night of the Lyceum in 1895, when the immortal bard's story of " King Arthur " was produced with scenes of uncommon splendour before a crowded and most distinguished house. The piece was dramatised by an able and scholarly artist of that day, one Mr. Comyns Carr. Irving, the greatest actor of his time—the warrior king, saint-like, " half divine "—melted the audience to tears by the exquisite and tender pathos of his words : " My sword is drawn! I want no scabbard now!" That beauteous and gifted lady, Ellen Terry, of whom you have often read, played Queen Guinevere. But alack! we have no Irving now!'

The present generation are more fortunate, and have their Irving in the flesh. Well for them is it that he discovered early in life that the dry details of commerce, to which he had been destined, possessed no charms for the soul, full of genius, that longed to spread its wings and to be free to soar into the world of art! Strange, too, that his first appearance on any stage should actually have taken place at the theatre in Sunderland bearing the same name as the one in the great Metropolis which is the scene of his continuous triumphs, and where he has so long endeared himself to the public.

Looking back through a heap of old diaries of the last score of years, it appears that your first meeting with the great tragedian occurred during an early revival of 'Hamlet,' on a never-to-be-forgotten occasion. It was at a brilliant social gathering at the house of an immediate relative—the late William Spottiswoode, President of the Royal Society—a man of profound learning, of grand and noble character, withal of singular modesty. Royalty was present and listened with rapt attention as the great scientist spoke on a favourite topic, and explained his researches into and his theories on the 'polarisation of light.' Presently, when the group dispersed, the passing stream of guests brought you into the near vicinity of your host, who was conversing with Mr. Irving about 'Hamlet.' While you stood listening with interest, an introduction took place. Faithful diary! It also records the fact that when the next evening came you were privileged to be admitted behind the scenes, received the promised welcome from Hamlet himself, and afterwards sat with sweet Ophelia—Ellen Terry—in her dressing-room between the acts.

During his first ten years or thereabouts of stage life Mr. Irving had his ups and downs too, in common with many another young actor who has since become distinguished, for not by a single bound did he leap into fame. He fulfilled many engagements in the provinces,

and for two or more years was engaged at the theatre in
Edinburgh, playing with Miss Helen Faucit, Miss Cush-
man, Robson, and other stars of that time. To this day
Edinburgh prides herself on having been his training
school, and when it is known that Mr. Irving proposes to
repair thither on one of his tours, the dignified old city
becomes excited, and he is received with more than an
ordinary ovation. And a severe training school it was,
for during two years or so he impersonated between two
and three hundred different characters, thus laying in an
enormous stock of experience for future use. These parts,
as may be supposed, embraced a wide range, and varied
considerably: now it was in pantomime, then in tragedy,
next perhaps melodrama, anon comedy, and not infrequently did it happen that he was called upon to play in
three separate *rôles* on the same evening.

There were early struggles at Manchester, too; but
they were all part of the training, not only in the young
actor's art, but in the formation of his mind and character,
and were leading him ever upward to his ultimate reward.
Hamlet had apparently always an attraction for him, and
he played in that part for the first time in Manchester.
It perhaps may not have been exactly his grand and
finished Hamlet of these later days, but it was all coming.
Ten years from his youthful entrance into histrionic life
found Henry Irving at a London theatre (the St. James's,
then under the management of Miss Herbert)—all preliminary difficulties vanquished, and a brilliant future
assured. Then followed a long period of leading *rôles*,
many of which are as fresh to-day in the recollections of
playgoers of that time as are those triumphs of subsequent
years. The mind reverts at random to his Doricourt in
'The Belle's Stratagem,' his Harry Dorton in 'The Road
to Ruin,' his Rawdon Scudamore in Boucicault's 'Hunted
Down,' in which the gifted Kate Terry played the heroine,
Mary Leigh. There was Joseph Surface in 'The School
for Scandal,' and the title-*rôle* of Robert Macaire; and

yet later, that delightful play, 'The Two Roses,' which ran over three hundred nights with such a cast—handsome young Montague, famous for his good looks and genial manner; George Honey—both, alas! gone over to the silent majority; Thomas Thorne, and Henry Irving as Digby Grant, polished, finished, and artistic.

It was at the Queen's Theatre that Mr. Irving and Ellen Terry first played together in 'Katharine and Petruchio,' and afterwards in 'Dearer than Life,' probably little dreaming then that the days were coming when they would have all the world at their feet. His Mr. Chenevix, too, in 'Uncle Dick's Darling,' was a masterpiece, but by and by, when 'The Bells' was produced, Mr. Irving broke fresh ground. He poured out his whole artistic soul into the part of Matthias with such depth of feeling that the audience sat spell-bound; and from the first day it was played—some twenty years ago—until its latest production, though one may have seen it fifty times, the wonderful representation invariably produces the same effect. 'The Fate of Eugene Aram,' 'The Lyons Mail,' Mr. Irving's dual parts of Joseph Lesurques and Dubosc, were further revelations to the public, and with each he strengthened his hold on their affections; no less than later by his Doctor Primrose in that touching and picturesque play, 'Olivia,' which displayed the extraordinary versatility of the actor's genius, and depicted him, with exquisite grace and simplicity, as the amiable and affectionate Vicar in an ideal parsonage: as much at home in his art as, when thrilling a crowded house night after night, he enacted the sad and melancholy Charles I., the sardonic Louis XI., the tempter Mephistopheles, the impassioned Romeo, the playful lover, Benedick, and hundreds of other varied and perfect *rôles*. Yet not only before the footlights has the great artist shown himself to be the man of his day. There is a thoroughness of organisation in the strongly practical element in his nature. One can scarcely realise the stupendous task of arranging details in such a vast work. The costumes—always correct to the minutest point—the scenic effects, each of which is a living picture of beauty, such as the celebrated Church scene in 'Much Ado About Nothing'—a faithful copy of the interior of a gorgeous church at Messina—the Brocken scene in 'Faust,' with its supernatural and lurid effects, the Court scene in the 'Merchant of Venice,' with its correct costumes, portraits, architecture, &c.; occasionally a stage with five hundred upon it at one time, where, so to speak, not one is lost in the crowd, but has his or her own presence carefully and methodically planned—truly only a master-mind could organise such gigantic undertakings; only a past master in art paint such vivid and harmonious pictures! The illustrious actor has already the proud satisfaction of looking back and feeling that his life's work of instructing, of elevating, and of refining the public taste will leave an undying record.

There is but little need to make more than a passing mention of Sir Henry Irving in private life. Kindly, genial, courteous, ever considerate and full of tact, his good works are countless and unobtrusive. His strict justice calls forth respect, while his tender heart and nobility of nature call forth something more, and that is the affection and devotion of his legion of friends.

MADAME ALBANI-GYE

IT may, perhaps, not be generally known that the famous singer, Madame Albani-Gye, who so delights the world by her rare gifts, and makes herself so beloved in private life by her gracious and sympathetic nature, adopted the name of Albani on making her *début*. It is usually supposed that it was chosen out of compliment to the city of Albany, where her singing at the cathedral, when she was but thirteen years of age, attracted considerable attention, and caused all present to predict a brilliant future—a prophecy that has been abundantly realised. According to an eye-witness on that occasion the sweet, pure, bird-like notes trilled through the vaulted arches, while the child-singer, with reverent mien and utter absence of self-consciousness, looked like an angel from heaven. As a matter of fact the name was selected by her singing-master at the beginning of her career, and is the extinct title of an old Italian family.

Her maiden name was Lajeunesse; Chambley, near Montreal, claims the honour of having been her birthplace, and her parents were French-Canadians. At an early age the little girl was sent to school at the Convent of the Sacred Heart, Montreal, and remained there until her father removed to Albany. At the convent the children and nuns would gather round her during play-hours while she sang with infinite pathos the chants, anthems, and portions of masses that she had heard at the services in the chapel; from babyhood, indeed, music was her chief delight, and she could reproduce any air that she had heard once and render it in faultless time and tune. The Mother Superior, too, an Italian lady, was wont to call the child to her and bid her sing. 'I used to make her cry,' says Madame Albani-Gye, softly; 'but in the chapel itself I was only allowed to sing at Christmas, Easter, and on other special feast days.' Up to that time her father, himself an accomplished musician, had been her sole teacher, but by-and-by, as the magnificent voice day by day further developed, it became necessary that she should receive more training than could be procured in America. Accordingly, it was decided in family conclave that she should be sent to Paris, and, under the care of the Baroness Lafitte, become the pupil of the celebrated master Duprez, for two years. During that time the young artist made rapid progress; later she passed on to Milan and placed herself under the tutelage of Signor Lamperti, a distinguished maestro of the day, and applying herself diligently to her studies for the next year she thoroughly mastered the technicalities of her profession. Then came the momentous occasion of her *début* at Messina, before which her master said to her, 'I have found you a name. You shall be called "Albani,"' and as Albani she has won her triumphs and made the world ring with her fame.

Almost immediately afterwards she sang at Malta, where she took the garrison by storm, so to speak, and received no less warm a reception than had been accorded to her at Messina. No such finished and exquisite singing and acting had hitherto been heard and seen at the place —it was a revelation to the inhabitants, and, according to the records of the papers of the time, 'the whole populace went wild about her.' Her next performances were during a winter season at Florence, before crowded audiences at the theatre of La Pergola, where the music-loving Italians warmly appreciated the Canadian nightingale, and manifested their approval by the most enthusiastic applause. One of her special successes at that time was the 'Mignon' of Ambroise Thomas, an opera that had actually been condemned in four different theatres in Italy; but the young singer saw great possibilities in it. When she had conquered the Italian public Madame Albani was invited to London and made her first appearance at the Royal Italian Opera, where she speedily won all hearts. A few years after her arrival here she married Mr. Ernest Gye, a son of the manager of Covent Garden Opera House.

'And here I have been ever since,' says Madame Albani-Gye, with a smile, 'varied, of course, by many foreign tours. I love the country and the people, who are all so delightful and so faithful to me, and I am always learning—always studying. I had three entirely new works to do last year for the Gloucester, Leeds, and Cardiff festivals.' But not only in England and in Italy is the gifted singer heard. She has made many tours in the United States and Canada. She travels at one time to Berlin, to St. Petersburg, to Paris, &c., anon to the Cape, and has sung before every crowned head in Europe, with the invariable result of universal popularity.

In such a long and varied repertory of operas, so well known to the public as to need few words, it is difficult to say in which part Madame Albani-Gye excels. Among the most popular of her *rôles* are Marguerite, in 'Faust'; Elizabeth, in 'Tannhäuser'; Desdemona, in 'Otello.' Her own favourites are Valentina, in 'Les Huguenots'; and Elsa, in 'Lohengrin.' Of late, Edith, in Mr. Frederic Cowen's 'Harold,' has given her much pleasure; and she speaks in hearty terms of the composer and his work, and of the prestige given to English opera, in that it is the first time it has been played at Covent Garden during an Italian season. For Sir Augustus, too, she has many kind words, and declares that she 'cannot sufficiently admire his great talents for organisation and he is always so nice to work with.' It is possible that Madame Albani-Gye's convent training, when she so early made acquaintance with the masses and requiems of the great masters, inspired her to turn her attention in after years to oratorio —to which her great gifts are so strongly adapted—as well as to opera. She is always engaged at the chief festivals, and is acknowledged to have no rival in oratorio. She sings in 'The Messiah,' 'Israel in Egypt,' 'Elijah,' 'St. Paul,' 'Judas Maccabæus,' and many others, and was the first to sing in 'The Golden Legend,' 'Redemption,' and 'The Martyr of Antioch,' as also in Mr. Cowen's 'Ruth,' and in his cantatas, 'St. Ursula' and 'Water Lily,' together with Dvořák's 'Spectre Bride,' 'St. Ludmila,' and Gounod's 'Mors et Vita.'

Her English home, situated in one of the prettiest spots of South Kensington, presents a picturesque appearance, and is filled with interesting souvenirs of her career. Here are the pictures given to her by the Queen, together with many gold and silver articles from her Majesty and the Royal Family. The large groups of figures in Sèvres biscuit china was a gift from the President of the French Republic, MacMahon; the painting of the house in Germany where she sang, from the late Empress Augusta; and there are valuable works of art too numerous to detail. Photographs, all signed, abound, of Royal personages in Europe; a portrait of her only child—a son—stands on an easel, and on all sides can be seen pictures of brother and sister artists. One of her most valued treasures is a beautifully bound album containing autographs, headed by that of the Queen. 'But, indeed,' says Madame Albani-Gye, 'it would be impossible to tell you of all the kindness I have received from her Majesty and her children, whom I know, admire, and love.'

GEORGE ALEXANDER

It is not uncommon to find that where nature and heredity have been most prolific in their gifts, the happy possessor of these good things is unusually modest in his own appreciation of them. No better instance of the truth of this theory can be found than in the person of the much-respected and popular young actor-manager, Mr. George Alexander, the charm of whose manly, unaffected character is only equalled by his frank, unassuming manner. His inheritances from both parents were singularly fortunate. His mother—an Englishwoman of singular beauty and delicate, refined nature—combined with a love of literature strong artistic tastes. To her he is indebted for this side of his nature, together with his personal and physical attractions, while to his father—a Scottish manufacturer —he owes the good business qualities, the practical, methodical habits, and the clear, level head which have contributed so largely to his successful career as a stage-manager.

But to no one does George Alexander owe his gifts for histrionic art. These originated entirely in himself, for no member of his family had at any time been before the footlights—his mother, indeed, had never been inside a theatre, while his father, a Presbyterian of the strictest type, looked on the whole thing as a positive sin and cut his son for going on the stage. George Alexander was born at Reading, and at the age of fourteen accompanied his parents on their return to Scotland. It was during his school-days at Stirling that his innate talent for acting manifested itself, though even then he was much divided in mind between religion and art. At one time he would be engrossed in the symbolisms of religion, in erecting miniature altars, and preaching—attired in a white nightshirt—to the boys in the dormitory; at another, his histrionic instincts would get the upper hand. Presently he suggested the idea of getting up a little amateur dramatic club at the school, but when the scheme was laid before the authorities the rector pronounced that a club would be too advanced, and, as a sort of compromise, Christy Minstrels were allowed. However, at some private theatricals at the Bridge of Allan, a classic burlesque called 'Jupiter Aeger' was performed, in which the young schoolboy made his first appearance on any stage, and played Mercury so ably that a great friend of the family who was present declared that he would rival Mr. Toole some day! Young Alexander's acting propensities were at that time greatly influenced by Mr. Davenport Adams, but the paternal eye frowned reprovingly upon these proceedings, for the father desired that his son should succeed him in business. As may be supposed, with such natural gifts the son frowned with equal disapproval upon the notion, and at last it was decided to turn him into a doctor, for which purpose he went to Edinburgh for the requisite course of study. But this after a short experience proved quite as distasteful, so to London he was sent, and there launched into commerce. It was not to be, however. The stars in their courses had ruled that George Alexander was to be an actor—and a successful actor. 'Needless to say,' he remarks, while a smile lights up the earnest, deep blue eyes, 'I devoted the whole time that should have been spent in learning business to the play. I became a regular "first-nighter," and from the pit or gallery watched the opening of each piece, and, indeed, passed every evening at the theatre. Of course, I thought myself an excellent critic in those boyish days, and ready to make or mar any actor who came on the stage,' but, he adds after a pause, with a genial laugh, 'having worked up from the lowest rung of the ladder, I find that I am not as good a critic as I was!' About this time Mr. Alexander joined the Thames Rowing Club and a company of amateur actors, where he soon took a lead. He played, among parts of all sorts and kinds, those of Jack Wyatt in 'The Two Roses,' Charles Courtly in 'London Assurance,' &c., then, at the brilliant private theatricals at Lady Freake's, the die was cast. His performance in 'The Critic' was so well received that, encouraged by Major John Holmes, a prominent member of the Club—and others—George Alexander took the law into his own hands, renounced the desk for good and all, left home while the family were at church, and joined the ranks of professional players. 'My first step,' he says, 'was to take rooms at Blackheath, where I knew no one, but I soon found out that the charming young lady who was my next-door neighbour was Miss Lottie Venne, the first actress I had ever met. She was most kind in giving me advice and encouragement. I silently adored her!' Soon after, the young player became acquainted with Miss Carlotta Addison, and with this delightful actress he played in 'London Assurance,' then, through Mr. Blackmore's agency, he obtained his first engagement at Nottingham, in Miss Ada Swanborough and Mr. W. H. Vernon's touring company, where he soon showed of what metal he was

made, and distinguished himself in many juvenile leads.
Towards the close of that time he was seen by an agent
in advance, Mr. Ward, in 'A Lesson in Love,' in which
it may be noted that Mrs. Canninge—now a member
of his own company—was also playing. Mr. Ward
strongly recommended the brilliant young actor to Mr. T.
W. Robertson, who was just then planning a tour with
his late father's comedies, and he was engaged to play
D'Alroy, Beaufoy, and all the *jeune premier rôles*. This
tour was succeeded by another, and was followed by a
well-merited and big jump upwards. George Alexander
may well have felt that good and earnest work—for, given
any amount of natural talent, each onward step has to be
gained by a man's own industry—had brought its reward
when so early in his career he was selected by Mr. Irving
to play the important part of Caleb Deecie in 'The Two
Roses,' a part that was for many years his favourite
representation. The character of D'Albery's brave and
gentle blind hero was well suited to the gifted young
actor's polished and artistic style. He remembers a little
incident connected with that play. The night before it
was produced poor Fanny Josephs slipped and hurt her
knee, which prevented her from going on, and her place
had to be filled by the understudy. He was dreadfully
nervous; in any circumstances it was anxious work to
play a part with one's eyes shut, but how much more so
with a strange leading lady with whom one had only
rehearsed two or three times! He and the distinguished
comedian, Mr. Howe, shared a dressing-room; the young
'Caleb' was plying the hare's-foot with trembling hand
which he vainly tried to steady, the while he cast furtive
glances at the older actor, hoping his embarrassment
would not be noticed. Presently he was glad to perceive
that Mr. Howe was sharing the same sensation. Taking
heart of grace, young Alexander whispered, 'I'm fright-
fully nervous, I shall never get through,' to which the
veteran actor replied, 'Wait, my dear boy, till you have

been fifty years on the stage as I have, and then you'll know what it means to be really nervous. I never knew a good actor who wasn't.' And it may here be recorded that for eight years Mr. Howe was an encouraging companion and friend to his young brother in art, and always ready with a kindly word and deed. As Caleb Deecie, George Alexander established his reputation, and made his way straight to the heart of the public, on whom, as time rolled on, he accentuated and deepened his hold. He spent altogether eight absolutely happy years at the Lyceum, only broken by a short period at the St. James's, where he scored further successes in the characters of Victor de Riel in 'Impulse,' Octave in 'The Ironmaster,' &c., and made a subsequent tour with the company, followed by a short season with a provincial Shakespearian company, where he played Benedick, Orlando, Romeo, &c. Now it happened that 'Romeo and Juliet' was unexpectedly called for one particular Saturday, and Mr. Alexander, who, from much experience, thought he knew that play backwards, had put off its further study until the others should be off his mind, feeling sure it would be all right. When it came to rehearsal, he discovered that the Mercutio was well up in the Cumberland edition, while he—trained under Mr. Irving—was versed in the actual text; the result was that when it came off they were all adrift, and his opinion is that a somewhat funny performance must have been introduced into the dramatic profession! The conclusion, however, was very far from being funny. As Romeo threw himself down to die, he discovered, to his dismay, that he had fallen on the exact line where the drop curtain must presently descend, which would have been awkward in its consequences In his deep sympathy with his part, Mr. Alexander was, as usual, feeling intensely the touching tragedy, and tears were streaming down his face, but he had the presence of mind to murmur to Juliet to raise his arm and draw him round towards herself ere the curtain fell. This she did dexterously enough, and the drop descended and hid them from view, but the actress scarcely realised that Mr. Alexander's emotion proceeded from the pathos of the play—not the situation—and she exclaimed, 'Oh! cowardy cowardy custard, to cry because you thought the curtain would fall and hurt you!'

Then back to the Lyceum for the remaining term of years, twice broken by trips with the company to America. Mr. Alexander cannot speak warmly and affectionately enough of Sir Henry Irving and Miss Ellen Terry's ready sympathy and kindly encouragement, both during those years and since he went into management for himself. He added a long and varied repertory to a large store of practical experience, and played among *rôles* too numerous to mention—Laertes, Bassanio, Don Pedro, Claudio, Orsino, Squire Thornhill, &c. When 'Ravenscourt' was to be produced there was no part suitable for him, and then Mr. Alexander decided to carry out a long-cherished wish and enter into management on his own account. Previous to taking the final plunge he accepted an engagement to create the leading *rôle* in 'London Day by Day,' at the Adelphi, where, in entirely different surroundings, his audiences appreciated him as fully as had those of the Lyceum. During the run of the piece he made all the arrangements for opening the Avenue Theatre with that most amusing farce, 'Dr. Bill,' which actually began before he was able to leave the Adelphi. He then joined his own company, and played the title *rôle* for nearly ten months, followed by Mr. Carton's 'Sunlight and Shadow.' The great success of his first venture justified Mr. Alexander's next move to the St. James's with the same play, which was succeeded by a long run with 'The Idler,' and followed in turn by 'Lord Annerly,' Mr. Comyns Carr's 'Forgiveness,' and 'Lady Windermere's Fan.' The 'youngest manager' in London had indeed changed the luck of the St. James's by his talents, wits, and excellent judgment, but there were more good things to follow. Mr. Carton's charming play, 'Liberty Hall,' proved no less attractive, while the sensation caused by Mr. Pinero's 'The Second Mrs. Tanqueray,' Mr. Henry Arthur Jones's 'The Masqueraders,' and Mr. H. V. Esmond's clever drama, 'The Divided Way,' is fresh in the minds of all playgoers. The latest addition is 'The Prisoner of Zenda,' by Mr. E. Rose from Anthony Hope's novel.

The house in which Mr. Alexander and his charming wife are located, is artistic in all its decorations, for she too has a keen appreciation of the beautiful, and a fine taste for home as well as for scenic effects. Proof engravings and a humorous series of drawings hang on the walls of his study, as also a large portrait of Mr. Irving as Becket and another of Mr. Pinero, called 'A Freak of Cameron's.' The deep, red-tiled hearth gives a fine bit of colour to the surroundings, and on the mantelpiece stands an autographed photograph of Princess Christian; well-filled bookcases, revolving and others, are all in the utmost order. Not a paper is awry on the handsome marqueterie writing-table. The telephone is close at hand, and under it stands a cabinet which opens with a spring, disclosing pigeon-holes alphabetically numbered and packets neatly docketed, among which, with a fine vein of irony, he keeps all his first theatrical refusals. And there is one specially valued reminiscence. This is a large volume of Shakespeare—as put forth in 1623—beautifully bound, which was presented to him by Mr. Ruskin in the name of the 'Tale of Troy' Company, of which play Mr. Alexander undertook the management, when Sir Frederic Leighton and other Royal Academicians arranged the tableaux.

Amid such a pressure of business it is difficult to imagine when the distinguished actor-manager finds time to learn his own lines, but this is done at all sorts of odd moments. In fact, he gets his words last of all, chiefly at rehearsal, and knows the whole of the rest of the play first, but confesses to having 'never been a quick study, perhaps slower now than ever.' Unspoiled by success, which he appraises at its exact value, Mr. Alexander is as great a favourite in his own profession and company as he is with the public, while in private life, among a large circle of friends, he is no less beloved than esteemed.

MRS. PARR

THE ancient landmarks of old Kensington are rapidly being removed. 'The old order changeth,' and in these later days there will soon be nothing left to remind the lover of historical relics of the days when Cromwell and Ireton met in the meadow in which Lord Holland's statue now stands—the same meadow in which the lovely Lady Sarah Lennox, whose beauty had caught the heart of the youthful George III., was set to make hay, that the sight of her charms as he rode past might lure back the royal youth whose confidence had been shaken by jealous tongues.

The old inn, where the Holland Arms now stands, is the house to which Addison repaired when his high-born wife, the Countess of Warwick, drove him out of Holland House, in the green lanes of which one could then see ghosts and hear nightingales. These interesting reminiscences are now all of the long past, as is also the salon of Lady Holland, formerly renowned for its brilliant and intellectual guests, such as Brougham, Addison, and Macaulay. Gone, too, is the charming house in which the immortal John Leech lived and died, and where he had as his neighbour Kenelm Digby, author of 'The Broad Stone of Honour.' In place of these old-world dwellings great blocks of lofty flats have been built, and rows of shops electrically lighted. The besom of so-called improvement sweeps away many memories, and even they who have been familiar with the old places forget them as they grow accustomed to the new.

In one of the houses where Sir David Wilkie painted 'Distraining for Rent'—now in the National Gallery—lives the talented author, Mrs. Parr, who came here on her marriage nearly twenty-five years ago. Built after a fashion familiar in the days when space was of no such value as in these, and when George III. was king, the house falls back from the road, and, being approached by a short garden, the busy hum of the incessant traffic is scarcely heard, and to ears accustomed to the sound is not noticed.

It needs but a glance inside to see that those who dwell here are great lovers of art; indeed it so happens that Dr. and Mrs. Parr have a taste in common in the love of the beautiful and of the artistic. The hall is lined with old prints, engravings, etchings, and rare views of old Kensington. The drawing-rooms are a study of choice specimens of pottery, china, and of genuine marqueterie work, and you are tempted to linger long over the fascinating art treasures, many of which have a story of interest and of association. 'They were collected,' says Mrs. Parr, 'in the days when taste and judgment helped more than now, and it was not so necessary to have a well-filled purse and a long pocket.'

The author's own little sitting-room is of a more simple description. Here she has gathered around her the gifts of friends and admirers, little treasures valued when a child, portraits, souvenirs of those dear to her; among these are many ornaments of an artistic importance, notably a fan hanging in a case on the wall, which belonged to a daughter of Bishop Burnet, the historian of the Reformation, who was born in 1643. He brought various letters from America from persons who claimed to belong to the family, and who were interested in this relic. Another fan, exquisitely painted, is of Louis

Quatorze day; a third, more modern, is perhaps the most valued of the three. It was designed by Mr. George Fox, and bears Mrs. Parr's monogram, crest, and motto, 'Amour avec Loiaulté.' This was a gift from her husband, and on each leaf an artist has left his sign-manual and autograph. Here are the names of Charles Keene, of John Tenniel, Farquharson, Boughton, Hamo Thornycroft, and of Henry Selons, whose portrait hangs opposite a fine etching of the author of 'Self-Help,' Dr. Smiles, by Rajon. On the mantelpiece stands a quaint Staffordshire vase given to Mrs. Parr by the old fisher folk with whom she lodged while at Polperro, where is laid the scene of her well-known novel, 'Adam and Eve,' a smuggling story founded on incidents that actually happened early in the present century, and which are related in Mr. Couch's 'History of Polperro.'

In order to get the briny essence of the sea into her nature, and to thoroughly imbue herself with its atmosphere and the spirit of its people, the author went down to the picturesque village 'which coucheth between two hills,' and wrote a great portion of her novel there. So faithfully is the place portrayed that a friend, led by his interest in the story to pay a visit to the place, said '"Adam and Eve" is a perfect guide-book to Polperro.'

'I used to talk to the old sailors,' says Mrs. Parr, 'and try to get from them all they remembered of bygone days, and I would get them to come in the evenings to the house and relate stories of the smuggling days. Later, they were much surprised and delighted to find that some of the things they said were in a book. These' (pointing to two pieces of magnificent brocade, woven in gold on a yellow ground) 'are portions of a gown worn by an old fisherman's mother, whose husband was a notorious smuggler; it had silver buttons, and the elbow ruffles were of lace worth a guinea a yard. The old woman's boast had been that on her wedding-day she curled her hair with five pound notes! I have a passion,' she adds, smiling, 'for relics and curios, old lace, old silver, all that there is of the most old.'

Born of a generation of sailors, Mrs. Parr has that love of the sea which comes as a heritage. Her father was an officer in the Royal Navy, and the early part of her life was spent at Plymouth. She says of herself, as of her heroine in 'Adam and Eve,' she was 'a sailor's child, and her inheritance was the love that is born in the hearts of those whose fathers, and their fathers before them, have gone down to the sea in ships and seen the wonders of the deep.'

With no hereditary leaning to literature, nothing seemed more improbable than that she should ever become a novelist. The talent, however, may perhaps have originated in her early school days, when she would write her own and her companions' themes with ease, while in return they would do her needlework, which she hated. Still, Mrs. Parr is of the opinion that she might never have written at all but for the encouragement she received, before her marriage, from her husband. He stimulated her intellectual faculties, and gave the impetus that she needed, and has ever been her most severe and her kindest critic.

Her first story, 'How it all Happened,' appeared in 'Good Words,' and was written under the pseudonym of Mrs. Olinthus Lobb. It was at once a success, and in a few weeks was applied for to be reproduced as a *feuilleton* in the 'Journal des Débats,' the editor apologising to his readers for departing from his rule never to take translations. The Queen of Wurtemburg then asked for it to be rendered into German. In America it was published in pamphlet form. Mrs. Parr may be said to have made a good start, but she is most anxious modestly to explain that she looked upon it more as a chance incident than from her own merits, but here her readers will be inclined to differ from her. It is a particularly bright, amusing little tale, and there is a humorous story connected with it. Some seven or eight years later her husband had asked a few friends to dinner. One of the gentlemen, during a conversation upon authors, said, 'I should much like to meet a Mrs. Olinthus Lobb.' 'Why?' asked his host. 'Because,' was the reply, 'she completely turned into ridicule the staff of the Jermyn Street Museum [he was the head of one of the departments there] and even caricatured my face and figure.' Great was the laughter when he was told that his hostess was the culprit, and assured that at the time the story was written she had never been to the Museum, and that the artist had never seen him.

She wrote 'Good Cheer' in collaboration with the Rev. Norman McLeod, and immediately afterwards was invited by Mr. Strahan to 'try her hand at a novel,' which was at first written as a short tale, called 'The Glovemaker's Daughter.' He returned it, saying it was 'too much like a Chinese puzzle, but would make a good three-volume novel.' The idea was carried out, and it afterwards became the successful work entitled 'Dorothy Fox.' After it had been accepted, on Mrs. Parr going to see Mr. Strahan, he said, while speaking in praise of the story, 'but I wish you had made me like Josiah Crewdon.' 'Give it back to me,' answered the author, 'and I will make you like him.' Taking it home she re-wrote half, entirely altering Crewdon's character. Mr. Strahan saw the improvement and predicted that the book would be very popular, a prophecy that was soon fulfilled, and Mrs. Parr declares that she always felt most grateful for the suggestion. By a strange coincidence the handsome cheque for this work arrived on her wedding morning. The story dealt with life amongst 'The Friends.' Its phenomenal success in America made her most popular, and invitations came from many of the Members to visit the States. The author received a variety of letters on the subject; some of the more emancipated of the Society were much pleased, but a few of the older and stricter sort made protests on the score of Josiah Crewdon being a portrait and well known in Leeds. This, however, was not the case.

Her next novel, 'The Prescotts,' is a West-country story, full of the humour that the writer possesses in a high degree, humour which from the first was recognised and welcomed by all her critics.

In the intervals between the production of longer books, Mrs. Parr contributed articles to various leading magazines, such as the 'History of Fans,' in 'Harper's,' illustrated by Mr. Boughton, and the series of 'Follies in Fashion' in the 'Pall Mall Magazine.' These last are most amusing, and are illustrated with *fac-similes* of old prints in Dr. Parr's collection. Some day she proposes to put into proper form a history of Kensington, for which she has been accumulating material for many years.

'Robin,' 'The Squire,' and 'Loyalty George' are the titles of other of the author's works. She is sometimes accused of making sad endings, but the fact is that she never shrinks from what she considers the natural, logical, and consequently the most artistic *dénouement*, to which the force of character and of circumstance has been working. To this quality may be due the reproaches sometimes addressed to her in private letters during the run of some novel in a magazine. On one occasion a letter was received by her publishers, saying that the writer should not shield herself with an 'i' instead of an 'e' in the name, for it was evident that she must know him, as the circumstances were exactly those of his own life. To this there was but one answer possible. She knew nothing of him, and as the character died in the next number, it was to be hoped that he would be satisfied of the truth of her assertion.

Mrs. Parr writes of the sea, in which she ever finds a fresh charm, of the winds and storms, of the great jutting rocks, and of the bold cliffs, with an atmospheric truth, in such graceful yet highly descriptive and vivid word-painting, that the reader follows step by step with breathless interest. She seems to hold one handle of the electric chain, whilst the other is in the hand of her public. Each character is admirably yet simply drawn from close observation of life, with conscientious care. In 'Loyalty George' there is one Mrs. Coode, who, with her quaint sayings and shrewd wisdom, falls no whit short of the immortal Mrs. Poyser, while Loyalty herself, Miss Anne, and Roger Coode are masterpieces of portraiture. Again there is a tragedy, and the book closes with a scene of rare dramatic power.

Undoubtedly one of the reasons why Mrs. Parr has the power of evoking so much sympathy in her works, is because, when she is going to write about any particular spot, she visits it, and spends much time there, so as to enter into its spirit and to be influenced by its surroundings. The coast has an effect upon her imagination that mountains and scenery without sea never possess. She has been a great traveller in Italy, in Algeria, in Sicily, and in France, but during these visits she has never been able to write; she invariably finds that her best work is done in some quiet, out-of-the-world village, where the only relaxation is to be found amongst the simple fisher-folk, and that the rough wild sea-coasts afford the most powerful inspiration.

A propos of 'Adam and Eve,' a few years ago Mrs. Parr was at Plymouth, and went into a shop to buy a photograph of Polperro. Selecting one, she asked the attendant, a true 'Devonshire maid,' ignorant of her customer, 'Is this one thought good?' 'Why, yes,' replied the girl; 'this is the place where Joan watched the fight from, and 'tis there that Eve stood to take her last look.'

'I felt very proud,' says Mrs. Parr, 'nearly as much so as when in return for a copy of the book sent, I had a letter from a rough old sailor who wrote, "I hadn't gone far afore I'd got to take off my coat to it, and there was

no turnin' in for me till I'd gone from cover to cover."'
The author laughingly contrasts this praise with the
admiration occasionally offered in the world of Society,
and with a fine sense of humour gives an instance. A
lady stopped her in the street to say, 'Oh! we have been
so enchanted with "Adam and Eve," we couldn't put it
down.' 'I hope you liked Joan?' replied Mrs. Parr.
'"Joan?" Oh, yes, by Rhoda Broughton. I've forgotten now what it was like, but I know we raved over it.'

There is yet one more recollection of this Cornish
story, and one that is of great beauty. The high oak
mantelpiece in the dining-room is set with Liverpool tiles,
representing the celebrated actors and actresses of the last
century in their favourite *rôles*. These tiles—of which a
similar set is framed in Kensington Museum—she brought
from Polperro.

Mrs. Parr remarks pleasantly that she is one of the
fortunate people who from the beginning have had occasion to speak well of publishers and the public. Perhaps
her amiable nature and unfailing tact may have something
to do with that. To young and struggling authors she is
well known as a kind and helpful adviser; one who is ever
ready to give them the benefit of her large experience, and
to comfort and warn them against discouragements,
while those who have the privilege of a closer acquaintance, can warmly testify to the strength and loyalty of
her friendship.

SIR AUGUSTUS HARRIS

A FULL history of the career of the great impresario, Sir
Augustus Harris, would fill two or three large volumes,
but until he, too, shall have given forth his 'Reminiscences' to the world, a brief summary of his life and
work will be found of interest. But first, a word of the

man himself, the courteous, genial, kindly gentleman who, with many gigantic enterprises on his shoulders and, besides, his coming opera season, generously accords you the favour of an hour's conversation and, without any semblance of hurry, walks up and down the room and relates a few incidents of a busy, eventful career. Blessed with an enormous talent for organisation, with a quick insight into every business detail, and a profound knowledge of human nature, he is also brimful of tact; the consequence is, that his huge machinery of people and of things runs on oiled wheels. But only those who are privileged to get a peep behind the scenes can at all realise the vastness of his undertakings, or the amount of physical and mental strength expended in bringing about such brilliant results.

His study—a harmony in white and blue—is a sight to behold, with its doors leading in every direction, and its well-filled book-shelves; a billiard-table forms his writing-desk, and is loaded with what may be called a tidy litter of proofs, scores, costume-books, plays to be read, photographs, &c. Two shorthand secretaries are hard at work, and a type-writer is at hand. Every few minutes telegrams and bundles of letters arrive. In the most methodical manner Sir Augustus glances over them, says a few words to one, dictates a message to another, anon resumes his walk and, going to a large portfolio opposite, leisurely and as if he had the whole day before him for frivolling, turns over and exhibits a collection of beautiful hand-tinted photographs, just received, of Japanese people.

He was born in Paris, and is the son of the late Mr. Augustus Harris, renowned for his skill as the finest manager of Italian opera in London, but who was looked on as the black sheep of the family when he was first known to enter the portals of a theatre. His grandfather was a Glossop, and his grandmother the celebrated singer Madame Féron; so on both sides he may be said to have inherited his artistic tastes. The last four years of his school-days were passed at the Collège Chaptal, Paris, during which time he was in the habit of spending his Sundays with Madame Patti, and pronounces it to be 'the best turn the Empire ever did him;' he had also the additional advantage of being constantly thrown into the society of the greatest artists, Rossini, Auber, Faure, Brandus, the musical editor of Meyerbeer, &c., and was *enfant de la maison* in all the cream of military and professional circles. Notwithstanding that his natural proclivities were fostered by such surroundings, and by being taken daily to the operas on the French stage—which he declares was then 'miles ahead of the English'—he was actually destined for business, and on his return to London he went to the Japanese College, and studied silk for a time at St. Katherine Docks. There Baron Erlanger offered him a seat in his office as foreign correspondent, at the end of which period he left for Paris, and entered the American firm of Tiffiny, diamond merchants. Six months later his father died, and the young Augustus Harris—not seeing before him the position to which he aspired, and with every thought and idea fixed on the stage—threw up a fine appointment, and elected to sink or swim on the waters of histrionic life. 'I began at the foot of the ladder,' he says, cheerfully. 'There was a revival of "Macbeth" at Manchester, and my first appearance before the footlights was as Malcolm with Miss Genevieve Ward as the Queen. Thence to Liverpool, where I played different *rôles* every night with Barry Sullivan, and had a hot time learning them!'

Then for a brief while the young player acted as stage-manager to Mr. Mapleson; and his next move was to Germany, where he was introduced to Madame Lucca, and through the influence of Prince Bismarck he obtained the *entrée* to the opera-house every night. A four years' engagement ensued as stage-manager to Mr. Mapleson, and on the departure of that gentleman to America, Augustus Harris 'went into pantomime' at the Crystal Palace; later, when 'Pink Dominoes' was to be put into rehearsal at the Criterion, Mr. Wyndham asked him to read the part of Harry Grunley; but one reading settled the matter, and he was put into the bill and played the character for 500 nights without a break. At its conclusion Mr. Harris heard that there was a similar part in Mr. G. R. Sims's 'Crutch and Toothpick,' about to be produced by Mr. Bruce. Thither the young actor repaired, to hear—though the place was not filled—there was nothing for him. 'Don't you want a stage-manager, or under-study, or anything?' he asked. But no; Mr. Bruce was in the happy position of wanting nothing! Not to be daunted, he dropped in another day, found Mr. Bruce busy over a play—'The Zoo'—and helped him so successfully that Mr. Bruce remarked drily, 'You had better stay on as stage-manager, or under-study, or anything,' which he did, and found himself one day, in conjunction with Mr. E. Rose, staging 'Venus,' which brought a small fortune to its owner.

But the present impresario had no idea of going in for comedy alone. This was all paving the way for what was to follow, and his ambition soared to have a theatre of his own. Drury Lane was then to be let; a backer was found; but though the young manager used all his ingenuity and diplomacy to bring him to book, the money promised was not forthcoming. Then did the stout-hearted spirit bestir itself and, after an infinite amount of trouble, succeed. 'Ultimately,' he remarks, reflectively, 'I managed to get the thing together, but that first year was a hard one, and there were many rocks to get through; however, it was good experience.' It must have been, indeed, an anxious time, as the first venture proved. Mr. Pettitt went to him and asked if, like other managers, he intended to produce Shakespeare only, or would give young authors a chance, further mentioning that he had a play written in conjunction with Mr. Merritt. An appointment was made to hear it read, but though not exactly what was wanted, the joint authors were told that if they liked to collaborate with himself in a play of which he had the *scenaria* in mind, the thing might be worked. Accordingly, 'The World' was put on. At first it did not make much way, though enormously applauded; for four weeks it looked very dangerous; it was in the dog-days, and the public came spasmodically. Then it woke up, took a long lease of life, and proved the first of many brilliant successes; the latest is the popular melodrama, 'Cheer, Boys, Cheer!' at Drury Lane.

But the perfect production of opera was what he yearned after. It had declined since the days when his father staged with much splendid spectacular effects 'Le Prophète,' 'La Juive,' 'Les Huguenots,' &c., and his desire was achieved in this wise. 'One evening,' he relates, 'I went to the opera in Drury Lane and was surprised to see what an awful performance it was. I then and there resolved to try my hand, and that I would revive it altogether or give it a decent burial; but it was at first a very bad patient!' he adds with a laugh. Needless to say, the 'patient' soon recovered under its new doctor—Augustus Harris, past master of practical detail and of scenic effects. His first effort, and one which he considers inaugurated a new era on the English stage, was the introduction of the Saxe-Meiningen Company at Covent Garden in 1882. Year after year the enterprising impresario has added to his triumphs. Being an excellent linguist, and always on the look-out for fresh novelties and the greatest artists, he has been able to produce opera in many languages. In the Jubilee year he won the well-merited order of Knighthood on the occasion of the late German Emperor's last visit to England. During 1894 he put forth light works in German at Drury Lane, together with twenty-one operas at Covent Garden, among which was Mr. Frederic Cowen's 'Signa.' The year 1895 welcomed Mesdames Patti and Albani (an event of peculiar interest, as these two artists had not been seen on the stage together for some years), Macintyre, Ravogli, Le Jeune, the brothers de Reszke, Tamagno, Pessina, De Lucia, and many other popular favourites, while 'Le Prophète,' 'Mefistofele,' 'Otello,' 'Lohengrin,' 'Il Trovatore,' 'Philemon et Baucis,' and 'Fra Diavolo' were among the rich treats provided—not to speak of the visit of the Saxe-Coburg Company to Drury Lane—by one who owns the proud distinction of having brought the opera to its present state of perfection. But—and as if this were not enough for one brain to conceive and carry out—Sir Augustus Harris must needs turn his attention to the regeneration of Pantomime, and some years ago waved his magic rod over this branch of theatrical art. A headpiece and the judicious expenditure of 20,000*l.*—where only between 2,000*l.* and 3,000*l.* had previously been laid out—enabled this remarkable man to produce such magnificence as can never be rivalled; though, to be sure, directly he achieved such marvellous work, many fresh Richmonds appeared in the field, invariably with the effect of doing no good for themselves, if indeed they do not get a tumble, or a rap over the knuckles! But it is ever thus: the great mind originates and carries out; the feebler imitates feebly; the former makes the success, the latter tries to take the glory away from it. The same spirit of improvement prompted Sir Augustus Harris long ago in melodrama. He desired to make comedy more dramatic with less of the 'blood and thunder' element, and what he sought to do in that direction he fully succeeded in doing. Again the same wish inspired him to take the Palace of Varieties; he designed to raise the tone of these entertainments, and when people asked him why he bothered himself about the improvement of music-halls, and what class of people he expected and hoped to get there, his reply was prompt and to the point—'The same who come to Covent Garden.'

As may be supposed, the charming home of Sir Augustus and Lady Harris contains all that there is of the most artistic within and without. It stands secluded in the most beautiful corner of Regent's Park, and is surrounded by fine old trees and undulating lawns that are gay with flower-beds. The approach is by a turfed lane, bordered on each side by trees, and on the left stands the Church of St. Stephen with its old-fashioned tower that forms a picturesque object in the foreground.

'The place has a musical reputation,' says Sir Augustus, as he leads the way out to the garden. 'Grisi lived here many years ago, but it has been much enlarged since then. It is so quiet and retired we might be miles in the country, and I do a good deal of thinking out and planning on these lawns.'

Lady Harris's delightful garden parties in this peaceful spot have a great renown. A perfect hostess, she and Sir Augustus here gather around them the most distinguished in the world of fashion and of art, and their home is enlivened by the presence of an only child, a sweet little maiden of ten years, who is the idol of her parents' hearts.

'I have stuck to my guns,' says Sir Augustus with a kindly smile, 'even when I have been mauled about by the enemy, which reminds me of a little story told me by Sir Evelyn Wood. When he was going up the Nile he didn't know how to cross the rapids; he was advised not to attempt it, but Lord Charles Beresford said, "Get through, or leave the ship's bottom stranded." It was the spirit of a soldier, and should be the same of a theatrical manager. Do or *die*!'

And it is precisely this spirit that has animated Sir Augustus Harris in his gigantic undertakings, and has won for him unprecedented success and the undying gratitude of the public.

SARAH GRAND

DESCENDED alike on each side from a race of artistic and talented families, of whom it might confidently have been predicted that, sooner or later, they would give to the world a poet, a painter, or an author of great note, Sarah

MADAME SARAH GRAND

Grand has fully verified these expectations, and proved that *bon sang ne peut pas mentir* by making for herself early in life a distinguished and unique name in literature.

Highly educated and accustomed from childhood to associate with cultured people, she was reared, so to speak, in an artistic as well as in a good social atmosphere, which has imbued her whole being, and led her to cultivate to the uttermost the intellectual gifts for which she is so renowned.

With every womanly grace and charm, a very gentle, quiet manner, and a low, musical voice, the young author is in herself a proof that it is generally the most highly educated of her sex who are the most refined; she holds the strongest opinions on this point, and maintains earnestly and on all occasions, that there is no reason why women who have attained unto knowledge should lose any of the charm of their feminine attributes, and that culture should not only stimulate them to increased efforts to stand by each other at all times and seasons, but also to preserve each in herself, in all its strength and glory, the respect and reverence due to womanhood.

'I always think,' she remarks quietly, 'that women who cultivate the best there is within themselves, will do more with a word than the too combative with their insistence and arguments, and they should never let it be supposed that because they advocate the " higher education," it unfits them for domestic duties or renders them unable to handle a baby, or darn a stocking. As it happens,' she adds, with a smile, 'I can manage to do both, I think.'

Sarah Grand's surroundings are in complete harmony with her opinions. In one of the oldest roads of historic Kensington, there has lately been erected a gigantic block of buildings that stand well back from the noisy hum of traffic, and by reason of their great height ensure the peace and quiet so necessary to a student. At the top floor of the further end of these mansions, a door opens into a broad, carpeted hall the walls of which are decorated with spears, quaint old daggers, swords and other warlike implements sent to her by her soldier stepsons, from Africa and Abyssinia, together with various cleverly executed etchings and drawings. On the left, the large, nearly square room where you presently find yourself, presents a bright and picturesque aspect. The four long windows in one broad flat bay running entirely across the south side with tapestry settees below, are hung with rich, gold embroidered Rose du Barri silk curtains. The rays of the summer sun stealing through their soft folds, cast ruddy tints on the amber-tiled fireplace and white Louis Quinze carved mantelshelf, a faint gleam of colour just resting on the central figure above a gravure of the 'Cruche Cassée,' after Greuze's painting in the Louvre. A thick Persian carpet of subdued tints with deep border of exquisite colouring nearly covers the polished floor; a restful looking Chesterfield couch with big down cushions, is covered with rare old Gobelin tapestry; in the further corner stands an ancient Chippendale writing-bureau with papers neatly arranged. Two large photographs, handsomely framed, stand on a small Sheraton table near, to which Madame Sarah Grand draws your attention. 'They are the portraits of my stepsons,' she explains. 'They do all the business of life for me, and are the greatest friends I have in the world.' Roses everywhere in abundance, gifts from many friends, who seem to have vied with each other on her *fête* day to bring to Sarah Grand the tributes she loves best. On yonder Chinese ebony stand with marble top is a gigantic bowl of old blue and white Delft full of roses, Maréchal Niel, gloire de Dijon, and the deep red, velvety blossoms of the 'Black Prince,' amidst which a bumble bee drones and hums, filling the air with languorous sound. A butterfly from the neighbouring gardens, attracted by the sweet breath of the flowers, has flown in and poises lightly with quivering wings on a fragrant bunch of mignonette. The pale China-blue walls with deeper tinted friezes are hung with choice original etchings of ' Morninquest.'

Madame Sarah Grand's taste in literature is indicated by many well-worn volumes in the bookcase. Never a great reader of stories, she prefers fact to fiction, and natural history, physiology, and also what may be called quasi-scientific books such as Nesbit's. She delights in Emerson's ' Essays,' and Oliver Wendell Holmes's ' Breakfast Table Series ' occupy a prominent place. ' All that warm one's heart and enlarge one's sympathies,' she says, ' all that are sweet, wholesome and most nourishing—amongst the poets, Shelley, Swinburne, Tennyson, Longfellow, according to one's mood.' The piano opposite has its own special use as an aid to thought, as when she wants to think out any serious thing, she sits down to play and finds that Beethoven and Chopin are the most helpful composers.

A small Chippendale table is laid out with a dainty little Queen Anne tea-service, and whilst your hostess dispenses the tea, her personality is rapidly committed to your memory and may be described as follows: Something over the medium height, and slight in figure, the face, of pure oval shape, is crowned with soft brown curly hair; a brow that indicates intellect and spirituality; eyes deep grey in hue; and a complexion of delicate colouring; a serious, somewhat sad, expression when in repose, but which relaxes into a smile of winning sweetness as she indulges you at your earnest request with a slight sketch of her brief literary career.

' I was neither particularly thoughtful nor studious as a child,' she remarks, as she hands you a cup of tea; ' indeed, I can remember getting into various scrapes at school, owing to over high spirits.' She loved out-of-door life, pet animals taking the place of dolls, whilst her special delight was an aquarium, for which she used to grub about in ditches in search of specimens; but at a very early age her imagination began to work, long before her intellect was fully awakened; for she used to tell serial stories some time before she had learnt to write them. She had always the run of a good library, and began to realise quite suddenly the depth of social questions; then the impulse to express her ideas grew strong in her mind, 'and,' she remarks thoughtfully, after a pause, 'I wrote simply because I could not help it.'

Her musical nature found vent at the age of eleven, when she wrote a song and set it to music, a remembrance at which she laughs now, though at the time she felt it to be a distinct grievance that it was not published. Gifted with keen powers of observation, she had been from youth up in the habit of always carrying a note-book, in which she recorded impressions of people and things, a habit which she pronounces to have been invaluable in her profession, and she has now a large collection of little volumes filled with these jottings.

Sarah Grand's first real start in literature was made with the production of 'Ideala,' a study from life, though she had previously written several short stories and essays. There was considerable difficulty with this work. After many rejections, the author, nothing daunted by failure, decided to publish it at her own expense, and having the courage of her opinions, she was rewarded by seeing the book pass into four editions. It is perhaps interesting to note, in relation to the late controversy about the three-volume novel that Madame Sarah Grand's first work was brought out by herself in one volume. That she succeeded in making herself heard and appreciated by the public is proved by the fact that, although it is eight years since 'Ideala' was written, a new edition of ten thousand copies has been lately brought out by Mr. Heinemann.

Her next important venture was 'The Heavenly Twins,' a work which was more discussed and more widely sold than any book of the day. Two years of much preparation and thought, of patient and earnest study—for such a book could not have been written on the impulse of the moment—were expended on this celebrated novel. Into it Sarah Grand put all that was best of herself. She sat down, not to write what is ordinarily meant by writing a novel with a purpose, but to depict a neighbourhood with its group of characters, types evolved by close observation, with the idea of developing them on natural lines, treating them without prejudice or making them answer to foregone conclusions. One great pleasure that this remarkable book has given the author, is the receipt of many letters from medical men, known and unknown, complimenting her on her accurate knowledge of physiology and of pathology ; another keen enjoyment has been derived from letters from absolute strangers, women in distant lands, telling her that she has done more for the cause of women and children than she will ever know.

But Sarah Grand's writings are by no means confined to abstruse physiological subjects. A keen sense of humour peeps out in the story of 'Ah Man,' the Chinese servant, and a note of indescribable pathos in 'Janey, a Humble Administrator ; ' while the other stories in 'Our Manifold Nature' are full of exquisite little episodes which betray the deep poetic feeling of the gifted writer.

She has enlarged her experience greatly by foreign travel. A prolonged tour in the East gave Sarah Grand a fine opportunity for making herself thoroughly acquainted with the various types of Oriental character and their manner of life. She passed through Egypt, Ceylon, the Straits Settlements, and so on to China and Japan, where, with her English maid and a Chinese cook, she spent some time in the house of the mayor of a little village, and there learnt much of native life from the inside. Then she returned through the beautiful Inland Sea, touching at Shanghai. Always a worshipper of the sea in its ever-changing moods and an ardent admirer of nature and of fine views, the picturesque loveliness of the Land of the Rising Sun, with its tranquillising and inspiring scenery, appealed strongly to Sarah Grand's artistic temperament. Strolling here and there as fancy dictated, she extended her interesting and instructive wanderings, and it was about five years before she turned her footsteps homeward.

An early riser, she devotes from eight o'clock to three daily to intellectual pursuits. She has no settled method of weaving a plot; but before a new work is in contemplation, as is the case at present, she has a general idea of the whole, with a knowledge of what she is going to do with a central figure or two in the foreground. Then the characters shape themselves as they develop, and sometimes, as she says, they run away with her; but she finds that the manifold interruptions and distractions of busy London are very serious hindrances to steady work, so, disliking crowds and retaining her early love of outdoor life, she is apt occasionally to make a temporary retreat to some lovely spot, where, among picturesque surroundings, in pure air and under the leafy trees, she can commune with nature and pursue her art in comparative solitude.

Not to all authors is it given to win fame and independence so early in life; but with Sarah Grand the prominent idea is to be sincere, thorough, and true to herself. 'Whatever thy hand findeth to do, do it with thy might,' she observes reverently. Like one of her own heroines, she possesses a 'mind of exceptional purity as well as of exceptional strength; one to be enlightened by knowledge, not corrupted.' The keynote of her nature is her intense and tender sympathy with the weak and the oppressed. It is undoubtedly this earnestness and thoroughness of purpose, this 'doing with her might,' that has stood her in good stead throughout her hitherto short but brilliant literary career

HENRY ARTHUR JONES

IT is curious and interesting to notice, if you go through life with observant eyes and a somewhat inquiring mind, how often that which seems to be the merest chance incident is capable of deciding that all-important matter—a man's career. Perhaps, if Mr. Henry Arthur Jones had not on one memorable evening when he was only eighteen years of age, dropped in at the Haymarket Theatre, it might never have occurred to him to turn his attention to dramatic literature. He might, instead, now have been one of the merchant princes of London, and the world might never have enjoyed the rich treats of such powerful and original plays as 'Judah,' 'The Dancing Girl,' 'The Crusaders,' 'The Middleman,' 'The Tempter,' 'The Masqueraders,' 'The Case of Rebellious Susan,' 'The Triumph of the Philistines,' not to mention 'The Silver King,' that universal darling of the public, old and young, which many years ago took the town by storm, ran over a year, and merrily pursued its course through the provinces, then travelled to America and Australia, with a success that has never yet seemed to tire. His latest play is 'Michael and His Lost Angel.'

The author was born in Buckinghamshire, at a large old-fashioned homestead overlooking the Vale of Aylesbury. About forty years ago railways were almost unknown in that part of England, or at any rate their influence had not begun to be felt. It was practically in the very heart of the country, all day long in the open air, that his childish days were spent. This early communing with mother-Nature has probably influenced his whole life, as even in these later days, whenever a particularly knotty point protrudes itself in his work, he is in the habit of rising early and going forth for a long day's ride or walk to where he can find most solitude and the prettiest views. Then the difficulty is solved, and the hitherto tangled skein is invariably unravelled and made smooth.

Blessed with a naturally keen perception of persons and things, with eyes and ears ever open to observe and to learn, even at that early age he noticed amongst the North Buckinghamshire villagers various types of rustic life. These types his remarkably retentive memory enabled him to recollect, and from the storehouse of his brain they were brought forth later and introduced into some of his plays.

At school he plodded and studied with dogged perseverance. While other boys were engrossed in the charms of cricket and of football, the young lad was absorbed in his books, among them his edition of Shakespeare was well scored and thumbed. At the age of thirteen he had already written many stories, and having made such good use of his time, he was considered sufficiently advanced in his education to leave school and to enter an office as a clerk. Here he resolutely turned his young mind to learning the business to which, uncongenial as it was to a youth of such pronounced literary tastes, he brought the strong will and unflagging perseverance that have stood him in such good stead throughout his career.

That these good qualities sooner or later bring their own reward, is proved by the fact that at the age of twenty-three Mr. Jones was able to marry and settle down into domestic life.

During his office years every hour that was not occupied in business was devoted to literature, although no idea of writing plays had as yet entered his mind. Tales, essays, articles, social and even political, poured from his pen. These were regularly sent to papers and magazines, but were as regularly returned. As fast as one editor declined them, they were despatched to another; however, he had determined to write at least one three-volume novel. It was fortunately not in the young author to be daunted by any failure. Having 'determined,' it stood to reason that he would carry out the intention, and accordingly the three-volume novel was written and took three precious years to accomplish. Although that literary effort shared the same fate as its predecessors, the work was not altogether thrown away, as a large portion of it was utilised in the production of 'The Silver King,' proving that what was pronounced by a 'reader' to be only 'a passable third-rate novel,' had stuff in it that was capable of making a first-class and very popular play.

Reared in the country and in somewhat narrow puritanical doctrine, it so happened that the boy had never seen the inside of a theatre. At last came the never-to-be-forgotten night which marked the turning-point in his life. He had now arrived at an age to think for himself. Having occasion to run up to town for a day or two on business connected with his firm, he bent his steps that evening to the Haymarket Theatre, and sat spell-bound through the famous play of 'Leah,' in which Miss Bateman so distinguished herself as to draw all London. Perhaps no better play could be found to stir for the first time an ardent and receptive mind. Certain it is that on the eventful evening Henry Arthur Jones may be said to have met his fate, as he resolved that some day—it might be in the far future—he would write a piece of his own. It is characteristic of the man with whom to *will* is to *do*, that twenty years later his 'Dancing Girl' was produced at that selfsame theatre and achieved an overwhelming success.

There were, however, many years of hard work to be got through before a first triumph was achieved. Every spare moment now was devoted to writing plays, every spare evening to the study of the drama. He would go night after night to the same piece to analyse its *technique* and composition. Looking back, Mr. Jones cannot recollect that he had any inherited talent for dramatic literature; but as his brother, under the pseudonym of 'Silvanus

Dauncey,' has also written several minor plays and one four-act piece called 'The Reckoning,' it is possible that the strain may be traced back to some remote ancestor.

Never crushed by disappointment nor beaten by the constant rejection of his compositions, the persevering young dramatist steadily toiled on. 'The race is not to the swift;' but with the goal ever before him, and the unconquerable spirit that would let no obstacle baffle him, it followed sooner or later that he was bound to come to the front. It came to him 'sooner,' for, before he was thirty years of age, being in a position to relinquish the cares of office life, he was enabled to turn the whole of his attention to the profession in which he has become so distinguished.

His first farce, 'Only Round the Corner,' was accepted in 1878 by Rousby, then manager of the Exeter Theatre. This little piece had not much of a run in England, although only two years ago, when brought out in America, under the title of 'The Organist,' it made a decided hit, and met with an amount of such favourable criticism as would have greatly encouraged the then struggling young writer.

'A Clerical Error'—a play that had been offered to and declined by every manager in London—was Mr. Jones's next effort. The piece was at once accepted by Wilson Barrett, who was just then leaving the management of the Grand Theatre, Leeds. Mr. Barrett, almost immediately after, took the Court Theatre, and brought out the piece during the following season. It was bright and witty, it created considerable attention, had a long run at home and abroad, and has since been constantly revived.

His foot had now climbed the first rung of the ladder, and in the next few years it rapidly ascended a good many more steps. His name was well before the public, and there was no longer any question of his ultimate success.

Miss Bateman brought out the next piece, 'His Wife,' at the Sadler's Wells Theatre, and, later, took it round the provinces. 'The Silver King,' in 1882, sent the author with a bound up the remaining stairs of the ladder. For a while he accepted commissions for such plays as 'Hard Hit,' 'Hoodman Blind,' 'The Noble Vagabond,' &c.; but it was not likely that a mind so entirely original in its conceptions could settle down to compose 'to order.' This method of work fettered and stifled him; he desired to soar on his own wings. Intensely disliking spectacular melodrama, and intent on depicting different phases of the English life of to-day, he resolved for the future to allow himself a free hand and to strike out in the direction of his ideal. The result of this decision is found in his succeeding plays.

'Saints and Sinners' ran for two hundred nights at the Vaudeville. 'The Middleman,' which 'caught on' at once, was played for even a longer time at the Shaftesbury. 'Judah' followed in 1890. 'The Dancing Girl,' which with many people was the greatest favourite of all, was played for nearly a year at the Haymarket. 'The Crusaders,' a strong and striking conception, filled the Avenue Theatre for over a hundred nights. To Mr. Henry Arthur Jones has fallen an honour which has never before come to the lot of an English dramatist. Besides being produced in America and Australia, most of his pieces have been played successfully in Germany and in Holland, in Austria, Denmark, and in Belgium.

'The Tempter' is the first play that he has produced in blank verse, though not the first he has written. Here he has broken entirely new ground, but the reception accorded to this powerful and poetic tragedy proved that he is as much in his element in portraying mediæval England as in depicting the less romantic life of modern times.

As may be supposed, Mr. Jones is a great reader, but not of modern fiction. He is naturally well versed in the old dramatists, the old English humourists, and in all the standard English poets. Ruskin and Matthew Arnold, the philosophical works of Huxley, Spencer, and Darwin are his favourite studies. His usual working hours are either very early in the morning or from six to eight in the evening. He always has three or four embryo plays seething and brewing in his brain, but until they are somewhat matured and arranged he puts no pen to paper. Once fairly started he writes off each succeeding act more quickly than the last. As far as the actual writing goes the strong emotional scenes are seldom retouched. The comedy parts are polished and re-polished. He is very particular about the names of his characters, and declares that he finds it almost impossible to draw them until he has hit on names that seem to describe them.

He works better at the seaside than in London, but he will sometimes takes a fancy that he cannot work well at one place and goes off to another. Thus, the first two acts of 'The Tempter' were written at Folkestone, the last two at Nice.

Mr. Henry Arthur Jones's home is ideal in all respects. Situated in the heights of north-western London, it commands a fine view of Regent's Park. The hall is hung with choice works of Albert Dürer and other proof-before-letters engravings. Here is one of Mr. Harry Furniss's witty etchings round the margin of his letter, there several interesting collections of playbills and programmes framed. The three reception-rooms lead into one another; the floor of one is curiously inlaid with narrow lines of ivory. There are a few handsome specimens of genuine old Chippendale bureaus, tables and chairs which stand out well against the soft tapestry hangings; and many bits of antique china. Everything is indicative of the highly cultivated and artistic taste of its owners.

By the way, an irreparable catastrophe occurred in the once beautiful study. It was formerly Alma Tadema's studio, and the exquisite ceiling was painted by the great artist's own hand with mythological scenes and figures.

Mr. Jones was busily occupied at his desk when he suddenly reflected that he would be late for an appointment he had made. He hastily rose and left the house. A few moments later, without sign or sound of warning, down with a crash came the beautiful ceiling. A large portion of the *débris* actually fell on the very spot where the author's old-fashioned, high-backed tapestry-covered chair had just been vacated.

Success has come to the accomplished playwright comparatively very early in life. A brilliant and intellectual conversationalist, he is also an excellent listener. With a singularly quiet, sympathetic manner, he has the happy knack of drawing out the best that is in those with whom he converses, and although besieged with business he yet never conveys the impression that he is in any haste; while the receptions held by Mr. and Mrs. Henry Arthur Jones are among the most attractive and intellectual in London.

MRS. CROKER

The scene is a lovely view of the Wicklow Mountains, which seem as if divided into groups separated by precipitous ravines, generally straight and narrow. The declivities slope gently downwards in many places, terminating in glens and valleys. The lofty promontory of Bray Head rises to the height of some 800 feet above the level of the sea and, overhanging it, makes a conspicuous sea-mark. The landscape is wild and picturesque. Facing all this grandeur of nature by the south, there stands, in about five acres of garden, lawn, and pleasure ground, a large, old-fashioned cottage, which has apparently been added to at different times by artistic hands that knew better than to destroy its original beauty. Protected by the great mountains from the wild, rough winds that blow up from St. George's Channel, the aspect of the cottage is such that even in mid-winter the whole is covered with roses and creepers which, clustering upwards, peep in at the bay-windows.

Nothing could be more disassociated with the scenes of death and battle than this quiet, peaceful spot; nevertheless, it bears the warlike name of Lordello, and was so called by the man who built it in memory of his brother, who fell in an engagement at the village of Lordello in Spain during the Peninsular war. But the place has been destined to have military surroundings, and is now the abode of Colonel Croker, lately retired from the service, and his talented wife, who is so well known to the world through her delightful novels of Indian life and experiences.

The tall, soldierly looking man who comes out into the hall has been a great traveller, and is a renowned *shikari*. The young girl yonder is their only child, and bears a striking resemblance to her father, with just a look of her mother, who is tall and very fair, with great Irish blue-grey eyes, in which a merry sparkle may be observed.

The interior of the cottage is all in keeping. The long, narrow hall, with two sitting-rooms on each side, is liberally decorated with tiger and leopard skins, Indian daggers, knives, horns and other trophies, whilst a magnificent stuffed tiger's head with gnashing teeth hangs over a door facing the entrance.

The pretty, bright drawing-room is daintily draped with silk embroideries from the East; the carpet was made at Agra; the piano has twice crossed the sea. Palms and ferns stand here and there among quaint Oriental carvings, brasses, and foreign ornaments of all sorts. On the walls hang several good water-colour sketches of places in India. Here a view of the blue hills of the Neilgherries, there scenes from the snow-covered Himalayan mountains.

Mrs. Croker's own little study has a French window opening on to the lawn, and has a warm, cheerful appearance with its bright-hued Indian carpet and easy-chairs, its great writing-table and bookcases. A good many novels can be detected behind its glass doors. 'Hitherto,' says Mrs. Croker, 'I have had no means of knowing my fellow-workers except through their books. It is always a matter of regret to me that, living so much abroad, or in garrison towns at home, I have never had the opportunity of becoming personally acquainted with many of my own profession; but in future I do hope to go occasionally to England and get into touch with those whose books I so much admire.'

Mrs. Croker was born in Ireland, and comes of old Puritan families on both sides. Her father, the Rev. W. Sheppard, rector of Kilgriffer, died in the prime of life when his only daughter was but seven years of age. He was a man of considerable intellectual attainments, a good writer and a brilliant conversationalist. The young girl was educated mostly in France, and being by nature a student, all her leisure hours were spent in reading. At school she distinguished herself by the fluency of her essays and the ease of her letter-writing, in which she depicted with equal reality the people whom she met and the places that she saw. History, geography political and physical, poetry and languages, were her favourite studies, but arithmetic and algebra were alike repugnant. 'Indeed, to be quite candid,' says Mrs. Croker, laughing, 'there used to be some sort of friendly exchange among the girls. Some, who were clever enough in other ways, would come to me in despair over a subject for a theme, such as "Memory," "Sympathy," and so on. I easily undertook their task and they in return took my algebra.'

Accustomed from childhood to the saddle, her favourite recreation was riding; on her return from school she became a famous horsewoman and used to hunt with the Kildares. Shortly after she became engaged to Colonel Croker, of the Munster Fusiliers, then a lieutenant in the 21st Royal Scots Fusiliers, and when very young she married and immediately afterwards accompanied him to India.

Up to 1880 no idea of adopting literature as a profession had entered her head. She had never thought of writing a novel, still less of getting it published, but being naturally a close observer of places and of persons, she had accumulated a storehouse of information which was destined suddenly to be opened and drawn upon.

It happened that the 'hot weather' of that year was abnormally hot; Secunderabad was more than usually scorched by the dry, arid winds of the Deccan. Ice was scarce, and even the incessant punkah day and night seemed to give no relief. The greater number of the residents had fled to the hills in search of cool breezes. Merely to amuse herself and to beguile the long weary days, she secretly drew out her pen. Then, as in a dream, everything passed swiftly before her: fleeting visions of places, people past and present, conversations, ideas, &c. The moment of inspiration had come and was seized; the hours now passed quickly enough; the intense heat —such as no one can imagine who has not passed a hot season in the plains—was forgotten, as day after day was spent in transmitting her thoughts to paper. But it was impossible wholly to conceal her occupation from the other ladies in the regiment, and after sundry veiled hints and delicate inquiries from her friends, Mrs. Croker, with many blushes, reluctantly revealed her secret and, after much persuasion, was prevailed upon to read aloud her MS.

'I called the book "Proper Pride,"' says Mrs. Croker. 'For many days we used to meet daily for these readings, but I never once thought of its finding its way into print. My friends kindly declared that it gave quite a new interest in their lives and unanimously pronounced that it ought to be published, but this was easier said than done. None of us had the slightest idea of how to set about getting a book printed. At last I sent it home to a publisher, and heard no more of it for a year; then, thinking that probably the parcel had been lost, I re-wrote the whole from memory.'

Although this first effort had not as yet seen the light, the young author had become absorbed in the fascination of story-telling, and, nothing daunted, wrote her second work, 'Pretty Miss Neville,' which again ran the gauntlet of her intimate friends only, in a series of private readings. In 1881 she and her husband went home with the regiment, and on their arrival the second MS. was sent to another firm of publishers. 'I remember that it was Christmas Day,' remarks Mrs. Croker, cheerfully —for she can afford now to laugh at these reminiscences— 'I received an unwelcome Christmas-box in the shape of a most polite letter from the firm, and I can recall the very words in it : " The story had no pretensions whatsoever to style or interest, and would not obtain even a passing notice from the public !" I was disheartened, but as my hopes had never been high, I was by no means a prey to despair. I supposed the verdict must be right, so I just put the whole MS. into a big grate where there was a fire smouldering and left the room. Luckily for me the fire was very low; my daughter, then a little girl, snatched it off and rescued it. She had heard the story read aloud and naturally thought a great deal of it. I then fell back on " Proper Pride," which was not lost but only reposing with string uncut in the office where I had sent it, and it was eventually brought out. Needless to say, I was charmed to see myself in print, but I awaited with terror the reviews. I said to myself, that as long as a certain great weekly journal does not mention it at all I shall not so much mind, for I feared its ridicule.'

But the author was needlessly alarmed. Her own modesty had led her to expect nothing more than an insignificant *début*, and she had scarcely even hoped that a mere amateur such as she considered herself would be noticed at all. She published anonymously, and no one was more surprised than she when the much-dreaded weekly, devoted to the novel two columns of that meed of favourable criticism so dear to the heart of a writer. The principal daily paper too, and others, reviewed it equally pleasantly and nearly all the critics spoke of it as the work of a man. The book passed into three editions in six weeks. Like all Mrs. Croker's subsequent works, it has been translated into German, running previously through a German paper, and appeared simultaneously in Great Britain, in Australia, the United States and in Canada. It is now in its twelfth edition.

A propos of this book the author has a little anecdote to relate. So well had she concealed her identity that none of her friends in England had associated her with it. She was in the habit of hearing it frequently discussed at dinner parties and afternoon teas. One day she met an acquaintance at the Dover bookstall where they mutually subscribed. The lady, after mentioning the novel as being so popular and so widely read, remarked, 'Someone actually told me that it was written by a Mrs. Croker in Dover, wife of an officer in the Royal Scots Fusiliers. Of course I laughed him to scorn. You are about the last person to write a book!' The author joined in the laugh. Presently the librarian came up and, bringing her own novel, whispered mysteriously, 'I kept a copy aside for you as you are such a quick reader; there is a wonderful run on it. They say it is written by a lady in Dover.' Mrs. Croker walked away with her book and made no remark.

Almost immediately after came the story that had been rescued from the flames, 'Pretty Miss Neville,' which was even a greater success. It has lately been dramatised, and is shortly to be played in Vienna. This was followed at intervals of a year by 'Someone Else,' 'A Bird of Passage,' and 'Diana Barrington.' These last two are the author's own favourites. Then came 'Two Masters,' 'Interference,' 'A Family Likeness,' 'To Let' (short stories), 'A Third Person,' 'The Poor Relation,' 'Married or Single,' and 'The Real Lady Hilda.'

These delightful tales of India are studies from life. The descriptions of scenery so graphically and artistically given are all true backgrounds to the stories. The natives are all real persons and described as the author saw them. She has indeed had peculiar opportunities for becoming so intimately acquainted with India. Owing to exceptional circumstances, she had been enabled to travel over the greater part of the country. Exclusive of trips home, Mrs. Croker has spent about fourteen years in the East, and has seen nearly the whole of the Madras Presidency, Burmah, the Andamans, the Deccan and the Neilgherries.

This long residence was not, however, altogether of their own choice. Colonel Croker had done one tour of India and then spent a few years at home when he was placed on half-pay, owing to one of the many Royal Warrants. He was subsequently brought into another regiment and despatched on a second tour to the East, when they visited most of the Central and North-West Provinces.

Of the Neilgherries the author speaks with much enthusiasm. She 'has an admiration almost amounting to a passion for these Blue Hills,' and declares them to be 'in all respects the most delightful and salubrious of ranges.' As she journeyed up, 'the close, tropical vegetation was left behind, the trees assumed a more European aspect, the air lost its steamy feel and became every instant more rarefied and pure. The path appeared to wind in and out through mountain-sides clothed with trees and foliage of every description. A foaming river was tearing headlong down a wide, rocky channel and taking frantic leaps over all impediments. Wild roses and wild geraniums abounded on all sides; enormous bunches of heliotrope were growing between the stones; lovely flowering creepers connected the trees. Before the windows of the hotel there was a hedge of heliotrope cut like box at home, so high and so dense that you could ride on one side of it and someone else on the other without either being aware of mutual proximity. It was one mass of flowers, and smelt like ten thousand cherry-pies, and was one of the sights of the Neilgherries; but for actual grandeur and magnificence of scenery even these hills cannot be compared to the Himalayas.'

Loving the beauties of Nature before all things, and having enjoyed the advantages of living amidst some of the finest scenery in the world, Mrs. Croker is peculiarly happy in her brilliant and vivid word-painting of the places she depicts. The reader can see with his own eyes the views that she describes. He feels himself to be one of those present whether in the home-life of a bungalow in the plains, or in the gay society of a fashionable hill-station in these most attractive and interesting pictures of life in India. He makes one of the group of passengers on board the P. and O. steamer, one of the party at the exciting tiger-hunts and pig-sticking adventures. The reason is not far to seek. There is an atmosphere of reality about her books. The very animals of which she writes seem to have an individuality of their own. The brightness and crispness of the dialogue cause each character to stand out and contribute its share to the development of the story.

She is equally at home in her description of fox-hunting in Ireland as in her race meeting and sporting scenes in India, and the reader would imagine that she must have been present at many a tiger-hunt, but this is not the case. Colonel Croker was, however, a keen sportsman and his experiences came in quite fresh to her; but this would not be enough without the special faculty of observation and the gift of forcibly expressing so much in so few words, that constitute the charm of Mrs. Croker's writing. The stories are told simply and with much vivacity. The most telling situations are concisely narrated and the interest is never allowed to flag. Certainly, she was never present on a field of battle, yet her stirring account of the Afghanistan expedition, and the camp-life of the troops in South Africa, are related with so much spirit and veracity that those who in the flesh, took part in both can vouch for their fidelity.

'There were a few things that were only too real to me,' says Mrs. Croker. ' I have twice been in camp when a tiger has been in the neighbourhood, and seen the mark of his pugs, after he had carried off a pet dog. Once a panther took a dear little dog out of the verandah of our bungalow, and I have often, to my sorrow, been up and down the six hundred steps described in " Diana Barrington," when we were at Ram Tek dâk Bungalow. It was the only means of getting down to the water. Ram Tek is a wonderful place, quite off the beaten track and but little known.'

Mrs. Croker has a volume of native stories and a new Indian novel in hand, which has, indeed, been on the stocks for two years. All are sketched out in the rough from copious notes taken on the spot. She never writes in haste, and finds it so hard to please herself that often one chapter is re-written ten times before it is allowed to pass. Her working hours are generally in the early morning, for she preserves the habit acquired in India of being up betimes. When deeply engrossed in a story and in writing mood, she is often known to work for ten or twelve hours for many consecutive days, until the people who are worrying her brain are drawn in black and white; but then someone in authority is apt to intervene, and his slightest wish is her law. She loves writing for its own sake, even if it were never to produce a penny. Luckily, however, it brings in a good many pennies ; but she maintains that the greatest pleasure she derives from it consists in the receipt of many letters from strangers and invalids, often at the other end of the world, saying that her books have wiled away many a long and weary hour of sickness, or have produced much temporary distraction and comfort when in anxiety or in sorrow.

With all her experiences of sport at home and abroad, Mrs. Croker is essentially gentle and feminine in her tastes and habits. She is bright and frank in manner, with a pretty wit, for which her Irish blood is partly responsible. She has plenty of practical good sense, and a happy, sunny nature which looks on things from the brightest point of view. Her concluding words are thoroughly characteristic. 'The press,' she observes, with much feeling, 'on which I do not know a soul, has always treated me most generously, and much of my encouragement has come from my unknown critics, to whom I am truly grateful.'

GEORGE R. SIMS

ACCORDING to Mr. G. R. Sims's own statement, he is 'a humdrum, old-fashioned, quiet individual, who has met with no adventures: never was in a railway accident, never wrecked at sea, and the only romance that he ever experienced was when he was once pitched out of his trap and alighted on his head, and even then was not injured enough to be in any way interesting.' He further asserts that he 'has no genius—only wishes he had—as genius comes down from the ceiling, and does your work for you, whereas he is only a hard worker, and has to do his work for himself.' Yet those who get a peep behind the scenes, and know something of the gifted writer's inner nature, will promptly contradict these statements. His literary works—numerous and versatile—speak for themselves, while under what he would fain make you believe to be a prosaic, stern, nay, cynical character, there lies the kindest, softest heart; a deep, poetic vein; an ever-working imagination, a brilliant originality of thought, with ample power of carrying it out, and a wonderful way of evoking the sympathy of those with whom he is brought in contact, even after a brief acquaintance. With an acutely strung nervous organisation—usually an accompaniment of true genius—Mr. Sims combines what is by no means one of its ordinary attributes. He is so scrupulously orderly, methodical and practical to the utmost detail, that in his house, which is a perfect dream of beauty and of art, and which must certainly contain more possessions than the contents of any three houses in the terrace put together, there is no appearance of overcrowding. Nor is it in any way stiff. Everything has its *raison d'être*, and is so arranged and disposed that, even with a bird's-eye view, it needs no perspicacity to determine that none but a master-mind and an artistic hand, guided by an inborn love of the beautiful, could have produced such delightful and unique effects.

Educated partly at Eastbourne, and partly at Hanwell College, George R. Sims manifested his literary propensities at a very early age. He was in the habit of writing his home letters in verse, and of composing little plays, for which he says 'he took chunks out of H. J. Byron's.' His first attempt as an essayist very nearly got him into trouble, for it was no less than a sweeping denunciation, in the 'College Gazette,' of the scheme of the school management, to which the head-master not unnaturally objected.

'But you ask if I inherit talent?' says Mr. Sims. 'My mother was a very clever woman, and various relations " did things." The doctrine of heredity is so large that I should have to invite you to spend a week with me to thresh it out thoroughly.' Moving on first to Germany, then to Paris, to learn languages, after a few years the young student returned to London and entered into business. From the age of fourteen he was a journalist and constantly sent stories and poems to different journals, that were nearly always returned, or, if accepted, were never paid for. With dogged perseverance he went on, and when, after thirteen years, his first book, 'The Social Kaleidoscope'—which had previously run as a serial through a magazine—was brought out and ran into a sale of 30,000 during its first year alone, G. R. Sims at last tasted the sweets of success. He remembers well his first guinea earned by writing. A chance meeting with an amateur actor led to his joining a Bohemian club, where he was introduced to a journalist on the 'Weekly Dispatch.' The result was a column on 'Waifs and Strays.' Then followed 'The Social Kaleidoscope,' which in book form brings him many guineas to this day. Thirteen years of rejections! Truly it was enough to have embittered and soured most young writers, but—and it is characteristic of the man—the only effect it seems to have produced on him is that, when shortly every journal was open to him, his heart went out in tender sympathy to those who were still enduring the sufferings he had known so well. From that time on it has been easy sailing. Resigning business, he set earnestly to work to study life and character in all its phases among the poor, visiting workhouses, slums, casual wards, and every place where he could sound to the depths the inner world of sorrowing humanity, and he depicted so forcibly and graphically their woes that he succeeded in stirring the whole of London into making researches as to the housing of the poor. And here, too, he would try, deprecatingly, to make you believe that it was 'all in the way of "copy," and paid for, and that he is no philanthropist, and while studying the wrongs of the people he really thought more about his own.' But the attempt is quite useless. His great work is too well known for that. His name is a household word in the East End of London, as elsewhere, and the doings of his right hand are carefully concealed from his left. The soul-stirring works, 'How the Poor Live,' 'Horrible London,' a series of letters which first ran through the 'Daily News,' 'The Pinch of Poverty,' 'Mary Jane's Memoirs,' and 'Mary Jane Married,' were the outcome of these visits at dock-gates, penny gaffs, &c., and are all more or less sketches of realistic life. They were followed by 'Memoirs of a Mother-in-law,' 'Memoirs of a Landlady,' 'Rogues and Vagabonds,' 'My Two Wives,' 'Zeph,' 'Scenes from the Show,' &c.—in all some twenty-five to thirty books. The readers of the 'Referee' would look blank indeed without Dagonet's popular 'Mustard and Cress,' which from the first issue of that paper in 1877, to the present day, Mr. Sims has never failed to produce weekly, though before that date he had contributed for three years to the pages of 'Fun,' after Tom Hood's death. A thorough hard worker—for Mr. Sims has ofttimes toiled eighteen hours out of the twenty-four—the unusual amount of business, literary and other, that he gets through is extraordinary. His plays are acted, his pieces are recited, his songs are sung wherever the English tongue is spoken. During later years he has turned his attention to melodramatic literature, and here his success has been unprecedented. 'Crutch and Toothpick' ran first for nine months at the Royalty, then went on touring in the provinces for years. Next came the famous 'Lights o' London,' at the Princess's under Mr. Wilson Barrett's management, followed by 'Romany Rye,' 'In the Ranks,' 'London Day by Day,' 'Mother-in-Law,' 'The Silver Falls,' not to mention the ever-popular 'Harbour Lights' at the Adelphi. But not only in melodrama is he the leading light; there were his delightful and witty burlesques 'Faust up to Date,' 'Carmen up to Date,' and the comic opera 'The Merry Duchess,' written in collaboration.

From the drawing room of Mr. Sims's beautiful house a fine view is obtained of Regent's Park, with its ornamental waters—whereon swans float up and down—and its undulating grounds beyond. Now that the beds are in flower and the trees in full foliage the scene is lovely and peaceful. The study—large and lofty—contains no less than six well-filled bookcases and two writing-tables.

Behind a glass-door a company of dolls, little and big, seem to be holding a party—dolls from Buda Pesth, from Germany, from France, &c., daintily dressed in national costume. These Mr. Sims declares to be his favourite playfellows, together with an army of soldiers—cavalry, infantry and artillery—all round the room, not to speak of a large box of bricks, a case of battledores and shuttle-cocks and a skipping-rope. Grotesque China figures and monsters are here by the hundred; multitudes of photographs and many pictures, notably a fine head of Pellegrini and one of Louis Wain's clever 'Cat' drawings—a gift from the artist. Two tall blue pedestals holding bowls filled with palms stand on either side of the window; the great inkstand mounted in silver is made out of the hoof of a deceased pet horse. But delightful as this room must be for a student with its luxurious rocking-chair and litter of pretty things, Mr. Sims does only certain portions of his writing here—journalistic work for which every paper lies ready to hand. He leads the way to the dining-room opposite, where everything is placed for another branch of literature—one form of comedy is done here. Then up the broad Japanese staircase, and you suddenly find yourself in an Oriental atmosphere. Verily it is a scene out of the 'Arabian Nights!' You almost expect Aladdin or Scheherazade to rise and greet you; but no, three gruesome and blood-curdling heads—models of murderers and demons of Eastern type—glare at you from the right. The walls are lined with gorgeous Oriental lincrusta; the white recesses, if they can be so called, are built out of fine Corean work over glass, and within are fitted with divans, cushions, and exquisite draperies on which the Turkish crescent figures largely. Every detail is minutely correct. Moorish rugs lie here and there on the matted floor; a banjo and mandoline of foreign manufacture stand on a deep lounge under the great arabesque window that opens out on a spacious, covered-in verandah, where Mr. Sims often sits in summer evenings among his orange trees. And mention must be made of the interesting collection of knives, daggers, and weapons in this wonderful room, from Toledo, Mexico, and all parts of the world. 'Plenty of wholesale murder on the premises,' says Mr. Sims, as he executes a few ferocious-looking manœuvres with these deadly instruments. This is the place where comic opera is written, and all the materials for that form of work are in their place. Drama is done in the Venetian room, which again is true in all its details, from the magnificent chandelier to the Italian wrought-iron work and delicate furniture of the country. But occasionally, when Mr. Sims is in a restless mood, and finds that even four rooms are not enough in which to work, he will betake himself to a bedroom, kitchen—anywhere. It is strange that the author, to whom the best box or stall at a theatre would naturally be open, never accepts either. He prefers to pay for his place, which is generally in the first row of the pit. He has an enormous correspondence with lunatics, who write to him on every conceivable theme—some so lucidly that once even he was taken in. There was a man who wrote every ten days or so a long letter in hot argument over one of his works. Mr. Sims went to call on his correspondent, and was received with the words, ' Have you an order? This is a private asylum.' 'I am a prey,' he remarks, ' to chronic melancholia, and sometimes feel as if a neurotic blizzard were passing over me. Then I flatten my nose against the window, and wonder if this be the best or worst of all possible worlds. I am excessively weak—morally, but,' he adds, with what he imagines to be a terrifying expression, 'I delight in horrible things!' But these words cannot be taken seriously from the great, tender-hearted, sympathetic man, who would not crush a fly, but would rather 'step aside and let the insect live,' whose love for children, animals, and all suffering humanity, is his strongest point, whose romance peeps out in every line of his plays and verses. He may be 'weak' secretly and

H

silently in the cause of charity; but no one detests cant or humbug more, no one is more manly, kind, and straightforward than the great journalist, novelist, and dramatist, George Robert Sims, the record of whose private and public work will long outlive him.

KATE TERRY

(MRS. ARTHUR LEWIS)

IN old-fashioned Kensington there stands secluded in about five acres of land, a large and imposing-looking house with a wide verandah covered with creepers, running along the south side. The approach is by a carriage drive which opens out on the right to a row of picturesquely built hothouses, and leads round to the great conservatory and billiard-room. The left side is sheltered by a high hedge of yew and holly, through which are obtained peeps of the fine old trees that stud the lawn. The birds are singing, and Nature seems in her most bright and festive mood. All is *en fête*, for it is the anniversary of a happy marriage that took place rather over a quarter of a century ago. The softly modulated Hungarian band discourses sweet music in the grounds, which are filled with a large assemblage of friends, who overflow from the French windows that open out of the reception-rooms to the sloping gardens. On the high ground of the path above, receiving her guests, stands the whilom bride, Mrs. Arthur Lewis, erstwhile the famous Kate Terry, whose brilliant career will be handed down to many generations of posterity, not only for an unbroken series of triumphs on the stage, where she never made an enemy and left none but friends to deplore her early retirement, but also for the winning grace, the charm of manner, and the tender, womanly heart that has so endeared her to all those with whom she has come in contact. The sweet sympathetic face—so thoroughly a 'Terry' face—is too well known to need much description. No touch of time is to be seen in the fair, smooth brow; the expression is one of serenity and contentment, of inward peace and happiness.

The little Kate Terry made her 'first appearance' in life at Falmouth. As both parents went on the stage soon after their marriage, her earliest associations were connected with the theatre. Bountifully provided with genius, it goes without saying that her infant footsteps naturally turned towards a histrionic career. At a very early age she developed a ready talent for mimicry, and when taken to rehearsals she would observe and carefully reproduce afterwards any particular attitude or gesture of the players. Song came to her as to the birds, and almost before she could speak plainly she could warble every air she heard in faultless time and tune. At the age of three she made her *début* on the boards of a country theatre, to sing between the farce and the principal piece the popular song of that day:

> 'I'm ninety-five, I'm ninety-five,
> And to keep single I'll contrive.'

'I think I see her now,' says one with whom you are in brief colloquy while strolling about the grounds. 'I was an eye-witness of that baby performance. She was dressed in character, in a long brocaded gown looped up over a quilted silk petticoat. She wore a great mob-cap and spectacles, and carried a crutch stick on which she leant. The sweet, childish treble, so pure and true, the modest little air of dignity that sat so quaintly upon her, and the utter absence of self-consciousness, which has indeed characterised her whole life, appealed powerfully to the greatly amused audience who vehemently applauded the tiny performer.'

At the age of seven she may be considered to have begun her real training, when she took the part of Robin in Charles Kean's revival of 'The Merry Wives of Windsor' at the Princess's Theatre, followed in the succeeding year by the *rôle* of Prince Arthur in 'King John.' By command of the Queen this play was performed at Windsor Castle, where the little girl acted Arthur for the first time, with Phelps as Hubert. Lord Macaulay, who was one of the audience on that occasion, was especially attracted by the performance, and on its conclusion the veteran historian called the child to him and, laying his hand on the bright, curly head, he warmly congratulated her on the grace with which she had impersonated the young Prince, and prophesied that before many years had passed she would make a great name. This favourable opinion was subsequently rendered historic, as in the 'Life and Letters of Lord Macaulay,' by Sir George Trevelyan, appears the following notice, 'The little girl who acted Arthur did wonders.' Later occurs a note: 'It is almost worth while to have passed middle age in order to have seen Miss Kate Terry as Arthur.'

While in her earliest teens she played Ariel in Kean's revival of 'The Tempest.' An anecdote connected with this play recalls itself, and speaks well for the presence of mind displayed in an emergency by the child-actress. The thunderbolt which always preceded Ariel's appearance used to fall some distance before her and disappear through a trap in the stage. One evening it was not thrown with sufficient force, and landed right in front of the ledge whereon she was poised. The heat was so great as actually to singe her silk drapery and scorch her feet. Although in deadly fear and pain, she gave no sign of fright, and Kean, who was playing Prospero, threw hurriedly into his part—unperceived by the audience—the impromptu words, 'Hold on, Katie, dear, hold on; don't give way,' until the obnoxious missile was removed.

Joliquet, in 'The Courier of Lyons,' was another of her juvenile parts, and when only fourteen she acted Cordelia to Charles Kean's King Lear! Kate Terry has the greatest veneration and affection for the memory of Mrs. Charles Kean, and considers her example as wife, manageress, and friend to have been unequalled. Being still too young at the end of Mr. Kean's management to play full-grown women's parts, she and her sister Ellen Terry, accompanied by their parents, went for two years' hard study into the provinces, where they gave entertainments on their own account. They often played in two pieces on the same evening, and constantly had a variety of four or five plays during a week. All this meant severe, incessant work, but Kate Terry looks back upon that time as an invaluable epoch in her career, as the seedtime of the rich harvest that was to follow. She had placed a high standard before her, and was determined to reach the goal. The more difficult or tiresome a part seemed to be, the more she resolved to master it, and to create it according to her own reading. Her patience and diligence were soon to be rewarded.

On returning to London, her next appearance was in Alfred Wigan's company at the St. James's Theatre. Shortly after, the management fell into Miss Herbert's hands, and then came the young actress's opportunity of giving a striking proof of her brilliant powers. One evening Miss Herbert was suddenly taken ill, and at a moment's notice Kate Terry was called upon to take the leading part of Mrs. Union, in the first English version of Sardou's famous play 'Nos Intimes,' called by its adaptor, Horace Wigan, 'Friends or Foes.' According to the principal dramatic critic present, 'she electrified the audience, and from that time her fortune was made.'

Presently she was invited by Mr. Arthur Stirling to Bristol for three months to play Juliet, Ophelia, and Pauline in 'The Lady of Lyons.' Here she scored enormous successes by her entirely original reading of these *rôles*. Her fame spreading rapidly, she was at once offered an engagement to join Charles Fechter's company at the Lyceum, where her creations of Blanche de Nevers in 'The Duke's Motto,' her Lena in 'Bel Delmonio,' her Ophelia to Fechter's Hamlet, are impersonations that have an undying record.

She then left the Lyceum to become 'leading lady' at the Olympic, where, in Mr. Tom Taylor's popular dramas, she originated *rôle* after *rôle*; perhaps the most striking may have been her Lady Panardon, in 'The Hidden Hand,' or the tender grace of her Countess de Moleon, in 'The Serf.' But where each success was the result of hard, conscientious study and unwearying energy, built upon her glorious, natural gift, it is difficult to determine whether this or that part were better. Her own favourite *rôles* were undoubtedly those of Juliet and Ophelia as affording more scope for varying emotions and original conceptions.

The young actress's method of study was peculiar. No one ever saw her at work, and this often caused her father considerable uneasiness, until at last he gave expression to the thought. 'The production of such and such a piece is only a week hence, Katie,' he would remark in anxious tones, 'and I have not once seen you open your part.' But the girl could always reassure him by answering, gaily, 'I have been letter-perfect for the last week.' She learnt her words in bed at night, and so absorbed was she in her art that no temptations could coax her into society. During rehearsal little bits of natural 'business' used to occur to her mind, and little peculiarities would strike her one at a time here and there; these she used to reproduce later and invariably found to be true inspirations. She learnt the words of Ophelia almost entirely in a cab going to and from the theatre, and a story is told of her that on one occasion so engrossed was she in the part, forgetting where she was, she sang the whole song aloud, causing the old cabman to pull up to inquire what she wanted.

Kate Terry's last creation was the *rôle* of Dora, in Charles Reade's play on Tennyson's poem of that name;

and her last appearance in London was in Juliet, when it had become known to the public that their idol, in the zenith of her fame, was about to quit for ever the scene of her triumphs to become the wife of Mr. Arthur Lewis. 'I was present on that occasion even as on the first,' says your informant, 'and I will describe it. The scene was unprecedented, and the expression of public affection and admiration that she received was most touching. Places could not be had for love or money. The Strand was blocked, and from an early hour in the afternoon there were crowds waiting, which was an unusual circumstance in those days. The excitement was tremendous. She was called and re-called, and at last, greatly agitated, and with tears trembling in her blue eyes, she said, in the sweet musical voice that we all know so well, a few simple words of farewell.'

Her final appearance on any stage took place a few weeks later at the Princes' Theatre, Manchester, where there was much the same sort of reception and farewell to go through again. The curtain had, however, fallen on the young player for the last time, and never since has she been prevailed upon to reappear.

Temptations of this kind have not been wanting. A few years after her marriage Mr. Tom Taylor implored her to create the part of Lady Clancarty in the play of that name which he had written expressly for her. Quite lately, indeed, she has been pressed to originate an important *rôle*, but all to no purpose ; and if, in the earlier years of her happy married life, knowing her own powers to be as great as ever, a poignant desire to exercise them may have come over her, she has long ago suppressed it, and has resolutely turned a deaf ear to all such entreaties.

When questioned—as she often is—on this subject, Mrs. Lewis is known to say, with a bright, winning smile, 'I have the strongest opinion on the matter. Art demands the devotion, the sacrifice, of a lifetime, and, once laid aside, it may not be taken up and dropped again capriciously.'

The assemblage of friends to-day is representative. Mr. and Mrs. Arthur Lewis's pleasant *réunions* are well known and always popular, not only for the kindness and hospitality accorded to each guest, but interesting as gatherings of the most distinguished people in the world of literature and of art; but on this occasion it is peculiarly noticeable. There are those present who have known and loved Kate Terry from her childhood; those who have grown up side by side with Arthur Lewis, and loved him from boyhood; and, again, those who have watched, with affection and interest, their children grow up from infancy to girlhood. Many here present were guests at Kate Terry's marriage, and feel the recollection of it as fresh in their minds as if it were but yesterday. There is no wonder, then, that there is an especial warmth and sympathy in the greeting of such old friends.

A large weeping-ash stands on the lawn, with great branches stretching far over the grass. It has supports all round, and is converted for the nonce into a supplementary refreshment tent. Under the venerable boughs are many well-known and distinguished persons. Sweet Ellen Terry stands just outside, surrounded by a group of admiring friends, amongst whom Sir Douglas Straight, the veteran Field-Marshal Sir Frederick Haines, Sir John Tenniel, and Mr. Frank Dicksee are easily recognisable. The young daughters of the house flit in and out on hospitable thoughts intent. The graceful form of Marion Terry is discerned here and there, always accompanied by an adoring tribe of little nephews and nieces. Her sister Flossie (Mrs. Morris) yonder, is the happy young mother of four of these dainty miniature Terrys. There strolls Fred Terry, so marvellously like his sister Kate, with his beautiful wife, Julia Neilson, talking to Mr. Boughton and Mr. and Mrs. Henschel. Henry Neville is sitting near a flower-bed in earnest conversation

with Beerbohm Tree. They are probably discussing the
bygone days, when Mr. Neville was so long associated
with the young Kate Terry in Tom Taylor's plays. Mrs.
Arthur Lewis's father holds his youngest grandchild in
his arms, whilst two more little ones, with sky-blue eyes
and auburn curls, gambol round him.

Another group consists of Mr. Linley Sambourne,
George Grossmith and his charming wife, and Charles
Terry with his daughter, 'little Minnie,' who played so
cleverly in 'Bootles' Baby' and 'A Man's Shadow,' &c.
She is now 'resting' whilst the process of education is
going on, and candidly avows that she prefers the stage
to her lesson-books.

But the afternoon wanes, and soon there is a general
exodus of guests, who unite in their affectionate and
hearty good wishes for Mr. and Mrs. Arthur Lewis, as
they stand side by side under the verandah—good wishes
that are warmly shared by all who know them.

JOHNSTON FORBES-ROBERTSON

THERE is a subdued dignity about the solid masonry of
the old-world, picturesque square where Johnston Forbes-
Robertson, the actor, has established himself and his
household gods. The imposing width and substantial
build of the massive structures tell a tale of a long past
generation, to whom the building of houses was a serious
and lengthy undertaking, and space apparently a matter
of no consideration.

There is scarcely a house throughout the stately
square that is not fraught with some historical anecdote,
or associated with some well-remembered name, and
while gazing at it, the imagination insensibly travels
back to the time when sedan-chairs, preceded by flaming
torches, traversed its broad pavements, and when powdered

and painted dames of high degree, with beaux in velvet coats, full-bottomed wigs and *queues*, were the order of the day.

Towards the close of the last century, when Bedford Square was a new and fashionable locality, the centre house on the east side, then the residence of Lord Chancellor Eldon, was the scene of an exciting adventure. During the Corn-law riots an angry mob attacked the house with such ferocity that Lord and Lady Eldon fled secretly in the dead of night, and made good their escape over the back wall into the friendly grounds of the British Museum. The large old mansion on the north-east side, then inhabited by Lord Mansfield, Lord Chief Justice, was also the scene of a similar outrage in the 'No Popery' riots of 1786; an infuriated crowd broke into the house and ransacked and burned his valuable collections of books and MSS. The great overhanging trees in the Square garden made a convenient shelter in those days for footpads, one of whom was caught, and, according to the custom of the time, was sentenced to be hanged for committing a street robbery outside Lord Eldon's house. When the Recorder subsequently presented his report to the King all the Ministers, with one exception, agreed that the man should be left for execution. The King, however, observing that Lord Eldon was mute, called upon him for his opinion, which the Lord Chancellor gave in favour of mercy. 'Very well,' said the King, 'since his lordship, who lives in Bedford Square, thinks that there is no great harm in committing robberies there, the poor fellow shall not be hanged.' And he was let off accordingly.

The garden gate stands temptingly open, and suggests a short cut to the opposite side, where the actor's house stands. The transit is easily effected, and you speedily find yourself in a spacious hall, where the first attraction is a beautiful line engraving about ten feet long, a hemicycle of all the most celebrated painters and sculptors, by Paul

Delaroche in the 'École des Beaux Arts.' The staircase is adorned with many valuable proofs from Holbein, Raphael, Reynolds, Vandyck and Domenichino; but only a cursory glance at these art treasures is possible at the moment, as a door is opened and you are shown into a lofty studio, where Mr. Robertson stands before an easel, palette on thumb, busily engaged in putting the last touches to a speaking portrait of young Mr. Irving, for the young actor is also a painter of no mean merit. He extends a hand of cordial greeting, pushes the easel further aside, wheels a chair to the right position, and bids you 'rest and criticise at your leisure.'

No more inviting retreat can be imagined than this quiet, peaceful studio, with its lofty ceiling and solid walls that shut out all exasperating indication of one's neighbours' amusements, such as a jingling piano or an unruly nursery—no small boon this to one whose tastes lie thoroughly in the art world, and whose chief object in life is its cultivation.

Oriental rugs partially conceal the polished oak floor. The walls are decorated with many portraits painted by himself. The picture of Ellen Terry was exhibited in the Academy of 1876, when the young artist was scarcely twenty-three years of age. She looks down from her frame, wrapped in furs, with a witching smile. Opposite is the Polish artist, Madame Modjeska, grand and stately, in a white robe. His mother's portrait hangs in a prominent place, and his brother Norman, in fancy dress of the fourteenth century as the 'Young Venetian,' with sword in hand and a loose cloak thrown lightly back. The fidelity of each likeness is striking. Among the other pictures there are two fine works of the late Mr. Val Bromley, brother-in-law of your host, a clever pen-and-ink drawing by Abbey of the 'She Stoops to Conquer' series, and a masterly etching after Rembrandt, together with groups of lovely child heads. On the mantelpiece stand some antique bronzes and a few bits of quaintly carved brass-work. The centre figure is an exquisite statuette by Miss Casella of a praying saint in monk's robes, with hands devoutly crossed; the rapt expression and delicate tracery of every line is produced with marvellous accuracy. A comfortable specimen of a couch of the first Empire is placed near a large marqueterie bureau of ancient design bound with brass, and covered with art and costume books, biographies, and the principal editions of Shakespeare. Judging by their well-worn and much-scored appearance they are largely studied.

His personality is so familiar with the public as to need but brief description. As you sit before the picture on the easel and glance up at the painter-actor, it cannot but strike you that the classical features, the tall, graceful build, the serenity yet gravity of the fair, broad brow, and the somewhat dreamy look in the dark-blue eyes, tell their own tale of the art-world in which he is absorbed; while, with singularly youthful mien, indications are not wanting, in the lower part of the refined and intellectual face, of a quiet but unconquerable determination of mind.

The eldest son of a good old Scottish family, whose every member displays the artistic temperament, reared in the very atmosphere of art, and in early childhood evincing a strong talent for drawing, Johnston Forbes-Robertson's career was evidently marked out for him as a painter. His school-days were passed at the Charterhouse, where he recollects constantly getting into trouble from the persistency with which he used to decorate the leaves of his lesson and copy-books with not too flattering portraits of masters and school-fellows.

Charterhouse days over, the young scholar was sent to Rouen, where he remained for several years, turning his attention principally to the English classics, yet stealing many an hour to devote to his favourite art. At the age of seventeen he returned to London, entered as a student at the Royal Academy, and for three years gave his whole mind to studying the technicalities of his profession. Among his contemporaries in student-life were the distinguished artists, Mr. Sam Waller, Mr. Waterhouse, R.A., Mr. Frank Dicksee, R.A., and Mr. Gilbert, R.A., the sculptor.

But 'the best laid schemes o' mice and men gang aft agley.' Up to that time Forbes-Robertson had no leaning whatsoever towards a dramatic life. Destiny cannot be credited with other than the most kindly interventions when she elected to interfere through the outward and visible medium of the late Mr. Wills, and to turn him suddenly into an actor ere he had reached man's estate. A chance meeting with the playwright, a few words, and the deed was done thus.

Mr. Wills (who was then bringing out his new piece, 'Mary Stuart,' at the Princess' Theatre) casually mentioned that he was hesitating how to cast the *rôle* of Chastelard, when suddenly the thought occurred to him, to which he gave immediate utterance, 'Why, Johnston, if you cannot act, you could at least look the part to perfection.' Young Robertson with much diffidence consented. 'The time was very short,' he says, 'but after a hurried process of drilling and rehearsal, I took my courage in both hands, and with much inward trepidation made my first appearance, and,' he adds after a pause, laughing at the reminiscence, 'no doubt I looked as nervous as I felt!' The criticisms, however, on this initiative performance were most favourable, and accorded to the young actor no small encouragement.

Although encouraged and reassured by this little success, Johnston Forbes-Robertson was as yet by no means even a little bitten by 'stage fever.' 'No, indeed,' he emphatically asserts; 'but at that age I naturally did not make much by my paintings, and I therefore hoped that by taking resolutely to the stage I might the sooner be in a position to earn an independence.' Not without a sigh of regret were the brush and palette temporarily relinquished, for even then his pictures had been favourably noticed; but from the early struggles of a young painter to ultimate success is a 'far cry,' and independence had to be achieved. Then came into play the sturdy determination of his character. Hard study in the provinces, perseverance, and zeal in his new profession gained the day. He never found himself out of an engagement, and thus it came about that his 'dream of independence' was early realised. Another dormant talent rapidly developed, and from that day to his Lancelot in 'King Arthur,' young Forbes-Robertson has steadily pushed his way on to the front ranks of histrionic art.

After that first almost accidental performance, the young actor was immediately engaged by the late Mr. Charles Reade to go on tour in the 'Wandering Heir.' This was succeeded by an invitation to join the stock company at the Princes' Theatre, Manchester, where he was so fortunate as to attract the favourable notice of the late Mr. Phelps, whilst playing under him for four years such parts as Lovewell in 'The Clandestine Marriage,' Falkland in 'The Rivals,' Joseph Surface, Cromwell in 'Henry VIII,' and Baradas in 'Richelieu.' The great tragedian, with that generosity which is so often observed among the higher lights of the dramatic profession, prophesied a successful future for his young brother-in-art, took him under his wing, 'and,' says Mr. Forbes-Robertson with much feeling, 'I shall never forget what I owe him for this; he coached me in all my *rôles*, especially in the Shakespearian characters, and showed me the greatest kindness. To Mr. Hollingshead, too, I am greatly indebted; he never lost an opportunity of pushing me forward, and was always most friendly.'

As years rolled by, and the young actor's position became more assured, he thoroughly realised the wisdom of his choice; but during a long run of any piece, when constant rehearsals were unnecessary, he gradually drew forth his partially neglected brush and palette, and devoted a few hours every morning to his first love. It was then that he painted the portrait of Mr. Phelps as Wolsey in his Cardinal's robes of scarlet silk and biretta, and Mr. Forbes-Robertson enthusiastically mentions his happiness when the Garrick Club bought the picture and hung it on its staircase. Later, Mr. Irving commissioned him to paint the famous church scene in 'Much Ado about Nothing,' which contained nearly two dozen portraits, himself the Claudio. But even while thus engaged he would conscientiously turn the picture to the wall and forsake the easel when the exigencies of a new part called for frequent rehearsals.

Pursuing the subject further, you express a desire to hear more of his histrionic triumphs; but as the word escapes he deprecates it, shakes his head, smiles, and substitutes 'experiences,' for one of the pleasantest characteristics of the young painter-actor is his extremely modest and unassuming manner. He fulfilled several engagements at the Olympic, Adelphi, Haymarket, and Lyceum theatres, and may probably be considered to have 'won his spurs' in his creation of Sir Horace Welby in 'Forget-me-not.'

Perhaps one of the most successful of his earlier efforts was his creation of Geoffrey Wyniard, in 'Dan'l Druce, Blacksmith' (W. S. Gilbert), a play that met with much favour more than a decade of years since. None who witnessed that charming idyll of the seventeenth century will forget its simple pathos: the young lovers, Johnston Forbes-Robertson and Miss Marion Terry, who played Dorothy, the Puritan maiden, with indescribable grace; Herman Vezin, in his masterly impersonation of the Blacksmith—a part in which the veteran actor rose to absolute greatness; and the concluding words ere the curtain fell on the graceful love story, when all misunderstandings being cleared away and the pair are at last united, Dorothy leans on her lover's breast whilst he whispers softly,

'And art thou happy, Dorothy?'
'Aye, and thou, Geoffrey?'
'Passing happy!'

Delicious tears were shed nightly over this play, report said not unshared by the players!

The young actor has had a long and varied *répertoire*, having acted in one hundred and twenty different parts. In 1878 he joined the Prince of Wales Company, and acted Count Orloff in 'Diplomacy,' and Captain Absolute in 'The Rivals,' for which he designed the costumes.

He made a provincial tour with Madame Modjeska, during which time he took the leading parts, having previously rendered them in London—Romeo to her Juliet, Maurice de Saxe in 'Adrienne Lecouvreur,' Armand Duval in 'Heartsease,' and Leicester in 'Mary Stuart.' His next tour was with Miss Mary Anderson in various Shakespearian and other characters, and at the close of these English wanderings he accompanied the American actress to the States, where he was most kindly received by the New York critics, and played Romeo and Ingomar among many other parts. On his return to London he took the *rôle* of Leontes at the Lyceum, a performance that lasted seven months. He was the original Claud Glyne in 'The Parvenu' at the Court Theatre, and was later specially engaged to play Claudio at the Lyceum when Mr. Irving produced 'Much Ado about Nothing.'

During an engagement with Mr. Bancroft he played the leading parts in 'Lords and Commons,' and the original *rôles* of Sir George Orman in 'Peril' and of Sir Charles Pomander in 'Masks and Faces.' At the opening of the Garrick by Mr. Hare, Mr. Forbes-Robertson created the parts of Renshaw in the 'Profligate' and Scarpia in 'La Tosca.' Rising, he opens a drawer in the bureau and takes out a morocco-case, containing a handsome pair of shoe-buckles presented to him by Mr. Hare at the close of 'La Tosca,' in memory of his Scarpia; also a silver cigar-box, the farewell gift of Mr. and Mrs. Bancroft; and from another drawer he draws forth two treasured family relics—a dirk picked up on the battle-field of Culloden, exquisitely carved, and in its original leather case, and a

plaid of the old 'hard' tartan, which actually belonged to
Prince Charlie, who gave it to Miss Johnston, an ancestor,
from whom it has descended to its present owner.

In 1891 the actor made another visit to America, being
lent by Mr. Hare to play the original part of the lover in
Sardou's 'Thermidor.' On his return he was again lent
to Mr. Irving to play Buckingham in 'Henry VIII.,' and
afterwards he rejoined Mr. Hare's company at the Garrick
in the revival of 'Diplomacy.' He has yet a later gift to
show, and one which he regards with pride—a beautiful
diamond pin, with Imperial crown and cipher, given him
by the Queen when he accompanied Mr. Hare to Balmoral
to play Julian Beauclerk in 'Diplomacy,' on which occasion he had the honour of being presented to her Majesty,
to the Princesses, and to the Empress Eugénie.

As Lancelot in 'King Arthur' at the Lyceum—the
last *rôle* he played before going into management—
Johnston Forbes-Robertson undoubtedly scored his greatest
triumph of all. The poet might almost have had a future
mental vision of this true artist when he created the character, so thoroughly is it suited not only to the refined
and *spirituel* countenance, but also to the harmonious
and sympathetic voice, which throbs with tenderness and
emotion in the beautiful blank verse that the actor loves
so well, for to him 'blank verse and romantic drama
have more attractions than any other.'

Now and then some odd little unrehearsed effect will
take place while acting, of which, happily, the audience
is ignorant. One evening, at the closing scene of 'Romeo
and Juliet,' as Romeo (Forbes-Robertson) mounted the
high steps to weep by the body of Juliet (Madame
Modjeska), he accidentally pushed them away, and thus
left himself in doubt how to descend creditably. Seeing
an expression of dismay come over his face, the dead
Juliet murmured from under her shroud, 'What is it?'
'The steps have slipped,' whispered Romeo, 'and I can't
get down!' 'Never mind,' muttered the corpse; 'jump!'

And jump he did, making a somewhat undignified descent, which, luckily, was not observed in front. Another time, after bidding Juliet an impassioned farewell on leaving her chamber, he rushed as usual to the balcony, threw his leg over the railing to make his exit, and found that by some mistake the stairs had been forgotten, and he dropped fourteen feet, which discomposed him not a little.

Shakespeare is Mr. Forbes-Robertson's favourite study and Leontes his favourite *rôle*. 'I prefer it infinitely,' he says; 'not only do I feel more at home in the plays of Shakespeare, but they are much easier to learn.' In 1895 he entered into the troubled waters of managership; and during the absence of Sir Henry Irving he opened the Lyceum with 'Romeo and Juliet,' the success of which venture justified his expectations. His latest production is entitled 'For the Crown.'

But as rehearsals are the order of the day, and time is on the wane, Mr. Forbes-Robertson must start for the theatre. Ere he leaves he bids you look at one more of his portraits in another room, whence many voices issue, and say if you recognise it, as it is of 'one who is very dear to him.' It is a life-sized painting of the artist's father, Mr. John Forbes-Robertson, who is well known in literary and artistic circles, and was for many years distinguished as an art-critic and historian. He is clad in a full suit of armour of the seventeenth century; the likeness is startling, but the ferocity of the accoutrements in no way detracts from the benevolence of the features, which are so well depicted by a faithful and loving hand. The family group here assembled consists of brothers and sisters who are striving—not unsuccessfully—for independence. One is a violinist, two are actors, one is an artist, and another an author.

Later, in the gloaming, you sit *tête-à-tête* over a friendly cup of tea with his mother, Mrs. Forbes-Robertson, and hear of many a pleasant incident that he has modestly omitted to relate. Always unassuming, gracious, and kindly, alike in the home circle and abroad, it is easy to see that triumphs have in no way turned his head. Small wonder, then, that he possesses innumerable friends, and that all, including his present chronicler—who has known Johnston Forbes-Robertson from his boyhood—have rejoiced over his success, and cordially wish him many more to follow as manager of a London theatre.

MRS. AMYOT

THE good fairies who presided at the birth of Carolina Catharina Engelhart were in a generous and even lavish mood. Not satisfied with knowing that she would inherit an artistic temperament from both parents—better fortune than comes to ordinary mortals—they endowed her with a creative talent and power of expression amounting to genius; then, waxing merry, they added a keen sense of humour to support her in trouble, and what is more to the purpose, a will-power and determination of character which would allow no obstacles or opposition to bar the way of her progress to ultimate success. Thus equipped, it is not difficult to understand how the popular artist has steadily made her way to the front.

A chance walk along the Strand has led you to the fringe of a crowd gathered before an office in that locality. Gently elbowing a way through, you stand opposite a large and exquisite painting exhibited in the window, called 'The Bridge of Sighs' (Hood). It is the property of Sir George Newnes, and is signed 'C. Amyot.' The scene is the Thames Embankment at daybreak. Two bargemen carry a drowned girl with lovely fair face up from the river.

> 'All that remains of her
> Now is pure womanly.'

A gentleman in evening dress and a gaily attired lady have just stepped out of a cab, and, bending over the poor dead, the lady recognises with horror her own sister. She has dropped her bouquet on the ground, and seems to realise in a moment the misery of her own brilliant life as she stands with left hand thrown out as if to push the man and her past behind her, while with the right hand pressed to her mouth she tries to suppress the agony to which she would fain give utterance. The man, calmly lighting a cigar, stands cold, indifferent, cynical; his cruel foot stamped on the flowers—he has crushed many fairer! The faces of the bargemen are most expressive. The elder turns in anger and reproach towards the modern Phryne, as if he resented her presence at the sanctity of death; the younger looks down with tender sympathy on the beautiful face—not long since in the agony of despair—now so still and peaceful. The old cabman, who has alighted, stands at a respectful distance, looking on with awe and pity, and forms an excellent and striking contrast to the cynical gentleman. In the background are the arches of the 'Bridge of Sighs' (Waterloo Bridge). The gas-lamps are still burning, and the reflection of the dawn on the river is most beautiful.

The picture is absolutely human and full of interest, but perhaps more French than English in its conception. Various admiring and appreciative criticisms fall from the lips of the persons gazing at it, and inspire you with a desire then and there to drive to the artist's studio, where, happily, more of her works may be inspected. Suiting the action to the thought, in half an hour you find yourself cordially received in a large and handsomely decorated house in Earl's Court Road, where, in imagination at least, you soon travel over various parts of the world. The studies and sketches indicate many foreign tours: Venice, Bride of the Adriatic—if the painted reflection of its glory can thus transport its lagunes where the skies seem to lie in the bosom of the seas, there must be a touch of the heavenly fire in the artist who can arouse in murky London such a sense of its loveliness!—Brittany, with its busy, crowded motley groups. A sunset over a flat, furze-covered common takes you to Norfolk, thence to far Cornwall, where, from a steep and picturesque street in the little fishing-village of Newlyn (with whose artists Mrs. Amyot has great friendship), a glimpse is caught of the green, foam-crested waves rolling in over the white sands. Two sketches of sky effects, in purple and orange before sunrise, imply that Mrs. Amyot is an early riser when work is in question. On the opposite walls, the silver waters of Coniston Lake, the delicate, misty Morecambe Bay, the cloud-enveloped Glenfinnan Hills, and the sunny meadows of Denmark are interspersed with compositions and sketches for works yet to come. Cats—Mrs. Amyot's favourite animal—largely figure in these studies. In the next room hangs the well-known picture, 'Three Guineas from the Queen,' justly described by a famous comic actor of the day as 'a comedy in colours,' also a replica—on a smaller scale—of Mrs. Amyot's great picture, 'The Return of the Penitent' (now in the possession of Colonel North), together with a speaking portrait of Dr. Amyot. The boudoir is exclusively devoted to photographs after her pictures: 'Tit-bits,' which has a double interest as being a likeness of her own boy; 'A Pleasant Task;' and a sweet girl's face, painted as a demonstration in two and a half hours. This shows that Mrs. Amyot, although a pupil of the highly finishing school of Bouguereau, can also sketch rapidly.

Carolina Catharina, afterwards called by the Russian form of her name, Cathinca, wife of Dr. Amyot, was born in Copenhagen, and is by parentage Norwegian. Her father, Christian Engelhart, held the responsible position of Manager of Departments in the Bank of Denmark. Her mother, Nathalia Röme, was a gifted and cultivated woman, who, notwithstanding the frail health which prevented her from going into society, devoted herself to the early instruction of the little girl who was for many years her only child. At the early age of four and a half, when she went to school, the little Cathinka could sew and knit, read and write. It was perhaps this somewhat too early stimulating of an imaginative brain and a retentive memory, that caused the child to be more than ordinarily restless and emotional, with pencil ever in hand, recalling in illustration the fairy stories with which her head was full, as well as with the more prosaic events and people around her. Every lesson-book bore marks of the talent that was within her, every copy book was illustrated with persons and places that she daily saw, and though it was considered necessary to punish her for these transgressions, parents and teachers alike exulted over the promise that she displayed. At the age of eight she accompanied her mother to the south of France. Here the latent talent speedily developed itself. Everything was new to an awakening mind, so susceptible of receiving impressions, and the seeds were sown of the harvest which was destined in later years to yield so rich a fruit. When taken to exhibitions, the child would inspect them with a gravity far beyond her years. On her return, when bedtime came, she would surreptitiously select the longest candle and in her room would strive to reproduce the subjects with her pencil, on the next visit carefully verifying, to correct, the different effects of light and shade.

When she went back to Copenhagen the youthful artist found herself a great source of amusement and interest to her friends, for being better able to express her impressions by pen and ink than by word of mouth, she would indicate by rapid sketches scenes that had struck her in the village: here a dance, there the quaint dresses of little French children, or the bright holiday costumes of the peasant women. After this journey she again went to school, and was allowed to take lessons in drawing in a feeble, amateurish sort of way, when she candidly confesses that she never distinguished herself. All her ideas lying in the way of composition—the copying of cubes, triangles, ivy leaves and plaster ornaments—were most repugnant. Her mother, becoming yet more of an invalid, the young Cathinka was entirely thrown on herself for companionship, and the only place where her imagination met with any kind of sympathy was the theatre; but this was a treat which rarely fell to her lot in those days. She was at a growing age, when the young are most susceptible, and the constant repression in which it was deemed salutary to keep the children of that country caused many different elements to ferment in her nature and to render her restless and unhappy. She would creep off to bed early in order to dream, and in her dreams she realised all that she desired but could not as yet grasp, while from childhood everything presented itself to her imagination in the form of pictures. 'Our house was just opposite the theatre,' remarks Mrs. Amyot, 'and in the winter evenings, weary with a long, dull day of small talk and domestic troubles, I used to slip out of the warm, brightly lighted drawing-room and go into a cold, dark room where, wrapped in a shawl, I could watch the brilliantly illuminated entrance of the theatre, the carriages setting down fashionably dressed people, and the crowd around—all seeming to me a paradise from which I was shut out. One evening my father found me there, sad and depressed. He said nothing at the time, —it was never his way—but the next day at dinner I found two stalls in the folds of my *serviette*. This was a supreme pleasure, and on my return from the theatre I stole upstairs on tiptoe and drew pictures of the actors and the scenes, which were duly recognised.'

Once a year an exhibition of paintings was held in Copenhagen. Two visits only were permitted to the girl, and these were events to be looked forward to and made the most of. They afforded the delight of sketching from memory—on her return—the outlines of a few of the principal pictures in miniature, and afterwards of filling them in.

Up to the age of fourteen the young girl had never

seen a painter at work in his studio, though she learned much from watching her father whilst engaged in wood-carving, at which he was an adept. It was about this time that a strong desire entered her mind to go abroad to study painting with a view of becoming a professional artist. 'But when I mooted it to my parents,' says Mrs. Amyot, laughing, 'the proposal was received with horror and dismay. The idea could not be entertained for a moment. A lady artist! A professional! Impossible! Such a thing was unknown in Denmark! A sort of hybrid creature that was associated in the mind with knickerbockers, a Tam o' Shanter cap, not improbably a pipe in its mouth! I should be looked upon as one who sought unbecoming notoriety, I should be socially ostracised. So, for some years, as the home opposition was too strong and at the same time too loving to combat, I relinquished the notion and contented myself with amateur work for my own amusement and for that of my family circle.'

Everything, however, comes to him—and presumably, to her also—who knows how to wait. As Miss Engelhart approached her coming-of-age year, and had never wavered in her resolution, her parents felt that the time had come when opposition was no longer to be maintained, and, urged by his wife, Mr. Engelhart gave the necessary permission for their daughter to go to Düsseldorf, only stipulating that she should go under the escort of her old governess. She had fixed on Düsseldorf as the great central point of a colony of artists and as the home of two great Norwegian painters of world-wide reputation, Tiedmand and Gude.

'It was all settled and we started three days later,' says Mrs. Amyot. 'I was so eager to get away, to go out into the world and to break away from all conventionalities, that I thought the whole universe would come to pieces to frustrate the realisation of my hopes and longings.'

Once settled at Düsseldorf, and having got over her home sickness, the young artist set to work with a will, and studied under Professor Vautier and Wilhelm Sohn. In the first year of her student life she painted, exhibited, and sold her first picture to the Art Union of Christiania. There were no public studios at that time for women, which made it difficult to study the academic subjects absolutely necessary for figure-painting, so for a while she curbed her ambition and contented herself with painting pictures chiefly of children. In this line her compositions were particularly happy, and all her work was sold as soon as it was finished. The life was congenial, and she was cheerful and contented in the society of several artists with whom she had gradually become acquainted through the introduction of her masters. A few years later the young artist returned to Copenhagen to paint some portraits, among others that of the celebrated Professor Madvig, Leader of the Danish House of Commons.

It was while on this visit that she met with the most awful experience of her life, and one which she never can recall without a shudder—an experience which probably never yet occurred to anyone. Hearing, on all sides, rapturous accounts of a young Swedish artist, Sophia Ribbing (a pupil of the great Belgian painter, Louis Gallait) and having seen her pictures in the Copenhagen Exhibitions, Miss Engelhart's mind was suddenly turned into quite a new groove. She was seized with a burning desire to meet the young Swede and to make her acquaintance, and through her to obtain information as to how she too could become a pupil of Gallait. Miss Ribbing was just then spending the summer at Copenhagen with an inseparable friend and companion. Miss Engelhart procured her address, and, without mentioning to her mother where she was going, started off to the lodgings, found the ladies were out, but learning from the landlady that they were painting in the Palace of Christiansborg, and determined to see them, she followed them thither.

This gigantic building, which was burnt to the ground a few years ago, contained all the State apartments, both Houses of Parliament and the whole of the enormous picture galleries, and was uninhabited. Miss Engelhart went in at the south side and inquired of the porter if he could direct her to the room where the ladies were painting. He made many difficulties, but finally told her that she should have applied at the north entrance, quite at the other extremity of the palace, but if she would follow his directions she could get there without much trouble. 'Alas!' says Mrs. Amyot, shaking her head ruefully, 'little did I know what trouble lay in store for me. It was a case of directions being more profuse than explicit; however, they contained a few leading features, such as corridors after endless walks through certain passages upstairs, turns to right, turns to left, then downstairs through the galleries, and at last, under the portico, a green baize door was to be reached, opening on to another similar door, on which was written "Fire-Plug." This, he said, would admit me to a staircase, which I was to ascend until I reached three doors, the left of which opened out into the room where I should find the ladies. It led from the ground-floor to the top of the building. I started on my lonely wanderings, ascending one flight of stairs to descend another, through long corridors and galleries where my own footsteps, sounding weird and uncanny, re-echoed. My heart beat fearfully, and I looked around on all sides, fancying that I was being followed by ghostly occupants. However, I at last hailed with delight the much-desired baize doors indicated, through which I should reach the one opening into the ladies' apartment. I opened one, found myself face to face with the "Fire-Plug," and emerged with much surprise and awe on the well-known "Queens' Staircase," so called from the statues of the queens of Denmark that ornamented it.

It was very wide, built of marble and designed with a double flight of steps that opened out *en perron*, and was only used on State occasions. I mounted what was apparently an endless flight of steps to the top, and there found the door that had been described to me ajar, and I heard muffled sounds of voices which seemingly issued from a back passage behind. I gave a sharp tap, and heard a woman's voice, in a high key in Swedish, say, "Someone knocked!" Then a door was opened and quickly closed as a second voice exclaimed, "No one is there!" I naturally found the situation somewhat awkward, being able to hear what was said, yet not able to make myself known. At that instant the great clock struck twelve! I tried the other door, which was half open, and, finding what I supposed to be a dark corridor before me leading to the room whence the voices came, I took two steps forward and—fell—down, down, into the depths of darkness!'

It was truly an awful moment, and must have felt like an eternity to the poor girl. All the events of a lifetime poured into her mind, her parents' ignorance of her whereabouts, the great uninhabited palace, the possibility of death by starvation, even if she reached the ground without a broken neck; for who would think of looking for her there!

All this and more flashed through her brain. A sudden instinct told her that it was a chimney into which she had fallen; bricks and mortar were tumbling down as with outstretched arms she presently found her alarming descent arrested, the right hand grasping the rough stones of a wall and the left being caught by a huge beam. The while she made no scream, and, as in the most sublime moments the most ridiculous ideas often shoot through the brain, she suddenly laughed aloud to think what an extraordinary introduction it would be to the two unknown ladies—a half-stunned, bruised and bleeding object, with torn clothes and dishevelled hair, arriving *viâ* the chimney! She had still sufficient sense to distinguish the voices. One said, 'A picture must have fallen.' Then another, apparently fearing something uncanny, exclaimed, 'Is there anything there?' A humorous thought occurred to the poor entombed prisoner, even at that terrible juncture, and she answered, quietly, 'A lady, to see Miss Ribbing.' 'But *where* are you?' said the voice. 'In the chimney,' said the girl, faintly; 'send for help.'

By the time this brief conversation was over, the ladies began to realise that a dreadful accident had occurred, and that a human life was in sore peril. Hastily shouting to her to be of good courage, and promising to bring help, they fled down the marble stairs and made their way to the custodian.

'It might have been one hour, or it might have been six,' says Mrs. Amyot. 'My footing was insecure. Holding on to the friendly beam with one hand, I stretched the other cautiously around and felt a piece of coarse sacking, so I concluded that I must have landed in the covered-in, disused fireplace of some room. It was pitch dark, and I didn't dare to move, fearing that I was perhaps only in a recess and might fall further—further down!'

At last welcome footsteps were heard, and men with ropes and ladder arrived. No one could, of course, get down to her aid, but the brave girl knotted the rope round her waist, tied it to the ladder, and was hauled up in safety. A bottle of milk, brought by Miss Ribbing, was the only refreshment available, and having partaken of that unstimulating beverage, the question arose, how to get home without alarming her mother. A cab was called, from which she alighted in the street adjoining her home, and stealthily creeping in at a side door she seized a large cloak to hide her torn and tattered garments. Then, going to her mother's room, she was greeted with the words, 'Is that you, dear child? Don't laugh at me, but at twelve o'clock I had the most terrible feeling of fear as if some danger were threatening you.'

When Mrs. Engelhart heard what had happened, she was greatly upset. The following morning her husband went to the Steward of the Palace, who was an architect. At first he absolutely repudiated the idea of there being any such doors, still more that if there were, they could have been left open. A plan of the Palace was procured, which disclosed iron doors that were opened at times to clean the chimneys. Mr. Engelhart insisted on their both going to the top of the building to investigate the spot, when it was found that the door *had* been left open, and the Steward, putting down the lantern with a cord, pointed out to his horrified companion that if his daughter had moved but an inch or two to the right when her descent was arrested, she must inevitably have fallen to the ground-floor of the Palace!

'In which case,' says Mrs. Amyot, quaintly, 'I should probably never have been found, and should have been one of the "mysterious disappearances" of which one sometimes hears!'

A short time later she was invited to Stockholm to paint two large historical pictures for King Oscar II. One of these hangs behind the throne in the Palace of Christiania, the other is in the Palace of Trondhjem. She spent nearly a year at the Swedish Court, and received much kindness from King Oscar and his mother, Queen Josephine. Although urged in flattering terms to remain and paint the whole series of portraits for the Throne room, a chance had arrived for her to become a private pupil of Bouguereau, and this opportunity could not be lost; she was, therefore, obliged to decline the Royal commission, and went instead to Paris for severe study.

In a few months she was able to send a picture, called 'Le Pauvre Amour,' to the Salon. It was hung on the line, and highly praised by the leading art journals. The following year the young student painted her largest and most important work, 'Le Retour de la Fille Repentante.' This too was exhibited in the Salon, hung on the line, and attracted much notice. It was reproduced by Goupil in 'L'Art pour Tous,' which only contained twenty-four of the principal works of the year.

Mrs. Amyot's few last Christmas pictures are too well known to need description. 'Tit-bits,' of which over 400,000 copies were sold, 'Scattered Tit-bits,' 'An Interval in Business,' and 'The Little Culprits.' A late painting commission, 'From the Sublime to the Ridiculous,' now stands on the easel. It is of the Georgian period. A lady in a pale blue satin gown reclines on a couch of white lacquer and yellow silk damask. By her side on a fauteuil sits her swain, reciting a love poem from a small volume of sonnets in his hand. Filled with enthusiasm and raptures, he does not observe that a little cat on his lady's lap, attracted by the irresistible bobbing up and down of his *queue*, has seized upon it, and, rolling on its back with outstretched paws, is engaged in the wildest frolics with the dishevelled pigtail. The contrast between the impassioned lover, unconscious of the kitten's gambols behind his back, proves too much for the fair one, who, taking the 'one step,' passes 'from the Sublime to the Ridiculous,' and gives herself up to the merriment of the situation.

The colouring is very striking, the beautiful old Georgian coat of a glorious red, the pale blue satin, the background of tapestry, and the delicate flowers on the tall stand, make a most effective picture; the kitten is delightful and humorous.

Paris and her artistic surroundings were a few years later forsaken, for the young painter there married Dr. Amyot and accompanied him to Norfolk; but after her marriage she was not idle, and her pictures appeared regularly at the Royal Academy. Amongst the works annually exhibited were 'The World Forgetting, by the

World Forgot,' 'Soap Bubbles,' and 'In Flagrante Delicto.'

While recalling with pleasure her happy student days, the brilliant life at the Swedish Court, the fascinations of Paris, Mrs. Amyot has long ago decided that her present life is the happiest of all. She has for many years now made her home in London. Although essentially a domestic woman, she is deservedly a great favourite in Society, and in this home of perfect love and sympathy, with a devoted husband and three charming and intelligent children, she pursues her art diligently, with ever-increasing success, while the good fairies show no signs of deserting her.

F. C. PHILIPS

THE first scene: outside, a wet, boisterous evening; inside, a charming domestic picture. It is the 'children's hour,' and the hard-working barrister, the talented author of 'As in a Looking-Glass,' has stolen a short interval from his legal and literary labours to devote to his home and the little ones, to whom he is a fond and indulgent father. A cheerful glow pervades the snug room. The firelight throws dancing reflections around; a tall, shaded lamp stands by the open grand piano, and casts soft rays on a marqueterie bureau of Dutch make. The tapestry curtains are closely drawn, and on the black fur hearthrug two thoroughbred pug-dogs romp with a lovely little maiden of four years, whose great violet eyes, fair curling hair and delicate colouring, give promise of considerable beauty in the future. Equally pretty, with gentle, thoughtful countenance, is an older girl, who attentively hands round the cups, and daintily does the honours of the tea-table. In this duty she is assisted by a fine, handsome boy of eight, just home from school, whose chief attention, however, is very properly paid to the fair young mother, to whom he is passionately attached. The group is completed by the husband and father, who stands leaning against the mantelpiece. He is above the middle height, strongly built, with great black eyes and moustache that must contrast well with his barrister's wig, but which undoubtedly give him a somewhat severe expression when in repose. This, nevertheless, is presently dispelled by some playful remark from his boy, whereat the author betrays that he can laugh as heartily and as genially as anyone.

Francis Charles Philips, who is but a year or two on the wrong side of forty, was born at Brighton, and is the youngest son of the late Mr. George Washington Philips. A discrepancy of nearly seventy years existed between father and son. 'He would have been about 112,' says the author, in a humorous tone of voice, 'if he were alive now.' (At this remark the intelligent youngsters prick up their ears, keenly expectant of one of their father's juvenile stories, but they are much too well-behaved to interrupt him.) 'He was a godson of George Washington, and was called after him on account of the friendship that existed between my grand-parents and the great American President, and because he was born whilst they were on a tour to the United States. We had a large picture of Washington which, after my father's death, was bought by the United States Government for somewhere about 3000*l*. My father owned large estates at St. Kitts, but when the British Government emancipated their slaves the family was practically ruined. He was an intimate friend of Wilberforce, and as he possessed much practical information concerning the slavery question, he was able to be of considerable service to the statesman when the Emancipation Bill came in, though he was a great sufferer thereby. My father was distinguished as a most humane slave-owner, and was a clever and highly gifted man, but unfortunately—or perhaps fortunately— he lacked ambition. But for that one failing there is scarcely any position to which he could not have attained. He subsequently came home, went to Oxford, took Holy Orders, and was certainly one of the finest preachers I ever heard in my life. He was offered a bishopric by Lord Derby, but declined it.'

The young Frank Philips seems to have inherited much of his father's talent, *plus* the much-needed ambition. At school he worked hard, though nobody exactly knew when. However idle he appeared to be, he was always found up to the mark when examination-time came on, and managed to take several prizes, chiefly for classics and for divinity. On leaving school, he had originally intended to go to Trinity College, Cambridge —and had he gone to that University he would certainly have taken a first in classics—but he was overruled by circumstances, and accordingly he 'went for a soldier.' For some generations his family had been associated with the Army, and with the Coldstream Guards in particular, two of his uncles having distinguished themselves in the regiment during the Peninsular War. A very short period of cramming sufficed, and he passed high into Sandhurst, and equally well out. He elected to join The Queen's Royals—famous as ' Colonel Kirke's lambs,' as his brother, then Captain Philips, was in the regiment, and being duly gazetted, he served chiefly in Ireland, and a year at Aldershot.

But the young soldier soon tired of military life. Possessing strong literary and theatrical tastes, and being perhaps somewhat of a Bohemian at heart, the monotonous routine of the profession grew irksome to him in the piping times of peace. Had there been any chance of seeing active service, no doubt Frank Philips would have buckled on his sword and gone off to the war with a light heart.

After resigning his commission, his next venture was a partnership with the late Mr. Henderson in the management of a theatre. Here for many years he was singularly successful. Under his auspices, ' Blue Beard,' with

K

Lydia Thompson, Willie Edouin, and Lionel Brough in the cast, ran merrily for the best part of a year, and the popular 'Cloches de Corneville' for over six hundred nights. In 1881 he retired from the management, 'and,' says Mr. Philips, 'I was not sorry to relinquish it. It is very hard work, and work that is never-ending. Trying to please everybody is always a difficulty.' It was then that he first seriously turned his attention to literature, and, as with him whatever has to be done must be done thoroughly, it was not long before he made his mark. Beginning first as a journalist, he contributed several leading articles to two London daily papers, short stories and 'Celebrities at Home' to the oldest weekly Society journal, and a variety of articles on general subjects to the leading magazines.

His first novel, 'As in a Looking-Glass,' was prompted by the idea that as it had been some forty years or so since a heroine of its particular type had been presented to the public, it was possible that a writer who created such an one would succeed. The book was immediately translated, and ran as a serial simultaneously through German and Italian papers, and in Paris through Madame Adam's magazine, 'La Nouvelle Revue.' It was immediately dramatised and acted, with Mrs. Bernard-Beere in the leading part of Lena Despard. Her clever and striking impersonation of the heroine made such an impression on M. Pierre Berton, that, thinking it would be a great *rôle* for Madame Sarah Bernhardt, he, in collaboration with Madame Vanderveld, rendered the French version. In consequence, to Mr. Philips belongs the distinction of providing the celebrated French actress with the subject-matter for one of her greatest triumphs. The success of this play in both countries is too well known to need further comment, while the novel upon which it is built has passed into some five-and-twenty editions.

À propos of Sarah Bernhardt, Mr. Philips has an amusing recollection of a visit that he paid her at her

hotel, Boulevard Pereire, in Paris. The door was opened
by a gigantic man-servant, standing some six feet six, a
Patagonian or Brazilian whom the actress had brought
back from South America. The *salon* into which he was
shown had no windows, but was lighted from the top as
in an artist's studio. The room was thoroughly characteristic, and contained many curious figures and bizarre nick-
nacks; but the *comble* of eccentricity was found in the
further corner, in the shape of a huge cage, rising from floor
to ceiling, which contained the great artist's young lions.
When Mr. Philips had somewhat recovered from his first
feelings of surprise at this singular development of room
decoration, he approached the cage, which 'Tigrette,'
Madame Bernhardt's tigress, had recently vacated, and
which now was tenanted by a leonine brood, and stood
watching intensely their gambols, not without some inward
terrors and quakings of spirit. The bars of the cage
seemed very slight, and the uncomfortable recollection
suddenly dawned on his mind that he had been told by
Bedel, the famous *dompteur*, that the large carnivora, when
reared in captivity, are far more dangerous than their
wild brethren. 'Are they quiet?' asked the author. 'Oh
yes,' replied the Patagonian Hercules, 'very quiet, especially Scarpia.' Thus emboldened, Mr. Philips stretched
out a hand to pat Scarpia's head, and was rewarded for his
temerity by a savage snatch, which made him jump backwards with the agility of a pantomimist. 'I thought you
said they were quiet,' he observed to the giant who was
smiling, enjoying the scene. 'Oh! yes, sir, so they are—
very quiet—that was only play when he grabbed at
Monsieur.' Presently the Patagonian left the room, returning with a great bowl of milk. To unfasten the cage
was the work of an instant, and before Mr. Philips could
save himself by precipitate flight, the mad things were
galloping all over the room, jumping from chair to divan,
and from divan to chair, dancing round him, crouching
at his feet, as though meditating a spring at his throat,

and then, to his inexpressible relief, dashing off again to the other end of the room where the milk was waiting for them.

'Madame not appearing,' says Mr. Philips, 'I took advantage of a favourable moment to place the *salon* door between myself and these pretty creatures, which I admired in exact proportion to the distance which separated us. When I called again in the Boulevard Pereire, a few days afterwards, I found that the lions had been removed, and their places taken by between two and three hundred birds, whose warblings and chatterings made it almost impossible to hear oneself speak.'

In 1884 Mr. Philips was called to the bar, and has ever since combined law with literature.

The next book was, 'A Lucky Young Woman,' followed by a collection of short stories, entitled 'Social Vicissitudes,' and 'Jack and Three Jills.' The succeeding novel, 'The Dean and his Daughter,' was originally written as a short story, but the characters ran away with the author. 'For instance,' Mr. Philips explains, 'I just get the main idea, and then I let the characters have their own way, and don't in the least know what they are going to do. Perhaps I do occasionally draw from life, but never so as to be recognisable,' and, he adds after a pause, 'I take a bit of one person here and another there, and so on. Many incidents have been suggested by things that I have observed in the courts, or when I was in theatrical management.'

On the morrow the second scene. The picture here reveals a totally different aspect of affairs: a square, severe room, with the neatest of writing-tables in the centre; another, on the right, holds a multitude of mysterious-looking packets precisely arranged, tied, and docketed. Not a pen seems to be out of place, not a sound can be heard without. Vast bookshelves line the opposite wall with cavernous cupboards underneath. What may not these cupboards contain! The windows

look out on the back of the Inner Temple Library. The
lad in charge is discovered comfortably curled up by the
fire, absorbed in one of his master's novels called 'Young
Mr. Ainstie's Courtship.' Asking him for another to
beguile the brief period of waiting, he affably hunts for
and produces a tattered Tauchnitz edition of 'Little Mrs.
Murray.' Soon, getting thoroughly interested, you are
inclined to wish that the case going on in Court may
detain the author for an hour or so ; but just as you have
reached an exciting chapter, Mr. Philips enters in wig
and gown (you do not fail to notice that the thought of
the previous evening *re* the wig is quite realised). He
hands you his special writing-chair—perhaps the chair
may afford inspiration ! Here he finds the quiet necessary
for his double profession. He dictates rapidly to a shorthand secretary, but cannot stand a type-writer in the
room, as the clicking sound 'knocks every idea out of his
head.'

Mr. Philips works at his novels very much as he
worked at school—at odd hours—but in the aggregate a
good deal of literary and legal business is got through
every day. He possesses not only facility in the art of
composition and the versatility that enables a writer to
vary his style at will, but he has a knack, quite his own,
of seizing the salient points of his subjects and of bringing
them out with vigour and with truth. He draws characters that are at once true and amusing; his stories are
alike artistic in construction and original in design, while
the wit is so keen, and the dialogue so crisp and bright,
that he sustains the interest to the final page.

He has tried his hand, also successfully, with three or
four farcical comedies. In joint authorship with Mr.
Charles Brookfield, 'Godpapa' was produced at the
Comedy Theatre, and in this remarkably humorous piece
Mr. Charles Hawtrey probably scored one of his greatest
hits. In conjunction with Mr. Percy Fendall he brought
out a most amusing and successful farcical comedy, called

'Husband and Wife,' at the same theatre, while his latest play, 'A Woman's Reason,' also written in conjunction with Mr. Brookfield, promises to be the greatest success of all. Two recent works, entitled 'Mrs. Bouverie' and 'A Question of Colour,' bear no sign of falling off. It may safely be predicted that in his erratic 'odd hours' the gifted author will continue to find abundant material for his brilliant pen.

SOPHIE LARKIN

To mention the name of Miss Sophie Larkin on your rounds among her brother and sister actors is at once to evoke hearty words of affection, in which a friendship of twenty years with the talented player enables you cordially to join. 'Is not she a dear?' says one. 'Is not she clever?' says another. 'How excellent she is all round!' remarks a third; while the fourth, a charming little member of her profession, naïvely exclaims, 'I do so want to know Miss Larkin; do ask me to tea to meet her!' No less warm is the appreciation of her by the public, before whom she is always to be seen as she pursues the even tenor of her calling without fear and without reproach. 'My critics are always so kind to me,' she says, quaintly, 'and—would you believe it?—I am not personally acquainted with any of them.'

She lives in a quiet, broad road near Chiswick, in an old-fashioned house whereat the frugal tramcar sets you down. The pretty drawing-room is flooded with sunshine on this bright autumn day, an indication of the actress's own happy, mirthful temperament. Under the mass of white curls and straight, black eyebrows, the dark brown eyes look out with a merry sparkle of fun, for she has a keen sense of the ridiculous, 'rather too much, unfortunately,' is her own opinion, yet it has helped her, not inconsiderably, through the battle of life.

No other member of her family has ever been on the boards, but at a very early age she was often taken to the theatre, of which she became so passionately fond that she soon began to copy and mimic everything that she saw, and in many little amateur plays got up among themselves she displayed so much ability that a friend who saw her act declared that she 'ought to go on the stage.' The late Mr. Benjamin Webster's brother Fred was just then holding a sort of dramatic class (in which Mr. John Maclean was at that time a student) to rehearse plays. The young girl attended it for a few months, and worked so hard that her instructor declared that he would take no more money from her; he had taught her all he could, and advised her to 'get an engagement.' Mr. Webster's son was getting up a benefit at the Strand Theatre, in which she was invited to play Widow Melnotte to Mr. Fred Belton's Claude. 'I was only too glad to play anything,' relates Miss Larkin, 'for the sake of acting. A short time after I saw an advertisement for a company to go on a Yorkshire circuit, of which Mr. Fred Belton was manager. I answered it, and was offered a "utility" engagement, playing anything and everything for the large sum of eighteen shillings a week. I accepted it, stayed one season, then joined Edward Gomersall's company (son of the celebrated "Napoleon" of Astley's) and remained on for two years as leading lady.'

In those busy years of unremitting toil, Sophie Larkin laid the foundation of her future success. Grounded so thoroughly in every variety of part and play, she laid in the large stock of knowledge and experience that has been so invaluable in her subsequent bright career. To give some idea of what work meant in those days, her own words shall be quoted. 'Yes,' she says, smiling, 'it was an incessant grind. I often played in two new pieces on the same evening; often, too, until it was over, I did not even know what would be played on the morrow. There were only two play-books in MS. between the whole party. How different from these days when everyone has a neatly typed copy for him or her self! After a performance I used to sit up until 4 A.M. copying out my lines, and got up at 7 o'clock to take the book to someone else in a similar strait. Rehearsal was called at 11 A.M., and was seldom over till three. Then back to the theatre at night. One great advantage of it all was, that one learnt what could be done under the pressure of excitement, but never could in cold blood. One finds out what suits one—an opportunity which the students of the present day miss. I remember one evening the manager said I must play the two leading parts the following night—both new—"Jack Sheppard" and "Susan Hopley." This is a specimen of the work night after night—sometimes blank verse, too, which, you know, people hear so critically. But for my beloved mother's constant companionship and help,' and here her voice trembles, and she adds, with pathos, 'I could never have got through it all. She arranged our *ménage*, our journeys, even my costumes, so I had nothing to think of except my profession.'

Miss Larkin has many a good anecdote and amusing incident to relate of her early experiences in these provincial tours. In those times there were none of the gorgeous upholstery and scenic effects of later years, and they had to resort to very simple means. On one occasion, in Yorkshire, 'Hamlet' was to be produced. The throne was composed of an inverted candle-box, covered with red baize, on which they had to sit in lieu of State chairs. Mr. Tom Glenny was the Player King; Miss Larkin the Queen of Denmark. The property-master's wife was cast for the *rôle* of the Player Queen—a most difficult part even for an experienced actress. She had been well coached, and was letter-perfect in the morning rehearsal, but, alas! when the evening came she was seized with stage-fright, and could not open her mouth nor gasp forth a word. The first speech should have been hers, but none was forthcoming. The Player King reeled off his sentences, but when it came to 'Madam, how like you the play?' Miss Larkin's reply, 'Methinks the lady doth protest too much,' was laughingly inappropriate, as the poor lady had been unable to 'protest' a single syllable, and the effect on the audience can be imagined. 'The Yorkshire people are great on Shakespeare,' says Miss Larkin, 'and could almost say every line backwards, which was all the worse for the poor Player Queen. The whole house became convulsed with merriment, and shouted so loud that it was some minutes before we could go on. I always laugh now when I think of it.' And she had once, when quite a girl, a terrible *contretemps* of her own, a portion of which must be suppressed. By an accidental transposition of two words, the perfectly innocent sentence became entirely altered, and turned into a ludicrous *double entendre*. This was at once grasped by the audience, who collapsed with laughter. It was an awful moment. For a second the poor girl scarcely realised what she had said; but as the meaning flashed upon her she felt sick with fright. At this moment a man in the pit, seeing her distress, shouted, 'All right, lass; go on, lass!' She pulled herself together; and, ably supported by Mr. Melville, she went on with the act, and received a storm of applause at its conclusion. 'But I think,' she says, laughing, 'we won't indulge anyone's curiosity by telling what the unlucky words really were. I grew hot and cold every evening after when it came to that bit.'

On the first occasion of her playing an old woman's part at Leeds a manager saw her, and said if she would engage to play only such *rôles* with him he would 'make her fortune.' Miss Larkin felt it 'a terrible jump from sympathetic and comedy characters to those of disagreeable old women,' but she accepted, on the chance of getting to London. A curious circumstance, showing upon what slight events fate often hinges, brought about the actual London engagement for which she had been wishing. By the accidental leaving of a letter—which would have bound her to the Prince of Wales's Theatre, Liverpool—at one door instead of another, it luckily arrived too late, and she was able instead to accept a much more tempting offer from Marie Wilton for the Prince of Wales's, London, where she made the first of her metropolitan successes which have gone on so uninterruptedly since. During the original run of the late Mr. T. W. Robertson's delightful plays, Sophie Larkin created the parts of Lady Ptarmigan in ' Society,' of Lady Shendryn in ' Ours,' and the Marquise de Saint Maur in ' Caste.' At the conclusion of that engagement she received an excellent offer from Miss Herbert to go to the St. James's Theatre to play in ' De Boots ' with the late Mr. J. S. Clarke, succeeded by a term of months with Miss Fanny Josephs at the Holborn Theatre in one of Mr. Burnand's extravaganzas. At the Globe, in poor Montague's time, she will be remembered as Priscilla Mervyn in ' Partners for Life,' with Messrs. James and Thorne ; as the Widow Warren, her ' pet part of all,' in ' The Road to Ruin,' with Mrs. John Wood ; in ' She Stoops to Conquer,' when she played with so much *éclat* the part of Mrs. Hardcastle ; and in multitudes of others.

In the immense range of her *répertoire* there are two plays which are peculiarly identified with Miss Larkin's name. One is the celebrated ' Our Boys,' in which she acted Clarissa Champneys for a run of four years and a quarter consecutively without a break ! She observes, ' It nearly made us all ill, the horrible monotony evening after evening. It seemed to be going on day and night too, like a well-wound clock. It got on my nerves, and at last I could not sleep. I had to send for the doctor, and the first words he said were, "' Our Boys ' ! that is what is the matter with you." We were all thankful when it came to an end.' The other piece was that most witty and laughable 'Confusion,' by Derrick; and what a remarkable cast it was! Mr. Henry Neville, Mr. Fred Thorne, Miss Sophie Larkin, Miss Winifred Emery, Miss Kate Phillips, &c. If it had been played farcically, it could not have escaped being 'broad;' but in such able and perfect hands, the vein of mock tragedy made it all the funnier to the audience, and it was wonderful how the players themselves could have got through it with such becoming gravity.

Countless are the characters that Sophie Larkin has impersonated. Her refined and vivacious Sophia, then, what she calls ' a lovely part ' in ' Loose Tiles,' in ' Nerves,' and 'The Pharisee,' in effective scenes with Marius; these are all well remembered. Also her Daphne in 'Pygmalion and Galatea,' and her Mrs. Hardcastle on the first morning of Mrs. Langtry's *début* at the Haymarket: while she was then engaged by Mr. Bancroft for *matinées* over and above the usual evening performance. Thus it will be seen that the talented artist has not spared herself. She has reached her prominent position entirely by her own merits, and made the good score 'off her own bat' unaided. That she is still strengthening her powers and increasing her reputation, the public saw for itself nightly in her late clever impersonation of Penelope Austin in the popular Adelphi drama, 'The Fatal Card,' since which time she has been engaged in the pantomime 'Cinderella' at Drury Lane.

FREDERIC COWEN

Of all the gifts assuredly good music is the one that produces the most refining and cultivating effects; therefore to the great composer and musician the public owe a deep debt of gratitude. For if his art can 'soothe the savage breast,' what measure of comfort and enjoyment can it not inspire in the sick, the sound, the sorrowful, the joyous

—rich and poor alike! Although his father was more or less of a musician, the talent with which Mr. Frederic Cowen is blessed originates in himself. He was born at Kingston, Jamaica, in January 1852, and at the age of four accompanied his parents to England, where they then settled. The elder Mr. Cowen was at once appointed treasurer to Her Majesty's Theatre, and remained in that post throughout the directorships of Messrs. Lumley, Smith, and Mapleson—a period of eleven years. Then, after the great fire of 1867, he moved to Drury Lane, and occupied a similar position under Messrs. Mapleson and Gye. Together with these duties he combined those of secretary to the late Earl Dudley for over twenty years. Thus it will be seen that the young Frederic Cowen, from his earliest years, enjoyed exceptional advantages in being brought in contact with the greatest artists of the day in public as well as in private entertainments, for which Lord Dudley—himself a devotee to music and one of the greatest patrons of art—was renowned. To the delicate, refined-natured child, no surroundings could have been more appropriate or better adapted to draw out and develop the natural gifts which have made the young composer so distinguished. When yet but a toddling infant he showed himself acutely sensitive to sound, and listened with intelligent delight to any good music, and with frowns to any disorder of time or tune. As long back as he can look he composed, and remembers standing at the piano—because he was too small to sit—and working out his ideas on the instrument ere he was old enough to write out the notes. He was educated at home, a circumstance he is somewhat inclined to regret, for he is of opinion that 'at a public school he would have lost an inherent shyness, though doubtless it has all been for the best.' Probably very much for the best. Reared in the very atmosphere of oratorio and opera, Frederic Cowen early acquired a thorough orchestral knowledge, which has served him in good stead as a composer. At the age of six he had produced a waltz, a song, and some quadrilles, which were written down for him by Mr. Henry Russell. Then his parents, fully recognising what was in him, began to cultivate the divine talent, and by the advice of Lord Dudley—who from the first had taken the keenest interest in the gifted child—persuaded Benedict to make an exception in his favour, and take him as a pupil for the piano, while he studied harmony with Sir John Goss. At the age of eight the boy had completed the music of an operetta called 'Garibaldi,' with the same aid to put it into shape. At twelve he was thoroughly at home in Beethoven's sonatas, in which he was just then heard by Thalberg, as also in some of that master's own work. Thalberg, much delighted, was enthusiastic over the boy's talents, and predicted a brilliant future for him. His first appearance in public was made at the age of eleven in the concert-room of Her Majesty's Theatre, where he gave a pianoforte recital that comprised several pieces by Bach, Heller, &c., without notes. The criticisms on this juvenile performance were so unanimously favourable—not to say flattering—that the following year the young musician gave a concert at Dudley House, at which Trebelli, Joachim, and Santley assisted—a trio of which the boy artist may well have been proud. It proved so great a success that he arranged yet another and last *matinée* some months later with Joachim and Piatti, before leaving for Leipzig to enter the Conservatoire. There Frederic Cowen, in his fourteenth year, studied under Reinecke for composition, Moscheles for pianoforte, and Moritz Hauptmann for harmony and counterpoint: Entering heart and soul into his work, he made such progress that he produced his first string quartette, and also an overture for orchestra, which was played with marked success a year later at the Covent Garden concerts. Then he returned to London, gave several *matinées* at Dudley House, and once more started—this time for Berlin—to resume study. 'I began my actual musical career,' says Mr. Cowen, 'when I was nearly seventeen, and have been at it ever since. My name came before the public so early that some people think I am an old man—the Americans especially. But with regard to my "method," of which you ask, the composition of music is most difficult to describe—there is nothing tangible in it. First the bare idea—the germ —and it gradually develops. I never believed in so-called inspiration. It does occasionally come, I admit, but as a rule I have always found my best ideas—if good they can be called—have come when I sought the hardest. It is like digging deep down into a mine with a spade.' But the mine yields rich treasures. Among his more popular early works, written while the young composer was yet in his teens, was the cantata 'The Rose Maiden,' produced in 1870 at St. James's Hall, performed by Titiens, Patey, Nordblom, and Stockhausen, and conducted by himself, succeeded by some incidental music in and an overture to Schiller's 'Maid of Orleans,' written for the Brighton Festival. In 1880 followed what is one of his most important works, the famous 'Scandinavian Symphony,' which has justly taken its place in Europe as one of the greatest orchestral works of modern days. Up to the time of the late Lord Dudley's serious illness he had continued to watch his young friend's career with deep interest and affection, and unbounded sympathy. One can well imagine the pleasure that such a work would have given so true a lover of art; but the kind-hearted peer passed away without hearing that or its exquisite successor. This was an orchestral suite called 'The Language of Flowers,' and from that day to the present it can be found and ofttimes heard in every orchestral society in England. Mr. Cowen's later works are too well known to need much mention—the delightful sacred cantata 'St. Ursula;' 'The Welsh Symphony;' 'The Sleeping Beauty;' the oratorio 'Ruth,' written for the Worcester Festival; the masterly opera 'Thorgrim,' for the Carl Rosa company, with its never-to-be-forgotten striking duet in the third act; 'Signa,' performed first in 1893, in Milan, and brought out later by Sir Augustus Harris. This opera, which abroad caused Mr. Cowen annoyances that are still fresh in the minds of the musical world, is dedicated, by permission, to the Queen, and was commanded by her Majesty to Windsor. Another work, a cantata called 'The Water Lily,' was written for the Norwich Festival of 1893. His latest opera, 'Harold,' was performed at Covent Garden, and he has now completed an oratorio for the Gloucester Festival. For six years Mr. Cowen had much practice as an accompanist.

As the art of accompanying is very much neglected, partly because it is not properly understood or considered of sufficient importance, his ideas on the subject shall be given in his own words. 'The very fact,' he says, 'of the nature of the art of accompanying ought to make it better understood. It should be entirely unobtrusive. The great requirements are that the accompanist must be a thorough musician in technicality and feeling, an excellent pianist, and a good sight reader. He must have an intense sympathy with all schools of music and a complete understanding of the nature of the voice that he accompanies. Then he must straightway forget that he possesses all these qualities! I gave it up some years ago, and though I came out as a pianist I was too nervous and not sufficiently robust physically to do that and to compose as well.'

Symphonist though he be, innumerable songs—tender, refined, and sweet, the outcome of the delicate, artistic soul within—flow from his pen. As director of the Melbourne Centennial Exhibition he spent nearly a year in that city, where his reception was most gratifying, and his concerts crowded. A great traveller in foreign lands, and with a love of Nature in all its aspects, Mr. Cowen is a keen mountaineer, and delights in all its dangers and discomforts. He is a slow composer, but a quick worker. The beginning of a big work takes him a long time, but when once he has got 'inside it' he writes rapidly, spending practically the whole day over it for months at a stretch. If worried over musical matters, the piano is the last resource to which he would fly, but if about more mundane things he finds its influence soothing. He has just been appointed to succeed the late Sir Charles Hallé in the conductorship of Hallé's Concerts, Manchester, for the ensuing season.

But under the quiet, straightforward manner, and the highly strung, warm-hearted nature, there lurks a fund of humour which now and then breaks out into witty, doggerel rhymes. Romantic and ardent in temperament, modest and unassuming after the fashion of genius, the slight look of gravity apparent on his face vanishes in an instant, and the thoughtful dark eyes flash out with merriment when any fun is in question. It has even been whispered that he has occasionally participated in the playing of a few practical but always kindly jokes.

Mr. Frederic Cowen's study, which is like a museum library, is filled in every available corner with books—chiefly humorous—first editions of Thackeray, Dickens, Leech, and Cruikshank; art books and illustrations. On a neat ebonised writing-table, in the post of honour, stands a picture of the sweet and gentle lady who presides over his home. 'My beloved and honoured mother,' says the famous composer, in a low tone; 'of whom it is impossible to speak too warmly or affectionately.'

EMILY GERARD (MADAME DE LASZOWSKA) AND DOROTHEA GERARD (MADAME LONGARD DE LONGARDE).

PART I.

THE subjects of the following sketch are the talented sisters who, singly and in collaboration, are the popular authors of many delightful novels. Together they wrote

'Reata,' 'Beggar my Neighbour,' and others, to which allusion will be made later; singly, 'A Secret Mission,' 'The Voice of a Flower,' &c. (E. Gerard) and 'Lady Baby,' 'A Queen of Curds and Cream,' &c. (Dorothea Gerard).

It is curious to trace how sometimes certain remarkable events which have convulsed whole nations, continue, long after their apparent influence has subsided, to mould the destinies of unborn generations. This influence will be found at work even in cases where cause and effect are seemingly as wide asunder as the poles, for, impossible as it may appear, it is undeniably true that the marriage of these sisters, who are Scottish by birth, was one of the results of the expulsion from France of King Charles X.

When his Majesty was dethroned, in consequence of the July Revolution of 1830, it was in Scotland that he first took refuge. The English Government placed Holyrood Palace at the King's disposal, and there he resided for nearly two years with his grandchildren, the Duc de Bordeaux (subsequently known as the Comte de Chambord) and Princess Louise, son and daughter of the Duc de Berri, assassinated in 1820. Sir John Robison, the Misses Gerard's grandfather, well known in Edinburgh at that time, had two daughters, Euphemia and Anne, who, as their ages corresponded with those of the young French Princes, were frequently invited over to play with them at Holyrood Palace. Between Euphemia (the authors' mother) and Princess Louise, a warm sympathy was soon established which, unlike the majority of such childish intimacies, became a life-long friendship. Although subsequently separated during a space of about thirty years, they always remained in touch and in correspondence.

Euphemia Robison married Archibald Gerard, of Rochsoles, in Lanarkshire. They had seven children, of whom three brothers were older and three sisters younger than the novelist, Emily Gerard.

The greater part of her childhood up to the age of fifteen was spent at Rochsoles, and from the fact of her brothers being mostly away at school, whilst the little Dorothea and two other sisters were still in the nursery, her life at that time was tolerably lonely, and she seldom had a companion of her own age. Long solitary rides on her pony, attended solely by a groom, and equally solitary rambles in the woods were her chief amusements. She was always fond of reading, and her mother often remarked that she was the only one of the children who had never required a reading lesson. Her brother Alexander, her senior by a year, taught her the alphabet, and she found out the rest for herself. Figures, however, seemed to be more of a stumblingblock; for, at the age of five, when the child could read with tolerable fluency, she was utterly incapable of distinguishing the figures with which the pages were numbered. Alexander was in the same predicament, and in order to supply their common deficiency, the children concocted a whole series of fantastic appellations by means of which to define and identify the Arabic designations. 'Some of these ingenious designations,' says Miss Gerard, ' have escaped my memory, but I know that 1 was called "the whipping-post," 3 "old crazy," 6 "the saucepan," 7 "the hatchet," and 8 "the lady" (probably because of her elegant little waist). Somehow, the idea of learning the real names of the figures never seemed to have occurred to either of us, and no one thought of investigating the matter until one day my mother's attention was aroused by hearing me reply, in answer to Alexander's question regarding the page of a story that he was seeking in a book, " it begins at the hatchet and the lady." After this we were made to learn the orthodox designations of the numbers, but I, at least, did this regretfully, and found them much less interesting and expressive than those of our own creation.'

Later, the little girl read pretty much what she could lay hands on, but her real passion for reading dates from a tedious illness when, at the age of nine, she was confined to bed for nearly six months. As an inducement to remain quiet she was offered the bribe of sweetmeats in plenty and an unlimited number of story-books wherewith to beguile the enforced captivity. Taking full advantage of both these offers, the rather melancholy result ensued that she gorged herself alike with fairy tales and bonbons, so that in after years the very sight of a box of chocolate or the mention of elves and giants was sufficient to produce nausea.

The girl's studies, up to the time when she went to school, were conducted by her mother. Mrs. Gerard, who was a singularly intelligent and accomplished woman and a brilliant pianist, gave herself up entirely to the education of her daughters, and during many years withdrew completely from the society of which she was so bright an ornament.

'I suppose that I must have been about eleven or twelve,' says Miss Gerard, 'when I first began to scribble in secret—poetry, of course; for what youthful writer at that stage of his or her existence would stoop to prose! Unfortunately I have not preserved any of these early effusions, which were mostly of an elegiac character, and chiefly suggested by the demise of some pet animal or doll. I can but faintly remember one of these poems, composed on the death of a favourite chestnut foal, which seemed to me so touchingly pathetic that it caused my tears to flow in torrents when I recited it to myself in bed, with my face well hidden under the sheets for fear of being caught by the nurse. She, not being of a poetical turn of mind, may possibly have failed to appreciate the beauty of this remarkable production, now, alas! lost to posterity! I can recall only the last four lines, which ran thus:

> 'Long years may pass, a thousand years,
> And yet no sigh or burning tears
> Can snatch one foal from death, and save
> It from its lone, untimely grave.'

These lines, together with some others composed about the same time, were shown to no one but one bosom friend, who, with the beautiful enthusiasm of thirteen, promptly declared them to be superior to anything that Burns or Sir Walter Scott had ever penned. I modestly felt inclined to agree with her at the time, but some years later, vague doubts as to her absolute reliability as a critic began to form in my mind, and I consigned these virgin productions of my muse to the flames!'

The lines at least showed that even at that age the little poet had fairly well studied her quantities in rhyming. At the age of fourteen, she wrote a fairy drama in verse, called 'The Magic Ring,' which was twice performed by her sisters and self before a select audience consisting of their parents and the household servants.

It was after this that her father and mother decided to send her, with her sister next in age, to some Continental school, in order to have the opportunity of studying foreign languages. The Sacré Cœur, in Paris, was first taken into consideration, but here Mrs. Gerard's old friend, Princess Louise de Bourbon, intervened, which caused a change of plans. Princess Louise, who in 1845, married Charles III., reigning Duke of Parma, had, since her husband's assassination in 1854, been acting as Regent for her son Duke Robert during his minority. Expelled from Italy in 1859, by Victor Emanuel, after the battle of Magenta, she had established herself in Switzerland on the shores of the beautiful Lake Constance, placing her two daughters at the Convent of the Sacré Cœur at Riedenburg, near Bregenz, on the Tyrolean side of the Lake. H.R.H. therefore suggested to Mrs. Gerard, that the object of obtaining fluency in French and German would equally be fulfilled were the girls to go to Riedenburg, instead of to Paris, while this plan would have the additional advantage of permitting their respective daughters to become acquainted and continue the friendship that had united their mothers for over thirty years. Accordingly, to Riedenburg they went, where they found a lively and a happy home, as well as two kind and devoted friends in the Princesses Marguerite and Alix, who were about their own ages. After the rather solitary life at Rochsoles, the change to a large boarding school was a delightfully novel sensation. The young Emily threw herself heart and soul into the studies, which possessed quite a new attraction now that the hitherto unknown elements of emulation and of rivalry had been introduced into them.

Being gifted with an exceptionally good memory and much perseverance, she quickly rose to the head of the class, notwithstanding the difficulty of pursuing studies in a language not yet wholly familiar. At the end of the second school-year, the young student had carried away every prize within reach, with the exception of those for calligraphy and needlework. Her taste for original composition also found a congenial outlet in writing odes, speeches, dramas and satires to be recited and acted by her companions on holidays. Then, as it became necessary to remove her to a warmer climate, the Duchess of Parma again influenced Mrs. Gerard's decision by suggesting Venice (her own usual winter residence) as the most natural and fitting place in the circumstances, at the same time proposing that as her own eldest daughter, Euphemia's particular friend, Princess Marguerite, was also to leave school about the same time, they could continue their studies together at Venice.

This plan was carried out, and from the autumn of 1863 until the spring of 1866, Venice became their winter home. Miss Gerard's joint studies with Princess Marguerite continued for about eighteen months, and after the Duchess of Parma's death they were carried on together at the house of the Comte de Chambord, uncle of H.R.H.

'I have, however, often regretted,' says Miss Gerard, 'that I did not make better use of the advantages thus offered, but being just then at that period of existence when balls present more attraction than books, and questions of toilette seem infinitely more important than the most fascinating mathematical problem, my thirst for knowledge cooled sadly down. Then, when, in addition to Latin, French, German, and Italian literature, it was decided that Princess Marguerite was to begin Spanish as well—by way of preparation for betrothal to her cousin Don Carlos—I fairly struck, expressing my conviction that my education was quite complete. It might be all very well for the Princess to learn Spanish, which indeed her position as the future wife of Don Carlos demanded; but as I had not the remotest chance of ever becoming Queen of Spain, and as I already could speak and write four languages with tolerable fluency, I did not at all see the fun of embarking in the dreary grammatical labyrinth that was to lead to a fifth. Now that I look back on that time, I keenly anathematise my own folly in having wasted such golden opportunities; but I suppose that most girls are alike on that point, and that to the end of time it will always remain a case of 'Si jeunesse savait, si vieillesse pouvait.'

Those years spent at Venice were at once the happiest and the most eventful of the young girl's life. In the joint novel by E. and Dorothea Gerard, entitled 'A Sensitive Plant,' she has endeavoured to retrace some of her impressions of that time, likewise in the earlier pages of the same work, Janet's solitary life at Glenmavis was chiefly suggested by her childish experiences. It was also at Venice that she made the acquaintance of her husband, Miecislaus Laszowski de Kraszkowice, who is descended from an old family of Polish nobility, for those were the days when Venice was still under Austrian legislation, and Austrian officers mingled freely in the pleasant little international circle to which the houses of the dispossessed Duke of Modena, the Infanta of Spain, and of the Comte de Chambord, imparted something of the charm and distinction of Court life.

Captain de Laszowski was at that time serving in a Hussar regiment stationed at Mestre, and came frequently to Venice with his comrades to take part in social amusements. It was then that his intimacy with the Gerard family began, although the marriage did not take place until 1869, when they met again at Salzburg. The disastrous campaign of 1866, (in which he so distinguished himself at the battle of Custozza as to be decorated), which for Austria resulted in the loss of Venice, having meanwhile intervened to sever the respective paths in life of the young couple, and to make it seem highly improbable that they should ever again converge.

'The Land beyond the Forest,' or 'Facts, Figures, and Fancies from Transylvania' (E. Gerard), was the result of two years' residence in that country, where General de Laszowski occupied the position of cavalry Brigadier. She has likewise been in the habit of contributing critical essays and reviews to various periodicals, and for nearly two years furnished the monthly reviews of German literature to the *Times*. 'Bis' is a collection of short stories, some of which had previously appeared in magazines. 'A Secret Mission,' a two-volume novel, was founded upon a tragic incident in Russian Poland, and this is the one that the author considers her best work. It is good, very good, but there is one yet more recent, which it is impossible to praise too highly. It is a single volume, entitled 'The Voice of a Flower,' a most sweet and tender story, powerful withal in conception and style. The characters are drawn with an unerring hand, and to sum up the whole in a few words, a more exquisite and artistic story has rarely been penned.

'A Secret Mission' possesses all the conditions for a powerful drama, and E. Gerard has often been advised to utilise it as such. She did actually attempt to dramatise it herself, and was decidedly successful in the effort; but having no connection with the stage, or with stage-managers, she has not yet attempted to get the piece attentively considered. Her latest work is 'A Foreigner.'

'I must tell you,' says E. Gerard, 'that I always remained in close and intimate contact with the dear and honoured friend of my early youth, Princess Marguerite de Bourbon, Duchess of Madrid, up to the very day of her death, which took place on Jan. 29, 1893, to the unspeakable grief of all who like myself had the privilege of knowing her intimately. She took a keen interest in all my literary work, and it was to her that I invariably turned to verify some doubtful historical or scientific question, or to trace the origin of a classical quotation. She had begun a French translation of our joint novel, " Beggar my Neighbour," which, however, was never completed, and another of her unrealised projects was that I should go some day on a long visit to her Italian country-place of Viareggio, and there write a novel in collaboration with herself. H.R.H. undoubtedly possessed all the qualifications which go to make up a novelist—a vivid and brilliant imagination, a keen sense of humour, a shrewd knowledge of human nature, and a truly marvellous memory, which always placed at her disposal the fruits of an exceptionally careful education, besides an extensive knowledge of the literature of five different countries. There is, therefore, every reason to suppose that our joint labour would have had considerable chance of success, and I shall always cling to the belief that with this unrealised air-castle has likewise perished the best novel to which I might have affixed my name.'

Madame de Laszowska's (E. Gerard) method of working differs considerably from her sister's. 'I am gifted,' she says, 'with far less patience than Dora. Some days I find it absolutely impossible to write at all, and have found by experience that it is of no use attempting then, as what I should write in these conditions would be absolutely worthless.' Weather also has an extraordinary influence on her, and when the barometer is falling, or snow—which peculiarly affects her—is in the air, she is incapable of working. On the other hand, when a writing fit is on, she has difficulty in restraining herself from working all day long, and has always then the feeling as though it were not she, but some invisible person standing at her elbow, dictating so fast that she can hardly keep pace with her pen; but her work is always done in her own little 'private den,' from which she excludes everyone.

Since 1885, when her husband retired from active service, with the rank of Lieutenant-General in the Austrian service, Madame de Laszowska's home has been permanently in Vienna; her trips to England have since her marriage been few and far between, and she has only twice visited her native country.

The family circle includes two handsome young sons. The elder, Arthur de Laszowski, is studying law at the Vienna University; the younger, Alfred, is serving as cadet in the same Polish Lancer Regiment which their father formerly commanded. The boys have been brought up to speak Polish with their father, and English with their mother, whilst their education has been chiefly conducted in German. German, too, is the language in which their parents converse, for he has never attained sufficient fluency in English, nor she in Polish, to enable them to employ each other's language for everyday use.

'Although for many reasons,' says Madame de Laszowska, 'we found it expedient to settle permanently in Vienna after my husband left the army, I have never been able to take kindly to town life, despite the undoubted intellectual resources which a capital affords. I have always preferred a country life, mountains in particular being my hobby, and it has become almost an imperative necessity for me to spend a week or so every year in really hard mountain climbing, my greatest delight being to set off alone with my elder son, who shares my passion, each carrying our own knapsack, and, if possible, dispensing with a guide unless for the ascension of any particularly high peak. By these means we have made many lonely, delightful walking tours in the Polish and Hungarian Carpathians as well as in the Austrian Alps.'

This passion for mountain climbing is rather a peculiarity with the Gerard family; not only her father, but several other members of the present family, are deeply imbued with it, and it is likewise not uninteresting to recall that a peak in the Himalayas, called 'Gerard's Peak,' was so named after Captain Gerard, a brother of the sisters' great-grandfather.

A year after Miss Gerard's marriage her mother died, and from that time forward, during a space of over ten years, Madame de Laszowska's three young sisters lived chiefly with her. It was at her house at Brzezany in Galicia that two of them became acquainted with their future husbands, thus clearly demonstrating the accuracy of the aforesaid assertion, that the revolution of 1830 was directly instrumental in bringing about their marriages.

PART II.

A BRIEF sketch of Dorothea Gerard's early days will bring the reader to the date when the two sisters just started on what has proved to be a brilliant literary career. She, too, was born at Rochsoles, and was the youngest but one of the family, and from her early childhood had been accustomed to compose little stories; and though as yet of too tender an age to write them for herself, she would dictate her compositions to her mother. One of these in that beloved handwriting is still extant, the moral of which shows that the child had a just turn of mind, and had even at that age a pretty way of expressing her thoughts. In those days they had a sort of literary club (of which Dorothea was the youngest member), the arrangement being that each of the young people had to supply a story once a week. A great part of her childhood was spent in Austria, and she and her little sister were chiefly educated at the convent of the Sacré Cœur, at Grätz in Styria. She was but fifteen years of age when her mother died, and soon after that sad event the girls passed into the charge of their sister, then a young bride, Madame de Laszowska (E. Gerard), whose husband's frequent changes of station gave them all good opportunities of becoming acquainted with various parts of Austria.

It was comparatively long before the sisters made the discovery that they each possessed a certain amount of literary facility which might be turned to a practical use, and they are both of the opinion that had they not happened to be together during those years, neither would have thought of touching a pen except for the purpose of letter-writing.

The sisters, however, are not the first of the family whose names have been known in literature. Their great-grandfather Professor Gerard's (of Aberdeen) works, 'Gerard on Taste,' and 'Gerard on Genius,' made considerable mark in their day, and are not yet wholly forgotten. Another great-grandfather, the Rev. Archibald Alison (father of the historian, Sir Archibald Alison), was likewise a no less celebrated writer.

It was not until 1877, that, being consigned to the deadly monotony of a little Hungarian country town, where the landscape was a desert and the society *nil*, the idea of writing a novel as 'something to do' was suddenly and almost without premeditation born in upon them.

It is curious to observe how much circumstances have to do with bringing out latent talent. Up to that time there certainly was in neither sister 'a deep poetic voice,' anxious to utter anything in particular. They simply wanted an occupation. The next thing was to find something about which to write. With the beautiful audacity of youthful inexperience, they never even thought of stooping to a simple story or novelette, by way of testing their powers, but blindly and recklessly they plunged head foremost into the gigantic task of a three-volume novel, at first merely by way of amusement, without thought of publication.

'We discussed and rejected all sorts of possible and impossible plots,' says Dorothea Gerard; 'and if the tale which goes against me be true, it was in the following manner that the idea of "Reata" first saw the light. I had knelt down beside my bed one morning to say my usual prayers, perhaps not with my usual attention to the subject. Two of my sisters were in the room. My prayers being finished, I rose to my feet and announced "I have got a plot for a novel." It was only a very rough idea, but it did actually become the basis of "Reata."'

Who shall say whence the inspiration came? The girls' hearts were so set on the matter, and with the idea they soon found the power to carry it out. As the book was written at first, it would have filled four stout volumes, for of course the young writers had no idea of proportion.

'For some reason or another,' continues Dorothea Gerard, 'we conceived the notion that something horrible and startling ought to happen in our book, and we therefore managed to drag a peculiarly unpleasant and superfluous suicide into the story; but later some right instinct fortunately told us that this was the first thing to remove, by way of curtailing a fourth of the matter, and accordingly we extracted the whole episode with far greater ease than we had inserted it.'

When completed, the sisters re-perused their composition, and tried a few chapters as an experiment on one of their brothers. Hitherto it had been kept a close secret. He, secretly delighted, with fraternal frankness pronounced it was 'not so bad after all, and deserved a chance of being printed.' The girls, however, were utterly ignorant of how this was to be achieved. They wrote at random to three firms, whose names they took from an advertisement-sheet of a paper. Two of these at once disappointed them. After some delay, during which the hopes of both sisters had sunk down to zero, they were suddenly electrified by the intelligence that it was accepted, with the only stipulation that it should be shortened by one-fourth, though the publisher declined to give any advice as to how this was to be done, considering it would be 'better that they should follow their own impressions.' Then the above-mentioned episode was cut out, and by-and-by, to their great joy, the young authors found themselves 'in print!'

'I should like,' says Miss Gerard, 'to pay a passing tribute to the memory of the late Mr. John Blackwood, for he it was who, by his frank, open-handed, and genial recognition of this first effort by two young and perfectly unknown writers, facilitated their literary career in a most unusual manner. Whatever subsequent success we may have achieved in literature may undoubtedly be traced back to that first stepping-stone.'

After 'Reata,' which first appeared as a serial in 'Blackwood's Magazine,' the sisters wrote in conjunction 'A Sensitive Plant,' 'Beggar my Neighbour,' and 'The Waters of Hercules.' This last was the result of two seasons spent at the watering-place of Mehadia, on the Roumanian frontier. They had likewise sketched out various other plots of stories which were hereafter to be written together, but none of these projects were destined to be carried out.

In 1887, Dorothea Gerard entered into a partnership of quite another kind, and became the wife of Captain, now Lieutenant-Colonel Longard, of the 7th Austrian Lancers. On her marriage a division of literary stock-in-trade became necessary: the skeleton plot of 'Lady Baby' fell to her share, whilst her sister received her compensation in the hitherto unpublished MS. of 'A Sensitive Plant,' which, though written long before, had been laid aside for further inspection and amelioration.

Ten years after it had been written, Emily Gerard drew out the MS. from its dark seclusion, and submitted it to a critical revision—'An ungrateful task,' says her sister, 'for it is as difficult to remodel an old story as an old gown, especially when the writer herself feels conscious of looking at many things with eyes that are ten years older than when the story was first penned.'

The very title, 'Lady Baby,' almost indicates the story—and it is such a fresh, easy story—with the lovable little heroine so full of individuality and of charm. Dorothea Gerard's habit of writing so much out of doors imparts a sense of open-air life to her work, and the reader feels himself to be one of the party at the gay country-house so gracefully described. There is the charm, too, of so much variety in the writer's books. If one story be laid in cheerful home-scenes where all goes brightly and merrily, the next is sure to be quite in another part of the world, with a sad ending. 'Orthodox,' a powerfully tragic story, would undoubtedly make an excellent drama. It is strange that this idea has not occurred to a playwright. Floods of delicious tears would be shed nightly over it, if relieved at times by a laugh over the oddities and wit of one Surcher Marmorstein, who figures therein.

Amongst many others, mention may just be made of three which are special favourites. 'Recha' is a one-volume tale that has been described as 'the one book in contemporary fiction that Julian Hawthorne might have written.' With singular strength it combines a vivid description and simplicity. 'Etelka's Vow,' a story of revenge, takes one in spirit to the countries the author knows so well—Austria and Hungary; but a most fascinating book, which, in the opinion of many, is the gem of the collection, is a three-volume novel, bearing the attractive title (taken from 'The Winter's Tale,' act iv. scene iv.) 'A Queen of Curds and Cream,' a story thoroughly original and entirely delightful in its vivacity, its knowledge of human nature, and its delicacy of touch.

It is manifest that all these interesting and talented works are from the pens of brilliant and highly cultivated writers, who have the advantage of being able to describe accurately the men and women as well as the manners and customs of diverse nations. The plots are uncommon, the tone pure and healthy, and the delineation of character invariably excellent.

Dorothea Gerard's present home, of which the surroundings are highly picturesque, is in Galicia. It is a cottage standing on the bank of a river, or rather at the spot where two rivers join, and is situated almost at the foot of the Carpathians, commanding a near view of the whole chain of mountains. So secluded is it that she has only one neighbour within visiting distance. Sometimes, indeed, she confesses to feeling the danger of forgetting her mother-tongue, and in order to avoid the chance of such a catastrophe she reads as much English literature as opportunity will admit.

'It is difficult to convey to you,' says Dorothea Gerard, 'or indeed to any civilised British mind, a correct idea of my present home. With the exception of my husband, I do not talk to a really educated person more than about six times a year. Of course, such things as society or lending libraries are entirely out of my reach, and really I find that I can get on very well without them. My husband has collected a tolerably extensive library, and the scenery is so fine that I can always go to Nature for effects and descriptions.'

As far as a writing-room is concerned, the author has none in particular. She has paper and pencil—she always writes in pencil—in a portfolio, and carries the parcel under her arm, and just settles down wherever it happens to be most convenient—in summer always in the open air. She is not disturbed by her surroundings, and does not even mind writing in a room with people in it, provided they do not talk too loud. Her literary work is all done in the forenoon, and seldom occupies more than two hours.

'If you were to ask me what I most enjoy reading,' remarks the young writer, Dorothea Gerard, 'I should reply, "The New Testament and Shakespeare;" but of the New Testament I am not at this moment speaking from a religious point of view, merely as of the most impressive and irresistible thing I know. Of the past English authors my favourite is Thackeray, of contemporaries the late R. L. Stevenson, of foreign authors of the present day Daudet and Tourgenieff.'

A late novel, called 'Lot 13,' first ran through the 'Monthly Packet' as a serial. The materials for the story were gathered during a visit that she paid to the West Indies a few years ago. Another work came out first in 'Blackwood's Magazine,' entitled 'The Rich Miss Riddell.' Her latest novel is 'The Wrong Man.' She owns to no particular method in forming a plot, but declares that if any such exist at all it is 'very untidy and indefinite.' She generally has the outline of a few novels 'lying by' for future use, but only in her head. Sometimes she will carry about with her the idea of a story for a year or so before starting on it; while at other times she invents a fiction and begins writing it on the spot; and she does not consider that the latter plan answers worse than the former. She loves to talk over her ideas with one person, though never with more than one, and since her marriage the 'one' has always been her husband; for, although Lieut.-Colonel Longard happens to be a cavalry officer, he certainly possesses a great many of the qualities of a novelist, having a vivid imagination, extensive literary acquirements, and, in particular, a very keen sense of the dramatic.

'My present studies of life,' says Madame Longard, 'are necessarily taken from my surroundings; Jews and Polish peasants, very far back in cultivation, are the people whom I have the best opportunities of observing. The peasants are desperately poor, but do not seem aware of it, and live contentedly in wretched huts. Their dress consists of the coarsest white linen (not always really white), over which in winter they wear sheepskin coats. Their ideas of civilisation are as yet very hazy. The Jews are all of the strictest "orthodox" class, and mercilessly prey upon the peasants in as far as it is possible to take something from someone who has nothing. Habits and ideas here are still refreshingly primitive. Here is an example which will help you to realise what I mean. Two of my servants, the kitchenmaid and housemaid, aged respectively fifteen and sixteen (at eighteen a girl of that class in this country is considered an old maid), are, not unnaturally, very fond of dancing! I can give them no greater treat than to play a waltz on the piano. The drawing-room is then left open, and the two big children whirl about in the passage outside, barefooted, and to their heart's content. When the performance is over they come in breathless and kiss my hand as a token of gratitude. Often when they have had a hard day's washing they send in a message to beg for a waltz by way of rest from their labours!'

Madame Longard has one only child, a little maiden of five years, who takes a great interest in her mother's books, inasmuch as when she sees her sitting down to write her first question always is, 'Are you going to write books, mum, or letters?' If her mother reply 'books,' the little Dorothea is somewhat depressed, knowing this to be synonymous with having to keep comparatively quiet; if, on the contrary, the reply be 'letters,' she generally gives a few cheers in order to give vent to her relief.

Both Colonel Longard and his gifted wife, Dorothea Gerard, alike enjoy art in every shape, while music is to them one of the chief pleasures of life.

WILLIAM TERRISS

THE experiences of the popular actor Mr. William Terriss have been more varied than those that have fallen to the lot of most people. He has been by turns soldier, midshipman in the Royal Navy, engineer, clerk in a bank, in the wine trade, tea-planter in India, sheep farmer at the Falkland Islands, horse-breeder at Kentucky, before he finally discovered his right vocation in life and settled to it. Since that time his career has been marked by a succession of brilliant triumphs.

The only member of his family who has ever been on the stage, William Terriss inherits many and versatile talents on both sides, together with a large share of personal attractions. From his father, the late Mr. Lewin, a barrister of good old Kentish stock, he gets strong, practical abilities and a keen aptitude for business; from his mother—a niece of Grote, the celebrated historian of Greece—his literary and artistic gifts. He was born in London, and was educated chiefly at the Bluecoat School and Windermere College. Later he matriculated at Jesus College, Oxford, with some idea of following one of the learned professions, but this was speedily abandoned. It was hardly to be expected that a lad possessed of such histrionic powers, with an exuberance of high spirits and an innate love of roving, should care for the dry details and monotony of a student life. For some few years he knocked about the world in different capacities, meeting with many hairbreadth and thrilling adventures, among which may be reckoned two shipwrecks. 'But I am not the first of my race who has met with adventures,' says Mr. Terriss. 'My grandfather, Thomas Lewin, was secretary to Warren Hastings in Calcutta, and on his way home he was chased by privateers, with a price on his head of two thousand pounds, dead or alive. Nevertheless, he bore his despatches to England in triumph. He had been a gallant of the French Court in his youth, and danced with Marie Antoinette, who gave him a ring, which is still in the possession of the family.'

On returning from one of his trips abroad William Terriss elected to go on the stage, and without any previous training he obtained employment at eighteen shillings a week at the Prince of Wales's Theatre, Birmingham, and played with Madame Céleste. A few months later he came to London, introduced himself to Mr. Bancroft, and asked for an engagement. The kindly manager, probably struck with the lad's handsome face, his grace, and charm of manner, gave him a small part at fifty shillings a week in 'Society.' His delight was so great that he at once had cards printed with the address of the theatre, and wired to his people that his fortune was made. By-and-bye the restless spirit of roving attacked him again, and he went off to the Falklands. On coming home he was shipwrecked, and spent some days in an open boat. On his return he went to Drury Lane and played Robin Hood in 'Rebecca.' Anon a trip to Kentucky, which was the last of his wanderings. Having married when he was barely twenty-one, and given hostages to fortune, he determined to be a rolling stone no longer, and his first engagement as Doricourt in 'The Belle's Stratagem,' lasting 250 consecutive nights, gave him just the encouragement he needed. In this piece he won his spurs, and there was no longer any question but that he would speedily rise to the top ranks of his profession. Everything was in his favour: a clear, rich voice, with so distinct an utterance that no word was lost, the easy yet spirited delivery, the charm of infinite variety, together with a bold, masterly grasp of subjects and the tender pathos he displayed, all marked him as a born actor, and he soon established a hold on the hearts of the public that time has but strengthened. Mr. Terriss has acted in comedy, tragedy, melodrama, Shakespearian characters, &c., and has no particularly favourite part beyond that in which he may be engaged at the moment. In earlier days he enacted Sir Kenneth in 'Cœur de Lion,' Romeo to Miss Wallis's Juliet, Molyneux in 'The Shaughraun,' with the Boucicaults, Julian in Mr. Wills's 'Peveril of the Peak,' both at the Princess's and the Adelphi. He also had a season with the lamented Adelaide Neilson at the Haymarket, playing Romeo and Orlando. Then he made a big bound upward in his impersonation of Squire Thornhill in 'Olivia' at the Court, followed by Sidney Sefton in 'Conscience Money' and Captain Absolute at the Haymarket. At St. James's he played the Comte de la Roque in 'M. Le Duc' and Jack Gambier in 'The Queen's Shilling' with the Kendals. In 1881 he joined the Lyceum company and acted Château Renard in a revival of 'The Corsican Brothers,' Sinnatus in 'The Cup,' and Cassio in 'Othello' in that ever-memorable cast consisting of Edwin Booth, Sir Henry Irving, and Ellen Terry. Among other *rôles* were Mercutio in 'Romeo and Juliet,' Don Pedro in 'Much Ado about Nothing,' and, again, Squire Thornhill. At the conclusion of that season he was presented with a silver tankard by the Lyceum company and a gold-headed whip by the employés. He has made sundry tours to America, one of which was specially remarkable as being the means of bringing over the delightful Daly players, whose first appearance in London was suggested and arranged by Mr. Terriss.

Several seasons at the Adelphi followed, where he played in the long runs of 'Harbour Lights,' 'The Bells of Hazlemere,' 'The Union Jack,' and 'The Silver Falls.' In 1890, he again joined the Lyceum company as Bucklaw in 'Ravenswood,' and, in the ensuing revivals, the King in 'Becket,' the title *rôle* of 'Faust,' afterwards Bluff King Hal in 'Henry VIII.' Since 1892, he has been exclusively at the Adelphi in 'The Fatal Card,' 'The Girl I Left

Behind Me,' 'The Swordsman's Daughter,' and 'One of the Best.'

No carpet-knight is William Terriss. He rather shuns general society, and is devoted to manly games and country pursuits. A long spin on a bicycle, the arrangement of his garden, a yachting trip in the holiday season—the rougher the weather the better it pleases him—are among his chief delights. A philosopher in the truest sense of the word, he goes through life easily with 'Carpe Diem' for his motto; he makes the best of everything, and has never once desired to enter into the troubled waters and responsibilities of managership. He has for many years made his home, which is ideal in all respects, at Bedford Park. The Cottage, as it is called, is a picturesque little building with red gabled roof, latticed windows, and nestles among chestnut, laburnum, and silver birch trees. The neatly tiled verandah at the back contains an aviary full of singing birds, and opens out to a miniature gold and silver fish pond, over which a fountain plays on ferns and flowers. Beyond is the lawn, divided on the right by a low apple-tree stretching across. In the front a glass-covered porch leads into the hall, and thence to the drawing-room, with its pretty red walls and panels let in below, its embossed ceiling and cosy recesses. In a Chinese cabinet, among a litter of art treasures, lies the Royal Humane Society's medals that Mr. Terriss gained for saving the life of a sailor boy at Deal and two lads at Barnes. The room is a museum of pictures of fellow-actors in different characters. A faded portrait of himself in his midshipman's uniform recalls a reminiscence. He was on leave at Weston-super-Mare, and a rumour got about that Prince Alfred was there. A demonstration took place, and, in spite of all protestations to the contrary, a gaily decorated carriage was sent to convey him to the station instead of the modest cab he had ordered. Among the family portraits are those of his two brothers, Colonel and Dr. Lewin, and their talented sisters, respectively the wives of Captain Banks Tomlin, late of the K.D.G., and of General Stevenson, governor of Guernsey; and Mrs. Terriss points with pride to the photographs of her three children— Ellaline, who has already made such a name for herself on the stage; Tom, who is also following in his father's footsteps; and Willie, who is seeking his fortunes in Western Australia.

MISS MARION TERRY

The very name of Terry evokes a long train of delightful remembrances. The mind travels back to many an hour of keenest enjoyment, spent both in the friendly intercourse of social life as well as in intellectual pleasures, as one after another of this gifted family has come before the public. A young actress of lesser capability would have found herself heavily handicapped by the fame of her sister predecessors, but sweet Marion Terry shines with no reflected glory. She has won her high position in the foremost ranks of histrionic art entirely by her own brilliant talents, her own personal grace and charm, her own tender and womanly nature, and, as she would be the first to confess, her own never-ceasing conscientious hard work.

An indomitable will also has done much for her in her successful career. Here is one page of Marion Terry's life, which will prove that obstacles which almost take one's breath away even to think of only stimulate her to increased efforts: 'Twelfth Night' was being played at the Lyceum. Ellen Terry was suddenly incapacitated from acting by an agonising operation on her thumb. Mr. Irving, in despair, asked Marion Terry by wire on Saturday if she could play Viola on the following Monday. The young actress was then enjoying a holiday with friends on the Lakes, and received the message on

Saturday at 5 P.M. She cabled back 'Yes.' A search was then made in her friends' library for a Shakespeare, but no copy was forthcoming. At last, when one was procured, it was not a theatrical version. She read the part right through before going to bed. On Sunday morning her hostess rowed her out on the lake, where she read and re-read for some hours. Back to luncheon, then out on the lake again for more study. Presently a twelve-mile drive in a dog-cart to catch the Scotch night express at the junction. The light was so bad in the train that she could not see to study, but she went over the lines by memory as far as she was able; and, tired in mind and body, she arrived in London in the early morning, drove home, and took two hours' rest. At 8.30 on Monday morning her brother Fred, who was playing Sebastian, called her, showed her the different 'cuts,' and how the scenes were arranged. Rehearsal was called for 11 A.M., and though she actually knew her part well by that time, she stumbled over every line. On that self-same night, however, all difficulties being overcome, she made no single mistake throughout, received rounds of applause, and retired completely dazed with fatigue and excitement.

Her present biographer (who has known and loved the talented actress from her 'short frock and long hair' days) has arrived at the pretty little flat near Victoria some ten minutes too early—perhaps on purpose, in order to make a few observations. There is a cosy little drawing-room with a sort of extension room beyond, where a grand piano stands. The walls are hung with proof engravings after Alma Tadema, Millet's 'Angelus,' and Dicksee, together with some fine landscapes in mezzotint. Tall palms, ferns, and flowers here and there; in the deep bay-window shelf are various bits of porcelain and china, and a litter of interesting photographs of her family, including a host of miniature Terrys, nephews and nieces. Near the 'silver' table, in a prominent place, is a portrait of Miss Terry's beloved and lamented mother, whose life was so bound up in her children's careers. The firelight throws dancing shadows over the white-tiled hearth and brasswork, anon glints across a marqueterie bureau and table, on which a dainty little Dresden china tea service is spread; but at this juncture Marion Terry, with that gracious punctuality and consideration for others that never fail her, comes in, looking so fresh and youthful that no one would guess she had just returned from a long day's rehearsal.

It was at Manchester that her *début* was made, as Ophelia in 'Hamlet'—a daring flight for so young a girl, but the late Mr. Tom Taylor, under whose auspices she came out, knew of what she was capable, and no better part could have been selected to prove it. A few months later she made her first appearance on the London stage in a totally opposite part at the Olympic, in 'A Game of Romps.' This was followed by another Shakespearian play, 'Much Ado about Nothing,' in which she enacted Hero. Then to the Strand to play Clara Mayfield in H. J. Byron's 'Old Sailors,' Lilian Gaythorne in 'Weak Woman,' &c. It was while playing Galatea in a revival of 'Pygmalion and Galatea' that Mr. Ruskin so happily pronounced her performance to be ' a serenity of effortless grace,' albeit so much sympathy and power lay behind it. A year later found her at the Court taking the place of her sister Ellen in the title *rôle* of 'Olivia.'

She speaks enthusiastically of a tour with Sir Henry Irving, during which she played Margaret in 'Faust,' Rosamund in 'Becket,' and, for the first time, 'Portia' —'and loved it.' 'Not that I have exactly any favourite part,' she goes on to say in the well-known melodious voice. 'They are all favourites, especially the one in which I may be playing at the moment. I am a slow study, and learn my lines with difficulty, reading them over and over again at night—often in bed—but I have a retentive memory. I always study well the whole play, and so find my own part comes easier when taken in conjunction with the others. I am painfully nervous,' she adds, with a smile, ' and become more and more so with each new play.' This, however, no one would imagine on seeing the grace and self-possession she displays, wherein lies the secret of the true artist.

Among many original impersonations, perhaps some of the most striking were her Belinda in ' Engaged,' Dorothy in ' Dan'l Druce,' Young Mrs. Winthrop, in the play of that name, &c. She likewise created the leading *rôles* of the heroines in ' Partners,' ' Sunlight and Shadow,' ' Forgiveness,' by Comyns Carr, and of Mrs. Erlynne in ' Lady Windermere's Fan,' and others ; nor will her sympathetic and artistic rendering of Blanche in Mr. R. C. Carton's ' Liberty Hall ' soon be forgotten. In the strongly marked contrasts between many of these characters Miss Marion Terry exhibits the great variety and breadth of her capabilities. She is as much at home in playing the simple, natural *ingénue*—high-minded and impassioned—as she is in portraying the dignity and polished *hauteur* of the *grande dame* of society.

A laughable incident occurred in earlier days which severely tested the young actress's power of self-control. She was playing the heroine in ' Far from the Madding Crowd ' at Liverpool with Mr. Cartwright and the late Mr. Kelly. It was just before the final drop of the curtain in the most powerful situation. Cartwright, who always makes such an excellent and realistic ' villain,' had loudly demanded the return of his ill-used and long-suffering wife. Marion Terry had made her way to the exit door, and, turning round, face to audience, with upraised hand, was on the point of delivering the last touching and dramatic words of the play when a resonant voice from 'the gods' indignantly exclaimed, ' Why don't someone tweak his nose ? ' The sudden revulsion of feeling from the sublime to the ridiculous was appalling. The two actors luckily had their backs to the footlights, so that no one could see that they were promptly convulsed with laughter. For one awful second, which, she says, 'felt like an hour,' Miss Terry was paralysed with fear lest she too should laugh; but with a mighty effort she choked down the impulse, preserved her gravity, and made her usual dignified exit, though it must be added that all the actors when out of hearing gave way to unrestrained mirth.

THE REV. PROFESSOR MOMERIE, M.A., D.SC., LL.D.

THERE can be but few of those who were privileged to be present at the Foundling Chapel on the Whit Sunday of 1884 who cannot even after this lapse of time recall their feelings of delight while listening to the scholarly utterances, the rare oratory, and the eloquent but simple language of the young and gifted preacher who then for the first time filled the pulpit. Combined with natural gifts of intellect there was an unconventionality, always tempered with good taste, and the power to deal with abstruse subjects so as to render them clear and attractive to his audience, that speedily caused his fame to spread far and wide, and brought brilliant and intellectual crowds to the Chapel Sunday after Sunday, content with standing room only if they might hear the powerful though brief discourses so concisely delivered. Statesmen and peers, literary celebrities, clergy of all denominations came to listen to him, some half fearing to hear unorthodox doctrines, but all wholly fascinated by his broad and liberal views on theological subjects.

During the six years that he held the office of morning preacher at The Foundling, the revenues of the charity benefited to the extent of about 1,000*l*. per. annum. At the end of that time he resigned his post, leaving a brilliant record that will not soon be effaced. Since 1890, he

REV. PROFESSOR MOMERIE, LL.D.

has preached but rarely in England, and has sought no
preferment, but has devoted his time to literature and study.

A rapid journey of about a second's duration in a lift
lands you at the comfortable flat in St. Ermin's Mansions
where Dr. Momerie has made his home. The long hall
through which you pass to reach his study is adorned with
the skin of a panther and many proof engravings. On
entering the study you at once recognise that he is an
intense lover of animals, for almost each picture is a well-
known print after Burton Barber, Caldwell, Paton, and
Roe's spirited paintings, such as 'The Distinguished
Foreigner,' 'The Foreigner Extinguished,' 'For the Safety
of the Public,' &c. &c. The large picture that hangs on
the north wall is of his old college at Cambridge, with
views of the exterior, the interior, and the Chapel, interspersed with portraits of the eminent men who have been
connected with St. John's, including Wilberforce, Palmerston, Ben Jonson, Wordsworth, Herschel, Selwyn, and the
present Master in the centre. On each side of the fireplace hang engravings of Stanley Berkeley's clever dog
pictures, 'A Disgrace to his Family' and 'A Credit to his
Family,' together with a humorous print of a dog wearing
a pair of *pince-nez* and a favourite photograph called
'Schmerz-vergessen,' a huge monkey curled up asleep
after a bad bout of toothache—'A world of sentiment and
of pathos in his attitude and expression,' remarks Dr.
Momerie, smiling. Close by a photograph of Trippel's
bust of Goethe at Weimar hangs a frame, to which he
draws your attention, containing the names of the sub-
scribers to the private testimonial that was presented to
him—a token of esteem which gratified him not a little—
on leaving The Foundling, by his friends and some of
the students who attended his classes. It is beautifully
illuminated by hand, and is quite a picture in its way
There are well-filled bookcases all round the walls. One
case is entirely devoted to works on philosophy and science,
another to poetry, a third to foreign literature, a fourth to

dictionaries and books of reference—all tidily arranged and for the most part well worn. The revolving chair and great knee-hole writing table stand in the bow window which commands a view of Christ Church, Westminster, with its trees in front, flanked by the high flats of St. Ermin's, which look something between a monastery and a college quad. 'But it is delightfully quiet,' says the Professor, 'and I sometimes feel like a monk as I sit here and work.' His appearance, however, has nothing 'monkish' about it. He is rather above the middle height, slight but wiry in build, and the dark eyes twinkle with a sense of humour which betokens that he is quite able to appreciate and to enjoy the ridiculous side of things, while beyond the customary white tie there is nothing in his dress to indicate the profession to which he belongs.

Dr. Momerie's morning hours are spent in the study of foreign and English literature, and he has, as may be supposed, a large and varied correspondence on all subjects from the works of Herbert Spencer down to the more mundane matters of every-day life. His literary work is done only in the afternoon. 'All my best work,' he remarks, 'is done from three to six, unlike my friend Adamson, a learned Professor in Edinburgh, who can only write when the gas is lighted. I never think of what I am going to say until, pen in hand, I sit down; the pen seems to bring inspiration. I am fond of languages, and, being a great traveller, I always contrive to pick up a little of the tongue of a strange country before I visit it.'

This bachelor establishment is presided over by a soldier servant who is proud of having drawn a Government pension for twenty-three years. The worthy veteran has done distinguished service for his country, and among other historical events in which he has taken an active part are the Indian Mutiny of 1857, under Havelock and Colin Campbell, and the burning of the Emperor's Palace at Pekin. He wears three medals and good conduct clasps, and, like many others who have come under the fascination of Dr. Momerie's manner, he is a devoted adherent. He informs you quaintly that 'The Professor and I seem to have been made for each other.'

His Celtic blood alone would keep Dr. Momerie from ever running in a conventional groove, for he is half French and half Welsh, and from his mother, who was a woman of great culture and refinement, a brilliant letter-writer and a deep thinker, he inherits his sensitive, highly strung temperament, his originality of thought, his vivacious and sympathetic charm of manner that acts now as a loadstone in society, where he is so deservedly a favourite, as it did in former years amongst the rough miners when he was a curate in the North.

Born in the same year that produced several other well-known men who have made their mark on the thought of the age, Alfred Momerie may fairly be said to belong to the glorious intellectual vintage of 1848. That he showed no special ability at school is borne out by the recent remark made to him by an old schoolfellow with more candour than politeness, 'I never thought you would come to anything, you were so slow!' His father was a Nonconformist minister whose ardent desire was that his only son should follow in his steps. The lad was accordingly reared in somewhat strict Puritanical discipline until he entered New College, Finchley Road, to prepare for the ministry; but it was hardly likely that one who studied German and Hebrew under the broad and liberal teaching of Professor Menner should return to the narrower views impressed on him in boyhood. The history of his gradual development of thought shall be given in his own words.

'I was still a boy,' says Dr. Momerie, thoughtfully, 'when I chanced to be present at a discussion between two learned men about Ferrier's lectures on Greek philosophy. It turned my mind in that direction, and I slowly but steadily passed out of sectarianism—I may say also out of ecclesiasticism—and step by step through slow stages of development until I altogether abandoned the orthodox notion of one infallible Church in favour of the scientific idea of universal religion. One prejudice after another almost unconsciously left me, and each change came distinctly in the form of evolution.'

After four years spent at the Edinburgh University, where he won two scholarships and took a first-class in philosophy, the young student passed on to St. John's College, Cambridge. He had been there but one year when he received the degree of Doctor of Science from his old college in Edinburgh. Three years of steady work at his favourite study resulted in his coming out Senior in the Moral Science Tripos. The next step was his ordination as curate of Leigh by the Bishop of Manchester, the late Dr. Fraser. Here for a year he preached almost exclusively to the working classes in the mining districts, but the shrewd sons of the soil appreciated the unusual discourses to which he treated them. They soon flocked to the church in large numbers, and would often discuss with him afterwards the stiff metaphysical questions that he made so clear. Drawn by his sympathy and extraordinary magnetism, these intelligent north-countrymen followed his sermons with the closest attention and the keenest interest.

At the end of his curate's year Dr. Momerie was ordained priest, and, as ordinary parish work was by no means in his line, he devoted himself for a while to the more congenial work of University Extension Lecturer on English Literature, in which capacity he travelled for six months in the northern counties. During this period he was elected Fellow of St. John's, and when but thirty years old he was appointed to the Chair of Logic and Metaphysics at King's College, London, and shortly after received the honorary degree of LL.D.

His classes, both for men and women, were largely attended, and the regret amongst the students was universal when, after an abortive attempt to censure him for the volume containing his sermons upon 'Inspiration,' his

Chair was removed to the department of Literature and the Divinity students were not allowed to study Logic and Metaphysics with him any more.

From 1881, to 1884, Dr. Momerie was afternoon lecturer at St. Peter's, Cranley Gardens, when he was appointed morning preacher at 'The Foundling.'

'My sole reasons for resigning the post,' he says, 'were want of leisure and the feeling that no man can preach continually and preach well. There were no theological reasons involved. My sermons were not altogether extempore; indeed, I consider that most extempore speaking is a synonym for slovenly thought, unless a man has been at it all his life and has his subject matter at his fingers' ends. I never preach without long preparation, but I have a good verbal memory, and when what I have to say is once written I remember it without difficulty; then the less one is tied down to paper the better; besides, when one is well prepared one is more free to catch inspiration from an opponent.'

And opposition frequently came to Dr. Momerie in the form of letters. Some of these epistles were anonymous and abusive, while others, signed by their writers, were courteous and suggestive.

He has added a long list of books to the theological literature of the world. The most conscientious preparation is manifest in each of these profoundly intellectual and instructive volumes. Deep and abstruse as are many of the subjects they treat, the reader becomes absorbed with interest as he—very often she—follows closely the working out of each problem, the whole being made clear by the author's freedom from subtlety and ambiguity.

That these works enjoy a world-wide popularity is evident, as 'The Origin of Evil' is now in its seventh edition, 'The Defects of Modern Christianity' in its fourth. These were followed at yearly intervals by 'Agnosticism,' 'Preaching and Hearing,' and 'Inspiration,' all of which have passed through many editions. Other works, also published by Blackwood & Son, are 'Personality,' 'Belief in God,' and 'The Basis of Religion,' while one of Dr. Momerie's later works, 'Church and Creed,' had an unprecedented success, for in little more than a month from the date of publication the first edition of 1,500 copies was exhausted.

It is only natural that these books, written by such a faithful and fearless exponent of the views of the Broad Church party, should have raised a storm of controversy, not only amongst the reading and thinking public, but also among clergymen of all denominations, as, with irresistible logic, clear reasoning, and unflinching vigour, he boldly attacks the old cherished prejudices, hitting hard, it may be, but always hitting fairly, while he insists on 'Righteousness as the sole requisite for membership in the Church of God.'

In the summer of 1891, Dr. Momerie delivered an oration at Princes' Hall, Piccadilly, on 'The Corruption of the Church,' before a large and representative audience. 'Everything that I have thought and done,' he declares emphatically, 'is implied in that lecture; my belief in the evolution, the development, and the final triumph of good; my detestation of cant, hypocrisy, and bigotry. What a man *does*—the life that he leads—is, in my opinion, of far more importance than what he believes.'

A second oration on 'Church and Science,' was delivered the following year. Here there was nothing to disturb the most orthodox of Churchmen. With a rare power of condensation, which is one of his great gifts, Dr. Momerie kept a large audience enthralled for two hours whilst he eloquently and with a fine vein of satire explained the history of the attitude of ecclesiastics towards science during the past 2,000 years, proving that a subject dry in itself can be made bright and interesting by brilliant treatment.

In April 1893, Dr. Momerie received an invitation to

go to America to attend the Parliament of Religions at Chicago, the most representative gathering of the kind that has ever been brought together by Churchmen of any country. He sailed for the United States the following August, and his reception was very gratifying. He found that, through his books, which circulate largely in the States, he was already well known, and his name was no sooner published in connection with the great Religious Congress at Chicago than more invitations to preach and to lecture reached him than it was possible to accept. He preached before the Universities of Harvard and Cornell, and at several of the principal Episcopal churches of New York, Boston, New Orleans, and Philadelphia, &c., &c. He also lectured twice before one of the principal theological colleges in New York; the second lecture was given by invitation of the students, and the subject was, 'The Art of Preaching,' by their special request. At the Boston Literary Society he gave, also by request, 'The Past and Future of the Church of England.' At the present moment he is home from a prolonged tour in Australia and a second visit to America, in both of which places he has been incessantly occupied in preaching and in lecturing.

It is just possible that Dr. Momerie may be induced in the future to spend a great portion of his time in America. It must be alike inspiriting and inspiring to find himself surrounded by those who are not afraid of listening to a man even when his views differ somewhat from their own. It is only by the sharp but friendly interchange of opinions that progress is possible, and there are many at the present moment even in this slowly moving England who have reason to bless the day that Alfred Momerie took holy orders in the Anglican Church.

The appreciation shown by America and Australia of his brilliant intellect and his many lovable qualities affords immense satisfaction to his legion of friends on this side of the Atlantic. In some respects, perhaps, the man is before his time, but it is safe to predict that he is one of those enviable mortals of whom it may be truly said that his work will live after him.

GENEVIEVE WARD

(*MADAME LA COMTESSE DE GUERBEL*)

GRANDE DAME to her fingers' tips, Nature has kindly supplied Miss Genevieve Ward with form and countenance to exactly suit the character. Tall and graceful, an oval face surmounted with slightly silvered hair, clear-cut features, large, grey-blue eyes with level brows, and a delicately sweet mouth displaying lovely white teeth complete the outward portrait. It would need far more words rightly to describe the courteous dignity, yet winning sympathy and charm of manner, that characterise the distinguished and aristocratic-looking actress. Under all these pleasant qualities lies a strong element of what may be called a practical nature. A first-rate woman of business, and greatly occupied in many matters apart from her stage life, she regulates everything in an orderly and methodical manner, and thus gets through an enormous amount of work easily. 'The busiest people have always the most leisure,' she observes with a smile. 'I always answer letters immediately, with a view alike to getting them off my own mind and saving my correspondents' time, waiting—perhaps temper, too!'

Genevieve Ward was born in New York and baptized in Cuba. Her mother, who had a great love of travelling, was a woman of highly cultivated artistic tastes and of great strength and refinement of character. She had advanced ideas on education, and when her little daughter was but four years of age she began her studies with her brothers' French tutor, and could already speak four languages—English, French, Spanish, and Italian. 'And she made me keep them up, too,' says Miss Ward. 'She used to talk to us alternately in each. We travelled always from one country to another, and saw everything that was worth seeing—an education in itself. My mother was a fine amateur, and most of the paintings you see around were done by her.' Some few besides are the work of Miss Ward herself, together with the cleverly executed busts in the corners of the room. Finally the family settled in Paris, where she married a Russian nobleman who is since dead.

Possessing a fine dramatic voice, Miss Ward had at first intended to adopt the lyric stage as a profession. She made her *début* in Italy and Paris, and for a time she sang constantly in England, at the Philharmonic concerts, at H.M. Opera, and Covent Garden, as Mdme. Guerrabella, but from overwork and fatigue she lost her singing voice, and was compelled to give up that branch of her art. Not her speaking voice, happily. This is remarkably clear and attractive, as all the world knows who has seen her in tragedy and observed the power and sweetness of her masterly elocution.

Coming of old Puritan stock, Miss Ward is of opinion that her forbears of two hundred years ago ' would turn in their graves could they but know their descendant had gone on the stage.' Perhaps they do ' know ' —who can tell ?—and have watched with joy the beautiful and spotless career of the accomplished actress ! It has certainly been a peculiar career. After a few months of study at New York she came to England, and made her first appearance at Manchester as Lady Macbeth. Since that promising *début* she has settled the question for good and all, and played the leading parts in ' Medea,' ' Lucrezia Borgia,' Catherine in ' Henry VIII.,' ' Adrienne Lecouvreur,' &c.

But there is one special part in which she has made the biggest success of all, and one with which her name will ever be brilliantly associated, and that is Stephanie de Mohrivart in 'Forget-Me-Not'—a play that she brought out first in 1879 at the Lyceum, when Mr. Irving was away, and in which she has acted, first and last, over two thousand times, in all parts of the world at home and abroad: amongst others, in India, in Australia, in South Africa, and New Zealand. A great event happened to her in New Zealand. She had a proposal from a Maori chief, and it happened in this wise. Miss Ward took a brief holiday, and went up to explore the celebrated silicate terraces—now, alas! no more. 'It was all very funny,' she relates. 'I was lying back in a big canoe on the hot lake Rotomahana, with arms extended on each side and hands alternately feeling the hot and cold water. Suddenly he burst out, "You marry me?" I replied immediately, "Yes, but you've got wives already." "Me all go wives away," he exclaimed, with a tragic gesture. Professor Tucker, who was in the canoe, took the matter up with an eye to business. "But have you any money?" he asked gravely. "Money!" shouted the Maori; "any amount." When he got to "any amount" he began to squabble with the guides, and we slipped off into another boat, and I escaped my fate.'

A propos of 'Forget-Me-Not,' it was in that play Johnstone Forbes-Robertson, who then looked little more than a boy, 'won his spurs,' and Miss Ward speaks with enthusiasm of his fine acting. She lately prepared a humorous little present for him in remembrance of his Sir Horace Welby, over which the young actor laughed heartily. Stephanie in one most tragic scene had to 'grab at his coat,' and as this was repeated for many nights the garment suffered considerably. One evening he remarked to her, 'A fellow at the club last night asked me what on earth was the matter with my coat. I told him Miss Ward was gradually tearing it to pieces.' 'Never mind,' said the actress, 'I'll give you a new one.' The other day, when the two players were recalling and laughing over the incident, he gravely reminded her: 'But you never gave me that new coat!' 'I'm having it made expressly for you,' she replied: and sure enough it was sent—a very tiny model of a perfect little coat in a very large box, with a paper affixed in her writing. 'The coat is too small for the man. The man has outgrown the coat!'

'I have wonderful health,' says Miss Ward, brightly; 'wonderful spirits, and I am always up to tricks!' But at this startling and unexpected announcement of the *grande dame*, the temptation to laugh is irresistible, and you suddenly collapse into merriment, in which the dignified-looking lady heartily joins. 'I lead a simple, natural life,' she observes when gravity is restored. 'I have ever been a total abstainer. Nature tells me it is better so, and if we all follow Nature we get on better. "Mens sana in corpore sano" is my motto, and I am always trying to impress it on the girls whom I coach. People often ask me why I play such "wicked parts." I tell them, "Because if I did not I should go to heaven at once, so I take out all my wickedness on the stage."'

Stronger than ever was Genevieve Ward in her late difficult part of Morgan Le Fay in 'King Arthur,' and she rises to the occasion in the last act in a most masterly manner. Lucky indeed that the character was in such able and artistic hands. Shortly before the rehearsals of this gorgeous play began she completed a tour with Mr. Irving, together with Marion Terry, who was taking Miss Ellen Terry's parts in divers pieces. Miss Ward puts in a pretty little word about this tour, and says, 'Marion is so sweet and so comfortable to get on with!'

To give some idea of the hard work that Miss Genevieve Ward can get through and the extent of her répertoire, on her last tour through South Africa she gave twenty-five plays—of which six were Shakespearian —in thirty-three weeks. During a pleasant time at Melbourne she made good use of one of her 'tricks.' She asked Lady Loch what good she could do for those who had been so good to her. The Governor's popular wife suggested a theatrical performance for the benefit of a terribly needed new lying-in ward at the Women's Hospital. Miss Ward bestirred herself, trotted about energetically, collected money on all sides, arranged to play 'Antigone,' 'coaxed everybody to give everything,' and was so heartily and generously supported by the Press with free advertisements, by ninety of the chorus, who gave their services, by managers, who lent scenery, by all who could contribute anything, that she cleared the magnificent sum of 2,680*l.*, the whole of the expenses being 10*l.* for workmen's services. Armed with the bankbook, she applied to the Government for their usual grant of the like amount earned. At first it was refused, but Miss Ward was not long to be resisted. She carried the day, and was thus the happy means of obtaining 5,360*l.*, the sum needed to build the wing, which was named after her.

Just before leaving Melbourne she received a most gratifying token of its appreciation. She shows you with pride a large morocco album, beautifully embossed and illuminated, containing the names of nearly 'one thousand of the women of Australia,' who, not being allowed to contribute 'more than five shillings, but anything under,' subscribed to present it to her, together with a handsome diamond star; and Genevieve Ward reads aloud melodiously the quotation on the final page of the album:—

'Farewell, my dearest sister, fare thee well. The elements be kind to thee and make thy spirits all of comfort! Fare thee well.'

G. A. STOREY, A.R.A.

PROBABLY no well-known artist in London has a simpler studio than Mr. G. A. Storey, A.R.A., or one less dependent on outward effects. Large, lofty, bright and airy, the great double rooms are divided with a white arch, while the floors are laid down with cool-looking matting and with no vestige of the orthodox Oriental rugs; but, with all its simplicity, there is an indescribable feeling of cheeriness and humour around that indicate the chief characteristics of the painter who made his name so early in life, and who, having had experience of the world in most of its aspects, yet pronounces it to be 'good to live.' There prevails, too, an air of domesticity, which is accentuated by the presence of the artist's gentle young wife and their only child, Gladys, a charming little maiden with heaven-blue eyes and long fair hair, who, hugging a doll nearly as big as herself, sits, good as gold, without disturbing the conversation. Casts and models are piled up here and there; the principal pictures on the walls are after the old masters, Vandyck, Titian, Sir Joshua Reynolds, Watteau and the Dutch painters; for Mr. Storey carefully avoids having any of his own work *en évidence* while painting, preferring to be surrounded by those he can enjoy and from which he can learn. But in some large closed portfolios standing against the walls he has hundreds of studies of landscapes, made in all sorts of places—including Spain—that he calls his 'Book of Nature.'

He was born in London, and originates in himself the gift which manifested itself at a very youthful age. His early scribblings being discovered by a friend of the family led to his being taken, when only nine years old, to the studio of Behnes, the sculptor, where he got his first insight into art, and was allowed to amuse himself by drawing and modelling. He remembers well, while engaged on a colossal foot of a Hercules, Charles Dickens came in one day and patted him on the head and said a kindly word of encouragement to him. That he had formed no idea of a future profession is evident from his answer on one occasion to a man who asked him what he intended to be. The little modeller paused and said gravely, 'An old bachelor for choice,' which reply caused much merriment to the questioner. At the age of fourteen he was sent to Paris to finish his education, where he came in for some of the horrors of the Revolution, and worked hard at the language, also at mathematics and other branches of science, studying painting and copying pictures at the Louvre under M. Dulong, to whom he declares he owes a debt of gratitude for teaching him to take pains with his work. Two years later he returned to London and entered an architect's office, but his real vocation was yet to be discovered. His drawings were shown to an influential friend, who at once pronounced the lad to be 'a painter, not an architect,' and introduced him to the late Mr. Charles Robert Leslie, R.A., one of the most refined and truly humorous of English painters. 'I felt it to be a great event in my life,' says Mr. Storey, cheerily, 'to be brought in contact with so distinguished an artist. The acquaintance ripened into an intimate friendship with the whole family.' His next step was to attend Mr. J. N. Leigh's art school in Newman Street, where he devoted himself to studying the technicalities of his profession, and was a fellow-pupil with Mr. Calderon and Mr. Stacy Marks. At the age of eighteen G. A. Storey exhibited his first picture at the Academy, and the following year he was admitted a student. About that time what was known as the St. John's Wood School came to be much talked of, and the young painter soon won his way into public favour by the grace and beauty of his compositions, which were fresh, pure, and cheerful. He impressed his own happy, sunny personality on them, and struck a note of humour and of character on every pose and expression of his figures that enabled his pictures to tell their own tale and to suggest their own title. From that time onwards he has exhibited regularly at the Academy; but, though his work was always well noticed, it was not until 1867 that he became famous.

An early visit to Spain, where Mr. Storey painted several portraits, was made the opportunity to study in the Madrid Gallery the works of Veronese, of Velasquez, of Titian, &c., where he got to understand and to delight in the translating of them into water-colour sketches; it was while thus engaged that he met John Philip, the celebrated Scottish artist.

The first picture that brought Mr. Storey prominently before the public was 'After You,' which was suggested while on a visit to Hever, a visit that he pronounces to have been 'a turning-point.' Another, called 'Breakfast at the Old Hall at Hever,' was painted at the same time and place; this work is now at the National Gallery at Hamburg. The unanimously favourable reception accorded to both these works established the young painter's reputation. Before this, however, he had turned his attention to historical subjects, and painted two large canvases, which attracted much attention, respectively entitled 'The Meeting of William Seymour and Arabella Stuart at the Court of James I.' and 'The Royal Challenge;' but Mr. Storey soon wearied of this branch of art, and struck out his particular line, which may be called a humorous vein, turning to the living, human subjects, the picturesque children and graceful maidens, the out-door life, the backgrounds and environments, that he is so peculiarly happy in depicting. In the halcyon days that followed, among a large number of works, perhaps some of the most popular were 'The Shy Pupil,' 'The Old Soldier,' 'Going to School' (portraits of Sir William Agnew's boys), 'Caught,' and 'Grandmama's Christmas Visitors,' which was engraved for the first Christmas number of the 'Graphic.' His celebrated picture 'Scandal' sold for a large sum, and won his Associateship. 'Mistress Dorothy' brought him a great many commissions for portraits, and recalls an anecdote. Mr. Storey's sister had gone to her milliner's and there beheld the hat that became so well-renowned as the 'Dorothy hat.' She was told by the modiste that she always went to the Royal Academy to study Storey's pictures for the most picturesque fashions! A painting called 'Little Swansdown' brought the artist many orders for portraits. 'The Blue Girls of Canterbury' and 'Lady Beaumont' were also celebrated pictures, while his 'Mrs. Finch' hangs in company with works of Vandyck, Sir Peter Lely, Kneller, &c., at Burley on the Hill, Rutland.

But Mr. Storey's portraits are not portraits only. They are pleasant pictures with which to live. What he does is to depict flesh and blood and human character with beautiful surroundings. He makes each part of his work help the rest in form and colour, in light and shade, even in atmosphere. He is often dubbed 'the modern de Hooghe,' from his rich colouring, his power of painting veiled sunlight and sunny interiors, which, however, he learned in Spain, and of causing the smallest objects in the background to invest themselves with interest. There is a photograph in one of the rooms of an early work, 'Godiva,' painted in 1865, and sold for 60l., but which in later days found a ready purchaser in a connoisseur at Munich for 300l. 'My own taste,' he says, 'leads me to figure painting. "Godiva" was far more to me than my historical "Arabella Stuart." I am almost an Old Master now,' he adds quaintly, 'having exhibited at the R.A. almost every year since 1852, and what makes me say I am almost an Old Master is that lately there was an exhibition of Early British Masters at Messrs Shepherd's in King Street, and two of my very early works were there, "The Burial of Juliet" and "Inspiration," painted in the fifties. When I called on Mr. Shepherd the other day to ask if he still had them, as a friend wished to see them, his reply was, "Both sold, Sir." "Oh!" I said, "I have more if you want them!" 'They must be early works," he remarked. "So what an age I must be!"' The artist modestly omits to add that the Press was unanimously complimentary about them; one distinguished critic remarking, 'these pictures of the early Pre-Raphaelite period by Mr. G. A. Storey come as revelations. They are delightful in colour, rich and voluptuous and admirable in sentiment; works remarkable for beauty, poetic grace of design, and general deftness of execution.' And mention must not be forgotten of a popular picture, 'The Violin Player,' which was bought by the Goldsmiths' Company and presented to the Corporation of the Art Society, Guildhall, and another, comically entitled 'The Hungry Messenger,' sold to the Corporation of Sunderland a few years ago. Mr. Storey's latest works in the Royal Academy of the present year are 'Reflection,' 'Coming Events,' and 'The Rivals.'

His fondness for his craft has led the painter to write a variety of books on Art, notably 'An Introduction to the Study of Drawing,' 'Living Anatomy,' 'The Mysteries of Colour, and How to Solve Them,' and 'Michael Angelo, a Sketch of his Life,' illustrated with tracings of that Master's works. He has also given many lectures on Art and written much poetry. One of his works, called 'A New Method of Perspective without Vanishing Points,' should prove of great use to students. 'Since a student has to learn perspective,' remarks Mr. Storey, 'he may as well do so intelligently, and without being bewildered by a confusion of vanishing lines, pins, strings, and all the cumbersome arrangements so delighted in by our Art Masters. The science is mathematical and quite simple; all operations can be done on the canvas itself without going outside the picture.'

He has of late been gathering materials for a book of 'Recollections,' which, written in his bright, amusing style, and full of anecdote, are delightful reading. For this purpose he is looking up old letters, old friends, old sketches. 'And, talking of old sketches,' observes Mr. Storey, as he turns up one of his MS. books, in which are the dates and particulars of all his pictures, 'I have something for you. Do you know how many years it is since I painted your portrait? Here it is, not finished yet—the hands in pencil only; still, very like you. Please accept it for old friendship's sake ! My " Recollections " include the names of many who have long since passed away, but they live over again with me as I write about them ! '

DORA RUSSELL.

A GREAT GALE is blowing. Torrents of rain flood the streets. The wind comes with sudden and mighty gusts, tearing down huge boughs of trees and howling round the corners of the broad, unsheltered roads of Hampstead. No vehicle can be found, and at length, with umbrella turned inside out and in weather-beaten, dishevelled condition, you thankfully arrive at what is verily a haven of peace and rest—the hospitable house of the popular author, Miss Dora Russell. She comes forward with kindly solicitude for your miseries, and in a few minutes, having recovered breath and become disencumbered from dripping wraps, you are snugly ensconced in her favourite chair by a bright fire, and the fury of the raging elements is temporarily forgotten.

'It is truly a most terrible storm,' says Miss Russell, in a soft, musical voice, with a touch of the North Country in its tones, ' but only think what it must be for the ships at sea. The lifeboats will be out, and we shall hear of many distressing wrecks to-morrow. It has disquieted me all day.' And in these words she has indicated the keynote of her character, which those who know her will not fail to recognise. She is blessed with an unselfish, sympathetic nature. She has in addition a fund of quiet humour, and a cheerful, happy temperament that invariably sees the best side of persons and of things.

And after all it is undoubtedly the best sort of disposition with which to go through this troublesome world. Here there is no fretting nor struggling nor pushing to be first and foremost. She has won her own position of independence, and has scored entirely off her own bat ; and if in earlier years she has experienced not a few sharp buffetings from fate, she has bravely battled against them, and remarks cheerily, 'No one is exempt. Everything was for the best, and I have met with much and unexpected kindness on all sides.'

The room is bright and lofty. Tall bunches of double chrysanthemums, of every shade and hue, are artistically grouped here and there. A few handsome bits of ancient Crown Derby from the old home stand on the marqueterie cabinet and high mantelshelf, together with two or three old blue china jars. A Japanese table is loaded with magazines and newspapers of all sorts, for Miss Russell is an ardent politician, and reads all the speeches with much interest. The great French window opens on to a flight of stone stairs that leads down to a large old-fashioned garden, at the far end of which are discerned sundry apple and pear trees. The house was chosen chiefly for the sake of this garden, in which Miss Russell works and takes a keen delight.

Born of a good family and connections in the county of Northumberland, Dora Russell was reared in comfortable and happy circumstances. There were large grounds in which to roam, ponies to ride, and every amusement and enjoyment that indulgent parents could provide. She was carefully educated by good governesses, and for a year or so was sent to school. Like many other so-called naughty little girls, she entirely declined to avail herself of these advantages. Agreeably with the orthodox custom of that day, all originality of thought and of character must be suppressed, and that which every other girl was taught she too must acquire. Accordingly, tasks such as music, drawing, and languages, to all of which she had no particular leaning, were pressed upon her, but composition and over-much reading were denied. Now it just happened that these were the studies to which her mind had a natural bent. Reading was a passion ; she devoured eagerly every book within reach, no matter whether it were poetry, fiction, history, or some musty old tome of ancient geography. It was all the same; but when sent to the piano, and supposed to be taking out the regulation hour in steady practising, someone was always sure to catch her with a book concealed in her lap, when the usual punishment followed.

It is possible that the young girl derived far more benefit from this desultory reading than if she had continued the usual routine of learning. After a time, seeing that the studies that she principally disliked would probably be productive of no very brilliant results, they were gradually discarded, and her reading was no longer restricted, but only judiciously guided by carefully selected books.

Although she inherited no literary tastes from either parents, Dora Russell from childhood amused herself by composing short tales that were never written. Her elder sister tells the story that the little Dora used to run up and down a long gravel path in the garden at the old home repeating aloud the most romantic histories and pieces of poetry, always in good metre and rhyme, woven out of her childish imagination, and she would keep a room full of children entertained by the adventures of her heroes and heroines. She met with a very real and serious adventure on her own account when she was but thirteen, and which for a few weeks banished all fictitious woes and joys from her head. Whilst walking with her sister in a shady lane, an infuriated bull, which had escaped from its attendants, came tearing along behind them, and lifting the young Dora, who was but a feather-weight, on his horns, tossed her high into the air. The child fell head foremost at his feet. The savage beast lowered his head to attack her again, when her sister bravely flung herself between them, brandishing her parasol in his face, which so startled the bull that he stepped back a few paces. The men arrived just in time to save any further catastrophe, and struck him hard with a heavy bludgeon. The animal leapt over the side fence into a field, where he was presently shot. 'Dora behaved like one of her own heroines,' says the elder sister, with emotion. 'She neither cried nor screamed, but showed much presence of mind. I shudder even now at the recollection.'

Mercifully no very serious or lasting consequences ensued, but the bull figured largely in subsequent stories.

'I can understand,' says Dora Russell, thoughtfully, 'what it is said that the drowning feel. In a moment every event of my short life flashed before me.'

It was not until many years later, during a time of great family distress and trouble, that she took seriously to what has since become the work of her life. Returning one day to a sadly overshadowed home, she saw an advertisement in the well-known 'Newcastle Chronicle' offering prizes for fiction and poetry. A small parcel of manuscript was packed up and sent in with much trepidation, and with a firm conviction that no more would be heard of it. But the young amateur need not have been so over-diffident of her own powers, though this modesty has accompanied her through all her literary career. In the competition, which was a very large one, she was fortunate enough to receive two prizes, one for a story, the other for a short poem. This was the first money that she had ever earned, and she can recall now the great pleasure and encouragement it gave her.

And still better was the news that this was not to be the end of it. Shortly after the editor of the 'Newcastle Weekly Chronicle' applied to her for a brief story for that journal, and in accordance she wrote 'The Miner's Oath,' which was so favourably received that it is read still in the mining villages round Newcastle-on-Tyne, and is become a household word among their families. It was afterwards published in book form and illustrated by Messrs. George Routledge & Sons.

This little book was the happy means of introducing

Dora Russell to the late Mr. George Routledge, of whom she speaks with deepest gratitude and regard. 'I can never forget,' she observes, 'the kindness and encouragement he gave me. He took me himself to the publisher of my first novel, "The Vicar's Governess," and used his influence in smoothing all difficulties from my path. Ten years later, shortly before his lamented death, he wrote and asked me to go and see him at his house in Russell Square. His letter—I preserve it still—begins with the kindly expression, "As I stood godfather to your earlier books," &c. I feel that Mr. Routledge's help in the beginning of my literary career was of very material benefit.'

This first novel proved very successful, and quite lately the fourth cheap edition has been issued. Her subsequent works have all been similarly successful.

About a year later, through the kindly editor of the 'Newcastle Weekly Chronicle,' Miss Russell obtained an introduction to Messrs. Tillotson & Son, of Bolton, Lancashire, whose well-known syndicate for supplying literature to newspapers has a world-wide reputation. The first novel that she wrote for the firm was 'Footprints in the Snow.' The book was not only very popular in England, but has been translated into many languages, and was a special favourite with Miss Russell's much-regretted and valued friend, the late Mr. Tillotson. From the date of this work until the present time Dora Russell's connection with the firm has been close and constant, and again she always speaks in the highest terms of their probity and kindness.

The scenes of her birthplace, with its rock-bound North-Eastern coast and the stormy wave-wash of its Northern Sea, have given a certain local colouring to many of the author's works. Indeed, during one terrible storm she was an eye-witness of the total wreck of an ill-fated vessel as it struggled to enter the Tyne, and from the shore she saw the heavy seas overlap and engulf the ship while every soul on board perished. This terrible incident she depicted with strong sensational interest in her story, ' Beneath the Wave.'

'Annabel's Rival' has a very good bit of character-drawing in the clever, worldly governess. ' Lady Sefton's Pride ' was humorously described by a critic as a good cure for toothache, as the reader would inevitably forget all about it in his interest in the story.

'The Broken Seal' and 'A Bitter Birthright ' are particularly noticeable for the ingenuity of their construction and the skill with which their plots are concealed. Other works of the author are entitled ' Quite True,' 'Crœsus' Widow,' 'Hidden in My Heart,' ' Jezebel's Friends,' and ' The Last Signal.' There is many a good sensational situation and much originality of character-sketching in these interesting works of fiction. The dialogue is bright, and she has the gift of writing in an easy and natural strain. Later works are ' An Evil Reputation,' 'A Hidden Chain,' 'A Country Sweetheart,' ' A Great Temptation,' ' A Man's Privilege,' &c., &c.

Dora Russell's method of composing is somewhat peculiar. She always fixes on the titles of her novels first, and the following morning, in the early dawn, a plot to suit her chosen title invariably rises before her mind, and goes on growing and growing until her story is written, without any notes whatsoever being required. She works about six hours a day with great facility and ease, scarcely ever changing a word or line in her MS.

Her study is a large, rather bare-looking room at the top of the house. The sole furniture consists of a huge writing-table and chair and a square of carpet, while reams of proofs and MSS. are methodically arranged against the walls. The only other chair—an easy one—is occupied by a little black-and-tan terrier, which never leaves her mistress day or night. Dora Russell has in truth a devoted love for all dumb creatures, and among her numerous pets she has a little colony of birds of much variety, who come for breakfast daily. Her pursuits are all thoroughly feminine and healthy.

She is a notable housekeeper, and has a very pretty taste in arranging flowers and decorating a supper table (whereof you presently have an experience), which is spread after the hospitable custom of the North-country. 'But my work,' says the author, 'is my greatest enjoyment. I am never so happy as when I am writing. I live in it.'

An hour later you take leave of the amiable and intellectual Dora Russell. She opens the hall door, and lo! a transformation scene has taken place. The gale is over. The wind has died out. The moon and stars are shining brightly, and all is as serene and peaceful without as it has been within.

GEORGE GROSSMITH

IF there be one thing more than another for which people as they go through this 'vale of tears' have to thank a comic actor, it is his power to make them forget their temporary worries and troubles in a good hearty laugh; and when this is accompanied not only with the true artistic finish and refinement, but also with touches of infinite pathos such as Mr. George Grossmith knows so well how to impart, it is all the more attractive. Who will ever forget him as the Merryman in that exquisite duet, 'I have a song to sing, oh,' in Gilbert and Sullivan's delightful opera, 'The Yeoman of the Guard,' which almost brought tears to the eyes, to be dispelled by laughter over his subsequent amusing speeches in that piece?

Now it is a fact that people like to know something of the inner life and surroundings of their favourites; and, as Mr. Grossmith is one of these favourites, their curiosity shall be gratified to some small extent.

There is a little domestic group at luncheon in a certain old house in an old-fashioned square situated somewhere about the north-west district of London. It overlooks a big garden in front, thus securing plenty of fresh air and no immediately opposite neighbours, and the birds will soon begin to twitter and to build their nests when the fine old trees awake from the long night of winter and unfold their fresh leaves. At the head of the table sits the popular entertainer, and at the side the sweet lady who, 'besides being his wife, is also his truest friend and his best adviser.' The prematurely silvered curls impart a picturesque beauty to the fair, youthful face, with its broad, smooth brow and large violet eyes. At the foot of the table is George Grossmith, junior. Then there are two young daughters present; the elder, who, though only just 'standing with reluctant feet where the brook and river meet,' inherits the family gifts, and is always to be trusted to read any new play or sketch or song and 'see if it will do.' A younger son, studying engineering, completes the happy family picture. Everything is very snug and comfortable, though quiet and unpretending, in this house of love and harmony. To those who like to learn such details, it will be interesting to know that George Grossmith and his charming wife may almost be said to have arranged this step in life when quite little children, when at juvenile parties they used to meet and nearly always danced together, 'because their steps suited'; and that the boy-and-girl friendship led on to a boy-and-girl marriage, which, 'Thank God, neither has ever had reason to regret for a single second.'

After luncheon you adjourn with your hosts to the actor's study behind, where you urge him to calm his nerves with a soothing cigarette; for, truth to tell, he 'positively hates talking about himself,' and only yields to the importunity of such an old friend as yourself. *A propos* of this old friendship, it is so sympathetic and harmonious that it justifies you in making a remark that in other circumstances would be an impertinence. You had lately had occasion firmly but, it is to be hoped, politely, to contradict a statement that 'actors earned their money so easily when at the top of the tree, and this one in particular drew a weekly salary that ran into three figures.' 'Ah!' replies Mr. Grossmith, with that grave air of fun that sits so quaintly on him; 'I'm very glad you told me. Now that accounts for the extraordinarily over-rated assessment of the income-tax collectors. I remember when I was playing at the Opera Comique, during the run of "H.M.S. Pinafore," at a salary of eighteen guineas per week, to the end of "The Pirates of Penzance," by which time it was increased to twenty and twenty-two (a period of ten years), I was accused by these gentlemen of not sending in "fair returns." I left their office, jumped into a cab, drove home, and returned with my agreement, of which I had luckily thought, and that settled the matter. They think I am a Rothschild, and won't allow me to know my own income!'

An American organ and neat little piano stand against the wall—but in this matter the house is well provided, for there are no less than six pianos in different rooms, besides the organ. The study walls are lined with many interesting photographs and pictures, among which are two characteristic and much-prized etchings, by Rajon, of Sarasate and Whistler. Almost every 'celebrity' is present. Here are some of the actor himself, representing his different parts, notably the Major-General in 'The Pirates,' with all the medals and bars placed in correct order—the V.C., the Crimean, Indian Mutiny, the Legion of Honour, and many others. These were lent by Lieut.-Colonel the Hon. Herbert F. Eaton. 'I used to see military men,' says Mr. Grossmith, 'gazing through opera-glasses, not at my face, but at my medals, to see if all were accurately placed. As Sir Joseph Porter, K.C.B., I had the greatest difficulty in getting the counterfeit collar and star made, as the originals were not to be procured, and I am most particular in having correct details.' The large writing-table is heaped up with letters, papers, proofs, scores, &c. It is not exactly an untidy table, though, but perhaps someone else may be responsible for that, as his wife laughingly observes that, 'except in appearance, he is by no means a "tidy man," and it would be no good giving him pigeon-holes in his desk, for he would never use them.'

As may be supposed, George Grossmith manifested his musical propensities at a very early age. When only eight years old he could play the piano, learning the technical details; while his correct ear, strong sense of humour, and power of facial expression made him a welcome and entertaining guest, not only at children's but at grown-up parties, where he would sing every variety of comic song, with great *aplomb*, to his own setting. He began life as a reporter at Bow Street, where his talent for observation received many an inspiration from the sometimes grave, sometimes ludicrous, scenes that came before his notice, and various *causes célèbres* were duly reported by him in the 'Times.' The next idea was the Bar, but his artistic proclivities very soon brought him favourably before the public. And in public estimation George Grossmith has deservedly and steadily, year after year, increased and strengthened his hold—this probably as much by his unceasing efforts and his well-known desire to give 'the very best that is in him to its service' as by his brilliant abilities.

Now, be it known, the actor is extremely nervous on 'first nights,' wherein his own opinion is that 'his performance is then worst of all; and, as a rule, he feels very grave, and unable to realise that there is any joke in the whole thing—indeed, it is as solemn as going to a funeral, though, to be sure, one is not nervous at that.' It is so difficult to judge at rehearsals what people will enjoy and laugh at when it is placed before them. Now and then, for his entertainments, he has taken two months over one musical item, and if it does not seem to make a hit at once, he will 'lay it aside with an aching heart;' while at other times he has knocked off a little sketch or song in a morning, which will 'catch on' at once—such as 'Baby on the Shore,' 'See Me Dance the Polka,' and the like trivialities. 'But it is the first duty of every actor to please his public,' says Mr. Grossmith, seriously. 'There is no nonsense about art; and, though I would not degrade my profession, of which I am so proud, by any buffoonery, nor, like a good bootmaker, "sell bluchers," I must give my customers what they like. It sometimes grieves me to find good work unappreciated, but anyhow I'll keep my score for people to see when I am forgotten.' But George Grossmith will not soon be 'forgotten,' so he need not trouble himself to think about it, and may the 'score' long remain in his own possession!

His first trip to America in the character of an entertainer was a big artistic success, though the expenses were necessarily so enormous that he did not realise enough to clear them. Neither husband nor wife can say enough of the great appreciation and hospitality shown them by their transatlantic brethren. Soon after his return from a second trip 'His Excellency' was produced at the Savoy. This 'first night' was even a more terrible ordeal than the preceding ones. Not only had Mr. Grossmith been suffering from depression of spirits, but fatigue and excitement had produced the demon insomnia. And, in this last annoyance, he humorously relates that, during the period of rehearsals, whenever he even dozed at night four dreams perpetually persecuted him like nightmares. First, that he had missed his train, and could not get to the theatre in time; next, that the Queen had arrived, and there were no chairs placed for her or any of the Royal Family; then that there was no audience nor orchestra; and last, and most agonising of all, that the most important garment of his stage apparel had been left behind; and these four dreams never ceased for a week nightly to assail him, after which all was again smooth sailing.

Mr. Grossmith is also acutely sensitive to criticism. A great 'believer in women' (a not infrequent experience with a husband who is possessed of 'the Angel in the House'), though not exactly of the 'New' species, he thinks it would be a capital idea to have women as well as men critics. 'There are women picture critics,' he says; 'why not women play critics?' On this idea you promptly seize, and generously make a present of it to all whom it may concern.

Of all his many successful *rôles* there is no need to speak, as they are fresh in the memory of every playgoer, from John Wellington Wells in 'The Sorcerer,' through the long runs of the 'Pinafore,' 'Patience,' 'Iolanthe,' 'The Mikado,' &c., down to 'His Excellency'; while his entertainments are always in request, and are an unfailing source of delight to his audience. His two latest and best Sketches are 'Wooings and Weddings,' and 'How I discovered America.' His bright, happy nature ever leads the popular actor to look on the sunny side of life, which he 'enjoys so thoroughly that its shadows sink into insignificance.' And with this genial disposition, his brilliant gifts, and his earnest striving to please, George Grossmith will long retain his proud position of a faithful and conscientious servant of the public.

KATE PHILLIPS

(MRS. H. B. CONWAY)

BORN of a good old county family of great wealth—the Goldneys of Wiltshire—nothing seemed more unlikely than that Kate Phillips should at any time be required to earn her own living; but, alas! her father was possessed of extravagant tastes, ran through three fine fortunes, and died leaving his wife and young family unprovided for.

Then did the brave-hearted girl buckle to with a will. As soon as she could in any way struggle for herself she began at the foot of the ladder, and, alone and unaided, got herself, at a very early age, an engagement to 'walk on' as an 'extra' for nine shillings a week at the Lyceum Theatre, then under the management of the Brothers Mansell. Gradually ascending step by step to her present good position among the leading comedians of the day, she has supported not only herself, in her simple, modest establishment, but her mother; 'for,' as she remarks tenderly, 'whosoever else had to "go without," that beloved mother never had.' Over and above this Kate Phillips has entirely educated her brother's child, Maude Goldney —to such good purpose that the young girl is now a *danseuse*, and has lately been on tour with Miss Cissy Grahame, and she will shortly make her *début* in London.

'No member of my family,' says the charming little actress cheerfully, as she recalls the reminiscences of early struggles, 'had ever been on the stage. Indeed, they were one and all horrified at my thinking of it. One of the collateral branches married John Bannister, the great comedian, but I had no interest, no influence, knew no managers, and never had a creature to help me.'

But she had, at any rate, been blessed with original histrionic talents; with sturdy perseverance and strength of will; likewise with a determination to get on—the which good gifts have carried the day; and as you gaze at the small, fair, curly head, with its broad brow and far-apart blue eyes, the slightly *retroussé* nose, the pretty little short upper lip, and the firmly moulded chin, it is easy enough to read these characteristics therein. And there is probably another reason why she has made such a good position for herself. From the first she worked desperately hard in provincial stock companies, laying in a store of experience, and as her success became assured, and she was engaged in legitimate business, she never hesitated, when her services were requisitioned, to take any part, good or bad, with the same unfailing alacrity. Her aptitude for playing 'bad' parts well has served her in right good stead, 'For,' as a dramatic critic remarked lately in a private chat, 'whatsoever be the character entrusted to Kate Phillips, one feels it will be always safe in her hands. She will cheerfully take one that many another actress will refuse, and which may really not be suited to her; but she invariably makes herself suit it, and works it up so thoroughly that it ends in being one of the hits of the play.' And this is an invaluable reputation to earn. Her *début* in London was made at the Globe Theatre in opera bouffe—'Les Brigands,' an adaptation by Offenbach. Oddly enough, though she was only engaged as understudy, in a short time she found her name on the bill. It happened one day that someone was suddenly taken ill. The manager, in despair, asked, 'Who can go on instead?' 'I can,' said the young girl. She had understudied not only one part, but each, and knew the whole piece by heart, and had stood nightly at the wings to watch. Thus it came about that she stepped in and made a complete success. Essentially a *comédienne*, the lines of Kate Phillips' career have been based on high comedy, with Mr. Irving, the Bancrofts, Mr. Hare, and the Kendals; but in her ardent, excitable temperament—systematic and thoroughly practical withal—there is a deep underlying pathos. With a clear, true mezzo-soprano voice, she can speak blank verse with fine, tender intonation and correctness, as all who heard her in 'The White Pilgrim' (in which she created the part of Gerda) will remember. 'It was brought out at the Court,' says Miss Phillips. 'Herman Merivale must have been inspired when he wrote it.' At your request she gives you the beautiful and touching recitation piece, 'Miscall me not,' in such pathetic and melodious tones, and with so much feeling, that for a few minutes after both reciter and listener feel a lump in their throats! After a pause she adds, in a voice of emotion: 'It is death personified!

Some time after I played it I had a long and dangerous illness, but those words were always in my mind, and for ever took all fear of death away from me.' Her voice, it may be mentioned, has been well cultivated under good masters, and is as good in singing as in speaking. On her recovery from this illness a grand *matinée* was organised for her benefit, of which Kate Phillips cherishes the most grateful recollections. 'I cannot speak warmly enough,' she says, 'of the kindness of Mr. Beerbohm Tree on that occasion. He lent me the theatre and himself paid all expenses; and oh! what a cast it was! So many of the great actors offered their services—Mrs. Kendal, Marion Terry, Carlotta Addison, Fanny Brough, Kate Rorke, Mary Anderson, Mrs. Bernard Beere, Mr. and Mrs. Tree, Mr. Toole, Edward Terry, Lionel Brough, James, Thorne, &c., &c.—I was proud of that bill. "Nabbs," too—a fox terrier who has been for many years my faithful and devoted companion—took a part.' Among her big *rôles* may be reckoned the Boy in 'Henry V.,' Phœbe to Mr. Toole's 'Paul Pry,' with John S. Clarke—who would have no one else—Lady Franklin in 'Money,' which fitted her to perfection, and Maria in 'Twelfth Night,' a *rôle* of which *The Times* critic wrote, 'she showed herself worthy to walk in the steps of Compton.' She was specially invited by Mr. Hare to play Audrey in 'As You Like It,' and indeed had three similar invitations from him, but was unluckily prevented by previous engagements. After a spell at the Gaiety Miss Phillips went to the Bancrofts at the old Prince of Wales', and, in common with many another young player, declares 'it was one of the happiest times of her life,' and her best engagement to have been Bessie Kebblethwaite in 'An Unequal Match,' with Mr. Bancroft as the sweetheart—a play in which there was so much natural merriment that Mrs. Bancroft used laughingly to declare she 'would have to give them the hot poker at Christmas if they "clowned so."' 'It was a delight to work with them,' says Miss

Phillips. She played for two hundred nights in 'The Rivals,' and for fifteen months consecutively in 'Confusion.' Anent this play—in which she created the part of the soubrette to perfection—it was at first only put on as a stop-gap for a few weeks while preparing for Byron's 'Open House,' but it deservedly proved so popular that it had an enormous run. At its conclusion the delayed play was somewhat hesitatingly produced. 'I went on rather in a rebellious spirit,' she says; 'but, to our surprise, it was a great success.' Naturally enough! To see those two perfect comedians—Mr. Farren and Kate Phillips—as Timpson was a never-to-be-forgotten treat; to watch their faces, their thorough sympathy, their every telling word and gesture—all so spontaneous and vivacious—was to learn how, in such skilful hands, comedy could be raised to the highest artistic pitch. Loud and universal were the commendations from the press and the public. Among many cherished private letters the actress shows two with pride—one from Dubourg saying her Maria was 'worthy to be ranked with those glorious chambermaids of Molière's.' But before this she had created the part of Jenny in 'The Queen's Shilling' at the St. James's by special request of Messrs. Hare and Kendal. Later came Dorinda Croodle in 'The Money Spinner,' Dot in 'The Cricket on the Hearth' at Toole's Theatre; also Mrs. Coventry Sparkle in Mr. and Mrs. Herman Merivale's play 'The Don,' and a part in their amusing piece 'The Butler.' Presently followed a long engagement with Mr. Irving at the Lyceum to play Cerisette in 'The Dead Heart,' Nerissa in 'The Merchant of Venice,' Martha in 'Louis XI.,' Susan in 'Nance Oldfield,' Marjorie in 'Becket'—a most difficult but creditable performance—and so on throughout the whole of the delightful Lyceum *répertoire*. And then came the recent trip to America with Mr. Irving's company. The Americans heartily appreciated her talent and the good style of the young actress's performance, and awarded her no small meed of approbation. During her absence a faithful and devoted maid carefully collected a bundle of press notices of her later parts in London, and put them aside. On her return Miss Phillips, who had a girl friend on a visit, had occasion late one night to fetch some trifle from below, and went down to the kitchen and opened a drawer. The first thing she saw was this little packet. The contents were all favourable, but one in particular, from a distinguished dramatic critic, was couched in such delightfully eulogistic terms that on reading it by the light of a 'farthing dip' the two friends looked at each other for a minute solemnly, and exclaimed simultaneously in tragic tones, 'And to think of this being found in a kitchen drawer!' 'I always study the first thing in the morning,' says Kate Phillips. 'I am very slow, and it is a great labour, but when I have got it by heart I've got it for good and all. It grows at rehearsal, but I play it quite differently after a week from the first night. I always wish the first night were on the seventh night—so to speak—which sounds rather like an Irishism!' Her latest performance was Honor Bliss in 'The Chili Widow,' justly pronounced by a great dramatic critic 'a gem of pure comedy.'

She was, on one occasion, on a tour with Mrs. John Wood, Mr. Conway, and others, when 'London Assurance' was to be played at Halifax, Yorkshire. A ridiculous incident occurred. In the last scene, when the duel is supposed to take place in the library behind, between Sir Harcourt and Dolly Spanker, it was suddenly discovered, to their dismay, that the pistols had been forgotten. What expedient could be resorted to? The moment was near at hand! It would be the play of 'Hamlet' with Hamlet left out! In a moment of inspiration someone called out: 'Paper bags!' An actor in stage costume ran round the corner to a neighbouring baker's shop, seized two of the articles in question from the much-astonished baker, and nearly expended his last wind in blowing them out as he breathlessly arrived, just in the nick of time. 'Two loud reports were heard,' said Miss Phillips, laughing, 'which really sounded more like cannon-shots, but they did their duty at the right moment, and the audience were completely taken in.'

Kate Phillips is not one of the lucky people who have had a 'part written expressly' for them, but has been a receptacle for the ideas of others, and has often had the difficult task of making 'dry bones live.' All honour, then, to the hard-working and gifted actress who has accomplished not only this somewhat unthankful work with ever-ready cheerfulness, but has shown herself to be so true an artist all round, without being indebted to anyone for help or favour throughout her successful career.

THE VERY REV. R. HERBERT STORY, D.D.
LATE MODERATOR OF THE GENERAL ASSEMBLY

THERE is no pleasanter tour on a warm, sunshiny day than a sail up the Clyde to the bustling, industrious city of Glasgow. 'The glory and the freshness of a dream' lie over the dark blue of the water, flecked with foam, and on the fair mountains that fade far away into space, as the steamer churns her way merrily along. Having elected this means of transit in place of the more prosaic railway to visit the Rev. Dr. Story at the University, it seems not amiss to tarry for a brief space at the little village of Roseneath, just opposite the Gareloch, in order to make acquaintance with the place associated with him and his late father for over half a century.

During the voyage a chance incident brings you into conversation with a fellow-passenger. On mentioning the name of 'Story' he imparts much interesting information concerning the family and the quiet, peaceful-looking village, which little looks as if it had been in bygone days the scene of much ecclesiastical notoriety, yet here many of the Scottish divines fled during the times of persecution and of strife in the old Covenanting days.

On a sheltered stretch of shingle by Camsail Bay stands the pier, and your companion volunteers his escort to point out the church wherein the late Rev. Robert Story ministered for forty-one years, and the manse where he passed away to his rest, beloved and lamented. It overlooks the Gareloch, and stands in a prettily wooded lawn and garden just by the gate of the church, which was twice enlarged and beautified during the twenty-seven following years of the incumbency of the present Dr. Story. In 1887, he too found a different sphere of usefulness, and leaving the home of his birth and the pulpit which almost seemed his by inheritance, he was appointed Professor of Ecclesiastical History at the University of Glasgow by Mr. A. J. Balfour, then the Scottish Secretary.

'When a parish minister,' says your informant, 'his church was always full, and his preaching was thought much of by those who do not care for noise and clap-trap. His delivery was fine, but very quiet, and he had no tricks of oratory or of gesture. An attached parishioner once remarked, ' If he wad but pit a leetle mair annemosity in til his mainner ! ' If he occasionally preached rather over the heads of his ordinary congregation, it was because he is a highly educated and scholarly man, and he could not always adapt himself easily to the intellectual standard of at least some of those who heard him; he is of a reserved and, as some think, austere disposition, and has a grave manner. In public debate he is inclined to be too sarcastic—so, at least, some say—but,' concludes the speaker, as he bids you good-bye with a kindly smile, ' at any rate, he contrives to make many friends ! '

During the former words an inward sinking of spirit had seriously caused you to think of turning back and leaving the late Moderator and the great seat of learning unvisited, feeling that it would be impossible indeed to venture on such intellectual ground, but the last clause of the sentence saves you. Taking heart of grace, the journey is continued, and an hour or so later the University buildings are in sight.

Situated on the summit of Gilmore Hill, on the north bank of the Kelvin, overlooking the West End Park, they consist of three fine courts, crowned with a lofty, massive tower, chiefly of the Early English style, built by Sir Gilbert Scott. The grounds are extensive and largely cultivated, and the inner courts, divided from each other by deep cloisters, present a gay aspect by reason of the throng of students who, as the hour-bell rings, hurry out of the class rooms, the juniors in the scarlet gowns which give a bright bit of colour among the arches. The outer court contains the houses of the Principal and twelve Professors on the old foundation, amongst whom are Veitch, the poet and historian of the 'Border,' Lord Kelvin, Dr. Gairdner, Dr. Dickson, the learned translator of Mommsen, and Edward Caird, now Master of Baliol. Turning in at No. 8, you find yourself in a high, roomy hall, where an old grandfather clock ticks away the minutes tranquilly ; a few large photographs hang on the walls, notably the Jove of the Vatican, the Apollo Belvedere, the Discobolus, and the Laocoon.

A door on the right leads into the library overlooking the college ground. Over the mantelpiece hangs a water-colour sketch of the Gareloch, executed by Lady Mary Glyn, and etchings of St. Margaret's College at St. Andrews. There is a small bust of Edward Irving—a gift from Mrs. Oliphant—a crucifix in a little shrine, and many odds and ends of all sorts. It is not altogether what might be called a tidy room, with its newspapers, examination papers, pamphlets, and a stray proof here and there lying about, but it has a look of comfort and of use. The walls on two sides are lined with books which overflow on to chairs, tables, everywhere. It is rather a mixed collection, but among them may be seen some that are valuable, such as black-letter editions of ' Peter

Martyr,' and of the Homilies, a large quarto of Baskerville's 'Catullus,' and several standard works of history and biography. On the top of one bookcase stand busts of Socrates, Dante, and Dr. Story, and various pictures and medallions are on the opposite walls. A large bundle of golf sticks in the corner indicates his favourite recreation. But here your inspection ceases, for the door opens and the Professor enters, fresh from a theological lecture, in his black Doctor's gown, with purple silk-lined hood and black velvet cap, such as is worn at Bologna, which Glasgow copies.

The cap removed discloses a broad, intellectual brow, crowned with prematurely silvered hair; large, thoughtful, dark eyes, straight features, and a silver-white beard complete the portrait. There lurks a suspicion of a twinkle in those brown eyes, which seem to say that the learned and so-called 'austere' Doctor of Divinity can temper his severity with mirth when occasion demands, and although his commanding presence and his well-known strictness in examination and discipline may be likely to inspire awe among those who come under him, his lectures have the reputation of being highly interesting, while the Professor himself is by no means unpopular with his students.

If the art of making others at ease consist in being at ease oneself, then does Dr. Story possess it to perfection. In five minutes the conversation has taken a lively, not to say frivolous, turn, and he laughs heartily while you confess to having felt a momentary feeling of trepidation at invading his retreat.

Amongst the more advanced of the Scottish divines, the Rev. R. Herbert Story, D.D., occupies a prominent position. A strong, broad Churchman of a type now getting old-fashioned in Scotland, he has no relish for co-operation with the dissent popular in some quarters, or the gushing evangelicalism occasionally to be met with in the older and stricter school.

'My theological bent,' he says impressively, 'was always away from Puritanism and Calvinism. My father's influence and that of the clerical friends he had about him was all in that direction, and I suppose that I imbibed it unconsciously. When I grew old enough to think for myself I could never have relapsed into traditional "orthodoxy." Dr. Robert Lee, whose life I wrote, Principal Tulloch, Norman McLeod, Dr. McLeod Campbell, and Dean Stanley all helped to influence my mind in the direction of freedom of thought, dislike of formulæ, and of all sorts of sacerdotal pretensions.'

An only son, he was educated entirely at home during the early days of boyhood under his father's careful supervision. On entering his teens he was sent to the Edinburgh University for some years, where he distinguished himself in classics, and for the ease and grace of his English compositions. He took sundry prizes for translations in verse from the Greek of Æschylus and Homer, also in Moral Philosophy, and wrote the prize poem in English literature. Then the young student, who from the first had determined to follow in his father's footsteps, passed on for his final session at St. Andrews. He had, however, wisely decided not to settle down into a groove until he had considerably enlarged his mind with foreign travelling. He spent the summer 'Semester' of 1853, at Heidelberg, and subsequently made a long winter tour in southern France and Italy, residing for some time at Nice, Rome, and Naples; after his return he received licence as a probationer, equivalent to the deacon's orders of the Anglican Church, and went for a year as assistant minister to St. Andrew's Church, Montreal. At the end of that time he returned to Scotland, being appointed by the Duke of Argyll to succeed his father in the incumbency of Roseneath, and there passed twenty-seven years.

'Not wholly uneventful years,' remarks Dr. Story. 'I liked my work as parish priest, and was interested in the great varieties of character—often very fine in type, and oftener quaint, shrewd, and humorous—among my rural parishioners, but my work here, I think, suits me better. I ever lament my country sun and sky, and my garden and trees, in the smoke and gloom of Glasgow, and I always regret the impossibility of keeping a dog here— with any pleasure to the dog or myself. I have never been without a terrier of the finest Skye species for thirty years. "Dizzy," "Pam," and "Toby" were their patronymics. I brought the last "Toby" with me to the college—a very dear friend—the most thoroughly gentlemanlike dog I ever knew, a manner of the old Court, a charming character, but,' and Dr. Story sighs as he adds, ' he drooped here without his usual rabbit-hunting and other exercise. I had him taken down and buried at Roseneath.'

For many years Dr. Story has been a regular member of the General Assembly, being returned whilst at Roseneath by his presbytery out of the usual rotation, and since his residence in Glasgow by the University as its representative. In 1886, he was appointed Junior Clerk of the Assembly, Professor of Ecclesiastical History in the University, and Chaplain to the Queen. He is Chaplain to the Clyde Naval Brigade of Volunteers, and has twice been Grand Chaplain to the Grand Lodge of Scotland. The last well-merited honour that was conferred on Dr. Story—and an honour that gave satisfaction in all quarters—was the Moderatorship of the General Assembly of the Church of Scotland, to which he was appointed in May, 1894.

All this time his pen has not been idle. He has contributed not a little to the theological, or perhaps one should rather say the ecclesiastical, literature of the day in the principal magazines and journals, such as ' The Saturday Review' and 'The National Review'; to 'Blackwood's,' 'Good Words' and ' The National Observer,' and is understood to be the writer for many years of most of the leading articles on Church questions in a leading Scotch daily paper. For three years he edited the magazine called 'The Scottish Church,' afterwards 'The Scots' Magazine.' Among his principal books are his biographies of his father and of Dr. Robert Lee, 'Christ the Consoler,' 'Creed and Conduct,' 'Health Haunts of the Riviera,' 'William Carstares'—a character and career of the Revolutionary epoch—&c. &c.; while among his pamphlets are 'Fast Days'—an almost extinct Scotch institution—'Continuity of the Kirk,' 'The Reformed Ritual,' &c., and he was the author of two of the 'Scotch Sermons' which, in 1880, created a stir among the orthodox. As one of the Scottish 'Church Service Society,' and convener of its Editorial Committee, he has had charge of its publication of 'Euchologion: A Book of Common Order,' now in its sixth edition. His last work of editing, 'The Church of Scotland, Past and Present,' now standard volumes, was planned by Dr. Story, and executed by carefully selected writers in the various departments of history.

The luncheon gong here creates a diversion, and is succeeded by Mrs. Story's entrance on hospitable thoughts intent. She, too, has been an author, but of lighter literature than her husband's, and one of her novels, entitled 'Charley Nugent,' a well-known story of military life, is still to be found in a cheap edition at railway bookstalls and in barrack-room libraries, where it never loses its popularity. She is also an accomplished musician, and has not given up the singing in which she is so proficient. The dining-room is bright and cheerful. The windows look out on the shrubbery and lawn between the houses, the cricket, football grounds and tennis-courts. On one side of this space lies the gymnasium, on the other the Western Infirmary, the scene of clinical instruction. Beyond the houses rising in the distance are the beautiful hills of Campsee and Kilpatrick. Over the fireplace hangs a fine portrait of Dr. Story's grandfather, of the Raeburn school, opposite a striking likeness of himself by Philip Burne-Jones.

The pleasant, sociable meal over, Dr. Story's two daughters propose a stroll round the College grounds, but first you desire to take a peep into the great drawing-room, which will presently be crowded with guests, as it is an 'At Home' day. This fine room, over forty feet long, has a fireplace at each end, and has a thoroughly home-like appearance, with its well-filled dwarf bookcases, valuable bits of china, old oak bureaus, ferns, palms, and bright water-colour sketches, among them a painting of 'Toby,' the beloved Skye terrier—now no more. The grand piano, vast heap of music, and open guitar case imply that a musical afternoon is in prospect. The photograph case, containing groups of the Queen and some of her family, together with two of her books, are Royal gifts, and bear inscriptions in Her Majesty's handwriting. These were presented to Dr. Story during his annual autumnal visits at Balmoral. The collections of portraits on easels and in portfolios include those of the Duchess of Argyll, the Duchess of Montrose, and of himself, done by Lady Emily Peel at her villa in Genoa, and many others, each signed by the donor; but the visitors' book is a curiosity, and would tempt the collector of autographs to commit a theft, with its numerous names of note, some few, alas! now gone over to the silent majority.

Some hours later, after dinner, in the sociable home circle of four, Dr. Story is prevailed upon to give some details of his whilom appointment of Moderator of the General Assembly. He speaks with much interest and eloquence of the various duties of the office, ecclesiastical and social, and was greatly pleased with the many proofs that he received of the satisfaction that his nomination gave to the Church generally. The question seems to sum itself up in a few words. Advancement and progress are the order of the day. Not only is a thorough knowledge of theology, ecclesiastical history and politics required for such an important post, but the task of maintaining principle without provoking unnecessary opposition and of justifying the Church's claims to the confidence of the nation, had to be achieved. Combined with these requirements, the tact, the cool head, the sound judgment, and above all the knowledge of human nature that this intellectual man undoubtedly possesses, carried him triumphantly through the ordeal of acting as Primate of the year for the Church of Scotland.

MRS. PATRICK CAMPBELL

IN the strange evolution of outward phenomena which is called 'life' it will now and then happen that a talent which has hitherto lain partially dormant is by some force of circumstances suddenly brought to the front, and lands its fortunate possessor almost instantaneously into name and fame. Perhaps no better instance could be found to illustrate this theory than the young actress, Mrs. Patrick Campbell, who bears her quickly won honours with so much grace and modesty. One year, seemingly but recent, finds her playing in amateur theatricals for amusement or in the sacred cause of charity; two seasons later and the discerning eye of the London managers—not to speak of universal public opinion—has rightly placed her in the topmost ranks of her profession as the 'leading lady' in one of the principal theatres in the metropolis.

A rapid transit of about two seconds in a lift and you arrive at a bright and airy flat in Ashley Gardens, facing the site of the new Catholic cathedral. A glance around the pretty square drawing-room is enough to satisfy you that art and comfort have been made to go hand in hand in its arrangement. The carved white wood shelves and mantelpiece show off to advantage many treasures in the way of bronzes and china; the quaint little marqueterie bureau overflows with papers and booklets; the piano is covered with every variety of photographs, and in one corner a venerable grandfather clock ticks the minutes tranquilly away. As your young hostess glides in, with swift and graceful movement, the thought promptly arises that she is in thorough harmony with her surroundings.

It is well known that Mr. and Mrs. Patrick Campbell took upon themselves the graver responsibilities of life at a ridiculously early age, for the child-wife was barely seventeen and the boy-husband but two years her senior. A picture that she hands to you represents her, a couple of years later, the proud young mother of a lovely, curly-headed, twelve-months'-old boy nestling on her knee. Her hitherto brief stage experiences have already been so ably chronicled that there would seem to be little to add. Suffice it to say that in herself she originates her talent for acting, no relations on either side having ever been before the footlights; but from her mother, an Italian of great beauty and of pure, ancient lineage, Mrs. Patrick Campbell inherits a passion for music, a love of art, and a warm appreciation of everything dramatic. Judging from a portrait of this lady, the young artist has also inherited something more—a tall, *svelte*, girlish figure; a pair of soft, dark-brown eyes, with a depth of thought in them; a clear, creamy complexion, and a wealth of dark, curly hair.

'My mother looks so young,' says the daughter fondly; 'we might pass for sisters.'

It was not until after the birth of her second child that Mrs. Patrick Campbell's dramatic power was developed. Once discovered—and, oddly enough, it was while playing in a piece appropriately called 'Buried Talent'—the rest soon followed. Her triumphs in 'The Second Mrs. Tanqueray,' 'The Masqueraders,' and 'John-a-

Dreams,' need but little comment; while the picturesqueness, the sympathetic charm of her acting, the depth of pathos in her full, musical voice, and her entire absence of self-consciousness are universally recognised.

Her method of study is as follows. Although she has no difficulty in actually committing the lines to memory, she generally begins by writing out her part. Then she will begin early in the morning, and go on uninterruptedly for five hours at a stretch; but so great is her ambition that she can scarcely refrain from working the whole day long. With regard to the actual study of the character, that never ceases from the day she receives her part to its last performance; indeed, it may be truly said that nature is the keynote of her method.

As may be supposed, Mrs. Patrick Campbell's next great ambition was to play some of the leading Shakespearian characters; to which end she applied herself, during a brief period of 'resting,' to ardent study of these parts. Shortly her desire was realised, and when Mr. Forbes-Robertson assumed the onerous duties of managership, and opened the Lyceum (during Sir Henry Irving's absence) with 'Romeo and Juliet,' he engaged her for the *rôle* of Juliet, in which she gained fresh laurels. Her latest *rôle* is Melitza in 'For the Crown.'

It is pleasant to hear her speak so enthusiastically of Mr. Robertson's management, also of Mr. and Mrs. Beerbohm Tree, and of all their kindness to her. These are themes on which she dwells, and here she calls your attention to an exquisite little silver chariot with prancing steeds that Mr. Tree presented to her, smothered in orchids, on the first night of 'John a Dreams.' She also confesses to a very soft spot in her heart for Mr. Pinero, to whom she is 'ever grateful.'

A most embarrassing little 'unrehearsed effect,' which would have tried the strongest nerves, took place just as she went on in the part of Andrea in 'The Trumpet Call' at the Adelphi—her first evening performance on any

London stage. Her skirt, which had been insecurely fastened, suddenly fell to the ground! The young actress, however, was equal to the occasion. With a deft backward movement of her arm she swept its folds around her, secured them with a pin, and went on with her part, receiving a perfect ovation at its conclusion.

Success has in no way turned the young player's head. She dislikes crowds, shuns notoriety, and has a horror of advertisement. Indeed, in the matter of the oft-recurring petitions for an 'interview,' she does violence to her feelings, and consents out of sheer kindness of heart, rather than hurt anyone by refusing. She cannot be coaxed to say much about herself, but dwells with pleasure and pride on her husband's shooting excursions in South Africa, declaring that he is more interesting to discuss than she.

But your host, too, who is as charming and gracious in manner as his wife, is modest, and declines to be 'drawn' on his deeds of prowess, though here and there Mrs. Patrick Campbell slips in a word prettily, with an arch smile, and says, 'He is a keen sportsman, not popping over rabbits two miles from London, *bien entendu*, but big game, lions, &c.' And a sly thought involuntarily crosses your mind that, if he left dead lions out at Mashonaland, he certainly came home to find a living one in his gifted wife!

To sum up pithily the capability and originality of this delightful young actress, the words of a great player may be quoted:—'The quality of her acting is entirely her own—something which she can neither borrow nor lend.'

HENRY BLACKBURN

IT is curious to notice the instinctive connection of ideas in the minds of people between a man's name and his work. For instance, to casually mention Mr. Henry

Blackburn is to immediately evoke the involuntary rejoinder from someone, 'Academy Notes,' and this gave rise to a little plot lately at a small and friendly gathering. On your alluding to this connection of ideas to a knot of acquaintances standing around it was agreed that as each new guest came in someone should bring in Mr. Henry Blackburn's name unintentionally, as it were. Every visitor was caught in the trap, and immediately uttered the words 'Academy Notes,' and when this occurred for the eleventh time consecutively there was an irresistible laugh, and the joke was explained. The 'little grey book' which 'caught on' from its first introduction, and year after year has found so much favour with the public, at once became the subject of conversation, and high were the encomiums passed on its merits, several persons mentioning that they had preserved each year's copy from the date of its publication in 1875, to the present time, and that one of its greatest charms was in the reminiscences and associations that it recalled. A brief history of the talented author of this famous 'little grey book' shall be told, and a few words given that will convey some idea of the time and labour required to produce it on the opening morning of the Royal Academy.

Inheriting from his father and grandfather the talent for drawing, Henry Blackburn cannot remember the time when he was not more or less an artist. Yet not only an artist; he is, besides, author of more than a dozen books; foreign correspondent and art critic for many London reviews and journals; lecturer on art at home and abroad; sometime editor of a magazine, and the originator of the system of illustrated catalogues of exhibitions. He was born at Portsea, where his father, the late Mr. Charles Blackburn, Professor of Mathematics, Cambridge, held an appointment in the Naval College. It is probable that he inherited something more than the artistic temperament from the scholarly parent, who also wrote books, albeit his son declares they were 'fearful and abstruse, as mathe-

matical works are wont to be.' The combination of this
practical element and the vein of romance in his own
nature have resulted in what has been the watchword of
Mr. Henry Blackburn's success, 'the value of a line,' than
which no artist has done more to substantiate. He was
educated at the Grammar School, Kensington, where he
maintains that he was by no means 'a deep student,' nor
did he in any way distinguish himself except in drawing.
His work, however, was to be done later in life. School-
days over, after studying for a time the mysteries of print-
ing and other kindred subjects, he obtained an appointment
in the Civil Service Commission, and subsequently became
private secretary to the Right Honourable E. Horsman,
M.P. But the claims of art soon asserted themselves too
strongly to be resisted; an opportunity arising to go to
Africa, in company with a party of French artists, Gérôme,
Constant, Regnault, &c., he started forth on his travels and
caught a glimpse of Horace Vernet painting his last picture, and witnessed the great gathering at Algeria when
all the tribes from the interior came in to pay tribute to
the conqueror, Napoleon III., bringing wonderful presents
of gold embroideries and ivories. 'It was a time of very
hard work,' says Mr. Blackburn, 'but I gained a great
deal of useful experience, and it taught one so much about
atmospheric effects and shadow. I brought away about a
hundred sketches; one or two of these you see on yonder
wall were done on horseback, and untouched afterwards.'
The series comprises several masterly water-colour drawings, each done in a day, of Algeria and Morocco, an Arab
cemetery, some landscapes and mosques, on one of which
the shadow of an aloe tree is projected with striking effect.
But his work is not confined to Africa only; he has made
many sketches in Normandy, Brittany, Switzerland, the
Pyrenees, &c., illustrations of which are to be found in an
interesting work of his entitled 'Artistic Travel.' The
outcome of this early visit to North Africa was a book
called 'Artists and Arabs,' which he pronounces to have

'set him going in literature.' Among other of his works are 'Life in Algeria,' 'Travelling in Spain,' 'The Pyrenees,' illustrated by Gustave Doré; 'Normandy Picturesque,' 'Art in the Mountains' (the story of the Passion Play at Oberammergau), 'Hartz Mountains,' and 'Breton Folk.' His latest volume is 'The Art of Illustration,' and there is one of which special mention must be made, for it is fraught with tenderest memories: 'Randolph Caldecott: A Personal Memoir.' Mr. Blackburn was one of the first to recognise the merits of this gifted illustrator and to introduce him to the art world of London. A young clerk in a Manchester bank at 70*l.* a year, Mr. Caldecott had sent up his drawings to various journals that had rejected them. Presently some of them fell into Mr. Blackburn's hands, and he, at once perceiving their merit, published them, and joined with other of his friends in persuading him to resign his desk and come to London, with the result that in the first year of his work Mr. Caldecott made 1000*l.* From that time a firm friendship was established that only ended with the artist's untimely death in Florida, and the history is touchingly told by Mr. Blackburn in the 'Memoir.' His book 'Breton Folk' is illustrated by his dead friend's hand.

The scheme of 'Academy Notes' was in the author's mind a year or two before he carried it out. It sprang from an idea that if one could not express in words the story of a painting to those who had no opportunity of seeing it, it could be done pictorially. This led him to cast about to inquire into the different methods of reproduction. From the first the book was welcomed by the public; the second year there was a rush on it; but Mr. Blackburn found considerable difficulties at the beginning. He had to draw the pictures as best he could, and the artists did not like it, as they said it did not give a fair idea of their work. Mr. Blackburn, however, with the peculiar tact and courtesy that characterise him, soon overcame their prejudices, and in the second year the artists volunteered to send in their own sketches, with the result that everyone was satisfied. These sketches consist simply of lines indicating the pictures, a kind of 'key-block,' and this year alone the author has received several hundreds. A few weeks before the Academy opens the rush begins, and Mr. Blackburn and his staff have a busy time of it. Everything has to be got ready beforehand, as he, of course, cannot know which pictures will be accepted. Then, when this is known, it leaves but little time to reproduce nearly two hundred blocks, and still less to print them. The compiling of 'Academy Notes,' which cannot be completed until the pictures are hung, is done in one day, and the letterpress written the same night. A vast army of operatives is then put on, and on the opening morning of the exhibition the 'little grey book,' with its summary in the beginning, its classification in different galleries in order all through, is not only in the hands of the London public, but on every railway bookstall throughout the kingdom within a few hours of its publication. One of the principal results of Mr. Blackburn's labours has been the founding of his studio in Victoria Street to follow up the instruction received at art schools and to enable the students to utilise the knowledge there acquired. He has created an art of his own, and, having studied well the various mechanical processes, he impresses on his pupils 'the value of a line,' and, in short, what not to do, as well as what to do, to obtain the greatest effect with the fewest lines, or it may also be called 'the art of leaving out.' Hundreds of pen-and-ink studies—the work of a variety of artists—in black and white, line the walls of the studios, so that the students may learn to avoid mannerism and to seek for originality. Another speciality of his is the starting of the system of 'Instruction by Correspondence' in drawing for the Press. He has pupils in China, in India, at the Cape, in Italy, in Germany, &c., who send their work and have it corrected, explained by examples, and returned. Mr. Blackburn is an excellent speaker, and has made five trips to America to deliver lectures, and freely admits that there is much to be learned there as regards illustration. He remembers an amusing experience on one of his travels, though the name of the place shall on no account be given. An exhibition of the works of English artists was to be held. On going to see it Mr. Blackburn observed that one picture had been hung upside down; nevertheless, in that position it had found a market. He pointed out the error, which was rectified, but the buyer then repudiated his purchase, so it was returned to England. At a lecture he subsequently gave at the Society of Arts he mentioned the circumstance, which led to the sale of the work in question.

Mr. and Mrs. Blackburn's flat is at the top of one of the largest and highest houses in Victoria Street. The walls are laden with treasures from the pen and brush of many well-known artists; among the most valued mementoes are some cleverly modelled clay figures of Breton peasants, which, together with a bronze bas-relief of a Brittany horse fair, are the work of Randolph Caldecott. A large oil-painting hangs in Mr. Blackburn's study—a life-size portrait by James Archer of Miss Blackburn clad in her grandmother's white gown with a coral necklace round her throat and a rose in her hand. The only child of the house, she inherits gifts on each side, and there are many decorative panels in natural tints and of her original designs that indicate her talent for art. Among many souvenirs is a quaint chess-board, painted by a friend, in patterns got by snow crystals; but perhaps the most cherished relic of all is a portrait of Longfellow, presented by himself to Mrs. Blackburn. 'These orange leaves,' she says, 'pasted at the back, he sent me in a letter from his study.'

MRS. L. T. MEADE

To beguile a weary wait for a train at Victoria you saunter to the bookstall, where your eye lights on a small volume, entitled 'Scamp and I,' by a well-known author, whom you are about to visit at West Dulwich. Promptly investing the modest sum of sixpence in its purchase, you presently become so much interested in the perusal that the flight of time is forgotten, and the half-hour journey seems condensed into about five minutes. But for the intervention of a friendly passenger, you might indeed have been carried on to some remote station on the London, Chatham, and Dover line without being aware of it, so great is the fascination of the simple, pathetic tale. On alighting a stiff hill has to be climbed, and on the top, just where three roads meet, stands a large corner house with garden back and front, and long flat bay windows on each side which command an extensive view all around. This is the home of Mrs. L. T. Meade, whose mission in life seemed to have been accomplished in her numerous and charming stories for the young, such as 'A World of Girls,' 'Polly, a New-fashioned Girl,' 'Beyond the Blue Mountains,' and many others which have found so much favour with the public. Lately, however, she has broken fresh ground, and in five novels, entitled 'The Medicine Lady,' 'This Troublesome World,' 'A Soldier of Fortune,' 'In an Iron Grip,' and 'The Voice of the Charmer,' she has proved that she can write equally well for children of larger growth.

The hall door opens on the left into a good-sized double drawing-room with a white arch division. Both Mrs. Meade and her husband have cultivated artistic tastes, and, given these, with Morris hangings and decorations, a few valuable and ancient family possessions and some remarkably fine photogravures after Burne-Jones's 'Briar Rose' series, the effect of the whole is just what might be expected. A few choice water-colour sketches are interspersed, notably one of the bold cliffs of New Quay an hour before sunset. The set of Wedgwood china on the mantelshelf dates over a hundred years back; a dainty miniature on ivory is evidently the author's grandmother, judging by the likeness; but two simple pictures, of a beautiful boy in one of the unconsciously graceful attitudes of childhood and of a couple of little fair girls called for good reasons 'Hope' and 'Joy,' with great wondering eyes, are more prized by their parents than any work of art that they may possess. A thoroughbred, but morose-dispositioned Persian cat, called 'Fluff,' curled up on the rug, and a handsome fox terrier, 'Jack,' completed the picture. (The two animals hate each other like poison, but this must be Fluff's fault, for Jack's manners are particularly cordial and sociable.) However, be their characters what they may, the twain are the beloved and inseparable companions of the little ones of the house.

'I always maintain,' says Mrs. Meade, by-and-bye, in the course of conversation, 'that our children have fully paid their own expenses for education in the many opportunities they have given me for the delineation of juvenile character and nature. I have received many an inspiration while observing their sayings and doings. I am naturally extremely fond of children, and several of my young girl friends have, unknowingly, sat to me for verbal portraits.' A peculiarly sweet and pathetic story, 'Daddy's Boy,' perhaps one of the most widely read of Mrs. Meade's large contribution to children's libraries, was suggested by her own boy when he was of very tender age.

Mrs. Meade is by birth Irish. She comes from Bandon, Co. Cork, and is one of a family of six. Her father was a clergyman, and her early years were passed at a pretty little vicarage in the heart of the country. Later the family moved to a larger rectory in another part of Ireland, where they soon found plenty to excite the imagination. It was a great, old-fashioned, rambling house with secret passages and mysterious staircases, whence uncanny sounds issued at night. 'It was said to be haunted,' says Mrs. Meade. 'Our parents concealed the fact from us, but I distinctly remember the noises we heard. One night in particular we were all awakened by what we supposed to be burglars. Everyone rushed out into the landing; the great mastiff growled, and then we heard with terror a sound as of a coach and horses being driven over the paving-stones of the large courtyard. The matter was thoroughly investigated, but nothing could ever be found to account for it, and I shall never forget it.'

From her childhood the young girl composed stories. The discipline of children was stricter in those days than in these. Her parents were afraid to encourage her in the habit, being unconscious of the latent talent that she possessed. All means, therefore, of writing her thoughts and ideas were carefully withheld, but she collected all the newspapers available, and on their margins were inscribed the little tales. One day the child went to her father and remarked gravely, 'I have not enough money; I should like to earn some. I think of writing a book. Some day I *shall*.' Her father was much shocked, and pointed out that it was a most improper proceeding for a girl to earn money. Her youthful prediction was in later years largely verified, for she has written not 'a' book, but about seventy.

Educated entirely at home, she was required to practise the piano five hours every day. Her mother was devoted to music, and hoped thus to inspire her daughter with a like fondness for it, but the habit had a distinctly opposite effect. Drawing, for which she had a passion, and also a strongly inherited talent, was not taught. She had intended to be an artist in after years as well as a writer, but, finding that to follow both pursuits would be an impossibility, she resigned the pencil and gave herself up, unreservedly, to the pen.

The young aspirant to literature was seventeen when her first work of fiction was written. It was called

'Ashton Morton,' and the characters were all more or less drawn from people whom she knew. Quite ignorant how to set about getting it printed, she sent it through a friend to the late Mr. Newby, who accepted it, and great was the delight of the young people at the rectory when a modest little cheque arrived, which was shared alike with each. Notwithstanding this first little success, some years elapsed before a second attempt was made. Finally the old home was broken up, and the young writer was able to gratify her strong desire to exchange a country for a town life. 'I came up to London,' says Mrs. Meade cheerfully, 'determined to fight my own battle and to abide by the result. It was at first a great struggle. Having hitherto always lived in Ireland, of course I knew but few people in London. Some friends had asked me to make my home with them. I crossed the Channel for the first time alone, and, after a terribly rough passage and a fatiguing journey, arrived at Paddington a poor, dazed weary traveller, and was met by these good people with the words, "Our house was burnt down last night, and we are staying with friends!" A temporary shelter was hastily procured, and directly arrangements could be made we joined forces and went to live in Sun Street, Bishopsgate, a most inappropriate name for the street, as the sun never shone there. I kept up my spirits and worked hard, going every day to the British Museum to study. Dr. Garnett, the superintendent, was most kind in directing my attention to the right sort of literature, and helped me to choose the name of my first book. It was called "Great St. Benedict's." Its *motif* was suggested by a doctor, and the subject was to be the way that out-patients were treated at the large hospitals. When it was finished I took it to a publisher, feeling that if he should say "No," then indeed I should consider myself to be a failure. A few days later I called again at seven in the evening, with palpitating heart, though outwardly composed. His first words were, "We will take your book!"

I could have jumped for joy, and,' she presently adds, ' I can recall it even now with pleasure.'

The 'joy' of success proved a great incentive to work. The same year the author thought of a title, and, without having written a word of the story, took the name and idea to the same firm. It was immediately arranged for to her entire satisfaction. The work was so congenial, the subject so thoroughly after her own heart! The girl went home and scarcely rested day or night till her task was accomplished. The words seemed to run down her pen. This book, ' Scamp and I,' was very soon brought out, and was so much in demand that it ran into many editions before it was eventually published in its present sixpenny form, and the author's difficulties and anxiety as to her future were at an end.

She has gone on year after year adding largely to the literature of the day for young people. Among many others, ' A Sweet Girl Graduate,' ' A World of Girls,' and ' Bashful Fifteen ' are probably the most attractive. Mrs. Meade has by no means confined her attention to writing books. Some few years after her marriage she started ' Atalanta,' a magazine for girls, and this she considers to have been the greatest idea and achievement of her life. She edited the paper successfully for six years, and thoroughly enjoyed the hard work that it gave her; it has been a great grief lately to be obliged to resign, but as the pressure of other writing became heavier and the children grew out of babyhood she found it impossible to be so much away from home, and was unwillingly compelled to give it up.

'It was harder work altogether than you can imagine,' says Mrs. Meade, ' much as I liked it. I had to breakfast at half-past seven to be ready for my shorthand writer at eight; from eight to nine I would dictate some three thousand words. Then I attended to household duties until my second secretary came, and worked till half-past eleven, when I always went to town for my editorial duties, which occupied me until seven. Then home to dinner, and I spent every evening correcting proofs, &c This lasted many months, and I had no holidays. An "eight-hours' day" would have seemed very little work to me!'

She likewise contributed largely to many other journals, to Messrs. Tillotson & Son's syndicate, and to the 'Sunday Magazine,' and Mrs. Meade speaks enthusiastically of Mr. Benjamin Waugh as one of her best and kindest friends.

'At the time of the passing of the International Copyright between England and America,' says the author, 'I was asked to contribute a three-volume novel to their International series by Messrs. Cassell & Co. I wanted my story to be exceptionally strong, and asked a friend—a very clever doctor—to help me. I had an idea of making a woman use an imperfectly discovered remedy indiscreetly. This was the origin of "The Medicine Lady." I was determined to punish her sufficiently for her presumption, but I could not have written it without the medical aid which was so generously rendered. I leave you to judge whether I carried out my intention,' says Mrs. Meade, laughing.

The novel is certainly a thoroughly original idea, cleverly worked out. It is extremely interesting throughout. The *dénouement* is strikingly artistic, whilst the 'punishment' is as severe and terrible as the whole faculty could desire.

'This Troublesome World' may perhaps to the general novel-reader have more of actual interest. It is well constructed and strong in plot, and is full of dramatic incident. The short scene between the Dean of St. Joseph's and Brian is exquisite in its touch. Again the 'family friend' partly collaborated, in as far as the whole idea was discussed with him, and he rendered extensive help in the passage exclusively connected with his own profession. But a barrister might have been consulted too, judging by the masterly way in which the trial scenes are handled. So anxious was the author to be absolutely accurate in all technicality and detail that she spent two whole days in court during a similar trial.

The same physician has helped her with a series of complete stories, entitled 'Extracts from the Diary of a Doctor,' which first ran through the 'Strand Magazine' and excited considerable attention.

Mrs. Meade's room where all these literary labours are carried on is small, but so well arranged that everything is at hand. The pictures are all good, from the photogravure of Mr. Watts down to the eight, in one frame, original drawings by G. M. E. Edwards of the author's successful book, 'A World of Girls.' A portrait that she greatly treasures is of Mrs. Meade's most valued friend, the late Mrs. Kingsley, and is inscribed in the deceased lady's own hand, 'On my 71st birthday.' She gave her also the portrait and volumes of her husband's works. These and Ruskin's are her favourite reading. Pinned against the wall are studies in water-colours of flowers and of landscapes done by little Hope Meade, who has not yet attained to the dignity of double figures in age. Here the inheritance of talent is strongly visible in the child's clever indication of tints and correct perspective. 'She is to be trained as an artist,' says her mother; 'she has the real gift, handed down from my great-uncle who served through the Peninsular War, and who was a genius with his brush.'

Mrs. Meade is frank and genial in manner. She possesses an indescribable magnetism that seems to inspire confidence. Presently she goes up to bid good-night to the little ones, and you hear something more of the gifted and sympathetic woman from a young and valued friend of the household.

'Mrs. Meade,' says the girl, with much feeling, 'is so full of tenderness. She cannot hear of any trouble or sorrow without not only wishing but doing her utmost to be of practical help and comfort. The religion that she lives and so instinctively teaches is essentially a religion of brightness and of love.'

MR. AND MRS. FRED TERRY
(JULIA NEILSON)

COMPARATIVELY brief as has yet been the career of these popular young players, it has hitherto been so brilliant, and promises such possibilities for the future, that a slight sketch of their home life and work will interest many who, only seeing them before the footlights, nevertheless love to hear something of the inner surroundings and doings of their favourites. Dame Nature, it must be admitted, has been bountiful to them at the outset in bestowing on both talent, personal attractions, and—what may perhaps be considered quite as useful—a passionate love of their art and a steady determination to work hard and to leave no stone unturned to rise in their mutual profession. Dame Fortune then stepped in and wisely brought them together, with the happy result that each stimulates and encourages the other to increased exertions.

In the old-fashioned neighbourhood of Gower Street there has lately been erected a handsome block of redbrick flats which give a bright bit of colour to the somewhat sombre character of its environs. It is in these buildings that Mr. and Mrs. Fred Terry have located themselves, in a bright and airy suite of chambers which, as may be expected, their artistic tastes have led them to make at once restful to the eye and home-like.

'I must tell you,' says the young actor, as you pause to examine a quaint old brass lamp of antique design, 'that we have both what may be called a positive mania for attending art sales, and we found this lamp in an out-of-the-way place; and, indeed, picked up most of our possessions in the same way.' A most noticeable 'possession,' however, became theirs in quite a different manner, and was a wedding gift from the Hon. John Collier of his own painting. It is a life-size and beautifully executed portrait of Julia Neilson as Drusilla Ives, in long *vieille rose* robe, which presents a fine effect of colour standing out against the background of crimson curtains in bold relief.

Those who remember sweet Kate Terry (Mrs. Arthur Lewis), erstwhile idol of the public, in the zenith of her brilliant but brief stage career, cannot fail to be struck with the strong likeness this youngest brother, Fred, bears to her. Indeed, the 'Terry' face, the 'Terry' charm and grace of manner, even the 'Terry' voice, so rich and musical, are strongly recognisable in each member of this gifted family. But the door opens, and the little group entering completes a living picture of happy domestic life. The beautiful, joyous girl, in all the pride of early motherhood, is Julia Neilson, 'Mrs. Fred,' and the fair, smiling babe in her arms is her son, while a lovely little maiden of about three summers clings to her dress, now hiding in pretended shyness, anon peeping out playfully to attract her attention.

Among many pieces in which Fred Terry and Julia Neilson have acted together there is one, called 'Tragedy and Comedy,' which will ever have a peculiarly tender association in both their minds, for it was then that they first met, he playing D'Aulnay to her Clarice. It seems, on looking back, but a slight stretch of years since you remember Fred Terry, when yet in his teens, scoring a success in the *rôle* of Bertie Fitzurse, with his sister, Ellen Terry, in 'New Men and Old Acres,' and later in Sebastian to her Viola; yet from that time to his late part of Robert Llewellyn, M.P., in Mr. Comyns Carr's play, 'A Leader of Men,' at the Comedy Theatre, he has played nearly a couple of score of original characters, such as Gerald Arbuthnot in 'A Woman of No Importance,'

Prince Léon d'Auvergne in 'The Tempter,' Christian in 'The Dancing Girl,' Philammon in 'Hypatia,' Gerald Cazenove in 'The New Woman,' &c., while at revivals he has had a large and varied *répertoire*, and has impersonated the leading parts of Prince Alexis in 'The Red Lamp,' the Dauphin in 'King John,' the twin brothers (George and Gerald Anstruther) in 'Marina,' and Eugene Lambert in 'The Pompadour,' &c. Nor must his Charles Surface be omitted, for his masterly and artistic rendering of that character won him special commendation.

'It really was quite by an accident,' remarks Fred Terry, 'that I went on the stage at all, and the whole thing seemed to be settled in about five minutes. I had come over for a holiday from Genoa, where I was being educated for business, and one morning I went with my sister Marion to her rehearsal. "Money" was then to be brought out at the old Prince of Wales's Theatre. Mr. Bancroft asked me if I intended "to cast in my lot with the players?" I replied "No, I'm far too nervous." Presently he invited me to "walk on," at a small weekly salary, by way of overcoming my "stage fright."' 'And,' he adds, after a pause, with a laugh, 'that was how I became an actor.'

Fred Terry's modesty, however, has prevented him from stating what his present biographer—who has known him from childhood and watched his each upward step with interest—is able to record—viz., that from his first speaking part he displayed such a strong talent for histrionic art, and so much ease of manner on the stage, together with plenty of shrewd, practical common sense and good judgment, that it was at once decided commerce should go by the board, and the study of art should take its place. A severe course of training in the provinces followed, and he served his apprenticeship in several tours with the late Mr. Charles Kelly, Mrs. Chippendale, and other good stock companies; later he made a trip to America with Miss Fortescue before beginning in good earnest his London career, which has been so distinguished.

Julia Neilson-Terry, too, in these few years has made her name in many original parts, such as the aforesaid Drusilla Ives in the 'Dancing Girl,' Hester Worsley in 'A Woman of No Importance,' Lady Isobel in 'The Tempter,' &c., &c. Having a strong gift for music, she had at first intended to adopt the operatic stage as a profession, and for that purpose she entered the Royal Academy of Music as a pianiste. Presently she found herself the happy possessor of a fine voice too, and, changing her subject, she directed her attention to its cultivation, becoming a pupil of Signor Randegger. Diligent study, combined with her own natural gifts, soon won for her the Westmoreland scholarship, the Sainton-Dolby prize, and, later, the much-coveted Llewellyn Thomas gold medal for declamatory singing.

'Here is the medal,' says the young actress, 'in our "silver" table, where we keep our most cherished souvenirs. The picture,' she adds softly and with pathos, 'you will recognise, as you knew her so well,' and she places in your hands a miniature of the late Mrs. Terry, so tenderly beloved, who passed into the 'great beyond' a few years ago.

Presently, over a friendly cup of tea, the subject of 'first appearances' is discussed, and Julia Neilson remarks, 'I owe a debt of gratitude to Sir Joseph Barnby. He was always most kind to me, and introduced me to Mr. W. S. Gilbert, who interested himself keenly on my behalf, and suggested a stage career.' After a few preliminary efforts, to test her powers, in amateur performances for some charity, Mr. Gilbert—ever so ready to advance and encourage a talented and promising *débutante*—took up the matter, and she made her 'first appearance' as a professional in his play, 'Pygmalion and Galatea,' as Cynisca, followed by Lady Hilda in 'Broken Hearts' and Silene in 'The Wicked World' at matinées. The next step was a

provincial tour with Mr. Beerbohm Tree's company in
'Captain Swift,' which considerably increased her practical experience. On her return to London she first fulfilled a long engagement at the Haymarket in 'A Man's
Shadow,' and this brought her to the time of the—to both
young players—ever-to-be-remembered 'Tragedy and
Comedy.' Now, although Julia Neilson laughingly confesses to being 'terribly nervous, yet always trying to hide
it,' it must be specially recorded that there is an entire
absence of self-consciousness about her which is, perhaps,
one of the young actress's greatest charms—no 'posing,'
or striving after effect. With all her personal attractions
she is just as natural and unaffected as her little daughter
yonder. The child is gazing up at a stuffed white pheasant
on the top of the mantelshelf, and asking for it. There
is a little story attached to this bird. One day Mr. Fred
Terry was invited to a shooting party. As he gets no
practice, and is, moreover, short-sighted, he had not expected to do much execution, but he was too good a shot
on that day. He was told that a rare white pheasant often
made its appearance, and its life must be tenderly respected.
Up rose a covey; he fired away, and just that one prohibited bird fell to his unlucky gun, and there it stands
looking plaintively at him—a mute reproach!

As Lady Chiltern in 'An Ideal Husband,' and in the
pieces that followed, it was universally recognised that
Julia Neilson made a considerable rise upward in her profession and exhibited a wonderful increase of dramatic
power and pathos. London, however, will see no more of
the young players for several months, as they are engaged
to make a long tour in America with Mr. Hare's
company.

KATE RORKE

(MRS. GARDINER)

IN a long, broad road, situated among the heights of north-western London, there stands in its own gardens a picturesque and unpretentious little house, built something after the bungalow type, with a gravel sweep in front and narrow flower-beds and trees around. The hall door opens and discloses the most bewitching little fair, curly-headed boy of some three years, with bright blue eyes, who hospitably bids you come in, holds up a little rosebud mouth for a kiss, and lisps, 'Auntie is coming.' In less than a minute his words are verified, and 'Auntie,' in the person of the popular actress, Miss Kate Rorke, appears.

Now it must be candidly confessed that if there be one thing in creation—nay, two things—before which you absolutely 'go down,' they are personal beauty and a rich, sweet voice. Nature has been very bountiful in these respects to Miss Rorke, and has likewise been lavish with many another gift, irrespective of her special and delightful histrionic powers. The voice may be described as a contralto with some melodious high notes in it while speaking. The slight, girlish figure, clear, creamy complexion, and deep grey eyes, with a laughing light in them, have an attraction all their own; and these outward charms are increased by the natural grace and sweetness of manner and the pure, true heart that beats within, which all conspire to make the talented young actress so winning and lovable.

Two long French windows open on to the lawn, where just in front stands a weeping ash, with boughs bending over to the ground; but though just now bereft of its greenery, in summer it is generally converted into a charming little *al-fresco* dining-room. Here Mr. and Mrs. Gardiner are wont to eat an early breakfast, ofttimes luncheon and dinner too, surrounded by an old mulberry tree and apple and pear trees which yield abundant fruit; but Miss Rorke sighs as she says that it is rumoured the railway company has cast a covetous eye on the place—indeed, further, that it has an evil and sinister design on it, in which case away will go the dear little house, trees, garden, and all; and the thought is already like a nightmare to both husband and wife.

There are many interesting and treasured reminiscences of her theatrical career to be seen. The great silver George III. bowl on the grand piano was a wedding gift from Mr. Hare, who also presented the silver-framed photograph of himself as Mr. Goldfinch on the one hundredth night of 'A Pair of Spectacles,' which, oddly enough, was his own silver wedding day. The exquisite gondola, lightly poised, as if in the act of moving, on a bronze and silver mount, was Sir Augustus Harris's marriage gift to Mr. Gardiner; and there is one much-prized relic to which Miss Rorke calls attention—a pair of old paste shoe-buckles. 'They belonged,' she says, 'to Edmund Kean; next they came into the possession of Mrs. Charles Kean, who gave them to the late Mr. David James, whose widow gave them to me.' The art-blue paper of the drawing-room walls makes a fine background for many good paintings and large Japanese plates; the Indian matting border brings into relief the subdued tints of a warm Persian carpet; and the high white mantel-shelf is adorned with many effective bits of oriental ware; two or three old marqueterie cabinets and bureaus, some comfortable lounges, and the fair child playing on a gigantic tiger-skin complete the domestic picture.

In herself Kate Rorke originates her artistic gifts. The only former members of the family who had been before the footlights were her mother's cousins, Nelly and Louie Moore, and her maternal grandfather, Mr. Thomas Whittall, a great Shakespearian student, known now only to playgoers of a past generation. Her husband is, of course, well known on the stage, and now her young brother, aged nineteen, Edwin Rorke, is going to follow suit. Her own first performance, when yet a child, was as one of a group of pretty little girls who 'walked on' in ' Olivia' with bouquets, which one or other offered to the leading lady; and she speaks of her delight when Miss Ellen Terry singled her out for notice, and asked, ' Won't you give me your bouquet to-night?' ' She was so kind to me,' says the young actress with enthusiasm. ' She used to take me to her dressing-room, and when she once put on a little coral necklet I had, I felt more proud than if the Queen had sent me a diamond collar!' Her next performance was at the Haymarket as one of the girls in ' School.' Miss Rorke's first big part came off in Albery's adaptation of ' Little Miss Muffet' at the Criterion. This was the crucial test when the young girl showed of what mettle she was made. ' Mr. Wyndham,' she remarks, ' who is such a manager for giving a *débutante* a chance, and such an able master, told me I looked the part, but if at rehearsal I could not manage it I must not mind being taken out.' Needless to say, she was not 'taken out,' and there scored her first success. Since that day each step has been upward. Triumph after triumph followed, and she has never been out of an engagement. ' In a good day and hour, be it spoken,' she quotes, laughing. At a *matinée* of Sydney Grundy's ' Silver Shield ' it will be remembered how she electrified the audience by the extraordinary power that she displayed in the strongly emotional part of the heroine. Dora, in ' Diplomacy,' was another of her happiest creations. She accompanied Mr. Hare to Balmoral when this piece was played before the Queen, and confesses to have been much delighted when the Empress Eugénie remarked to her: ' You have a beautiful contralto voice.'

It was after the conclusion of ' The Profligate ' (at the Garrick), in which she impersonated with such infinite pathos and strength the leading *rôle*, that Mr. Hare asked her to take the original part of Mrs. Goldfinch in 'A Pair of Spectacles,' but to refuse if she did not think it suited her. Kate Rorke, however, had no such feeling. She took it heartily and made it all her own. 'The pretty comedy with a funny little exit,' she calls it. The play ran for eighteen months.

An awkward little incident happened in the very early days of her career, when she was but a child. She had to open the play as a servant girl, and come on to make some slight remark and look for something; but the next to follow made a mistake about the cue, and did not appear in time. Then came a most embarrassing 'wait.' Her presence of mind was equal to the moment. She improvised suitable words, moved about, looked up the chimney —everywhere, 'though the minutes felt like hours,' she says, laughing—and carried it off, luckily, unperceived in front.

Kate Rorke describes her histrionic career to have been 'more than commonly happy, and the season of "Diplomacy" perhaps the happiest year of all. A stage life,' she explains, 'is in many respects an extraordinary life. There must be hard work—there may be some disappointments, some worries, but these are to be found in all lives; but I can honestly say that in my experience I have never heard a word to blush for in the green-room or seen anything that I should be ashamed for a daughter —if I had one—to see. Certainly most of the people with whom I have been brought in contact have been charming. Indeed, now I come to think of it,' she adds, reflectively, 'I believe they have been all charming!'

And the beautiful young wife's words bear their own significance.

EDWARD TERRY

IF a man's surroundings in any way indicate his temperament, it needs but a glance at Mr. Edward Terry's house and well-appointed grounds at Barnes to be assured of his artistic tastes and of his happy, optimistic disposition. Within all is bright and beautiful; but, as the day is far too fine to spend indoors, the popular and kindly comedian suggests a stroll round the gardens, which are his special delight. The long French windows open on a wide verandah, whence, apparently, a human voice utters a cheerful 'Good morning,' but it proceeds from a grey parrot—a first-rate mimic and a great pet with the family. Steps lead down, terrace fashion, to the lawn, which is dotted with fine old trees—deodars, araucarias, chestnuts, and almonds in blossom, and one of the largest maples in England. Flowers are everywhere, and on the right is the tennis ground; extending further is a large kitchen garden and various glass-houses for peaches, vines, orchids, palms, and ferns. Winding paths lead to a rosery on the left, and secluded, shady walks branch into the orchard, which contains, among a variety of fruit trees, mulberry, quince, and walnut. Quite in the foreground stands a picturesque ivy-covered ruin, which looks as if it might have been there for centuries, but Mr. Terry laughingly pronounces it to be only a 'dummy,' and its age about fifty years. The elms are of the time of Cromwell, and there is one particular old tree where the doves pair every season. There is a thorough absence of formality and an old-world air of quiet and restfulness throughout this charming place that banish the very thought of the great metropolis, which lies so near. 'I love every sign and sound of country life,' says the famous comedian, as he leads the way to the well-kept poultry yards and stables. 'I love to be awoke by the songs of birds, and never allow any to be destroyed. I would rather lose my fruit and save my feathered friends. Up yonder I am laying out new fern banks, and the ground will be carpeted with my favourite flowers—violets and primroses. No ribbon borders for me! I planted that sweetbriar hedge near to waft its fragrance into the sitting rooms.' The little study is reached through the long window at the back, and here Mr. Terry stores his curios from many foreign countries, for he has been a great traveller. The old alpenstock is a reminiscence of his ascent of Mont Blanc; the quaint sundial of the Himalayas; another, carrying out the same idea, he found in North Norway; the old carved brass ball-lamp at Jeypore. 'Yes,' he says, 'I have been to many parts of the world—India, Australia, Ceylon, Russia, Spain, Lapland, Poland—almost everywhere except to Monte Carlo!'

Edward Terry inherits his histrionic gifts from his father, who, however, had left the stage before his son was born. He supposes the talent 'broke out somewhere,' for he had had other views of a career, and after schooldays soon began to act in private theatricals. His first public appearance, while yet in his teens, was at Christchurch, Hants, followed by tours through Guernsey, Isle of Man, Belfast, Newcastle, &c. He made his *début* in London at the Surrey Theatre as Finnikin Fusselton in 'A Cure for the Fidgets,' and the following year he appeared at the Lyceum as the First Grave Digger in a revival of 'Hamlet.' Then, joining the Strand company, he made his first big hit as the King of Toledo in H. J. Byron's burlesque, 'The Pilgrim of Love,' where his comic singing, dancing, mock-melancholy, and extraordinary powers of facial expression kept the house in roars of laughter. Among a host of early original parts he played Kalyba in Burnand's burlesque of 'Sir George and a Dragon,' Polyphloisboie in 'Orion,' Lieutenant Lamb in Byron's comedy of 'Old Sailors,' and Cassidy in his 'Old Soldiers.' Then, in Mr. Farnie's burlesques, 'Nemesis' and 'Jack Sheppard,' Mr. Terry played respectively Calino and the

Widow Sheppard, succeeded by the *rôle* of Captain Ginger in Byron's popular comedy, 'Weak Woman,' which, after twenty years, is still so great a favourite that, when on tour, especially at Dublin, if the play be not produced, the people 'write to the papers' to complain. He next joined Mr. Hollingshead's company at the Gaiety, and among a variety of parts played the original *rôles* of the King of Spain in 'Little Don Cæsar de Bazan,' Devilshoof in 'The Bohemian Gyurl,' Mephistopheles in 'Little Doctor Faust' (burlesques), and the title *rôle* of Burnand's comedy 'Jeames.' In later years, and before he went into management, some of his parts were Beppo in 'Fra Diavolo,' Ali Baba in the 'Forty Thieves' (where he originated the saying, 'We are a merry family, we are,' and imitated Chaumont so well), 'Robbing Roy'—a real travesty indeed—Camaralzaman and Petit Pois in 'Blue Beard,' in which he sang the famous song, 'Off to the Bodega,' and executed the well-remembered dance. Mr. Terry was the first to introduce the Polyglot song in French, German, English, and Welsh languages, for he is a great linguist. Indeed, on one occasion, when he had given a performance in Wales, it was remarked in a local journal that his fluency in Welsh was marvellous. Some Englishman, however, contradicted this, and said there was nothing 'marvellous' in it, as it was not Welsh at all, but just gibberish; whereupon he was severely censured by the same journal for 'fooling' the people, until it was discovered that it was real and very good Welsh after all. There was a song, too, in 'Camaralzaman' that he used to give in five different tongues, including Russian, and, though all the words were nonsense, he sang them in the correct language of each, and in very good Russian and rhyme. While waiting for the completion of his own theatre Mr. Terry took the Olympic and brought out the amusing play, 'The Churchwarden,' carrying it on later to Terry's Theatre, where it had a good run, and was followed by one hundred and twelve nights of 'The Woman-

Hater.' Mr. Pinero wrote for him the comedies of 'The Rocket' and 'In Chancery,' in both of which he played between five and six hundred times. Of only eight plays that Mr. Terry has found it necessary to produce during his eight years of management, that most touching and exquisite piece of Pinero's, 'Sweet Lavender,' ranks high. No less than six hundred and seventy times did he impersonate, with so much power and tender pathos, the hero, Dick Fennell, in London alone, besides over three hundred times in the country. 'But what a Ruth Rolt Carlotta Addison made!' he remarks, adding presently, in a meditative voice, 'Charming actress—charming woman! The sorrows of those two characters were very real to us both! I had a letter from a clergyman during the run of "Sweet Lavender," asking if I thought it right to make such a hero for people to laugh at—he had not seen it then—but later, when he had found it to be one who made people weep instead, he wrote me I was quite right.' It was while this play was going on that Mr. Terry was asked to read a paper at the Church Congress on 'Amusements in Relation to Christianity'—a non-combative and highly successful address, which he had to give again at an overflow meeting. Mr. Pinero's play, 'The Times,' held the theatre for four months. There was one terribly tragic situation with which Mr. Terry so completely identified himself that night after night his imagination ran riot in it, and he suffered the actual pangs of the hero so severely that it had what he describes as 'an awful effect' on him. A late play that was brought out was 'An Innocent Abroad,' which was written in England but never produced; then, taken to America, re-written, and brought to him, again made ready for playing, and proved a great success. Its run had to be cut short to make way for 'The Blue Boar'—his latest of all in London—which, in its turn, came to a too early end, as he had let his theatre for the season.

As may be supposed of an actor so full of quiet, refined

mirth, he has a fund of humorous stories, and enjoys a joke. It struck him as 'funny' when one day the oldest inhabitant—then unknown to him—stopped and said, sadly, 'You are Terry, the comic actor?' 'Yes,' replied the comedian; 'but why?' 'Ah!' remarked the old gentleman, more cheerfully, 'I buried Drinkwater Meadows, and I remember him and Charlie Mathews when they used to play about on the village green like a couple of boys.'

An expert at the fire appliances of a theatre, Mr. Terry was invited to be the judge by the Society of Arts when a prize was offered for the best method of putting out fires. In his own building he has inaugurated a system of which when a question was asked in the House of Commons the answer was in its favour. His check-takers are all trained firemen—eleven in number—an organised body gathered from the Metropolitan Fire Brigade Association. Behind the scenes he has 'sprinklers' enough to drown a stage, and a fire drill is held once a fortnight. So experienced has this well-disciplined staff proved that four times they have been called out to extinguish fires in the neighbourhood. For fifteen years Mr. Terry served on the Board of Guardians for the parish, and, with the relief of the needy members of his own profession ever at his heart, he founded the Strand Theatrical Provident and the Actors' Benevolent Funds, for both of which the Covent Garden Fund—also founded by a comedian—gave him the idea. He is also trustee for the Dramatic Sick Fund, and did his best to save the Dramatic College, but found it a forlorn hope. Though 36,000l. were earned for it by the profession, the eleven inmates only got 300l., while it took 1,300l. a year to keep it up, and it was, through his influence, accordingly closed.

Mr. and Mrs. Terry have an only son, who has joined the stage—hitherto chiefly with country companies—and shows fair promise of following in his distinguished father's footsteps. One daughter has lately married, and one fair young maiden is at home, but the mention of the family would be incomplete without the introduction of 'Sentry,' a fine dog of the St. Bernard species.

A courteous gentleman, a good friend, the polished and delightful actor is naturally extremely popular. His managerial duties seem to sit somewhat lightly on his shoulders. 'The public and the Press,' says Edward Terry, 'have always treated me very kindly, and taken me as a friend. I have never been concerned in a *fiasco* as yet; but though I love my profession well,' he adds, with a smile, while a mischievous twinkle lurks in the merry blue eyes, 'I think some of my happiest hours are spent in pottering about among my ferns, animals, birds, and flowers.'

MARY MOORE

(MRS. JAMES ALBERY)

In one of the broad terraces commanding a fine view of Regent's Park there stands a certain white house where the popular actress, Miss Mary Moore, has lately established herself. The interior has a distinctive character of its own; evidences of refined and artistic tastes are at once noticeable, and, without any particular display, there is a sense of fitness and restfulness all round. The subdued tones of a thick Persian carpet throw up the prevailing scheme of pale pink and white, and set off to advantage the white furniture of the Empire period and the pure white woodwork and delicate Goupil pictures on the walls. Close by the arch (draped with tapestry hangings) that divides the two rooms stands a low table on which is placed a quaint old jar filled with sprays of the graceful white lilac blossoms drooping over its edges; the fragrant yellow mimosa grouped here and there mingles its sweet perfume, and a few choice specimens of Sèvres china add their old-world tints to produce a harmonious whole. 'I chose the house,' says Mary Moore, 'principally for the sake of the fine air and the beautiful view. I dislike being shut in, and it is so delightful to see the trees and grass in front. It is almost like being in the country.' And, indeed, it is difficult to realise that this terrace is actually not a mile from the heart of busy, bustling London, for as far as eye can travel, right and left, and opposite, there is an expanse of fresh, green grass; multitudes of birds are singing merrily in the grand old trees of the picturesque park, now breaking out into young spring foliage, and all Nature seems awake and rejoicing in the bright sunshine of a cloudless morning.

Altogether unlike the career of most of her sister artists in the theatrical profession has been that of Mary Moore. She had no histrionic inheritances, no opportunity of long study on provincial tours, no moving about from one theatre to another, but the whole of her art life has been confined to one theatre, and under its able manager, Mr. Charles Wyndham, she has so developed her natural talents that she has during the last few years won for herself the position of leading lady at the Criterion. Neither did she come before the public in children's parts, nor even begin to act at all until after her marriage; though, as that event took place at the early age of sixteen, she may fairly be said to have made her start as a young girl. She had, however, always been devoted to the theatre, and had a great wish to go on the boards, and on marrying Mr. Albery, the well-known author of 'The Two Roses,' she naturally began to take a still keener interest in all things connected with the profession. She used to attend regularly all the rehearsals of her husband's pieces, and make herself acquainted with the 'business,' and thus the longing increased to cast in her lot with the players. Mr. Albery was at first opposed, and would often jokingly tease her by saying he had got a part which would exactly suit her, but when it came to the point he would hesitate and refuse. However, a day arrived when circumstances further stimulated her desire; but then came the question how to get a start. Mary Moore took her courage in both hands and went round to many friends—Sir Augustus Harris, Messrs. James and Thorne, and others—who were all very kind, but said they could do nothing until she had had some experience. But it needs help to gain experience, and this help was kindly given to her by a great friend, Mrs. Bronson Howard, who coaxed her brother, Mr. Wyndham, to take the would-be *débutante* in hand. He gave her an engagement as understudy in his country company, then starting on tour with 'The Candidate,' with a promise of a small part within a few weeks. 'But it was only his kind way,' says Mary Moore, 'of putting money into my pocket, for I found out that he had never really meant me to play at all. He told his sister I looked far too sad for the stage.' And the large, melting brown eyes have, perhaps, in repose, a somewhat saddened expression—for she has had her share in the sorrows of life—but the least change of thought alters this, and they flash out into a bright beam of mirth, and a happy smile lights up the pale, sweet face when she speaks of having 'fought with these troubles and surmounted them, and looking forward to a cheerful old age, when, having worked to educate her children, they will be a help and comfort to her.' All this seems to be ridiculous just now, and to be 'looking forward' a long way; for with slight, lithe figure, youthful face and calm, unruffled brow, Mary Moore looks like a girl just out of her teens. After a hearty laugh together over the cheerfully drawn picture of the future, you settle down to hear of the past and the present. 'As you will imagine,' she says, 'I could not entertain any such idea, kind as it was. A few weeks later I duly reported myself at Liverpool, where the company was playing, then hastened back to town, and arrived just before the performance was over at the Criterion. Mr. Wyndham was surprised to see me, and asked what I was doing there, as I ought to be in Liverpool. I told him I realised his kind intention towards me, but that I was too independent to avail myself of it, even if it could have benefited me, which was impossible, as a salary then would not keep me in the future, and I wanted practice in the profession I had chosen. I said that it depended entirely on him if I went back to Liverpool, as it was useless to do so unless he promised me a part.' Seeing her determination, the kindly manager consented. She returned, played Lady Oldacre in 'The Candidate,' for the remainder of the run, and then came back to London and renewed the *rôle* with him at the Criterion Theatre. Having got her footing, Mary Moore took good care not to lose it, and there she has remained ever since, working hard, so that each step might lead her upward. Her next part was in a farcical comedy called 'The Man with Three Wives.' Quite different was the succeeding *rôle* of Lady Amaranth on the revival of 'Wild Oats.' Mary Moore's quiet, innocent young face and manner were exactly suited to the demure, modest little Quakeress, and it was her first chance of making a big success. She won universal commendation by the simplicity and good style of her acting, and this led on to the part of Ada Ingot in 'David Garrick,' a character that she has impersonated many hundred times both in English and in German, and one in which she never fails to please. She has two valued souvenirs of her Ada Ingot; a beautiful diamond and ruby brooch, presented to her by the Czar when she played it before him at St. Petersburg, and a handsome album given to her by her Teutonic colleagues after her performance at Berlin. Later, Mary Moore acted Mrs. Mildmay in 'Still Waters Run Deep,' Grace Harkaway in 'London Assurance,' Miss Hardcastle in 'She Stoops to Conquer,' Jessie Keber in Henry Arthur Jones's 'The Bauble Shop,' &c. &c. These good comedy characters, always well thought out and well studied, were excellent parts in which to gain experience for an actress who combines, with so much delicacy and refinement, a bright, vivacious sparkle of humour. They brought out all the force of character that lies under the calm exterior, and when the time came for the production of 'An Aristocratic Alliance' her friends all agreed that never had she played more charmingly nor more sympathetically than as Lady Forres, the shy, devoted, but jealous wife. The above are but a few of the *rôles* she has enacted; probably her best of all is her creation of Lady Susan Harabin in Mr. Henry Arthur Jones's delightful piece 'The Case of Rebellious Susan,' in which she displayed an earnestness and devotion that raised it to the dignity of fine art. Her latest performance is Adeline Dennant in 'The Squire of Dames' at the Criterion.

Among many reminiscences of her stage life, scattered about here and there, are two dainty feather screens. These are souvenirs of a visit paid to Sandringham, when she accompanied Mr. Wyndham's company to play in 'David Garrick.' Shortly after the Prince of Wales sent her a hamper of game, and, selecting the finest pheasants' feathers, she designed and carried out the screens as a memento of the occasion. The photograph, standing on a cabinet, signed 'May of Teck' is a Royal gift. During several visits to the Engadine Miss Moore had the honour of meeting the Duchess of Teck and her daughter, then unmarried, and describes them as 'always very gracious' to her. She sent a photograph in her possession to Princess May, and asked her to sign it, which H.R.H. not only did, but explained that she was also sending another that she liked much better for Miss Moore's acceptance, and this is justly a valued treasure. Another is a picture by Mr. Whistler on a white wood easel, a gift from the artist, accompanied by a letter saying that he 'sent it as a compensation for having been so dull the evening before when he met her out at dinner.' 'To this,' says Miss Moore, laughing, 'there could obviously be but one reply—that, though I had not perceived the dulness, I should be glad if he were equally so on the next occasion if it always produced such happy results.' There is one feature of her own design in the room that is particularly attractive, and this is a white wood arrangement for holding photographs. It extends nearly all round, and here, side by side, are portraits of many friends in and outside the profession.

The two chief characteristics of the charming player are her ardent desire to please and her extreme modesty regarding her own performances. Never resenting criticism, when she observes in Press notices any suggestions which strike her as being desirable to adopt, she will frankly think them well out and act accordingly. Hence her clever impersonation of Lady Susan—artistic and striking as it was at first—gained considerable power and charm. 'But I am a wretched " first-nighter,"' says Mary Moore, shaking her head ruefully, ' and I owe any success that I may have made to Mr. Wyndham's careful and excellent system of coaching.'

CLIFFORD HARRISON

IT speaks volumes for Mr. Clifford Harrison's powers of entertaining that, on a succession of Saturday afternoons in midsummer, with the rival attractions of Sarasate at St. James's Hall, sundry *matinées* at theatres, polo at Hurlingham, not to speak of river parties and other country amusements, he can, single-handed, keep a crowded audience enthralled and spell-bound for two hours. Now he brings his hearers to the verge of tears by his exquisite and tender pathos ; anon peals of subdued laughter ripple through Steinway Hall as, with an incomparable sense of humour and with the utmost delicacy and refinement, he indicates the comic side of a situation.

Mr. Clifford Harrison's home is situated at the corner of a great square, just where the garden terminates in a

MR. CLIFFORD HARRISON

point—opposite St. Saviour's Church—which makes a picturesque object in the foreground with its creepers and line of trees running down one side; from the left can be seen the barges floating up and down the river. Within the house a recess, half-way up the stairs, forms a perfect bower of palms, ferns, and flowering plants; the long French windows of the double drawing-rooms open out on a broad verandah, with wicker chairs and little tables under the awning, which makes a pleasant retreat on a sultry evening. The polished floors are partially covered with thick Persian carpets of subdued tints; the carved white woodwork overmantels hold specimens of china collected from many lands; while a big jar of deep crimson Oriental pottery, high up on a bracket, throws down a bright bit of colour on the collection. The great marqueterie and several other bookcases, in every available space, are loaded with books, for Mr. Harrison is a student of Nature, and declares that 'if a reciter is to hold his own at all he must dig deep in the field of literature, and to study Browning alone requires a mining process, though whenever he opens a volume of that poet he finds a fresh gem.' A little glass-covered table is filled with odds and ends, souvenirs from friends, and on it stands a quaint model of a sedan chair of the past century beautifully painted by hand. In the inner room is a Steinway grand pianoforte, a treasured gift, flanked by more bookcases, on one of which is a formidable line of books of recitation, those of each author in a separate compartment. Comfortable lounges, saddle-bag chairs, Eastern screens, inlaid tables, and Egyptian curios complete a picture of the quiet home life of one who, so thoroughly imbued with artistic tastes, is under the necessity of leading a comparatively placid existence outside his professional career. A long and serious illness, which left a delicacy of the chest, obliged Mr. Clifford Harrison to eschew society and festive gatherings, where he was so bright an ornament, and to betake himself for six months of every year to the more genial climate of the South of France.

The paintings on the walls are chiefly by old masters—Berghem, Domenichino, Zaccarelli, Canaletto, Salvator Rosa, &c.—but among them is an effective little water-colour sketch of the impressionist school which he regards with peculiar affection. It is a view of Montreux, a place endeared to him by many recollections. Going there when utterly broken down in health, he declares that in his time of desperate illness he received such devoted kindness from his friends as he can never forget, while in his opinion 'there is something in the splendid air of the place that is peculiarly nourishing to all forms of kindness.' Altogether he will remember, with life-long love and gratitude, a spot that had such beneficence of healing in it, and the skill and care which brought that healing home to him.

From his childhood Clifford Harrison was trained in the atmosphere of art. He was born at Henley, and is the third son of the late Mr. William Harrison, so renowned as the manager of the English Opera Company that was called by his name. It will be remembered by playgoers of a quarter of a century back that he created the tenor part of Wallace's 'Maritana' and that of Thaddeus in Balfe's 'Bohemian Girl.' He possessed many physical advantages; he was strikingly handsome, of dignified bearing and of noble presence. He was likewise gifted with strong histrionic powers, a thorough love of music, and a beautiful tenor voice; indeed, his rendering of the famous song, 'When other lips,' can never be forgotten by those who were privileged to hear him. On the maternal side Mr. Clifford Harrison also inherits dramatic talents. His grandmother, Mrs. W. Clifford, daughter of a leading physician at Bath, acted with Macready and the Kembles, with Edmund Kean, and with Mrs. Siddons. She was in the original cast of the 'Lady of Lyons,' and distinguished herself as Lady Macbeth, Meg Merrilies, &c., and was a friend and contemporary of Helen Faucit (Lady Martin). His mother, too, Ellen Clifford, was on the stage a short time before she married; and from her Mr. Harrison inherits the wonderful memory and quick study that enabled her when quite a girl to learn in one day the whole part of Goneril in 'King Lear' and to play it letter-perfect the same night. It had happened that Mrs. Clifford, whose *rôle* it was, found herself one morning taken ill with acute headache, and the young Ellen went to Macready to explain that her mother could not possibly appear that night. Macready insisted that the girl should take her place, which she protested she could not do, not knowing a word of the lines. The great actor, however, coaxed and entreated her, with the result that, beginning at two o'clock, she learned the whole in a few hours and acquitted herself to perfection.

What more natural than that Clifford Harrison should have determined early in life to go on the stage? During schooldays he had visions of being a poet, an actor, a dramatist, a painter, and an author! In a measure all these ideas have been more or less realised; for he wrote a play and introduced two songs, which Balfe set to music; he has written books, one a volume of poems, which is still paying; another in prose called 'Stray Records,' bright, interesting, and full of literary merit; while a third work, entitled 'Lines in Pleasant Places,' is now in the press, and will shortly be issued by Kegan Paul, Trench, & Co.; and it consists of thirty-six rondeaux, each accompanied by a full-page illustration, reproduced from pen-and-ink sketches by himself. Thus it will be seen that his early ambition has been gratified. Shortly after the death of the Prince Consort the decline of the once popular English Opera Company set in. This effected the ruin of its manager—who, from being a very rich man, suddenly became poor—and on his death young Clifford Harrison began his short career as an actor.

He made his first appearance at the age of seventeen

on the boards, at the Theatre Royal, Manchester, and followed it up by a six months' engagement at Sheffield, studying and playing no less than ten or twelve parts every week—in comedy, tragedy, melodrama, and farce. He was in the very last of the old stock companies that are now things of the past; he relates an amusing incident of his enthusiasm as Catesby in 'Guy Fawkes,' when he was so anxious to be shot that he fell down headlong just half a second before the volley was fired, which caused roars of merriment among the audience. It was while at Sheffield that he gave his first public recitation, at the benefit of the leading lady, and chose 'Locksley Hall,' in which he laughingly declares that his youthful audacity and inexperience in selecting such a poem 'between the excitement of melodrama and the laughter of a farce were rewarded, to his surprise, by a recall.' Then for a short time Mr. Clifford Harrison left the stage and went to Cambridge, but the claims of art asserted themselves too strongly to be resisted, and he relinquished college life and returned to the theatre. For a season he played in Byron's comedies with the author, and his last engagement was with Mrs. John Wood at the St. James's Theatre. A chance incident discovered his real vocation. In 1877, Mr. Clifford Harrison gave a recital at St. George's Hall, and at once 'struck oil.' No such scholarly, artistic, and, it may be said, original recitation had yet been given. In a few weeks he had more engagements offered than he could accept, and in a short time he rose to the post which he has long held as the foremost of English reciters. During his first year as a popular entertainer he gave four recitals, the following year twenty-four, and so on, continuously, until 1888, when he was compelled by illness to go abroad. Of late years he has appeared only in summer months at the Steinway Hall, and is forbidden by his medical advisers to accept many private and nearly all public engagements, including flattering offers from America and Australia. In fact, he says his 'private life is now that of a hermit, and he has been obliged to cut the Gordian knot by going nowhere.'

It was soon after his father's death that Mr. Clifford Harrison was brought in contact with the late Rev. Charles Kingsley, rector of Eversley, with whom his brother, the Rev. William Harrison, was then curate. The young actor was in the habit of spending all his spare hours with his brother and their widowed mother at that pleasant country retreat, and became a frequent guest at the rectory. The atmosphere that surrounded Kingsley, at once so intellectual and inspiriting, exercised a powerful influence over the young receptive mind, attuned to noble and elevated desires, and that influence has been ever-abiding. Under Mrs. Kingsley's hospitable roof he enjoyed the advantage of meeting many distinguished visitors, among whom were Froude, Wilberforce, Professor Seeley, and Dr. Benson. In subsequent years the tie between the families was cemented by the marriage of Miss Kingsley— the talented Lucas Malet—to the Rev. William Harrison, now rector of Clovelly. One of Clifford Harrison's best and most popular recitations is 'A Reminiscence of Charles Kingsley,' while in later days his friendship with Browning, Ruskin, George Eliot, Adelaide Anne Procter, &c., further enriched the gifted reciter's large and varied repertory. When the pleasant home at Eversley was broken up he came to London, where his mother shared his home until her lamented death some years after—an event that left a blank in the life of her devoted son over which a veil must be drawn.

Though Mr. Clifford Harrison's art is so true as to seem spontaneous, and thrown off at a minute's notice, as it were, it involves long and continued practice. He spends half the day in rehearsals at his piano, and studies a new piece for months; his musical compositions are all his own, but none are written down. One of the most appreciative of his admirers is H.R.H. the Princess of Wales. He has had the honour of reciting on many occasions at Sandringham, where he was received with much kindness and cordiality, though in his modesty he never advertises the names of his illustrious patrons on the playbills. To see the long, slender fingers glide over the piano and to hear the delicious and soul-thrilling chords which fit in with his story is an intellectual treat. Among many pieces, which to hear once is to remember for ever, the delightful and pathetic compositions, 'The Bel's of Is' (by himself), Ruskin's 'In the Clouds,' Marie Corelli's 'Story of the Priest of Philomen'—a powerful bit of writing magnificently interpreted by Clifford Harrison—Browning's 'Saul,' Edwin Arnold's 'Great Renunciation,' A Tocata of Galluppi's, Rossetti's 'King's Tragedy,' Walt Whitman's 'Passage to India,' enter the mind at random as displaying the poetic and devotional element in his character. But there is one peculiar effect —alike instructive and ennobling—produced by this true artist, an effect which is universally acknowledged; and this is that he introduces his hearers, so to speak, to literature in such a way that when they go home each is fired with a desire to turn up the passages and to search deeper, for him or herself, in perhaps hitherto imperfectly explored books. And after every visit to Steinway Hall one has the sensation of being led upward and onward.

MISS LE THIÈRE.

WHILE climbing up to the second floor of a little house not far from Brook Street a fearful sound of hammering is heard. Can it be possible that you have mistaken the number, and are unwittingly on the way to an undertaker's? But no; the door opens, and, with one last hard hit on the parcel before her, Miss Le Thière rises and greets you smilingly. She has been preparing some wood for carving, whereat she is an adept, and sundry specimens adorn the walls of her modest little rooms, notably a broad frame made out of a single block of wood with grapes and vine leaves beautifully chiselled. Tiny growing plants are hanging here and there; at the south side several little paroquets are chirping in a small aviary, and two pugs, 'Cadawallah' and 'Baby,' nestle close to her, and are her cherished companions. 'My poor friends, wood-carving and lacework, make up my life,' says the actress in the clear, resonant tones so well known to the public; 'but I have a big scheme in the future of which more anon.' But a question naturally arises about the histrionic art life in which she is so distinguished, and to answer it she goes back for a while into an interesting past.

Roma Guillon Le Thière is the daughter of the late Guyon Le Thière, formerly in the Imperial Guard at Waterloo, afterwards a civil engineer. Her grandfather, Captain Augustus Bizet—who was shot in the retreat from Moscow—was Member of the Paris Institute and Director of the French Academy at Rome, in which glorious city she was born. His widow—one of the Harvé D'Egvilles—re-married, and was the celebrated Madame Michau of Brighton, ballet 'master,' teacher of dancing, and mistress of the ceremonies to Kings George IV. and William. Roma Le Thière was brought up by her mother—from whom she inherits her artistic talents—in strict Evangelican doctrines. On the death of her father, pecuniary circumstances made it necessary that the young girl should do something to provide for herself and her beloved mother. Her first step was to write to a valued friend, Mr. George Augustus Sala, and ask his advice. He replied, 'Go on the stage,' to which she answered, 'Have you lost your wits? I know nothing about it.' The journalist knew better. 'Go on the stage,' he reiterated; 'if I know you aright, you will make your way.' Accordingly Miss Le Thière determined to try. 'It was the funniest thing,' she remarks brightly, 'and quite like a little poem. I was a perfect novice, had no idea how to set about it, and, being extremely ignorant, I flew at high game. Off I went to Drury Lane, sent in my card, and requested to see the manager, Mr. F. B. Chatterton. He was engaged, and I made that little pilgrimage ten or eleven times. At last I was told to walk into the greenroom and he would see me. After keeping me waiting for a long time he bustled in, stared hard at me, and asked what I had done. I said it wasn't much. Evidently in despair at the calm young woman who would not be ruffled, he asked testily, "To whom on earth do you belong?" It quickly flashed through my mind that he was not likely to know a single creature belonging to me. After a pause I said, "I am a granddaughter of old Madame Michau of Brighton!" The stern look melted, the little man beamed; he came up and wrung my hands warmly. I was amazed, and could not imagine what had caused the change, but I was still more bewildered when he said, "from this day you belong to my company!" I gasped out "But why?" "Why, indeed!" he remarked with emotion; "for a very good reason. When my father and uncle were struggling young artists they managed to go down to Brighton, and were introduced to your grandmother, and she contrived that they should play before the King, and they subsequently became his harpists!" So you see,' adds Miss Le Thière reverently, 'the bread cast upon the waters came back after many days. He was from that time the best friend I ever had, and to him I owe the inestimable advantage of having been the pupil of Samuel Phelps. In justice to a man against whom much was said let this fact be recorded.' Among many parts, the actress will be well remembered in earlier days as Emilia in 'Othello,' in 'Hunted Down' at the St. James's, in 'Life for Life' at the Lyceum, in 'Ours' at the Prince of Wales's, Helen McGregor in 'Rob Roy,' &c. In later days she created the *rôle* of the tender but stately Marquise de Rio Zarer to perfection. She was engaged by Wilkie Collins to play

Janet Roy in 'The New Magdalen,' at the Standard, with Miss Ada Cavendish in the title *rôle*, and remembers a funny anecdote connected with that piece. Miss Le Thière remarked to her, 'They won't understand Janet Roy down there,' to which Miss Cavendish replied, 'You are mistaken,' and so it proved. At its conclusion on the first night ' Magdalen ' was called and came off laughing. 'What do you think I have just heard?' she said to 'Janet.' 'One gentleman in the gallery shouted to another on the opposite side, " Let's have the h'old woman out!" to which the other indignantly retorted, " She h'aint a h'old 'ooman, you pig, she's a lady!"' Amidst roars of laughter 'Janet' took her call, was applauded to the echo, and speedily became a great favourite. On the last night of the piece Sothern was to take a part in the second play, and while talking to him at the wings Miss Le Thière took off her cap and wig, quite forgetting the ' h'old woman ' would be called. When the call came there was no time to readjust them, so she simply walked on with them in her hand; for a moment the audience hardly recognised her, but presently ringing cheers broke out. ' I thought they would never let me go,' she adds merrily. In 'The Cabinet Minister,' under Mrs. John Wood's management, she played the tyrannical old lady so realistically as to cause two people, who were discussing her, to suggest that she must be ' the most horrible and wicked old woman ever seen,' but this was too much for a girl friend of Miss Le Thière's who sat near and interrupted the speakers with a piteous, ' Oh! no, please don't think Grannie' (as her intimates fondly call her) ' is a bit what you say--dear old thing!' Lady Ashton in ' Ravenswood ' at the Lyceum was another of her characters. ' But the hardest and queerest little bit with which I ever had to deal,' she remarks, ' was the Queen in " Henry VIII." There is nothing I have not played, from the Queen in " Hamlet " down to a rollicking Irishwoman at the Adelphi. I have never hesitated to take anything offered to me;

one of the *rôles* I enjoyed most was a dual part with Rose Leclercq in " A Woman of No Importance." It was delightful to play with her.' The last pieces in which the actress has been seen are ' A Leader of Men,' and ' John a-Dreams,' with Mr. Beerbohm Tree, at the Haymarket.

The lacework of which Miss Le Thière speaks as being a favourite pastime is truly a wonderful production. Judging by the enormous bundles lying here and there, there must be some miles of this fabric, made after old designs in early English, French, and Italian. But there are other bundles also of her own work—knitted woollen garments of every sort, which chiefly find their way to her ' poor friends,' for the actress has a large district in the City, and delights in carrying help and comfort thither to the sick and the afflicted. Although a strict Churchwoman, she makes no distinctions, and the warm, tender heart is open to all alike; but her aid is given in a methodical and practical manner. She wins the confidence and affection of these humble friends, and speaks with joy of their many proofs of appreciation, such as in the case of habitual drunkards, when several took the pledge on her birthday ' because it was the only present we could give you, miss.' ' And they kept it, too,' says Miss Le Thière impressively, while the good, earnest face beams with interest. ' My visits to my district have often comforted me in my own troubles, but I never let my skeletons dance in public. I keep them to perform their little fandangos in strict privacy at home,' she adds, laughing.

Though only in the prime of life, Miss Le Thière meditates retiring from the stage in a year or two in order to devote herself to the great scheme she has in contemplation, which will, however, only bind her more closely to its interests. With a strong talent for organisation and a keen eye for practical business details, she is about to start a new school for the training of *débutantes*.

She has been occupied for two years in the search for suitable premises, but has at last succeeded in her quest. The schoolroom is being built in the form of a large stage. There are no less than six baths in the house, and the whole place is so planned that there shall be plenty of fresh air and light, while the sanitary arrangements are of the most perfect modern type. She intends to have French attendants, for the sake of the language, and the pupils will have the advantage of not one master, but several. For instance, one week old comedies will go on under distinguished teaching; another week Shakespearian plays; and so on. Each department will be provided with the best instructors; dancing, drilling, prosody will be taught, and all the different versifications and rhythms. In short, it is to be in London what the Conservatoire for girls is in Paris, and what they teach there will be taught here. Herself brought up after the sensible manner of French families, where the girls are educated in thrifty habits, and are early made conversant with every domestic occupation, each detail of this admirable establishment will be Miss Le Thière's special care, and will doubtless prove to be of incalculable benefit to the rising generation of young players. Their moral and intellectual training certainly could not be in better hands than those of the noble-hearted and accomplished actress, who, alike in her public and private life, has manifested by her work and her example what a woman with a pure, womanly nature can do for the good of her fellow-creatures. 'All I desire,' she says, in a low voice of pathos, as she bids you good-bye, 'is that when I am gone people will remember me with a kindly "God bless her! She has done what she could."'

W. H. PREECE, C.B., F.R.S.

ALTHOUGH only seven miles away from the busy hum of the Great Metropolis, the high ground on which stands the house of the eminent electrician, Mr. W. H. Preece, might be in the heart of the country from its quietness and picturesque surroundings. Situated on the very corner of the great common at Wimbledon, it commands an extensive view of the neighbouring country, with the woods of Coombe Park in the extreme distance.

The fresh, pure air comes unsullied over the vast open ground; the trees are in full foliage, and the whole place is bathed in the bright sunshine of a clear summer afternoon. Glints of light fall on an old-fashioned, pointed-roofed house, of Gothic build, which, covered with creepers and facing west, stands back in its own grounds from the road.

Originally constructed in the last century, it has been constantly added to and improved by its present owner, who holds the opinion that 'the more beautiful you make the home the more you keep the family together.' In the present instance nothing could have been worked out more satisfactorily. The lines of beauty have been well preserved, while every detail of modern comfort, combined with thorough appreciation of art, are to be observed on all sides. A range of buildings without, on the right, comprise the neatly tiled sloping roof and teak sheds where the electric light is manufactured. This is done by gas instead of steam, and Mr. Preece rightly maintains that he 'is the best friend of the gas companies.' The engine, which is in the first room with the dynamo, works two or three times a week to charge the accumulators, which—stored all round an inner room—are ready to be drawn upon as required.

Beyond the stables and cowhouse, where a lovely soft-eyed Alderney cow—a great pet with the family—chews the cud of contentment, is a long hot-house filled with ferns and palms ; a path leads round to a spacious lawn of undulating ground shaded by great overhanging trees of ancient growth, old medlars, pink and white thorn, apple trees, and well-grown araucarias ; but the great feature of this delightfully old-world spot is the Deciduous Cypress, known to be the tallest in England. The garden was formerly the orchard and musk-garden of Queen Henrietta Maria. It was chiefly the picturesque undulation of ground that decided Mr. Preece to take the house some twenty years ago, the winding paths, rockery, and shady nooks adapting it alike for a merry afternoon party as for luxuriously idling away a hot summer afternoon in solitude.

The back of the house is somewhat of a surprise, and gives an idea of extensive space, with its photographic studio stretching away on one side and the many sexagonal flat bow windows, lattice-paned, above the arched, covered-in verandah—a favourite place for afternoon tea. But if the back of this charming retreat be a surprise, the interior is at once a surprise and a delight. The inner hall, decorated with curios from Australia and South Africa, and one long hanging Persian tile dating from the thirteenth century, opens into all the living rooms, which branch out right and left, the further being a little ante-room with Persian tiles, carpet and hangings and a cosy corner. A few words must be said of the drawing-room, for it is perfectly unique, and has the additional merit of being entirely original in design. An oblong room of pale tint, which displays to the best advantage the collection of blue Persian china on the walls ; two white arches, one leading into the broad flat bay window (looking sideways into the greenhouse), with comfortable lounge below, the other, at right angles, indicate an extension or sort of inner room. In the recesses are imitation doors, made of teak wood, in geometrical designs, with stars and borders of fretwork backed in mirror. Ispahan embroidery, *por-*

tières of gold embroidery on velvet, prayer carpets, choice cabinets, carved Persian chairs and a profusion of flowers; but, with all this wealth of artistic beauty, the room has a thoroughly home-like and domestic appearance. The sunshine throws dancing beams around, lighting up the great arm-chair, where, with her knitting, sits a sweet-faced elderly lady—Mr. Preece's sister—whilst his three young daughters flit about with tea and muffins, and are eagerly watched by a handsome Dachshund (Max) and an odd nondescript sort of dog, who looks as if he had been meant for a poodle but has somehow developed into a miniature Newfoundland. In spite, however, of his obscure and doubtful origin, he has his good points—of character at least—and these are displayed in his amiable nature and fidelity.

The group here assembled is completed by the third son of the house and the distinguished electrician himself, just returned from a committee meeting from some remote part of town. Here for a brief space he throws off the cares of business, and a lively chat follows. Presently, leaving the bright, happy, young people deep in the discussion of some projected amateur theatricals, Mr. Preece takes you to his study, where, notwithstanding the piles of papers, reports, plans, manuscripts, &c.—it is true that some are placed on the floor, but all are neatly heaped up, and it may be called a tidy litter—it is easy to see that he is a man of extreme method. An enormous bureau stands before the octagonal flat bay-window—which has recently been thrown out—with multitudes of drawers, and his writing chair of Savonarola work brought from Florence. Bookcases, of course, on all sides, well crammed; the lowest shelf of one looks as if it contains gigantic volumes, but each is in reality a box, alphabetically labelled, containing notes, memoranda, and slips concerning various scientific matters, upon which he can at once lay his hand if required. The arrangement for electric light is, as may be expected, perfect. Softly shaded, the large centre lamp diffuses its light over the room upwards, and, being reflected from the ceiling, there is none of the glare which is sometimes experienced.

Carnarvon claims the honour of being his birthplace, and King's College, London, may be proud of turning out the brilliant scientist. At school he made his mark as much in athletic sports as in an aptitude for study. He was captain of the eleven and foremost in all games. He had originally intended to enter the army, but his father's death caused a change of plans; other fields of work opened out, and he entered Mr. Edwin Clark's office as a civil engineer.

The young student soon began to show of what mettle he was made. His original scientific bent was fostered and largely developed by his attendance, early in life, at the Royal Institute Lectures, those of Professor Faraday especially interesting him. Possessing unusual ability, indomitable industry, a thirst for knowledge, and a clear, logical mind, he took the keenest delight in the stiff scientific subjects that he heard discussed. Before he became of age he was appointed to the charge of the Electric and International Telegraph Company, and shortly afterwards became superintendent of the Southern District, and of the London and South-Western Railway Company, also engineer of the Channel Islands Telegraph Company. The electric telegraph companies were then private property, but in 1870, when they were transferred to the State, Mr. Preece's services were taken over by Government. Steadily working his way upward, he was appointed Engineer-in-Chief and Electrician to the General Post Office in 1892.

He was made a Fellow of the Royal Society in 1881. His latest and well-merited honour was the dignity of Companion of the Bath conferred upon him by the Queen in an autograph letter from Mr. Gladstone, written on the venerable statesman's eighty-fourth birthday. It is interesting to note that on the day after the notice appeared in the Gazette Mr. Preece received telegrams of congratulation from New York, Adelaide, Sydney, Calcutta, and Ispahan, among many hundreds of letters and wires from Great Britain and the Continent, a testimony to his popularity which has gratified him not a little. From between this large collection a curious post-card drops out bearing the superscription, 'To the clearest-headed Electrician in the General Post Office Buildings.' Post mark, 'New York.'

His remarkable gifts as a lecturer on science have brought him prominently before the public, and it is safe to predict a big crowd in the halls of the Society of Arts or of the Royal Institution when it is known that he is to discourse on some of the marvellous inventions of the electric world of the day. Gifted with a profound sense of humour, he has always some appropriate anecdote or amusing incident to relate; but while it detracts in no way from the dignity of the abstruse subjects on which he speaks, it adds an interest and brightness to his words; indeed, it is on record that on one occasion, when he was asked to deliver a lecture at some learned Society, there were one or two who objected on the ground that 'he was so frivolous!' Besides being a Fellow of the Royal Society, he is a member of more intellectual bodies than one could count—such as the Physical, the Meteorological, the Royal Institution, the British Association, and the Society of Arts. He is likewise a Fellow and a Member of the Council of King's College.

But it is perhaps at the General Post Office, where he is chief over about four thousand persons, that the lovableness and geniality of his nature stand out preeminently. Blest with a great talent for organisation and a thorough worker himself, he has the gift of getting the best work out of his subordinates, and, with the remarkable influence held by a master-mind over his fellow-men, while his discipline is strict he never requires to be severe, and it is well known that his employés would do any mortal thing for him, so strong is their belief in his absolute justice and capability. With the simplicity and modesty that are almost invariably allied to genius, he decided, since his employment in Government service, never to take out patents for his inventions, and he would always rather give the credit of these to his assistants than keep it himself.

Mr. Preece is indeed a hard worker; he certainly may be said to 'burn the candle at both ends,' and, if report be true, he not unfrequently breaks the pieces in order to have more ends to burn; for instance, after a long day at the office or a journey of several hundred miles, he arrives home late, and his scientific work of notes and writing will be done principally at night; then he will 'turn in' and get a brief period of repose; anon he awakes and does three hours' work in bed. This he declares gives him 'a fine pull over his neighbours, and he can always drop off to sleep again.' Doubtless his extremely methodical habits enable him to get through so much work. It is a difficult thing to catch him at home, and an appointment on aught but serious business generally necessitates a three months' notice, during which period a series of forty or fifty letters will generally ensue; for, just as you think that you have fixed him to a date, you find that he has been summoned off in hot haste to Scotland, Ireland, or Wales, on some important committee. Anon, within twenty-four hours of a hoped-for appointment, he has fled to Manchester, Birmingham—where not? As for the list of papers that he has written, they are calculated to make the non-professional head spin. Among several hundreds of these may just be mentioned one, 'On the Co-Efficient of Self-Induction in Telegraph Wires;' another, 'On the Form of Submarine Cables for Long-distance Telephony;' a third, which sounds as if it might have a vein of fun running through it, is called 'A Peculiar Behaviour of Glow-lamps;' whilst a fourth interprets 'Delany's System of Synchronous Multiplex Telegraphy.' His inventions have been not a few. For instance, his new method of duplex telegraphy, of working miniature signals by electricity to assimilate electric signals with out-door signals on railways; locking signals on railways by means of electricity; his new telephone, &c., &c. His latest lecture at the Society of Arts was on the transmission of electric messages without the medium of wires, and for over ten years he has been engrossed by the, to him, fascinating study of signalling through space. Not only has this marvel been actually accomplished, but he has now obtained certain effects which have convinced him, as he in that lecture conveyed, 'that the radiant waves of electricity sent off from a wire running along the cliffs are reflected back as soon as they strike the surface of the water, just as in the case of light falling within the angle of total reflection.' Such signals were sent over five miles, his experiments in Scotland enabling speech to be maintained across an air space of a mile and a quarter. 'So that there is now,' he says, 'no difficulty in communicating with outlying islands without the expense of laying a cable.'

After this miracle of science, who shall say that the great electrician may not shortly project some ingenious contrivance which shall enable him to communicate with the moon and stars? for to one who so faithfully and conscientiously searches into the deep well of science she will yield her richest treasures.

A propos of telephony, Mr. Preece had an amusing reminiscence. Some years ago, when it was getting into work, the Queen was anxious to test its powers, and accordingly arrangements were made to put Osborne, Portsmouth, and London in telephonic communication with each other. With this view Mr. Preece went to Southampton, and it was agreed that a band should play in London at nine o'clock, so that Her Majesty might hear the music. Some slight mishap occurred to the Osborne section of the wire, and the Queen's coming was

delayed. The musicians, after playing some time, were
dismissed. Shortly after, to his consternation, Mr. Preece
received a wire from Osborne stating that the Queen had
arrived and was ready to hear the music. What was to
be done? The band had departed, and there were no
means of providing another! On the impulse of the
moment he decided to perform himself, and hummed
'God Save the Queen' through the telephone. He then
enquired whether Her Majesty had been able to recognise
the tune. 'Yes' was the reply; 'it was the National
Anthem, but very badly played!'

A little later the family group is assembled round the
dining table; the scene is bright and cheerful; over the
great carved sideboard and mantel are displayed Persian
weapons and chain armour, together with sundry Cingalese
daggers. The two bold, spirited paintings by the
American artist Gilbert Munger represent scenes in the
Rocky Mountains. During the sociable meal Mr. Preece
is the life and soul of the party; jest, anecdote, and
repartee fall from his lips. Your young hostess who
presides over the large establishment does the honours
with infinite grace. Inheriting much of her distinguished
father's cleverness and his genial, kindly disposition, she
and her sisters are alike thoroughly domestic in their
tastes and habits.

Two elder sons are already out in the world carving
their fortunes in their father's profession, the third has
elected to 'go in for law,' and the fourth is in France
studying the language.

After dinner there is just time for a peep through the
little picture gallery of Fellows of the Royal Society living
and gone before, among whom hangs an excellent portrait
of the late William Spottiswoode, President. This
passage leads into the lately erected billiard-room, which is
decorated with armour, breastplates, swords, and skins of
beasts. The over-mantel is crowded with prizes, tankards,
cups, &c., trophies won by 'the boys.' A door on the

east leads into the conservatory, electrically lighted, where orchids, camellias, and a variety of other flowers are in full bloom.

But at the hall door Mr. Preece stands, with true hospitality, to 'speed the parting guest,' as the last train to town must be caught. Escorted by the young embryo lawyer, you take leave of your intellectual and scholarly host, while he laughingly remarks, 'When the moon and planetary system are in thorough telegraphic communication with the earth, you shall be the first to be told!'

OLGA NETHERSOLE

WITHOUT any actual fostering of an innate gift—for no member of her family had at any time been on the stage —the ardent, artistic temperament of Miss Olga Nethersole seemed to grow spontaneously. The union of strong dramatic instincts and a love of the fine arts on her mother's side, and on her father's an extraordinary facility for acquiring languages—for he could speak in seven different tongues, and was self-taught—would seem to have produced in the young player a solidity of thought together with an intense earnestness of purpose; and these, with a large share of natural talent and a highly strung nervous organisation, have combined to bring her so rapidly to the front ranks of English actresses.

'A lavish planet reigned when she was born,' which happened to be at Kensington. As a child she was somewhat sad and morbid—never, as it were, flirting with life, but inclined to look upon everything too seriously, which, perhaps, may have taken away, not the brightness, but the trivialities of childhood's days. At the age of seven she became, as she laughingly explains, 'the victim of circumstances, and got taken to school accidentally.' The whole family escorted her two elder sisters to Holland, where they were being educated, and though there had been no previous intention of leaving her with them, the governess prevailed upon her mother to allow her to remain and to become a pupil. Two years later, however, she returned to London, and attended the High School, Chelsea. A quick student, the little Olga absorbed knowledge, and, without exactly learning her lessons, contrived to get outside them, as it were, without difficulty. Even in those early days of development her vivid imagination and strongly sympathetic nature called forth the love and companionship of those around her. In that way she gained the confidence of people much older than herself, and drew out their experiences. In her strong desire to know people and life she became a great reader, and soon realised that what lay within her was a longing desire to interpret the ideas of others and to clothe their thoughts with words. In this gradual awakening of her soul her mother's training and guidance were of the greatest help. Together they read and discussed poetry, plays, and metaphysics, and the young receptive mind threw itself heart and soul into these studies, and eagerly imbibed the feeling and the spirit of the writers. Little as anyone foresaw it at the time, this mode of education was all leading up to what was to follow. It happened that when Olga Nethersole was nearly fourteen her sisters and brother got up a little amateur performance during the holidays and omitted her in the cast. She—the spoilt baby of the family—wept bitterly at being left out, whereupon they introduced a servant into the piece and gave her the part, which she played with so much *aplomb* that a doctor friend who was present begged that she might be allowed to act in a farce to be given at the Colney Hatch Asylum. Consent was given, but when the day came the little girl experienced a momentary shock, which almost overcame her. A lunatic fixed his eyes on her, which so alarmed her that no words would come. Bravely conquering the feeling of stage fright, with the consciousness that if she did not then she never would, she continued her part, and won her first public applause. Soon after, while on a visit to Torquay, Miss Nethersole made the acquaintance of Mr. Nutcombe Gould; he was then an ardent amateur, and was arranging a performance for the benefit of the hospital. One of the company was taken ill; and he, seeing how enthusiastic the young girl was about the stage, offered her the part, which she played so cleverly that later, when Mr. Gould determined to adopt the profession, and was organising a provincial tour, he invited her to join. 'At first my mother was strongly opposed to the idea,' says the young actress, 'and for many days would not speak about it. It was the only disagreement we ever had, but she was the wisest and noblest of women, and when she saw how much it affected me, and that I was not "stage-struck," but felt it must be my vocation, she yielded, and to the day of her death helped me. Accordingly I started on my career without any training. Indeed, when girls come to me and ask me how to begin to learn, I always tell them to learn on the stage from experience only. It is the only way to do it. I was offered three pounds a week, to my amazement, for I could not believe I was worth that to anyone.'

Her first appearance was made at Brighton, in her early teens, as Vera in 'Moths,' followed by Clara Douglas in 'Money;' then she was engaged by Mr. Charles Hawtrey to play Lettice Vane in that beautiful piece, 'Harvest.' She went next with Miss Amy Roselle and Mr. Dacre on tour for four months in Mr. Merivale's 'Our Joan,' succeeded by a part in ''Twixt Kith and Kin.' In 'The Double Marriage' she played Miss Ellen Terry's part—Claire de Beaurepaire—and in the same year she acted with Mr. Lionel Brough in a farcical comedy entitled 'Modern Wives.' Then, returning to town, she fulfilled an engagement at the Adelphi as Ruth Medway in the 'Union Jack.' 'It was my first meeting with Mr.

Grundy,' she remarks. 'The acquaintance deepened into a firm friendship, and I have the greatest admiration for him and his work. That was my first pathetic part, and it was very real to me.' During the run of the piece Miss Nethersole was obliged to leave, being under agreement to originate the *rôle* of Miriam St. Aubyn in Mr. F. C. Philips' play 'The Dean and his Daughter,' and here she tasted largely of the sweets of success. She identified herself so thoroughly with the heroine, and in a subtle manner and with true art so developed the character, that she seemed to be growing older in each act. She made a big bound into public favour, and it was remarked that her receptions were such whereof Bernhardt, Siddons, or Rachel might have been proud. Two seasons with Mr. Hare followed; but until the Garrick was ready to be opened he lent the young player to create the part of Lola in 'The Silver Falls' at the Adelphi—a *rôle* in which her inheritance of Spanish blood from her mother served her in good stead. At the Garrick she took Janet Preece in 'The Profligate,' and then came the grandest opportunity she could have had. During the run of 'La Tosca' Mrs. Bernard Beere was taken ill, and Olga Nethersole came to the rescue; without a single rehearsal she played the title *rôle* with so much fire and pathos that she received a perfect ovation at its conclusion. Then came a ten months' tour in Australia with Mr. Charles Cartwright. During this visit she added so largely to her repertory and her experience that, on her return to London and to the Garrick, where she created the *rôle* of Beatrice Selwyn in 'A Fool's Paradise,' one of the most eminent critics remarked: 'She had gone away a student and come back a master.' While acting every night at the Garrick Mr. Hare allowed her to perform in *matinées* at the Criterion, with a whole company of stars, in 'The Silent Battle,' where a very great personage told her that her Agatha had made him weep, and he was not ashamed!

A long run of 'Diplomacy' followed; this was the first time the young player had seen Mrs. Bancroft act, and she expresses herself as having been 'so proud to act with her.' In the revival of the piece it will be remembered that Miss Nethersole took the part of the Countess Zicka, and played it with true artistic finish and an earnestness that was absolutely thrilling. Her next venture was to take the Court Theatre and, under her brother Mr. Louis Nethersole's able management, to produce 'The Transgressor' (by Mr. A. W. Gattie), herself the Sylvia. 'It was a great responsibility,' she observes, 'but my brother has a peculiar gift for organisation, and is so experienced a manager.' 'Need I say,' she adds presently, with a smile, 'he is also the most delightful companion in the world?' 'The Transgressor' made an enormous success, and it is scarcely surprising that Miss Nethersole's rendering of Sylvia brought her fame to the ears of many American managers. Among four offers that she received she chose Mr. Daly's, and after making a provincial tour with her own company the brother and sister sailed for the States. Here she had a right royal time, as is well known, and, from the President downwards, met with so much kindness, favour, and encouragement, that she declares 'it developed her to what she may be more than aught else.' She played Juliet for the first time, never having even seen it, and knowing nothing of its traditions. Camille in 'La Dame aux Camélias' was an absolute triumph, also 'Frou Frou.' Before its production her appearance as Camille was called 'an unwise move, as it almost invited comparison with Sarah Bernhardt, Duse, and Jane Hading;' but she carried it all through brilliantly, and won golden opinions on all sides. The last two performances of Camille at Boston brought in the sum of 780*l*. ; on her return from America Miss Nethersole had contemplated taking a theatre in London and appearing in the same characters she had impersonated there with such marked success; but, instead of doing so, she was induced by Mr. Hare to take up the part of Agnes in 'The Notorious Mrs. Ebbsmith.' 'I was deeply interested,' she explains, 'in the psychology of the character, which is one of the most complex I have ever played. It is terribly realistic, and I had the idea of Louise Michel ever in my mind.'

Since that performance Olga Nethersole has again enjoyed a series of triumphs. Two American managers, Messrs. Daniel and Charles Frohman, joined forces in order to star her on a tour of twenty-four weeks in the United States; and, under the contract, Paris, Berlin, St. Petersburg, and many other capitals were visited, while she is under agreement shortly to appear in a magnificent Shakespearean production.

The gifted actress has made her name early in life. As she modestly puts it, she 'has been lucky enough to be successful right away from the beginning.' Strongly emotional and realising vividly the salient points in every part she represents, she studies the flesh, blood, and brains—so to speak—of each with earnestness and enthusiasm; while each suggests delicacy of treatment and the refinement of her own nature. 'But I did not understand what real feeling was,' she says, 'before I went to America. The audiences are so encouraging and sympathetic; they seem to hold out a hand and draw one along with them!'

JOSEPH HATTON

ON the high ground of St. John's Wood, about a stone's throw from Lord's, there stands a long, old-fashioned, detached house, with garden back and front, and a high wall which ensures absolute privacy. The charming interior is in thorough keeping, and betrays an originality in design and arrangement that indicates artistic tastes and culture. In conversation with the eminent novelist, Mr. Joseph Hatton, it transpires that Mrs. Hatton has a genius for art decorations, and naturally the first step taken on obtaining possession of the premises, some years ago, was to entirely remodel the inside, and to reconstruct it according to her own ideas. The effect is particularly happy, and, although it has the appearance of being entirely unstudied, every detail has evidently been thought out carefully, from the snug 'cosy' corner to the comfortable drawing-room recess yonder and the antique candelabra in the ceiling.

The first door in the little entrance-hall opens into the drawing-room, which has a deep bow window with lattice panes on the immediate left; on the further end, on the right, high French windows lead on to the tennis-ground at the back, a judicious arrangement of light that sets off the large collection of engravings and studies in black and white to the best advantage. Another latticed window, facing due west, has a shelf below filled with choice specimens of Venetian glass, on which a brilliant sunset sheds every sort of colour. The great oak mantelpiece was modelled after one in Haddon Hall, and the quaint fireplace within is an old-fashioned revival of Coalbrookdale. The highly polished floor is partially concealed by Indian matting and a few Persian rugs of subdued tints, which throw into relief an old oak settle, a Chippendale bureau, and a marqueterie cabinet, standing beside a great copper vessel filled with long-leaved plants, and a large Nuremberg jug, of the same metal, a gift from Mr. Willard.

Among the principal pictures that adorn the walls are a proof-before-letters engraving of Orchardson's well-known painting, 'Hard Hit,' and two masterly engravings after Margetson (son-in-law of Mr. Hatton), one of which represents the boat scene in 'Charles I.,' with autographs of Sir Henry Irving, Ellen Terry, and Mr. Terriss below. Mr. Hatton specially directs your attention to three charcoal drawings which he values highly—bold, spirited sketches by Volkmark, Vance, and Burns (celebrated for his marine pictures)—as they are cherished reminiscences of a certain evening at New York, when a reception was given to him by the Salmagundi Club. 'The artists worked while I chatted,' he remarks; 'and the result was these black and white sketches, which were made on that evening and finished the following morning.' Amidst a group of interesting portraits are two that are particularly attractive—respectively, Miss Bessie Hatton as the Prince of Wales in 'Richard III.,' and a picture of Sir Henry Irving at his desk, that is certainly one of the finest portraits of the great actor that exist.

Not only as a novelist has the brilliant author of 'By Order of the Czar,' and some thirty other books, made his mark in literature. A long apprenticeship to journalism, a vivid imagination, and a deep poetic strain, combined with much foreign travelling and close observation of human nature, have given his versatile pen the ease and fluency, the profound interest and instructiveness, that distinguish his works.

He first saw the light at Andover, Hants, but has no recollection of his birthplace, as his parents shortly after moved, and made their home at Chesterfield—the town of the crooked steeple—where his father founded one of the first of the penny papers, the 'Derbyshire Times,' which afterwards became so successful. At school he declares that he in no way distinguished himself, except in English composition, music, and calligraphy, and, being passionately fond of the Derbyshire dales, fishing, and every sort of country sport, he confesses to having frequently played truant. 'My school has been a newspaper office,' he remarks pithily.

Notwithstanding the fact that he came of an artistic and journalistic family, and on his father's side of a race of musicians, the young lad was designed for the legal profession, and was placed in the town clerk's office to learn the rudiments of law, but his natural proclivities soon asserted themselves, and, disliking intensely the preliminary dry studies, he speedily abandoned the idea. Many of his leisure hours even then were spent in study. He learned shorthand, had a private tutor for French and a coach for Latin, his chief recreation being music, in which, when yet quite a boy, he acquired sufficient skill to enable him to take solos on the piano at local concerts. At the age of seventeen he went on his father's paper as 'reporter, free lance, compositor—anything!' 'The Editor,' continues Mr. Hatton, 'was a man of considerable intellectual acquirements, and was somewhat severe in regard to journalists' work, and he looked upon me as too young, and perhaps scarcely appreciated my efforts, whereupon I took the matter into my own hands, left home, and determined to seek my fortune, in the direction of journalism, with such knowledge as I had obtained in my father's and the town clerk's offices.'

His perseverance and steady determination met with their due reward. Almost immediately the young writer obtained the appointment of reporter on the 'Lincoln Gazette,' which was followed after a time by the post of sub-editor of the 'Bristol Mirror,' now better known as the 'Bristol Daily Times and Mirror,' and before he was quite of age he became the editor of that oldest and most important journal in the West of England.

'Those were delightful days at Bristol,' observes Mr. Hatton. 'We were young, bright, happy, newly married, and prosperous!'

Young indeed, considering that the boy-bridegroom had barely reached the age of man's estate, whilst the girl-bride whom he had wedded had as yet not attained her seventeenth summer!

In those light-hearted, youthful days the young journalist, like his intimate friend Mr. Toole, was somewhat inclined to practical jokes. On one occasion, when he was a reporter on a provincial paper, a crowd had

assembled to witness the arrival of a criminal connected
with a sensational murder case. The man, with some
difficulty, was placed in a cab, while a second cab, containing representatives of the press, followed. The joke
was extemporised by these lively spirits, who indicated
to some of the people that Mr. Hatton was the perpetrator of the deed. The young reporter acted the part
to perfection. Crouching back on the seat of the cab, he
put on a cowed, terrified air, and preserved his assumed
character so well that, thoroughly taken in, a mob
gathered round, and, the situation and demonstrations
becoming too warm to be pleasant, his identity had to be
revealed. An eye-witness of the incident remarked that
nothing could exceed the serio-comic drollery exhibited by
the youth on that occasion.

If the talent for journalism be Mr. Hatton's by inheritance, the gift of novel-writing is entirely originated by
himself. He had been accustomed from his earliest years
to write in secret accounts of views that he had seen, of
people whom he had met, and of every particular incident
that he had heard, weaving them more or less into
romances. His first novel, 'In the Lap of Fortune,'
written when he was quite young, largely exploited the
journalism of that period, and was suggested by his
experiences at Chesterfield. The next was 'Clytie,' where
the scene was laid in his own house in the cathedral
precincts at Durham, described as the residence of the old
organist and his daughter. This work had at once a
success; it was translated into German, and is, after this
lapse of years, being now rendered in Swedish.

But romances were for a time only interludes in his
newspaper work, and Mr. Hatton continued to contribute
articles to a variety of journals, notably to the well-known
'Newcastle Chronicle,' where so many distinguished writers
have found a field for their labours. London was naturally the goal of his ambition, and, after some years
of interesting and instructive provincial experience, he

accepted a small engagement and made his way to the great capital, where, however, he was destined, on that occasion, to make but a brief stay. 'I came up almost unknown,' says Mr. Hatton cheerfully, 'and went to the Hummums in Covent Garden. London had never seemed so big and so serious to me. That same evening I picked up a number of the "Athenæum," and saw an advertisement in which an editor was wanted for an important county paper with prospect of partnership. Under the depression of a solitary walk down Fleet Street and a certain sense of responsibility that belongs to the happiness of having a wife and two children, I answered it, and received in reply an invitation to dine at the Queen's Hotel, Norwood, where I found a very pleasant county gentleman of means and position, Mr. R. W. Johnson, who was also proprietor of the paper in question, "Burrows' Worcester Journal." His proposals were so tempting that I at once accepted them, and wired to my wife to join me at Worcester instead of London—to her great disappointment.'

In the historical old city Mr. Hatton soon took a prominent place. He became town councillor, hospital visitor, captain of volunteers, and was drifting in the direction of the mayoralty when he became wearied of local politics, and projected, with his friend Mr. Johnson, high sheriff of the county, the first illustrated paper for the provinces, 'The Illustrated Midland News,' with its headquarters at Birmingham. Those were the days before the invention of process-blocks, and wood engraving was a costly necessity. Great things, however, were accomplished with the help of Mr. Swain, the famous 'Punch' engraver. The small school for this art, founded in Birmingham by Mr. Hatton, still exists.

The much-desired London as a permanent abode followed, where the industrious writer was already editing the 'Gentleman's Magazine.' Having entered upon those duties during his residence in Worcester, under Bradley and Evans' management, he had an exceptional staff, consisting of Tom Taylor, Shirley Brooks, Mark Lemon (the Druid), Luke Limner, Blanchard Jerrold, and other well-known writers. For seven or eight years he was the special correspondent in Europe of the 'New York Times,' and filled a similar post on the 'Sydney Morning Herald.' He was also one of the specials of the 'Kreuz-Zeitung,' of Berlin. He has edited the 'Sunday Times,' and has founded one or two successful journals, besides contributing special articles to 'Harper's,' 'Scribner's,' the 'English Illustrated,' and other leading magazines.

The author's study upstairs is as bright and cheerful as Morris' decoration and a brilliant sunset can make it. Stray beams, indeed, seem to be flitting all over the room. It has a sort of attic roof and verandah overlooking the tennis-ground. At every odd corner well-filled white bookshelves are fitted over the Indian-matted dado. The old Dutch tiles were brought from Holland; on the mantel-shelf stands an ecclesiastical candlestick in deep crimson pottery of two 'jolly monks,' presented by Mr. Toole with the remark that it was 'a comedian's idea of Becket and his friend going home together.' There is but little room for pictures, though you find autograph portraits from Bret Harte, Sir Arthur Sullivan, William Black, Miss Braddon, and other old friends, besides a notable picture from Victor Hugo and a portrait of Mr. Hatton's ideal monarch, the little Queen of Holland in her Friesland dress.

Curios from Borneo and Upper Congo are scattered here and there, and two fetish idols, from Doongoo Villase, with looking-glass eyes, that present a quaint but fierce appearance. These were gifts from young Mr. Ward, of Stanley's party, who was the last white man to greet Mr. Hatton's only son on his last expedition in the vast island of Borneo. (This beloved and lamented son has since passed into that 'great beyond' of dreamless sleep and silence unbroken.) A modest-looking automatic desk-table stands in the corner, and on Mr. Hatton's pressing a spring a complete Remington typewriter rises from within. This ingenious contrivance is one of the first that were made, and the first sent from America to London, where he saw it and promptly made it his own.

Two large photographs by the window represent Mr. Willard in the dual *rôle* of John Needham and Joseph Norbury in the author's book 'John Needham's Double,' which later, as a play, gave Mr. Willard two of his finest parts. The novel first ran through Tillotson's Syndicate, and was afterwards dramatised by Mr. Hatton.

Among his many works, too numerous to mention, perhaps the most popular are 'Three Recruits,' 'Christopher Kenrick,' 'The Queen of Bohemia,' 'A Modern Ulysses,' 'The Princess Mazaroff,' 'Cruel London,' 'Under the Great Seal,' and 'When Greek meets Greek.' A work entitled 'By Order of the Czar' achieved the distinction of being prohibited in Russia. It is now in the fourteenth edition, and is being translated into Swedish. This intensely interesting work is powerful in description and picturesque in detail, while every incident is admirably worked out. It is by no means a soporific, for it has the effect of getting the reader into such a state of thrilling excitement that he is apt to lie awake half the night after reading it, and, when he drops off to sleep, to dream of it the other half, and he will probably lay aside his usual morning duties in order to finish it!

There is, moreover, a delightful vivacity and originality in all Mr. Hatton's situations; in fact, as Charles Reade once remarked to him, 'You write a new story every time, and your people live,' a compliment that pleased him very much, though of course the bigger compliments he receives come largely to him in the public endorsements and in the recognition of America and foreign countries.

Mr. Hatton always has plots in his head that may go on for years. He conceives an idea, and, if it particularly impress him, his brain takes care of it, and it then goes on growing and developing on its own account.

Touching the question of 'pointing a moral' as well as 'adorning a tale,' Mr. Hatton says 'there is always a lesson in a good story, always a moral in the conclusion of the adventures of a man or woman, either in fact or in fiction. In my novel of "Clytie" my leading idea was to expose the abuse of the statutory declaration, but the adventures and perils of a country girl in London were sufficiently strong to keep the motive of the story in proper subjection. I think as much may be said for "Under the Great Seal," the pivot of which was the unrighteous treatment of the first settlers in Newfoundland; and in "By Order of the Czar" I have not allowed the business of exhibiting the condition of the Jews in Russia to do more than colour the dramatic and tragic action. You are right in thinking that Hannah Klostock must be one of my favourite creations, and I take delight in her champion, Andrea Ferrari, whose fight with the mob at Czaronva almost put me into a fever when I wrote it. I had to take my coat off in the middle of the fray, and I did it at one sitting. One of my earliest and one of my latest novels are two of my most successful works, and I hope I have given them a companion in one of my latest.'

This Mr. Hatton has undoubtedly done in 'The Banishment of Jessop Blythe.' It is an English story, its people and scenery English, and of the present day. It begins with a dramatic incident which is entirely new, and there is an element of surprise in the story that never flags. The opening scene describes one of the most impressive of Nature's handiworks, musical with the labour of God's creatures, the song of birds, and the continual plash of a subterranean river.

His working hours are from 11 A.M. to 3 P.M., then a walk and talk, and not unfrequently a night of labour to follow. He is a rapid writer, but, as he remarks significantly, 'When I have thought slowly I write fast.' Though not always in a writing mood, he makes a point of 'coming to work' at his desk, for, as he observes, 'If one can't write one can at any rate read and think,' and when thus disinclined for actual work he has a peculiar recreation. He has half a dozen gigantic folio books of personal memoranda, in which he pastes letters, notes, photographs, and incidents associated with people whom he knows or has met. These volumes cover many years, and should be valuable even as souvenirs of distinguished people.

Mr. Hatton is a great reader, and particularly fond of books of travel, biographies, essays, and fiction. There is one little peculiarity noticeable in his library; many of the books have printed notices pasted into them, and not a few are annotated by his own hand. He laughs at your discovery, and remarks, 'I fear I don't treat books very well, but, at any rate, I treat them better than Wordsworth did, for I don't tear or destroy them; but I cannot help marking them, and often paste in printed or manuscript notes connected with the subject of the work. I am not much of a classic, but I read Plutarch in my youth, and even to-day I find Tacitus not more instructive than entertaining, the style as interesting as Macaulay and as picturesque as Froude.'

The talented author has had an interesting career, that is, if being behind the scenes of many exciting events, knowing many important people, having crossed the Atlantic many times, and for many years living in the heart of London life and work make an interesting career. He has done most things in journalism and literature, and been most things—reporter, editor, proprietor, foreign correspondent, literary adviser, novelist, biographer, and playwright. Among his most pleasant work for some years back and at present is a newspaper feature entitled 'Cigarette Papers,' which he contributes to a limited syndicate of journals, through whose columns, every week of his life, he addresses at least eight or nine millions of people in all parts of the world.

'It is better to wear out than to rust out,' he remarks

with a genial smile; 'besides, one has to be busy—the tendency of household expenses in these days is always upward.'

PHYLLIS BROUGHTON

THERE is a subdued dignity about the large and solidly built houses in a broad, quiet 'Place'—which might justly have been called 'Square'—not far from Oxford Street. The hand of time has mellowed the work of man, and there is none of the garish appearance of modern days in the massive structures. No outward or neighbours' sounds can be detected, which is wonderful, considering the near proximity of one of the noisiest and most bustling streets in the great metropolis, and this is a blessing which the fortunate inhabitants duly recognise. Most especially is it appreciated by Miss Phyllis Broughton, whose home lies within the old 'Place' with a kind, indulgent step-father, a fond mother (General and Mrs. Hutchinson), and a happy family circle comprising likewise two brothers and a little sister.

Although the exterior is somewhat sombre, the interior is bright enough, and her own private 'den' makes a suitable background for the chestnut-coloured hair, soft brown eyes, and straight, delicate features which give the popular young actress such winning yet piquante beauty. But besides her outward personal attractions she has what is most pleasing, and that is a perfectly simple, natural disposition and pretty cordiality of manner. Her first thought is of your creature comforts as you arrive somewhat weather-beaten in the teeth of a raging gale, and she comes forward eagerly to divest you of sundry storm-garments, looking so bright and happy that it is easy to see that her late well-earned holiday has braced her up afresh to carry on the battle of life. The room carries you back in imagination to a long past visit to Japan, but there are no 'three-three-farthing' imitation fans or the like shams. The whole, with one exception, is carried out in severely orthodox fashion, with its finely matted floor, great bamboo chandelier, and bamboo-work ceiling corners from which depend four quaint Japanese dolls. Even the little piano is cased in bamboo, which Miss Broughton says 'makes it look rather like a tea caddy.' The wall hangings and *portières* are all of Japanese silk and gold embroideries, and two great blue bowls of the same country's ware give a fine bit of colour to the room. 'The whole idea,' she remarks, 'grew out of them. I had to live up to those blue bowls! When "Cootie"' (as she affectionately calls her stepfather) 'and my mother gave me the room for my own I worked it all out gradually. The very chairs I would have covered with matting and braid, but then I found nobody would come in, so I had to get that "one exception,"' which is a luxurious and altogether desirable Chesterfield couch with big down cushions. But 'Cootie' had to interfere in one small particular. The hanging lanterns threatened to exterminate the house, so he bought her those grotesque dolls, which she promptly executed and hung up instead.

The love of dancing was born in her. As soon as she could run alone she would dance in perfect time to any piano or barrel-organ she heard from her nursery window. It was when 'only a tiny mite' that the young player made her first bow to the public in a ballet, 'The Forty Thieves,' attired as a snowball in little white, swansdowny skirts. From that day to this she has been constantly on the boards, principally in long engagements at the Gaiety, Avenue, and Prince of Wales's theatres. She studied elocution in Macbeth, Juliet, and other Shakespearean characters under Mr. Villiers, of whom she speaks with gratitude and affection. Later the two families became connected by the marriage of his son to her sister, Emma Broughton. By and by Mr. Villiers suggested that his

pupil 'wanted deportment,' and this led to her going to a
dancing master, M. Dervinne, under whose tuition she
improved so rapidly that she was soon engaged at the
Gaiety, where she had only four lines to speak and a solo
dance. 'And, oh! how terrified I was,' she says, with a
little shiver at the remembrance; 'my knees knocked together; but I got more and more nervous with each new
part.' At the Gaiety she remained for five years,
taking Miss Kate Vaughan's *rôles*, and there she made her
name and established her reputation firmly in the eyes of
the public. 'It was real hard work, though delightful,'
says the young girl reflectively. 'Two hours with a
governess in the morning, for my mother would not allow
any neglect of my education, three hours practising dancing
in the afternoon, and the theatre at night!' But Phyllis
Broughton reaps her reward in the long engagements she
gets and in the warmth of her receptions. When the
Avenue Theatre opened with 'Kenilworth' she played
Lydia Thompson's part, and in a subsequent three years'
engagement she acted with Mr. Arthur Roberts in
Planquette's musical pieces, such as 'The Old Guard,'
'Indiana.' At the close of the season she received a
pleasant testimony to her merits in the form of a handsome diamond and enamel brooch from the management,
together with a letter containing a few neat and appropriate words of praise and thanks. She is a rapid study,
but thinks out her lines and 'points' with much precision,
and while at private rehearsal in her own room little bits
of 'business' suggest themselves which at real rehearsal
invariably come off all right. Next came a grand opportunity, of which the young player made the most. When
the Carl Rosa Company opened at the Prince of Wales's
Theatre, Phyllis Broughton was offered a three years'
engagement in 'Paul Jones,' 'Marjorie,' and 'Captain
Thérèse,' in *ingénue* parts with 'a little singing, more
acting, and most dancing.' 'I haven't much of a voice,' she
remarks frankly, 'but I am content and thankful if it

carries me through.' The voice, however, 'carried her through' successfully enough as Cicely in 'Marjorie,' for it will be well remembered that the duet in which she and Mr. Hayden Coffin sang used to be encored five times nightly! Then, as she comically expresses it, she was 'sublet' by the Carl Rosa Company to Mr. George Edwards at the Opera Comique to play in 'Joan of Arc,' 'Blue-eyed Susan,' &c. Thence to the Prince of Wales's for 'In Town,' which was subsequently transferred to the Gaiety, and ran over a year. Three different companies were at one time or another in that play, but at its conclusion Miss Broughton was the only one of the original members left. Yonder portrait represents her in 'La Mascotte,' together with the cat that appeared nightly in the play. 'But the cat,' she observes quaintly, 'got sick of being so much photographed, and expired soon after!' A later performance, and one which she thoroughly enjoyed, was Lady Virginia (Miss Lottie Venne's original *rôle*) in the famous 'Gaiety Girl'—a play that ran merrily several hundred nights—after which a severe illness obliged the young actress to rest for a season to recruit her health. Never had she a more gratifying reception than when she again appeared at her old place in the Prince of Wales's Theatre, where, as Mrs. Ralli Carr in 'Gentleman Joe' with Mr. Arthur Roberts, she was once more seen at her best in the new songs and dances introduced for her. When two comedians, who have been accustomed to act with each other, meet after long separation the effect is noticeable; they play into each other's hands with additional brightness and with a mutual sympathy that cause the piece to run with extra zest.

In common with all young players, Phyllis Broughton has her experiences in the form of curious letters and little unrehearsed effects. Of the former her mother takes possession, as she says 'Phyllis is so careless, and always tears up everything, but I keep them as curiosities.' They are indeed 'curiosities.' Here is one from a stranger in

New Zealand, beginning 'Respected Miss,' and asking her in all good faith to go out and marry him, but begs her, if she has other views, to suggest a friend or relation instead.' He explains his own qualifications and those required in a wife—'they' must be this, 'they' must have that, and so on. He encloses his photograph, but acknowledges it was taken 'before he had time to wash or do his hair.' She is to send 'them' out, or indeed gallantly offers 'to go home and fetch 'them'! (Can the man want two wives?) Another is one of a series of registered letters from a religious maniac—who went nightly to the pit to see her—and each encloses drawings of coffins, cross-bones and skulls, warns her repeatedly of the 'sin of the stage,' and names a certain Thursday which is to be her last on earth. But this was too much, and Miss Broughton was so terrified that General Hutchinson had to interfere through the police, and the nuisance was stopped. She had a terrible experience once in 'The Old Guard,' in which she had to dance in *sabots*. It had been well rehearsed, but on the first night a carpet was unfortunately laid down. The effect was disastrous. Down she came, but in an instant she was up and flew to the wings, threw away the *sabots*, returned and went through the dance to the end in her 'stocking feet.' The young player has contrived to put a good deal of successful work into comparatively a short career. In the home circle her bright and happy nature causes her to be the 'life and soul of the house.' 'She is a good daughter,' says her mother fondly, 'and a good sister, and has never given me an hour's anxiety.'

FITZGERALD MOLLOY

NOT unfrequently does it happen that the boy who at school is pronounced dull and dreamy, inapt at learning, and with no particular bent, blossoms out in after years and makes his mark on the literature of the world. Many such instances might be quoted. The intellectual faculties have lain dormant, latent talents have remained undiscovered, or have been deprived of the stimulus necessary to their development by want of perception and of sympathy on the part of the instructor.

Just such a lad was Fitzgerald Molloy, who has now for years been climbing the 'thorny path,' with ever-increasing success, achieving distinction by means of his social histories of the Georgian and Restoration periods, his biographies of theatrical celebrities, and his novels. Now, having reached his fortieth year, and published upwards of thirty-two works, his popularity may be said to be firmly established.

His house, situated in a secluded quarter of St. John's Wood, is an ideal home for a writer. Lying far from the road, the French windows of the dining and sitting-rooms open on a delicious little garden, shaded by poplar, beech, and pear trees, crowded with old-fashioned flowers and screened by dull red-brick walls, half covered with fig trees and clematis. It might be removed a hundred miles from town, so peaceful is it, so refreshing in the greenness of its surroundings.

This colour would seem to the author the most harmonious and restful, for not only is the house painted green, but the hall, the stairs, and every room it contains are in apple and olive green, while the Morris papers are in kindred shades of the same colour. His work-room, with its Turkish rugs and Eastern potteries, is full of interesting memorials of the countries he has visited. That richly wrought dagger he bought at Toledo; the painting of Fra Angelico's 'Angelo' hails from Florence; the curious old brass box is from Amsterdam; the quaint instrument hanging on the wall he picked up in an Algerian café; the old censer was given him by a Capuchin monk in Rome; and the string of praying beads by an Arab pilgrim. The beautiful book-case and desk, with their elaborate brass-work, belong to the Louis Seize period, but the carved oak chest, which contains manuscripts and proofs, is English, and dates from the reign of William and Mary.

In one corner is a planisphere, or map of the heavens, by which the motion of the heavenly bodies can be traced, for Mr. Molloy studies astronomy and astrology, in which latter he has implicit belief; in another corner stands a piano, for he is passionately fond of music, and turns to it as a restful resource when mentally wearied. On the walls are some old engravings after Morland and Cosway, while the book-cases contain many presentation volumes from fellow-workers.

The descendant of a good old Irish family, Fitzgerald Molloy was educated by a private tutor, and afterwards spent some years in St. Kyran's College, Kilkenny. Soon after leaving school he, having always had the idea of becoming an author, came to London with an introduction to Mrs. S. C. Hall from a relative of that distinguished writer. Mr. Molloy cherishes the most affectionate remembrance for this charming old lady, who at first would dissuade him from being a writer, but who eventually abetted him in joining the ranks of literary workers, from which she had long retired. Their friendship was formed from the first. Not only was she a native of his country, but she had passed the earlier years of her life at Bannow, the scene of more than one of her delightful Irish novels. Coming from her own people, and from her beloved Ireland, of which she used to say, 'Every blade of grass that grows upon its soil is dear to me,' both she and Mr. S. C. Hall received the lad with open arms, gave him words of advice and encouragement, employment as amanuensis, and made him a son of the house. Mr. and Mrs. S. C. Hall, who had been friends and associates of Lady Blessington, Count D'Orsay, Lady Morgan, Lytton, Disraeli, Moore, and indeed of all the distinguished men and women of an earlier day, preserved all the grace, courtesy, and charm of manner belonging to the old school that is so sadly missing from modern life.

Encouraged and stimulated by the intellectual society of these excellent people, to whom many now successful authors owe a deep debt of gratitude, Fitzgerald Molloy soon began to write short stories and poems, which his friends read, corrected, and criticised with a kind spirit. Mr. Hall subsequently obtained for him a clerkship in the 'Art Journal' office, where, during the illness of the sub-editor, he was appointed for a brief period to the post. His next promotion was under the late Mr. John Cashel Hoey, then secretary of the New Zealand Government Office, and when that office was dissolved he became private secretary to Sir Charles Gavan Duffy, a friend of his parents. In that capacity Fitzgerald Molloy acknowledges that he received his first real insight and training into literary work, of which he has since made good use. Evidently Sir Charles saw that his young secretary gave promise, for on one occasion he remarked to him, 'I know you have a career before you, though in which direction it lies I cannot say.'

The practical advice that he received from so able and experienced a writer, together with his association with so clever and distinguished a man, left their impression on a young and receptive mind. On the departure of Sir Charles to Southern Europe, Fitzgerald Molloy, loving art and liberty more than all else, determined that he would seek no other appointment, but would strike out for himself, to sink or swim upon the uncertain waters of literary life. Since that decision he has supported himself entirely by his pen.

His first real success was 'Court Life Below Stairs, or London under the First Georges,' from 1714 to 1760, a work that entailed a vast amount of literary research—a training in itself. These volumes may be said to have taken the reading public by storm. In three weeks a second edition was announced, which in three months was out of print. Much new and hitherto unpublished matter was collected from the pamphlets, manuscript letters, diaries, and correspondence that he found in the British Museum. These he ingeniously wove into a lively and stirring picture of the times, touching but slightly and with delicate and refined pen on the *risqué* but sadly veracious points of that era.

The rapid sale of the book caused the publishers to suggest a sequel in continuation of the epoch. This work, 'Court Life Below Stairs, or London under the Last George,' contained some remarkable extracts from the famous Molesworth correspondence regarding the Court, which had never before been printed, and now caused a lively sensation. It speedily passed into several editions before being issued in one-volume form. Some discussion arose in certain high quarters as to the advisability of suppressing the work, on account of the scandals therein relative to the ancestors of various distinguished families, but the idea was finally abandoned.

By this time the young author considered that he had fairly earned a partial holiday, so on the proceeds of his last book he went to Rome, where he spent four months in sightseeing and recreation, writing home a weekly letter on social subjects for a society journal of good standing. Returning to London invigorated and refreshed, he wrote 'The Life and Letters of Peg Woffington,' which was ready for publication the same autumn. This book was dedicated to Miss Ellen Terry in a letter in which he told her, 'You have idealised your impersonations. You have realised the highest poetical conceptions. You have delighted the most cultured intelligences of two worlds.'

He works from ten to three continually, but he always thinks out his plots after dinner, in the dark, when knotty points disentangle themselves, incidents suggest themselves, and what seemed barren soil in the morning produces rich harvests. The germ of a story has frequently been in his mind for two years before he puts it on paper. 'Stories often turn out differently from what I originally intended,' he says. 'Quite recently I began a novel for the sake of its *dénouement* which I saw must be abandoned as unsuitable when I got half way through. Again, a story which I intended to write in five thousand words ran to about eighty thousand—to a serial or two-volume book. All my novels are written for serial publication and to order. The length of instalments and of the story itself are always arranged for beforehand by the editor or manager of the syndicate who gives the commission. This is almost invariably the case with authors nowadays.'

Among other works by Fitzgerald Molloy is 'Royalty Restored, or London under Charles II.' This is the author's own favourite. It contains a graphic account of the ever-thrilling and interesting history of the Plague, of the Fire, and of the conspiracies of Titus Oates. In this book the true history of the Plague was written for the first time, the pamphlet on which Defoe founded his description of the scourge that devastated London several years before he was born having been found by Mr. Molloy and largely utilised in his pages. 'Royalty Restored' also gives vivid if somewhat scandalous pictures of the manners and literature of the times, together with the social and domestic life of the 'Merrie Monarch,' and his Court, with its array of frail beauties and witty courtesans.

Early in the autumn of 1886, Mr. Molloy started for a tour through Spain and Algeria, and it was while in the north of Africa that he met an Arab adept whose strange personality, sanctity of life, and remarkable powers impressed him and influenced his mind in a direction towards which it has since steadily turned. One of the most remarkable gifts of this venerable Mahommedan was his wonderful power of healing. His fame was so great that people flocked to him from France, Spain, and Italy, not as to a magician, but as a healer of disease. From this individual, the author—who somewhat reluctantly speaks of the subject—states that he first learned from personal experience of the latent possibilities and inherent powers which lie in all men, of their capability of development, and of the uses to which they can be applied. The following year he published 'A Modern Magician,' which now, in its two-shilling form, continues to have a large sale. 'The Life and Adventures of Edmund Kean,' which contained much that was new concerning the great English actor, came next. A visit to Italy in 1890, was made the occasion to produce a series of articles in the 'Illustrated London News' descriptive of Italian cities and sites of interest.

Quite a new departure is the late work, 'The Faiths of the Peoples,' which first ran through the columns of a London Sunday paper. This most interesting and instructive book, which involved much study and research, deals with the religious beliefs of all denominations. It contains no theological discussions, but throws a bright light upon many persuasions, and is written throughout in a simple and eloquent style with a strict justice and impartiality which most of the Church papers recognised and praised.

The author's latest book is a biography of his brilliant and beautiful countrywoman, published in two volumes, and called 'The Most Gorgeous Lady Blessington.' The work gives a wonderfully vivid insight into the literary circle which surrounded the Countess in the middle of the century, and contains many interesting letters from those who were at the time most prominent in art, in fashion, and in literature. If the 'prime of life' be the 'prime of work,' the public may in the future confidently expect much more bright and entertaining literature from Fitzgerald Molloy's graceful and versatile pen.

GERTRUDE KINGSTON
(MRS. SILVER)

PASSIONATELY attached to the theatre and to all things dramatic, Miss Gertrude Kingston received her first strong ideas and longings to adopt the stage as a profession from watching Mr. Irving when as yet but a child, and declares that, in common with most enthusiastic young creatures, she madly adored him. Never a first night did she miss, and every friend was coaxed to give her the greatest possible treat and take her to the play. Then for a few years she actually refrained from going at all, fearing the desire to join the ranks might become too ardent. This abstention showed a distinctly well-regulated mind at an early period; the combination of highly artistic tastes on the side of her mother, and solid practical qualities on that of her father, resulted in the cultivation of many accomplishments and languages, and a somewhat exhaustive system of education, fundamentally. It likewise fostered a habit of thinking and judging for herself so impartially that, if at any time she were a creature of impulse, her cool judgment and level head invariably prevent that impulse from running away with her. 'I was born in London,' says Miss Kingston in soft, tuneful accents, as she nestles back in an easy chair. 'I have no drop of English blood in me; my father was German, my mother Italian—and wonderfully handsome. They had what may be called instructive talents, and we were kept at studies all day long. I was a most melancholy infant,' she adds with a laugh, 'always writing diaries, poems, and stories of early deaths. Ours was a cosmopolitan education; we had Italian and German governesses—one remains in the family to this day—French maids and teachers of every sort and kind—a good many more than I cared for then, for I did not see the necessity for so much learning for girls.' It has, however, all proved very useful. Miss Kingston can take a part in French as easily as in English, and in other languages, too, with equal fluency and accent acquired in the countries which she constantly visited. The youngest of four sisters—all of whom, as she says, 'have married and lived happily ever after'—she had at one time thought of painting as a career, and—schooldays over—before she came out in society she went abroad to study under Gussow, where she made the acquaintance of Miss Röderstein, the favourite pupil of Carolus Duran. This lady befriended the young girl—the only student from England—and Miss Kingston speaks with enthusiasm of the kindness she received from her. When continuing her studies in Carolus Duran's studio a couple of years later, the first person she met was Miss Röderstein, who said she should not go away this time without being painted, and the result is a fine life-size portrait of the young actress, which hangs in a good light on the wall, and is a gift from the artist. Reproductions of Miss Kingston's own works—many done for a German firm—are on the other walls. These are mostly humorous, and their originals long since published in her clever picture-books for children. But the day was hastening on when Gertrude Kingston's early longing for a histrionic life was to be gratified. Her father died, and she desired to earn money; she wrote to Mr. George Alexander and asked for his advice. 'Go to Miss Sarah Thorne,' he replied. However, before she took this step she played with Mr. W. S. Gilbert in his 'Broken Hearts' at Mr. Boughton's private theatricals, and also in 'The Tale of Troy' at Lady Freke's entertainment at Cromwell House, where both Mr. Beerbohm Tree and Mr. Alexander observed that she gave considerable promise. Eventually she acted on the advice given, and went down to Margate. 'Dear Miss Thorne,' says the young player heartily, 'I should like to record my gratitude to her. Nearly all the present generation of

professionals have passed through her hands. She was
such a good friend to me! I never enjoyed any time
so much as with her. Those might be called impressionist performances: a few rehearsals and "on," and
such a variety of parts. She is an excellent teacher, and
brought me good luck. I was playing Zoë one night in
Boucicault's "Quadroon Girl," and Mr. Tree was present,
though I did not know it. He had come to recruit, and,
by way of a change, dropped in at the Theatre Royal,
Margate. He wrote me a charming letter, and, what was
more practical, wired to me a month later offering me a
big *rôle* in "Partners"—Mrs. Harkaway, a wicked, fashionable woman. I came up to town at once, but such a part
has its disadvantages, and had one evil result. I found
myself compelled for the next five years to play adventuresses, which I cordially hated.' Now this is a very
modest way of putting it. Miss Kingston's performance
of Mrs. Harkaway was so powerful and realistic, and
combined with so much individual refinement and pathos,
that it was no wonder she was called upon to impersonate
characters of the sort. Another of the same kind was
Rachel Denison in ' Tares' at the Opéra Comique, and in
this she particularly distinguished herself, though she felt
it to be a great ordeal to come after Miss Eyre, who had
created the part so magnificently. Among many early *rôles*
she played Mrs. Fizzleton in that humorous farce ' Nita's
First,' Enid in ' Mr. Barnes of New York,' Clara Dexter
in ' Woodbarrow Farm,' Mrs. Selwyn in 'A Fool's
Paradise,' Lena in a revival of ' The Harbour Lights,' and
Octavia in ' New Lamps for Old.' During the last three
years her chief performances were the original parts of
Mrs. Glyn Stanmore in ' The Idler' at the St. James's
with Mr. Alexander and Madame de Sivori in ' Lord Aner-
ley,' followed by a season at the Court to play the Honourable Mrs. Chombleigh in ' Marriage,' a part in which she
delighted. Gradually the ' adventuresses' were shaken
off, and she found mitigation in Inez Quesnel in ' The

Case of Rebellious Susan,' a play that she declares to have been 'murdered by the influenza,' and her part one that she found it 'great fun to act—sympathetic and pleasant,' adding that she was 'greatly surprised' by the good notices she received. A late part that attracted much attention was in 'The Passport' at Terry's Theatre, under Mr. Dana's management, as Mrs. D'Arcy—the lady with the inconvenient memory, who complicated matters by forgetting who was her real husband.

Under a calm exterior and a peculiarly quiet manner, Gertrude Kingston possesses much strength of character and a great sense of justice. She had once an occasion to exercise it, and her method of so doing shall be given in her own words. 'I was engaged,' she says, 'in the autumn of 1893, to play Mabel Wentworth in Pettitt's melodrama, "A Woman's Revenge," at the Adelphi. During its run I was seized with a severe throat attack, and asked for a three weeks' holiday to go to La Bourboule, Auvergne—a place celebrated for throat treatment. Another actress was chosen to fill my place temporarily; on my return I was told that my *locum tenens* had made a success of the part, and I had better look out for another engagement. Now, I am not pugilistic, but I do like fair play, and this was an opportunity to help my brother and sister artists in the profession and to establish a precedent in a law which enables a manager to restrain a player from performing elsewhere than in his own theatre, but renders an actor powerless to prevent a manager from engaging another in his or her place. My answer was to take out an injunction to stop anyone else taking my part. Unfortunately the case came before a holiday judge, who could not create a precedent in another court. He took twenty-four hours to consider the question, but, though he admitted that I had been badly treated, he was sorry to be unable to grant an injunction; but he added that it was clearly a case for damages. I could not, however, conscientiously say that not being allowed to act at the Adelphi would damage me in any way. Moreover, since then I have more than trebled my salary; so I dropped the matter, and have often laughed heartily over it.'

But it was before she went on the stage at all that Miss Kingston had quietly arranged another portion of her life for the future. While on a visit to friends at a large country house in the North there arrived a good-looking, sunburnt young officer, Captain Silver, fresh from the Soudan—with all his medals—who took her heart by storm. The young couple became engaged, and a few years later the marriage took place. Yonder hangs his portrait in the uniform of the gallant 42nd Highlanders—the Black Watch—close to a photograph of her brother, who inherits the family abilities, and, though only twenty-five years of age, holds a high position in the Bengal Civil Service. 'My husband,' she remarks, 'is devoted to the stage, and if he had 10,000*l*. a year he would love to give me a theatre of my own!' Essentially feminine and gentle in all her ways, Miss Kingston delights in a country life and in all out-door amusements. Yachting is a passion, together with a morning dive overboard for a swim. She is a great horse-woman, but on one occasion met with a sad misadventure in the Row, and was thrown on her head, and picked up as dead. By an odd coincidence, the young gentleman, Mr. John Mackey—then a medical student at St. George's—who flew to her assistance, conveyed her to his hospital, and dressed her wounds—acted with her in 'The Passport.' At rehearsal she pronounces herself to be 'the despair of the author and a most lamentable study;' up to the opening night she never lays down her book, and gets the sense of the play long before the words. However, when the evening comes she is 'as firm as a rock.' In appearance she is tall with slender figure, expressive grey-blue eyes that sparkle with mirth under the level brows; straight features and a wealth of chestnut-coloured hair coiled carelessly round a classically shaped head.

Miss Kingston's pretty little red and white house stands in a road near Belgravia, and gives a bright bit of colour to the somewhat dull-looking terrace. Two rooms open into each other, the great bay windows of the further one looking out on to a gay little garden. The walls are hung with a beautiful and unique paper of softly tinted peacocks on branches of trees; the deep crimson tiles of the fireplace give a warmth to the pale green of the hearth and harmonise well with the carved overmantel after Adams of the last century. A grand pianoforte, Hampton Court chairs, Chippendale bureau, and tiny Davenport, together with a revolving bookcase and many ferns and plants in full bloom, complete a picture of domestic comfort. Success achieved early in her career has in no way relaxed Miss Kingston's efforts. She takes it very quietly, and is always working for something higher; and 'Onward, ever onward,' is her motto.

REV. PROFESSOR SHUTTLEWORTH

JUST on the bend of Lambeth-hill, nestled amid ungainly warehouses, and in the very heart of the busy, bustling City, stands a pretty red-brick Queen Anne house, which forms a strange contrast and gives a bright bit of colour to its unlovely surroundings. In 1883, when the Rev. Professor Shuttleworth was appointed Rector of St. Nicholas Cole Abbey, he asked his friend Mr. George Birch, architect of 'Ye Olde London Streete' at the Health Exhibition, to build him a residence in what he calls this Tower of Babel, and the result is the artistic house of which the exterior and the interior are alike picturesque. A square oak staircase leads up to the rector's study at the back, where a broad window stretches across one side, terminating in a little balcony on the left. The look-out is on a quad, with garden in front, containing a solitary tree and bounded on each side by warehouses, while at the further end can be seen the red roof and lattice windows of the new club, in which its founder, the rector, is so keenly interested, and of which more anon. An aviary with singing birds adds its brightness to the scene—two tame canaries fly about the room, and frequently alight on his shoulder, for he 'loves to have living things around him.' Over the mantelshelf hang two fine etchings—portraits of Frederic Denison Maurice, the prophet, and of Ruskin—with a Bartolozzi picture in the centre of the famous Dean Colet, of St. Paul's, this last a gift from Mr. Aldam Heaton. A valued possession, presented to him by his people, is a broad, roomy writing-table of light oak, with innumerable cupboards and drawers reaching halfway up to the ceiling—one of the chief merits of which, in its owner's eyes, is that he 'can be as untidy as he pleases, and the revolving lid shuts it all in.' On its corner stands a charming portrait of a young and graceful woman, with dark eyes and hair, and serene, thoughtful expression. 'My wife,' he says with a smile as he hands it to you, 'and the best helper I have.' His secretary's desk, before the window, presents a different aspect, and is as neat as can be desired. Bookcases, tall, dwarf, and revolving, in every available space, are crammed with books, while from a cavernous-looking, half-open cupboard below a vast heap of MSS., proofs, and music may be dimly discerned.

The genial, boyish-faced professor was born in Cornwall, where his father held a living, and is descended from a good old Lancashire Jacobite family, many of whom sacrificed their lives for the cause outside the walls of Preston. He was educated entirely at Walthamstowe, where he became a distinguished athlete, and carried off every attainable prize. Thence, in 1869, to Oxford, where he first entered St. Mary Hall and took a scholarship, migrating later to Christ Church, where among his friends who afterwards achieved fame were Sir Ellis Ashmead-Bartlett; James Hannington, the martyr bishop; George Russell, the present Under-Secretary for the Home Department; Ingham, Bishop of Sierra Leone; and Wilson, the first white man found at Uganda. In 1873, the young student took his B.A. degree with high honours, and, as from boyhood he had always determined to be a parson, was duly ordained, got his first title to Holy Orders at St. Barnabas, Oxford, and soon became absorbed in the work. With the curacy he held the chaplaincy of Christ Church—a somewhat unusual circumstance—and remained for three years. In 1876, he was appointed a minor canon of St. Paul's Cathedral, with which election his strong musical gifts and the possession of a fine baritone voice had probably something to do; but it happened that a special kind of man was wanted who could influence and manage youths. As the young minor canon had always at heart a longing desire to do something for young men and lads, no more fitting appointment could have been made. Here was a grand opportunity, of which he availed himself to the uttermost. He continued for seven years at the post, and got to know a great deal about the deep, throbbing heart of the City and its inner life and conditions—an experience which has proved very valuable since. While yet at St. Paul's he was appointed, in 1883, one of the lecturers in the Faculty of Theology, at King's College, London, and, in 1890, he succeeded Dr. Swete—who became Regius Professor of Divinity at Cambridge—as Professor of 'Pastoral Theology.' At the age of thirty-four he was offered by the Dean and Chapter the Rectory of St. Nicholas Cole Abbey.

'The church is of Wren's architecture,' remarks Professor Shuttleworth, with something between a smile and a sigh; 'and very ugly. It is like a great hall, though we have made it as beautiful as possible with interior decoration. But my choir'—and he brightens up visibly—'I am proud of my choir; it is quite unique. At first, as there were no boys to be found, I got ladies to sing *pro tem.*, and they proved so satisfactory that I have never wished to make an exchange. They are so efficient, earnest, and tractable; the men are surpliced.' Together with the musical rector and the able choir-master, Mr. Henry Cooper, and the organist, Mr. Ralph Norris (whom the rector brought from Oxford), this well trained band of men and women produce most effectively on one Sunday afternoon in winter months and on one evening in each month, portions of such oratorios and sacred music as Gounod's 'Gallia' and 'De Profundis,' Mozart's 'Requiem,' Handel's 'Passion Music,' Sullivan's 'Light of the World,' &c. The whole idea bears on and grew out of Professor Shuttleworth's work at St. Paul's Cathedral. In the summer months there is no afternoon service, as he says that people are much better out in the open air. His preaching is too well known to need much mention. Entirely extempore, but carefully prepared, he possesses great fluency, and never hesitates for words. He seldom exceeds half an hour, feeling that if a man has something to say people will not grudge him time to say it; but it is when he has nothing, and takes three-quarters of an hour to give it words, that they do not like it. One characteristic of his work is that he endeavours to cater for different classes of people: for instance, on Sunday mornings the services are remarkable for their rather elaborate music, simple but dignified ritual, with no fuss, which appeal to the more refined type of devout mind. On alternate Sunday mornings there is no sermon; but a Bible exposition, with the latest criticism, is given. In the evening it is a plain parochial service with simple chants. The wisdom of this plan is evident, for whereas when Professor Shuttleworth first came as rector the congregation consisted of four or five old people (who were paid to come), now, though the church is in the City, and so far out of the way, there is scarcely standing room for the crowds that flock in, of which a noticeable feature is that they are largely composed of men. Another successful work was the institution of a series of lectures, apart from the services, dealing with social or general questions—of course, from the Christian point of view—delivered sometimes by himself, sometimes by other clergy, and these attract large audiences, especially when the subject be of more than ordinary interest. Among such lectures have been: 'Some Churchmen and their Influence on English Life and Thought,' 'The Church and the Public Health,' 'John Keble the Poet,' and 'John Colet the Reformer.'

St. Nicholas is open every day for six hours for people who seek a quiet half-hour's rest from their labours, and that this privilege is appreciated is manifest by the many who go in and out. 'I am dead against the pulling down of the City churches,' says the rector earnestly. 'It is a scandal and a shame—not to say a penny-wise pound-foolish proceeding. I am of the opinion that the day will come when people will return to the City to live. If it were not for the Inhabited House duty, not the heads of firms, but the foremen would be able to occupy the empty top floors of all these warehouses—and what an advantage to them it would be!'

At this juncture the door opens and the children enter to exhibit a bowl of gold fish just presented as a birthday gift to the youngest girl. These bright, healthy-looking little ones show no trace of a city life, but the Embankment is close at hand, and there they get plenty of fresh air and exercise. It is for their sakes that the rector has striven to make the interior of his home so attractive, for he holds the theory that beautiful environments are essential to the dawning intelligence and to the development of artistic tastes of the young. Wherefore the high latticed windows shut out all that is unlovely without, and are gaily decorated with boxes of plants in flower, while the thickness of the well-built walls deadens the sound of the teeming out-door traffic.

From the time he entered on his duties at St. Nicholas' Professor Shuttleworth had formed a scheme which soon grew very near his heart. This was the inauguration of a club on a social basis with one original feature—that it should include women as well as men members. 'I desired,' he says, 'to provide a comfortable place of social intercourse, culture, and recreation for young men and women, chiefly, though not exclusively, those employed in the City.' A thorough organiser, and gifted with remarkable energy and tact, Professor Shuttleworth was not long before he elaborated his scheme. At first he hired and furnished two floors of a warehouse in Queen Victoria Street, which soon extended to three. The club opened in September 1889. Then, as the members outgrew the premises, he took the freehold site opposite his study windows and built the new club, which he is striving to place upon a permanent and self-supporting basis. During the past five years he has collected 5,000*l.* for this purpose, and now only needs 2,000*l.* more to start it free of debt. The new premises — which were opened by the Lord Mayor—consist of a large drawing-room where reviews, magazines, and newspapers are provided, and contain a permanent stage for entertainments, lectures, &c. At the back is a ladies' toilet room; there is a spacious library for reading, conversation, and work; a reference and also a circulating library, besides a large games room with two full-sized billiard-tables; a refreshment room and bar, with the usual club meals and smoking room. This admirable institution, for admittance to which there is no religious test of any kind, is under the patronage of the Lord Mayor and the Lady Mayoress, and is managed by a committee, of which the rector is president, and among the nineteen or twenty distinguished names of vice-presidents are those of Mrs. Shuttleworth and Miss Ellen Terry. It is an indescribable boon to many hard workers, who here find a resting-place such as they cannot get elsewhere, while the joint admission of the sexes is attended

with the best results. A close and careful observer of
men and manners, Professor Shuttleworth has noted with
joy the good effects upon different phases of character
which this judicious system has brought about—how the
shy, awkward young fellows have become more refined and
polished and less selfish; and many weary, depressed girls
have grown brighter and happier in the healthy, social
atmosphere of a mutual meeting-place whose privileges
have never yet been abused. For amusements they have
in winter, monthly Cinderella dances, smoking concerts,
and tournaments of billiards, whist, and chess; while in
summer there are cricket, tennis, and croquet clubs in
connection with the club at Bowes Park.

All of which speaks volumes for the sound, practical
judgment and the robust common-sense of the young
rector of St. Nicholas'. Brought up a High Churchman,
he has had much experience of the world, and has emerged
from any narrow grooves, though what his views are is
best indicated by what he has done. He is an ex-president
of the National Sunday League and a member of the
committee of the Christian Social Union, and may be considered of the same type of man as his friends the Rev.
Canons Scott Holland of St. Paul's, and Gore and Eyton
of Westminster. He is, besides, lecturer on literary and
historical subjects at the ladies' department at King's College, Kensington, and does a good deal of drawing-room
lecturing with the object of raising money for his club.

Before you leave, Professor Shuttleworth shows you
other rooms in his charming house, and points out a fine
oil painting of his grandfather, Post-Captain Cary, R.N.,
who was a midshipman in the 'Victory' at Trafalgar.
When he bids you adieu at the hall door he says, with a
merry laugh, 'I call myself professor of sanctified common-
sense, since Pastoral Theology defines the practical and
parochial side of clerical work.'

x

MISS FORTESCUE

THERE is a sense of reposeful dignity in the stately buildings known by the name of St. Ermin's Mansions, near Westminster. The great courtyard looks not unlike a college quad, and certainly no inhabitant requires to keep a clock, or has the smallest excuse for unpunctuality, for the sonorous tones of Big Ben roll out the quarters over the peaceful precincts with unfailing regularity. Their quiet, too, is undisturbed by the excruciating itinerant brass band or the ubiquitous organ-grinder, while the solid structure of the interior is so well arranged with regard to acoustic properties that even a neighbour's piano is not distinctly enough heard to be an annoyance. So well is this fact recognised that the great mansions are continually filled with members of Parliament, reading and thinking people, and students of art, literature, and science. It takes but a moment to glide up by the lift and to land at the picturesquely appointed flat where Miss Fortescue is located with her mother and sister, and it needs but a glance at the sweet lady—who rises from a comfortable Chesterfield sofa and greets you with a clear, silvery voice—to see from whom the young actress gets her inheritance of personal attractions—the straight Greek nose, the short upper lip, the classical contour of face, and the abundant masses of fair hair, which in the elder lady's case the hand of time has mellowed into pure white.

The artistic decorations of the delightful drawing-room merit a special word of comment. Art has not been allowed to interfere with comfort. The polished floor is liberally strewn with great Oriental rugs, in the broad window recess stands a carved blackwood couch, thrown into relief against the richly embroidered curtains. The actress's own ebonised writing-table is severely neat, and on a shelf above stand a few treasured photographs—notably one of her only sister, known on the stage as Miss Helen Ferrers. Bookcases in every direction—revolving, dwarf, &c., and all well filled. A principal feature above the iris-papered walls is a narrow Japanese frieze—bound in bamboo—of which there is only one other in England. Flowers and palms in abundance; valuable old Indian and blue china here and there—among the latter two beautiful Spode plates; and Miss Fortescue is justly proud of her fine collection of proof etchings, among which can be seen Mason's 'The Gleaner' and 'The Return from Harvest,' Fred Walker's 'Bray and Cookham.'

Miss Fortescue was born in London in the lap of luxury, and was educated at home with extreme care under the most cultivated teachers of English, French, German, and Italian. She laughingly pronounces herself to have been a 'real naughty child,' but here the mother, with a tender smile, murmurs a deprecating word, and says, 'It was all high spirits, for she loved riding, boating, and all country and out-door life.' These tastes, together with a love of travelling, have strengthened in her, but the excellent training of her childhood soon bore fruits. Being blessed with great determination and force of character, she applied herself diligently to her books and studies, and, without relinquishing the healthy amusements that she so loved, laid in a store of knowledge, and cultivated a love of literature and a natural gift for music and languages. 'These two last talents,' says Miss Fortescue, 'I inherit from my mother and her family; they are all good linguists and excellent musicians, but not one of my people has painted a picture, written a book, or previously faced the footlights.' And nothing was further from her own intention until the day came when her father unfortunately embarked in some speculations which turned out to be unlucky; then the young girl cast about in her mind for some way to earn money, and soon discovered that the openings were few for people who had no technical knowledge and no technical training on definite subjects. Nature, however, had been kind to her in the matter of outward appearance of face and form, and no less generous in endowing her with a sweet disposition and a happy, sanguine temperament that would only view circumstances through rose-coloured glasses. But Miss Fortescue lays most stress on her educational advantages. 'From the first,' she explains, 'we were taught to speak well and easily, and to pronounce with clear enunciation, in which our mother excelled ; and, still further, we were encouraged to think for—but not of—ourselves, and to avoid all nervousness and self-consciousness.' All wise and judicious training, which was shortly to produce good results ! Certainly no girl could have found the *entrée* into theatrical life more easy than Miss Fortescue, though she acknowledges that in the present day the difficulties of such a step have increased a hundredfold. A friend gave her an introduction to Mr. D'Oyly Carte, who was then going to mount 'Patience'—a play which contained three minor parts in addition to the two chief *rôles*. At the suggestion of Mr. W. S. Gilbert, to whom so many *débutantes* owe their subsequent success, and whose discerning eye saw that here was promising material, Mr. Carte offered her the part of Lady Ella, and she was bidden to rehearsal. Never in any circumstances at an amateur performance—not even in a charade—had she previously tested her powers. The self-dependence to which she had been reared came into use, and if, as she naïvely remarks, she felt that 'fools rush in where angels fear to tread,' her utter absence of self-consciousness and of nervousness stood her in good stead. The part of Lady Ella was singularly well adapted to the young player's fine personality, while her musical gifts—singing studied under Randegger and music under the late Sir George Elvey, organist of the Chapel Royal, Windsor—proved to be valuable adjuncts.

During the two and a half years that Miss Fortescue remained in Mr. D'Oyly Carte's company she followed the excellent advice given to her, and, besides playing in the evening at the Savoy, she acted in as many *matinées* as possible, thereby largely increasing her experience. At the conclusion of that time she fulfilled an engagement with Mr. Cecil and the late Mr. Clayton at the Court in a revival of Mr. Gilbert's play 'Dan'l Druce,' with Hermann Vezin in his original *rôle* of the village blacksmith, and, later, went on to the Strand and played in the revival of ' Our Boys.' Her next step was to take a long tour on her own account and with her own company. She opened with ' Pygmalion and Galatea,' and took this *rôle* for the first time. ' I never think of Galatea,' remarks Miss Fortescue brightly, ' without recalling a most humorous incident connected with it. My two pet dogs —a collie and a particularly intelligent black poodle, Buddha—are in the habit of accompanying me to the theatre, and, except on that occasion, have always behaved with great discretion. One evening, just in the scene where Galatea, awakened into life, descends slowly from her pedestal, to my horror Buddha gravely walked in, marched up to the empty pedestal, sniffed for a moment, then sat on it, calmly surveying the audience with a self-satisfied expression. The humours of " Black and White " were well illustrated, but the contrast between the jet black poodle perched where the marble-white Galatea had just descended was too much for the audience, who simply fell into paroxysms of laughter. I turned round and gave the dog one look, from which I do not think she has yet recovered ; but she took the hint and retired in the same dignified manner in which she entered, and she has never since transgressed—but it was an awful moment!' The provincial tour was followed by a prolonged visit with her company to America—a visit that Miss Fortescue greatly enjoyed, and to which she looks back with pleasure—where she ' made many friends and received much kindness.' She played for nine weeks in New York, and at all the principal States and in Canada. Since that time she has alternated between the provinces—with her own company—and in London, under other managements, and she has lately made a successful tour in South Africa and Australia. Her repertory comprises nearly two hundred characters.

'I like the hard-working battle of life,' says the actress with enthusiasm. 'I love my profession, but a dramatic career becomes more and more of an exotic and less of a garden flower—more, so to speak, of the hot-house atmosphere. I find prose more difficult to learn than poetry, and blank verse easier than either. I am rather a slow study, and like long preparation.' Miss Fortescue has the keenest sense of humour. She is very short-sighted, which she declares 'to have its advantages, as, seeing nothing in front, she is never disturbed by people moving or any eccentricities.' But if she cannot see, she is particularly sensitive in feeling the spirit of an audience, and if they are going along with her or not; she pronounces the difference of the sensation of the mental atmosphere of audiences in different places—perhaps only fifty miles apart—to be perfectly extraordinary. She is as fond of country life—at its best—as in the days of her childhood, and delights in riding, rowing, and all outdoor exercises. She has 'read hard' all her life, and is now more than ever an omnivorous reader—memoirs and history of every sort and kind being a passion—while historical research into unpublished papers from the muniment rooms of great houses—the Paston Letters, Maxwell Lyte's Cecil papers from Hatfield—are perfectly fascinating to her. But she frankly avows that she 'hates science,' and attributes it to 'a kink in her brain, an absence of a faculty—call it what you like.' She is extremely adaptable, and in her foreign trips is wont to enjoy mixing with and talking to the peasants in Germany, Italy, and France in their own language. She confesses to a 'great capacity for hero-worship, and that no one was more bitten than herself by the Napoleonic craze,' adding quaintly, 'If I had been Napoleon's door mat I should have looked down—or up—with disdain on the hatstand of lesser lights.'

TIVADAR NACHÈZ

It is with almost a feeling of awe that you gaze at the violin, reposing in its case, at the pretty little flat in the West End of London, where the world-renowned violinist, Mr. Tivadar Nachèz, has made his home. The instrument—

> 'That small, sweet thing,
> Devised in love and fashioned cunningly
> Of wood and strings'

—on which he evokes the exquisite melodies that have caused his fame to spread throughout the kingdom, is a genuine Stradivarius of the grand pattern which cost one thousand guineas, but it has probably repaid its price many thousand times over in the skilful hands of its gifted owner, as, with his extraordinary executive power, his clear phrasing, and perfect technique, he pours out his whole poetic soul with the bow on its strings.

It is a strange fact that Mr. Tivadar Nachèz has in no way inherited the divine gift of music, nor can he trace back any such inheritance in his remote ancestry. He was born at Buda-Pesth in May 1859, and is one of five children of Major Nachèz, an officer in the Austrian army, who distinguished himself in the Revolution of 1849. Ere yet he could speak plainly he would sit on the floor listening with delight to his mother while she played on the piano, and, with one bit of stick under his chin and another in his hand, he would pretend to accompany her on the fiddle. Before he was five years of age the talent manifested itself so strongly that his grandfather bought him a little violin and paid for his lessons from Sabathiel, leader of the orchestra of the Royal opera in his native town. The great Liszt, who was then president of the State Academy of Music, was a frequent guest to play whist at the house of Major Nachèz, and took the keenest interest in the musical education of the gifted child, and at a charity concert given by Liszt in aid of the sufferers by an inundation he insisted that the young Tivadar should play. At this entertainment, at the age of seven, he performed in public for the first time, and gave the violin concerto by Lipinski. During the next three years he played at a series of *matinées* given by Liszt for the benefit of the students in company with the illustrious master in such pieces as Schumann's sonatas, and in many of Beethoven's works, and it was this period that influenced his whole subsequent life. But on reaching his eleventh year it became necessary that his general education should be considered, for which purpose he was sent to the Catholic States Gymnasium, the preparatory school for the university. Now, it is the law in Austria that every man shall serve his country, and at the end of his school career the young student would have had to take active service for three years, but, having applied himself with such hearty goodwill to his tasks, he passed the Matura examination, which confers the right to reduce the usual period under arms to one year. On leaving the Gymnasium he entered into competition for the three years' Government scholarship for music, and won it out of 346 candidates. This scholarship was one of four that were founded to commemorate the crowning of the Emperor of Austria King of Hungary, and enabled him to proceed to Berlin to be trained under Joachim, with whom Tivadar Nachèz studied for three years, while at the same time he took lessons from Professor Kiel in harmony. Later he went on to Paris, worked under Leonard, and devoted himself to the technicalities of his art.

Mr. Nachèz has a peculiarly touching remembrance of a

concert at which he played when only sixteen years of
age, at the Cirque d'Hiver, under the conductorship of
Pasdeloup. He had performed the very difficult Concerto
in F sharp minor by Ernst, and the widowed Madame
Ernst was among the audience. 'She came into the
artists' room,' he says, 'at the conclusion, and said many
kind, complimentary words on my rendering of her husband's music, declaring that it had brought tears to her
eyes. She then invited me to her house, and gave me this
bow that you see, which the famous composer had used.
His spirit seems to have been with me ever since. It was
while I was still at college that I met Richter, who had
just come to Buda-Pesth fresh from the influence of
Wagner. He woke us all up with his Philharmonic
concerts, to which my teacher took me to play at the first
desk, and my soul awakened to the beauties of Mozart,
Beethoven, and Schumann's symphonies.

At the age of twenty-two Tivadar Nachèz decided to
spread his wings and come to London. His first step was
to apply to Mr. Manns at the Crystal Palace to give him
a hearing. That gentleman at first demurred, saying he
had no free day, and he had Joachim, Neruda, Sarasate,
&c. Not to be daunted, however, the young musician
coaxed the *impresario* to hear him, with the immediate
result that he was offered five guineas to play at the
Saturday concert. 'Guineas were scarce with me then,'
he remarks pithily, 'and I jumped at it!' The impression
he made was so favourable that he was at once engaged
for the next concert, and the basis of his success was
established. From that time his reputation was assured;
he was invited to play in all the principal towns throughout Great Britain, and has never since lacked engagements
or admirers. He has the proud satisfaction of feeling that
he has conquered the public entirely by his own merits
and made the score off his own bat. During many tours
through Germany, Switzerland, Russia, Austria, &c., he
has performed before nearly every crowned head in Europe.

After the first of these Continental wanderings Mr. Nachèz returned to England and played at the Philharmonic Concerts, at Princes' Hall, at the London Musical Society's Concerts, and at one of the Royal Amateur Orchestral Society's Concerts at which his old friend Liszt was present. And then came a terrible catastrophe that threatened to extinguish an exceptionally brilliant career. While tricycling he fell and broke his bow arm, which kept him a cripple for nearly a year; during this time he travelled in Germany and Vienna, where the skill of the renowned Professor Billroth restored to him the full use of the arm. Mr. Nachèz has a pleasant recollection of two concerts at the Guildhall, Plymouth, in 1891, when the Duke of Edinburgh was first violin. At the conclusion of the second concert the Duke addressed the members of the orchestra in the artists' room, and, after speaking in the warmest words of appreciation of Mr. Nachèz' solo, proposed that he should at once be elected an hon. member of the Royal Amateur Orchestral Society. The proposal was unanimously carried, and His Royal Highness took off his own badge of membership and fastened it on the young violinist's breast. His artistic achievements soon brought him before the notice of the Queen and the Royal Family, and he has repeatedly been commanded to Balmoral and Windsor by Her Majesty, who signified her approval in the most gratifying terms. It will be remembered that he was also specially summoned, together with Madame Albani, by H.R.H. the Duke of Saxe-Coburg Gotha, to perform again before Her Majesty and other Imperial and Royal guests at the wedding festivities of April 21, 1894, on which occasion he was presented with the first class of the Saxe-Coburg-Gotha Family Order and with other valuable souvenirs.

Year after year Tivadar Nachèz has performed at all great musical meetings, at the Patti and Albeniz concerts, at Sir Augustus Harris's operatic concerts, together with private entertainments at the most fashionable houses in

London. Among some of his chief triumphs were three violin recitals that he held in St. James's Hall during the season of 1894, where, in spite of the hot weather and the classical nature of the music, the great hall was filled to overflowing with critical and enthusiastic audiences. He was then engaged for a tour in company with Mr. Ben Davies, and played at Leipsic, Stuttgart, Berlin, Munich, Prague, Vienna, &c., not omitting his native town, Buda-Pesth. At these Continental concerts he put before the public programmes classical to the highest degree, including Bach, Schumann, Corelli, Beethoven, Mendelssohn, but always introduced one or more pieces by English composers. Among some thirty to forty of his own compositions the most important are a concerto for violin and orchestra (dedicated to his old master Dr. Joachim) and his world-famed Hungarian Dances, which are in their seventeenth edition, and have been reprinted in six different countries. Nor must a Swedish Rhapsody be omitted, for thereby hangs a tale. A few years ago, when at Stockholm, he was invited to play at Stockholm, where the Queen of Sweden, though lying ill, was desirous of hearing, even if she could not see, him. The Crown Prince asked whether he could play a Swedish air, and he tried to play a soft, pathetic, Swedish national melody, improvising on it. This was attended with happy results, and moved the King so deeply that he gave the young artist a command to write a work for the violin on this melody. His engagements of late have included many at private houses—notably at one very distinguished reception—where, with no other vocal or instrumental help, he kept the attention of fashionable but critical audiences riveted for three hours with selections from Handel, Wagner, Bazzini, &c., and some of his own compositions.

Never was a favourite of the public so completely unspoiled by success. Simple and genial by nature, perfectly unaffected and full of bright conversation, Tivadar Nachèz has won the hearts of all those in the country that he loves to call 'the land of his adoption,' though, he adds with a smile, 'of course my own Hungary must come first. But when I have been abroad, and return to see the white cliffs of Dover, I know that I shall find a place for my weary head to rest, and I forget my present shortcomings in the country and among the people that I regard with so much estimation and affection.'

BEATRICE WHITBY

(*MRS. PHILIP HICKS*)

THE bright sunshine and soft, balmy breeze make the morning stroll very pleasant as you wend your way through the handsome, scrupulously clean streets of Leamington towards the house which has lately become the home of the well-known author, Beatrice Whitby. Strictly a modern town—for sixty years ago it was only a tiny village, without even a butcher's shop—it covers a good deal of ground considering the number of the inhabitants. Of late years it has become so popular as a hunting centre and 'pleasure place' that it has actually joined on to Warwick, and is even reaching out arms to Kenilworth. The broad streets are airy and well lined with trees, which seem to have made rapid growth; the buildings are handsome and well constructed, and there is a general well-to-do appearance all round.

In the main road that runs from end to end of Leamington stands the big house to which Dr. Hicks brought his bride. She is, however, by no means a stranger in the town, and by an odd coincidence her present residence happens to be the very same house that her father formerly occupied for many years. Her recent marriage has taken Beatrice Whitby away from her late home in Devon, but here she has no intention of giving up her work; and in this new step in life Mrs. Hicks has won the good wishes and congratulations not only of her many personal friends, but also of a large section of the novel-reading public. The house within is charming. The drawing-room is gay with flowers and luxuriant maidenhair ferns; a handsome black retriever, 'Sweep,' is stretched on the hearth-rug, and inspects you critically, but, apparently satisfied with his scrutiny, comes forward and presents a huge paw by way of greeting. 'He knows everything,' says the young author, smiling, 'and is a valued friend. He has been at my heels indoors and out for eight years. I am delighted with everything,' she continues presently, as you take furtive glances around. 'My husband has picked up all sorts of antique furniture, Chippendale and Sheraton—there are few legs in the house that are not "ball and claw"; the old prints and engravings are also a hobby of his. He has arranged a delightful room for my study at the back.' To this study, in which there are many reminiscences of her late home in Devon, you both adjourn. Among various pictures on the walls there is one which Beatrice Whitby regards with peculiar affection. It represents a long, two-storied, old-fashioned house, with sloping roof and wide verandah-top overhanging the great windows below, which command a lovely view of the valley, framed in hills, and of a widely-spreading lawn opening out into four acres of gardens and orchards. It is Ridgway House, Ottery St. Mary's, her birthplace and home for twenty-three years. Close by this picture hangs one of 'Larkbeare,' where Thackeray lived for many years, and where, in the surrounding neighbourhood, he laid the scenes of 'Pendennis.' Here, too, is a photograph of Ottery and the house where the poet Coleridge was born, and another of a favourite church —'very beautiful, very old, very interesting,' she says. 'Charles Lamb, in his play "John Woodville," alludes to the bells. The chimes in monotone are the sweetest I ever heard.' The cleverly executed pastel portrait on an easel, of Miss Whitby herself, is the work of the promising young artist Miss Maud Coleridge, who has caught the likeness admirably. The talented young author of 'The Awakening of Mary Fenwick' and other novels is one of a family of eight, and is a daughter of Dr. Whitby. Her mother was a Welsh woman, Miss Philipps of Llwyncrum in Carmarthenshire, and niece of the celebrated beauty, Lady Owen of Orielton, Pembrokeshire, who, judging by the many photographs that are to be seen representing handsome brothers and sisters, has handed down her good looks to the younger generation. Yonder noble-looking youth was a lieutenant in H.M. 17th Regiment, and met with a soldier's death in the Afghanistan war. Young as he was he had made his mark in journalism, and was editor of 'The Khandahar News' when he was killed in battle. Another, in a cricketing suit, was a renowned bowler at Oxford during his four years' residence at that University. 'The celebrated swift bowler's sister,' wrote a kindly sporting editor to her, some time later, as he warmly congratulated her on the success of her first (published) book.

All these young people had healthy, athletic tastes as well as considerable literary ability. 'With the exception of a year at Hamburg,' says Beatrice Whitby, as she leads the way into the dining-room, where luncheon is spread, 'I was educated entirely at home. We were all quick at writing and fond of reading, and our studies were made agreeable by patient and cultivated teachers. We used to tell each other tales, as I suppose most children do; the woes that came my way I lamented in poems, and as soon as I left the school-room I set to work to write a story.' Of the practical making of printed books the young girl was naturally profoundly ignorant. In those days there was no 'Society of Authors' to enlighten her (or, at least, if there were, she knew nothing of it). For the forming of such a society experienced and inexperienced authors can never be sufficiently grateful to Mr. Walter Besant. The fate of her first story was unfortunate. Miss Whitby sent it in answer to an advertisement for MSS. to London, where neither MS. nor advertiser could subsequently be heard of. With 'Mary Fenwick' she deemed it safest to go to a firm whose name she copied from a book in the library. 'But I fell into good hands,' observes the novelist. 'Messrs. Chatto and Windus at once accepted it. I had judged it to be the length of a shilling book, but heard, to my surprise, it would form a three-volume novel. I am a particularly slow writer, and my people used to get impatient over the time that I spent in seclusion. I remember that we had Anthony Trollope's "Life and Reminiscences" in the house, and from it they gathered that Mrs. Trollope—his mother—has written her best novel in three weeks, during the intervals of nursing a sick child, and it had taken me an unjustifiable nine months of hard work to write my story! No,' she continues in answer to a question, 'I was not at all elated at the prospect of authorship as the time of publication came on, though one of the three people who had read my MS. assured me that she "had often read more stupid things in print ;" a second wrote me to "be sure and prepare myself for the very worst," while the third remarked pithily, "reviewers don't take off their hats to *ladies*—only to good *writers*!" Even the man at the bookstall volunteered that "a nasty, slashing review, Miss, will often do a book more good than harm!"'

All well meant, but very discouraging to a girl-writer whose own opinion of her merits was particularly modest. However, the book came out, and so did the reviews, and there was nothing 'nasty' or 'slashing' in any of them. On the contrary, they were all so kind and encouraging that Beatrice Whitby, after a short period of rest, was emboldened to begin again, slowly and deliberately, as is her wont, and during a residence at Leamington re-wrote the story that had been originally lost, called 'Part of the Property.' This was by and by followed by others, entitled 'One Reason Why,' 'In the Suntime of Her Youth,' 'A Question of Skill,' &c.

Her first work went into a second edition in a couple of weeks, and has since passed into many more. It brought, as her later books have done, many letters of commendation from unknown correspondents in Tasmania, America, and other countries. A sequel is entitled 'Mary Fenwick's Daughter' (now in its third edition), wherein the reader meets again with renewed interest the old friends who proved so fascinating in the former story.

The peculiar sensation of quiet and peace in the views around her beloved and native county Devon, where most of her work was done, has largely influenced the life and work of Beatrice Whitby. With a keen sense of humour and an intuitive perception of peculiarities, alike in persons and in things, she has a strong appreciation of the beauties in nature, which she has cultivated to the uttermost. No effect or scene escapes her notice. Her characters are at once natural and easy, while the purity and innocence of the tone in no way detracts from their vigour and interest.

Beatrice Whitby is, like her novel, 'in the suntime of her youth.' Much of her life is in front of her. If, while yet in her teens, she could write such a story as 'Part of the Property,' and follow it some few years later by 'The Awakening of Mary Fenwick,' what possibilities may not be in store for her in the future?

ARTHUR à BECKETT

THERE is scarcely a corner in Mr. à Beckett's bright and artistic house, standing in the west side of Eccleston Square, that is not fraught with relics and memories of a peculiarly interesting and eventful career. The hall and staircase are lined with framed collections of valuable letters, pictures, autographs, and etchings—reminiscences from most of the well-known people of the day as well as of those who have gone before.

MR. ARTHUR W. À BECKETT

Beyond the great double drawing-rooms, divided by a white arch, there can be seen an extension recess; the pale-tinted yellow walls are hung with original drawings by Sir John Tenniel, Sambourne, and Du Maurier; the art-blue felt is strewn with Persian rugs of subdued tints, and on the carved white overmantels and genuine old Chippendale bureaus and cabinets stand many choice specimens of old blue and Oriental china; but there is one special corner which takes you back in imagination to the last century—every detail is correct, from the old-fashioned and quaint mirror and ancient grandfather clock to the framed 'Mask of Flowers' programme of the entertainment given at Gray's Inn which Arthur à Beckett arranged, edited, and produced, and in which he was chosen by H.R.H. the Duke of Connaught and the other benchers to act as Master of the Revels. The original drawing is in the possession of the Hon. Society of Gray's Inn, with which seat of learning the names of three generations of à Becketts are associated.

Arthur à Beckett is the third son of the late Gilbert Abbott à Beckett—Metropolitan Police Magistrate—who was on the original staff of 'Punch' with Thackeray, Dickens, Douglas Jerrold, and other literary giants. He was born at Portland House, close to the Addison Road Railway Station—'Punch's Railway' it was called, because the elder Mr. à Beckett used to chaff it in that humorous journal when the line—at first an utter failure, now valuable property—cut through and spoilt his garden. The young Arthur was first sent to a private tutor, Mr. 'Dominie' Birch, who had been an officer in the army; the result was that, hearing so much about facings, drills, and other military matters, nearly every boy under his care obtained a commission in the army as he would have done himself had he been allowed. Later, when the family moved to Hyde Park Gate, he attended the Kensington Grammar School, where the late Dr. Payne Smith, subsequently Dean of Canterbury, was head

Y

master. Thirty years after, when Mr. à Beckett went down to Canterbury to inquire into the disturbing of the bones said to be those of St. Thomas à Becket, he strolled into the minster to hear the service, and from behind a pillar, where he could not see, he at once recognised, in the reader of the lesson, the voice of his old master. After the service the Dean, too, recognised the face of his whilom pupil before he mentioned his name! Among the boys at the same school was Mr. R. A. Bayford, a great athlete, and in the eleven at Cambridge—now Q.C.—in whose chambers Arthur à Beckett subsequently read after he was called to the Bar.

Accustomed from childhood to be much in the society of the most distinguished wits, men of letters, and celebrities of all sorts, and inheriting from his father a strong literary bias, it was only to be expected that the young student should make his mark at his next schools, first Honiton and later Felsted—the while athletic and field sports were by no means neglected. At both he organised debating societies and started magazines; at the age of twelve he carried off the divinity and history prizes—the latter rather for excellent composition than for correct detail, as he had got up the whole from his father's work, the 'Comic History of England.' The late Dr. Mackarness, afterwards Bishop of Oxford, was then head-master at Honiton, and it is worthy of note that Mr. à Beckett has recently taken the chair at the respective dinners given by the 'old boys' of both schools.

Of his father Mr. à Beckett speaks with peculiar affection. 'I have the greatest reverence for his memory,' he remarks; 'he treated me more as a grown-up friend than as a child, and frequently took me to his court. Only the other day Mr. Toole told me that my father took the chair at the first reading of "Trying a Magistrate." At the end some man got up and angrily protested that it was meant for himself—oddly enough the name was the same—and Toole said my father had to interfere as chairman, and put everyone into good humour by his dignified geniality.'

Up to the time of his lamented father's death Arthur à Beckett had been destined for a university career with a view to Holy Orders. Circumstances, however, altered this intention, and at the age of eighteen he entered (thanks to a nomination from Lord Palmerston) the War Office, where in the same rooms were John Norman Lockyer, F.R.S. (the great astronomer), Tom Hood, Clement Scott, and other distinguished men. When landed at the War Office it was but natural that a youth possessed of such strong journalistic propensities and surrounded by so many literary spirits should find the routine of a government bureau somewhat monotonous and uncongenial. Out of office hours, however, he found plenty of amusement assisting at Mrs. Milner Gibson's private theatricals with Mr. Merivale, the late Sir Charles Young, Mr. B. C. Stevenson, Quentin Twiss, &c. Here, too, he met Mrs. Gibson's son-in-law, Mr. Robertson—Registrar of Designs at the Board of Trade—who was just then intent on starting a new evening paper in conjunction with the members of the Old Arlington Club. He invited the young member of the Civil Service to act as his private secretary, and to help in organising 'The Glow Worm,' which opened with a distinguished staff consisting of Mr. F. C. Burnand (editor), Mr. à Beckett (sub-editor), Messrs. Archer, Tom Robertson, Halliday, Mortimer Collins, Walter Austin, Arthur Sullivan, Douglas Straight, Dion Boucicault, T. H. Escott, and F. C. Clay. After three weeks Mr. Burnand found the duties too irksome, and resigned his post in favour of his young 'sub,' who, before he was twenty-one, found himself in charge, and was known as the Boy Editor. 'I kept the staff together,' says Mr. à Beckett, 'for three years, and then I too resigned. I remember it was suggested that we should put the whole proceeds of the paper on a horse—we will call him "Snuffbox"—that was to run for the

Derby. The secretary tried to prevent it, and the directors passed a resolution of want of confidence in the young secretary, but—Snuffbox won !' The next ten years were passed in editing successfully many magazines and comic periodicals. Then came a long rest from such duties, and the young journalist went to France and Germany as special war correspondent for the 'Globe' and 'Standard.' Travelling up the Rhine, he visited the prisons in which the French were confined, and found the poor prisoners, in that most severely cold weather, starving, and much illness and death ; through his exertions the 'Standard' called attention to their sufferings, and on the strength of his letters a fund of some five or six thousand pounds was collected for their relief.

On his return to England Mr. à Beckett was immediately appointed private secretary to the Duke of Norfolk, and while in that capacity he practically acted as whip of the Catholic party in the Lords and Commons, which led to his becoming intimate with an early friend of his, Cardinal Manning. In 1873, he began his connection with 'Punch,' on the invitation of Mr. Tom Taylor, and it is a notable fact that for thirteen consecutive weeks his contributions were quoted in the 'Times.' Shortly after this he was asked to join the 'Punch Table,' and he has ever since written almost without a break for 'Punch,' thus carrying on the traditions of his father, who always made it a point that some of his own work should appear weekly in that periodical. Since Mr. Taylor's death—when Mr. Burnand became editor—Mr. à Beckett has acted as chief of the staff and *locum tenens* when the editor is away. Among his contributions have been a series entitled 'Papers from Pump-handle Court, by A Briefless Junior.' All these years he has been engaged in general literature, and has besides written several novels and two three-act plays, called 'About Town' and 'L. S. D.,' also some short pieces, principally 'Long Ago,' 'On Strike,' and 'Faded Flowers.' He edited the

'Sunday Times' successfully for four years, and was elected President of the Newspaper Society for 1893-94, in which post his immediate predecessors had been Sir Algernon Borthwick, Sir Charles Cameron, and Sir Edward Lawson. Notwithstanding these multifarious occupations, Mr. à Beckett carried out the intention he had always had in mind of reading for and being called to the Bar, feeling that a knowledge of the law of libel was very important to anyone connected with literature. For a few years he practised with a fair amount of success in the Probate division, his most notable brief being in the Holloway Will case with Sir Edward Clarke—who won the verdict—as opponent. Mr. à Beckett held a brief for one of the sisters, and on his own responsibility, and without instruction from his client, suddenly rose in court and proposed that an annuity should be given to the lady, which was at once granted. It was while in chambers that the young barrister undertook the heavy task of editing and revising his father's well-known work, 'The Comic Blackstone.' 'The book,' he relates, ' was written before I was born, but when I was reading for the Bar my coach strongly urged me to get it up to help me to pass my examinations. It was not of much use, as the law had changed considerably during the thirty years since it was written, so with a view to help students in the future, and also to carry out my father's intention of doing some good by combining amusement with instruction, I revised and brought it up to date, with all the law correct. It is illustrated by Harry Furniss.' Among other of Arthur à Beckett's works are 'Hard Luck; or A Murder at Monte Carlo,' 'Tracked out; A Secret of the Guillotine,' while his latest is 'Green-Room Recollections' (Arrowsmith), which, to quote his own words, had 'a trial canter through the pages of the periodical press.' It is delightful reading, and full of bright and amusing anecdote.

A picture of Mr. à Beckett stands near in the uniform

of a captain in the Fourth Battalion (Militia) of the Cheshire Regiment, for his early training in the art of self-defence and his soldierly proclivities have never deserted him, and he is as keenly interested as ever in all things military. The opposite table holds a treasured portrait of a beautiful and talented boy whose promising young life was cut short at the age of fifteen; but there are yet two fine, intelligent lads left, who gladden their parents' hearts and inherit their brilliant abilities—for Mrs. à Beckett—Susannah Frances, a daughter of the late Dr. Forbes-Winslow, and granddaughter of the late Captain Thomas Forbes-Winslow, 47th Regiment—also possesses considerable literary talents, and acted as reviewer of books for several years on the 'Sunday Times.' These charming boys, dubbed by a friend 'The Heavenly Twins,' though there is a difference of a year between them, are as bright and clever as their namesakes, though by no means as full of tricks and mischief. Gifted and thoroughly original, they can sing, act, and dance, and withal are so entirely well-behaved and tractable as to prove delightful companions, and are deservedly great favourites with Mr. and Mrs. à Beckett's large circle of friends.

As may be supposed, both husband and wife are extremely popular in society; their 'afternoons' are peculiarly attractive, and there are few literary, artistic, and social gatherings where they are not to be found. Arthur à Beckett's kindness of disposition, his ever-ready advice and encouragement to fellow-workers in journalism, however low in the scale they may stand, are well known. A charming conversationalist, full of sparkling wit and fun, and an excellent listener, the benevolent, genial nature may be at once detected in his fine, beaming countenance and sunny smile.

LOUISE JOPLING-ROWE

Those who can remember a certain old, dilapidated house in Kensington, ugly within and fallen by long neglect and disuse into partial decay, will in no way recognise it in its present condition. Whilst searching for an abode with sufficient ground to allow of the building of a studio for herself and an *atelier* for her pupils, the experienced eye of Mrs. Jopling-Rowe lighted approvingly on the premises, and, at once foreseeing great possibilities of their being transformed into all that there is of the most comfortable and artistic, she set to work to demolish the greater part of the house, and to reconstruct it, with the happiest results, on her own lines.

The front door opens into an anteroom whence the reception rooms branch out, each with its great French windows leading on to the lawn dotted about with standard rose trees and a good-sized garden with serpentine paths. A rockery and fernery lie on one side, and beds of purple iris, daffodils, wallflowers, and other sweet-smelling old-fashioned blossoms on the other, shaded by apple, pear, and lilac trees; here a great bush of holly, there a weeping willow. The *atelier* stands at the further end, partially concealed beyond a raised bank of shrubs, and is to be inspected later. The lawn is bright and gay with groups of well-known and distinguished people, for it is Mrs. Jopling-Rowe's 'At Home' day. Ellen Terry is a centre of attraction, and flashes a winning smile of recognition as she strolls past discoursing on her latest American experiences to Mrs. Hungerford, the popular author of 'Molly Bawn,' &c. Mrs. Stannard's (John Strange Winter) merry-rippling laugh is heard as she rests on a rustic garden seat, surrounded by friends, under the shadow of the great lilac tree, with a huge tortoise reposing near her feet. The gallant soldierly man yonder is General Stevenson, the popular Governor of Guernsey, accompanied by his talented wife and her accomplished sister, Mrs. Bankes Tomlin, the latter a handsome, picturesque woman with prematurely white hair, who is unmistakably the original of a charming painting by your hostess entitled 'Summer Snow.' These ladies are the sisters of the favourite actor Mr. Terriss, and bear a strong resemblance to him.

A passing shower presently causes a general movement into the house through the dining-room, where tea is laid out. The walls and decorations of this artistic room are all in white and yellow, and here, over the mantelpiece, hangs Millais' famous life-size painting of Mrs. Jopling-Rowe, which was exhibited at the Grosvenor, the Grafton, and the Paris galleries. Here, too, are some of her own pastel portraits of Lady Colin Campbell, of Rose Norreys, and Mr. Rowe. Proof engravings after Millais are dispersed in a sort of inner or extension room, which is fitted up with old oak and a quaint little Sheraton corner cupboard, which displays behind its glass doors an array of silver cups and goblets, prizes won by Mr. Rowe and his brothers in athletic sports. Many surprises in the shape of electric light are to be found in these rooms; lamps on every convenient table or stand, each with its own separate little wire of communication.

The studio lies on the right out of the drawing-room, whereof the principal features are the ancient tapestry and a large carved Cairo screen of Mushabeer work, from ceiling to floor, which encloses a Persian divan in a cosy corner. A descent of two steps on one side and you find yourself in a broad and lofty studio with pretty arched ceiling, quaint south gallery, and parquet floor strewn with Oriental rugs. The red-tiled hearth of early English design gives a bright bit of colour to the whitewood fireplace, niches, nooks and corners which were designed to be in character with the room, and contain choice bits of pottery and *bric-à-brac*. An exquisite little Sheraton writing-table of satin-wood is pushed on one side opposite an old oak dower-chest and Japanese cabinet. Near the grand piano stands a striking picture, which is presently to be despatched to a foreign gallery. It represents a priest's funeral winding its way along the narrow footpath by the side of a canal leading to one of the open spaces surrounding the old Palazzo and Church in Venice. The procession of lay brothers, carrying banners and candles, vanishes away into the distance; the foremost figures are priests in gorgeous vestments, while two graceful Italian girls on the right gaze with awe-struck expression. The reflection of the pellucid sky on the water is exquisitely rendered. Speaking portraits stand on easels here and there of Marion Terry, of Piatti the popular violoncellist, of Bernard Shaw, and of the veteran Dr. Smiles, on its way to Paris.

Louise Jopling-Rowe is one of a family of nine, and lost her mother at an early age. Her father, the late Mr. Goode, was a civil engineer of great repute, but from neither parent did she inherit the gift which has made her famous. It dates back to a great-uncle, Colonel Phelps, a self-taught artist, who, after the Peninsular War, was appointed to the command of a small garrison to guard Napoleon at Elba. Two interesting pictures of his are treasured by the family, the one representing a long, low bungalow where the mighty conqueror of the world lived in exile; the other a portrait of himself, which bears a strong likeness to his descendants. Mrs. Jopling-Rowe's talent for drawing, which showed itself from childhood, was rather checked than encouraged by her father, on the ground that 'it was a selfish amusement, and led people to shut themselves up too much.' The artistic nature, however, could not be wholly repressed, and found vent in writing, music, and sketching portraits. At the age of fifteen she wrote a thrilling love story, which found its way into the 'Family Herald;' nor were domestic accomplishments neglected. An expert with her needle, as she has so long been with her brush, sundry pieces of exquisite darning and of elaborate embroidery are still cherished possessions of her sisters.

It was not until after her marriage and subsequent departure for Paris that her training in art began, and then it may be said to have been an accident that caused it. She had always been in the habit of making sketches of her friends and catching a likeness faithfully, and when one of these drawings fell into the hands of Baroness Nathaniel de Rothschild, that lady, recognising the talent it displayed, persuaded her to take up art in real earnest. Selecting the studio of Mr. Chaplin, she devoted herself to studying the technicalities of her profession with such resolute will that during the second year of her student life she was able to exhibit at the Salon two chalk drawings, which were at once sold. On returning to London she drew for 'Punch,' and, taking a studio, began to paint portraits and figure pieces. This work she infinitely prefers, and uses landscapes only as a setting.

'I remember,' says the artist, meditatively, as you pause to contemplate her latest painting, 'reading long ago a novel called "Hirell," the Welsh for light, the heroine of which so deeply interested me that I drew a fancy portrait of what I imagined her to be like. I called the picture by the same name, and while it was being exhibited I received a letter from the author asking if it were accidental, as it was the exact image of what he wished his heroine to be.'

But the accomplished artist has many and versatile gifts. She is a sweet singer, and is an adept at private theatricals. Indeed, it is on record that on one occasion, at a party at Mr. Joachim's, a practical joke was arranged in which she took part. It was given out amongst the guests that Sarasate was expected that evening. It so happens that Mrs. Jopling-Rowe and the great violinist have much the same cast of features. After dinner she slipped upstairs, and presently reappeared enveloped in a long travelling cloak, and was announced as Señor Sarasate, and so well did she impersonate him that several well-known musicians who were present were entirely taken in. She also acted in a Greek play, Dr. Todhunter's version of 'Helen of Troy,' adapted by Godwin, when Hengler's Circus was temporarily converted into the exact model of a Greek theatre.

Year after year finds Mrs. Jopling-Rowe well represented at Burlington House, at the Grosvenor, and at other exhibitions at home and abroad. Among innumerable works, her 'Five o'Clock Tea,' her portrait of Ellen Terry, which adorns the supper-room at the Lyceum, and her 'Auld Robin Gray' are perhaps most familiar.

Her working hours are long indeed; as she remarks, she works 'like a man in the City, and seldom goes out of doors whilst daylight lasts.' At her School of Art at the end of the garden she finds rest from her own labours, and, as the sun shines out brilliantly again, you seize the opportunity to pay it a visit. A winding path leads into the large and lofty building with arched roof and parquet floor. At one end is a high gallery, which is reserved solely for the use of the class, each member having her own locker. At the other end a door leads into a room entirely devoted to studies of the antique, of still life, and of anatomical subjects. Opposite the north-light window hangs a gigantic tapestry of great antiquity after Raphael. On the walls are fastened various studies and sketches by the pupils. The origin of this school, which is so popular and successful, sprang entirely from an accidental circumstance. It happened that Mrs. Jopling-Rowe was visiting at a country house, and while indicating by a drawing something she wished to explain, her host, struck by the rapidity and accuracy of her design, said, 'Why don't you teach others how to draw?' 'That,' replied the artist, laughing, 'is just the one thing that I could never do!' The idea, however, took root, and the result is the now famous *atelier*, which is conducted on exactly the same principles as are those in Paris. Here some twenty-five or thirty pupils are found busily engaged in study; but, as the hour for closing is at hand, a bright, clever-looking girl, whom her companions call 'Biddy' (Miss Macdonald), descends from her high stool before an easel and volunteers an explanation of the method of instruction, which shall be given in the young embryo artist's own words:

'We work,' she says, 'from 9.30 until 4 o'clock; three days a week we study figures, the other three head models. Once in a week we work at black and white sketches for illustration purposes. These'—taking you to one side, where a number of little studies are grouped together—'are they, and the two that you indicate as especially clever are done by Edith Morris, one of the class. An especial feature in the school is our drawing from memory of any sketch done in the studio, and another interesting lesson comes once a week, when we have a subject given us, and we interpret it according to our ideas and make compositions out of our own heads; every day we do a time study, and are given one hour to work it out.' Many of these drawings are pinned on a screen, and are amusing as indicating the various 'interpretations' of a given subject, such as 'Spring-Time,' 'A Scare,' 'An Old Curiosity Shop,' &c., &c. 'Yes,' continues the young student, smiling, 'naturally we all adore Mrs. Jopling-Rowe, and look forward to her many daily visits, when she goes round suggesting, exhorting, and encouraging.'

The pupils are all attired in long, picturesque blouses of varied make and materials. These artistic garments are composed by Miss Florence Goode, whose School of Art Needlework is close by in Earl's Court Road, and grouped here and there are some exquisite embroideries and tea-cloths designed and executed by her skilful fingers. Many distinguished artists visit from time to time this interesting *atelier*, amongst whom are recorded the names of Sir John Millais, Mr. Corbould, Mr. Luke Fildes, Mr. Calderon, &c.

Mrs. Jopling-Rowe's *salon* has long been renowned as

a happy meeting-place for all who are most distinguished in literature and in art, while in society, where she deservedly holds a prominent position, she is esteemed as much for her lovable and kindly disposition as for her great talent.

CICELY RICHARDS

ALTHOUGH Miss Cicely Richards began her career on the stage ' very low down indeed,' and merely ' walked on ' as a slight slip of a child at the Vaudeville, she had the unusual experience, very soon after, of getting an engagement that lasted nearly 1,400 nights consecutively and without a break, and to make a phenomenal success, clad in a tattered print frock with a big smut on her face and a housemaid's stair-broom in her hand. Without interest or influence, with no one belonging to her on the stage and her parents rather opposed to the idea, on account of the uncertainty of any prospects, she begged to be allowed to try her chance, and consent was at last reluctantly given. She went to the theatre, and by good luck caught Mr. Tom Thorne in his office, and diffidently stated her wishes. The kindly manager listened attentively, bade her come as understudy and to ' walk on,' and promised that if she showed any talent he would give her the first opening—a promise he faithfully kept. 'The School for Scandal' was then having a long run, and the young girl, looking out for opportunities, wisely made herself at home in all the business of the piece and quietly understudied every one. Soon the chance came. The actress who was playing Lady Teazle was delayed by some accident on her way to the theatre, and the one who acted Maria was put in her place. The prompter flew behind, and hurrying to Miss Richards, asked her, if she knew Maria's words, to say them then and there, which she did. ' You will do,' he remarked pithily. ' I ran up hastily and changed my dress,' she says, with a laugh, 'and went on in an agony of fear. While waiting for the cue I almost regretted that I had said I knew the lines, and at first I did not recognise my own voice!' The stage fright, however, was soon overcome, and then followed the unprecedented run of 'Our Boys,' when Cicely Richards was allotted the part of the ever-memorable Belinda, the lodging-house slavey. By her careful and intelligent study of the part and her clever interpretation of it she made a bound into public favour, and, to use the words of a distinguished dramatic critic who was present, 'She got the chance we predicted for her; she availed herself of it just as we expected she would, and brought down the house. The chief honours of the evening were carried off by her and Mr. James; the acting of these two should certainly be added to the art gallery of the year.' And never did honest, hard work vindicate itself more fully! It was only to be expected that during such a tremendous run a few little unrehearsed effects should occasionally take place. The monotony of it was a severe trial to one and all of the players. 'It got upon my nerves,' says Miss Richards, 'to such an extent that it made me quite ill. Over and over again, when I had my hand on the door to go on, the words would temporarily escape me, though, once on, they luckily always came back.' There was an evening when Belinda's faithful chronicler was present that a most terrible 'stage wait' occurred—the longest on record. Just in the middle of a speech Mr. James suddenly experienced a total loss of memory. He appealed to Mr. Farren and Miss Richards to prompt him, but neither could at the moment—in fact, no one could do anything. To give an idea of the dreadful length of the pause—which, however, must have seemed far longer to the poor players than to those in front, it must be stated that the employés, after setting the scene, had to go out, and were not allowed in again until after the act for fear of noise. Someone near saw there was a wait, and he had to go first to the hall-keeper to explain why he wanted to get out, then to find the prompter, who returned to his desk, got out his book, and asked, 'Where are they?' No one could tell. The audience were in fits of laughter. Mr. James tried two or three times, but the people shouted 'Oh no, we've had that!' Suddenly the words came back, and the act continued, and at its conclusion the popular actor was called again and again and loudly encouraged and comforted. One great benefit resulted from Cicely Richards' performance of Belinda. After a short time it was the means of her being introduced to Mr. Horace Wigan, who was present. He was most kind and encouraging, bade the girl go on and persevere, and from that time forward did her more good than anyone in the profession by the advice he gave and the interest he took in her. 'And I must not forget,' she adds prettily, 'to record how much gratitude I owe to Mr. Thorne and to the late Mr. James in the beginning of my stage life.' Her next part was in 'Our Girls,' which fell somewhat flat after its brilliant predecessor, and then came a long provincial tour, under the management of Messrs. Bruce and Tom Robertson, as Meg in 'Retiring,' a tour she thoroughly enjoyed, while every spare moment was spent in studying fresh parts. On her return to town she was engaged at the Princess's to play Biddy Roonan in Jeaffreson's melodrama 'The Shadows of a Great City,' which had a long run. Vera, the Russian flower-girl in 'Siberia,' was a favourite *rôle* that she describes as 'a bright little part of a good girl.' The next engagement was at the Princess's to play Mrs. Rolleston in 'The Mystery of a Hansom Cab,' and while acting every night in that piece she took part in five *matinées* a week besides, among which were Mary O'Brien in 'Little Lord Fauntleroy' and Miss Potts in 'Dorothy Grey.' There was considerable variety in these performances—Mrs. Rolleston being a little comedy part, Miss Potts an American girl, and Mary O'Brien Irish—and, but for the fact that she is able to imitate these last two accents capitally, Miss Richards might have got a little mixed. As it was, however, she laughingly declares that she was always in fear of getting her Irish tongue Americanised, and *vice versâ*. After fulfilling a special engagement at the Vaudeville in a comedietta, the hard-working young actress passed on to Toole's Theatre to play in Mr. Fred Horner's amusing piece, 'The Bungalow,' which ran over nine months. Then back to the Princess's for a summer season in 'Fate and Fortune,' followed by an invitation to the Strand to take up Miss Fanny Brough's part of Mrs. Stewart Cross in 'The Late Lamented.' Some seven or eight years ago 'Our Boys' was revived at the same theatre, and ran nearly a year, and Cicely Richards resumed her original *rôle* of Belinda; but she and Mr. James were the only two members of the old and brilliant cast, that had consisted, besides, of Mr. Farren, Mr. Thorne, and Mr. Warner, Sophie Larkin, Kate Bishop, Amy Roselle, &c., and, now that these are all scattered and Mr. James is no more, Miss Richards devoutly hopes the play may never again be revived. She has a comic incident to relate *à propos* of 'The Bungalow.' In one scene Miss Larkin had to open the door after leaving, put in her head, and utter a shriek and disappear. Miss Larkin had a severe cold for some days, and, though she was able to get through her words, she had no voice left for the shriek, and asked Cicely Richards to stand behind, and when she opened her mouth to give it for her. 'It came off correctly for some nights,' she observes demurely, 'but the last night there was a *contretemps*. I had not got near enough to Miss Larkin in time. She opened the door—and her mouth; just as she had closed the latter I uttered what must have sounded like a yell! The audience gave a tremendous shout of laughter, and the manager came bustling round to see what was the matter—but he had not the heart to scold us, for it was so funny!' Miss Richards remained at Toole's through the run of 'Mrs. Othello,' which went on in what she calls 'a business-like manner, and then set out on tour with the piece, taking the title *rôle*. In 1894-95, she played for the first time in pantomime (Mr. Barrett's, at the Grand Theatre, Birmingham) as the fairy godmother—which she pronounces to be 'a delightful part to act.' Her fine mezzo-soprano voice and knowledge of music assisted her materially, and her reception and notices were most gratifying. And mention must not be forgotten of a recent performance at the Trafalgar in a merry little farce called 'The Chinaman,' for on her shoulders fell the chief burden of the play. Seizing the full grip of the situation from first to last, she acted with so much artistic *verve*, vigour, and *esprit* as to win universal commendation. Her latest character was Markham in 'The Passport' at Terry's Theatre—a part she sustained with her usual cleverness.

A quaint little spiral staircase leads up to the top flat of an ancient house in one of the busiest thoroughfares of London, where Miss Richards has established herself and her household gods. Small but very bright and cheerful are her rooms—an index of her own happy, sunny temperament. Extremely quiet alike in manner and in tastes, there is a sense of refinement and of culture around. The terra-cotta tinted walls are hung with several paintings from nature—the works of her own brush—together with fine photogravures after the well-known foreign artists Hald and Constant, and a picture of Garrick as Richard III.; the quaint bronze temple was picked up at Antwerp, and the dainty bits of Sèvres and Dresden are an inheritance. A novel arrangement of photographs stands over the low mirror; the Benares brass-work and Kuska screens—the fragrant perfume of these last waft one back in imagination to India—are gifts from a brother who holds a position of trust at Calcutta; a tambourine is a special treasure, and is adorned with autographs of many familiar names. The open piano and heap of music indicate a favourite resource, and her well-filled bookshelves yet another. She is a great reader, but not much of fiction, and prefers Shakespeare,

Byron, histories, travels, &c. Yonder on a tiny Davenport stands an excellent portrait of the youthful Belinda. 'I remember,' she remarks, 'that I had some trouble to get the frock; I borrowed an old one from the cleaner, had it washed, and then—to get it properly soiled to suit the maid-of-all-work—I rolled in the dust and cobwebs below the stage.' The actress is much taller now than in those juvenile days, but there is the same smooth, soft complexion, the same thick, curly hair, and the same mirthful yet determined expression in the earnest grey eyes. And it is this steady determination that has enabled Cicely Richards, alone and unaided, to win her way to a modest independence. Miss Richards can recollect the turning point in her early childhood. She had been an idle little girl at school at Wellingborough, and one day her mother sorrowfully remarked that it was waste of money and time to send her at all. Stung by the mild reproach, she shut herself up, did her own little studies, and from that time on was one of the hardest workers. 'I love my profession dearly,' she says very gently. 'Everyone must love it. I have had my ups and downs—my little hardships and disappointments like others—but it is a happy life, and I am content, and have much for which to be thankful.'

ANNIE S. SWAN

(*MRS. BURNETT SMITH*)

LET Kensington sneer as it will and Belgravia 'turn up its noble nose in scorn,' but there is a fascination in the absolute peace and quiet of the old-fashioned, old-world Camden Square of which the gay West End knows comparatively little. It is not without its beauties either to those who love plenty of room in which to breathe. There is a broad space in front with a large garden and fine old trees that in early spring are the homes of thousands of birds, while the garden is then gay with lilacs and pink and white may-blossoms which impregnate the air with delicious fragrance. Built according to the good solid custom of nearly a century ago, when there was none of the rush of these later days, when the word 'scamping' was unknown, and when a row or terrace was not intended to be 'run up' in three months, the time-honoured houses of Camden Square have weathered many a gale and storm, and will probably outlast many a new structure in more fashionable quarters. To a hard-working student the quiet ensured by thick walls, large rooms—and plenty of them—a garden back and front, and neighbours within reach but out of sound, is an indescribable boon.

The corner house on the south side is inhabited by the well-known young author of some twenty-five or thirty books, Annie Swan, and her husband, Dr. Burnett Smith.

> 'Hear, Land o' Cakes and brither Scots,
> Frae Maidenkirk to Johnny Groat's;
> If there's a hole in a' your coats,
>   I rede ye tent it;
> A chiel's amang you takin' notes,
>   An' faith he'll prent it!'

And as your hosts come forward with hospitable greeting, the first words they utter proclaim them as fellow-countrymen, and a cordial comradeship is at once established.

'Yes,' says Annie Swan, laughing merrily, 'we are very, very Scotch, I know; we have spent nearly all our lives north of the Tweed. It is only within the last few years that we have deserted the old country and come to settle permanently in London.'

She was born at Leith, and was one of a family of seven, 'the middle or "odd" one,' as she describes it, 'of a particularly merry, united, and happy family.' There were apparently no hereditary tendencies to literature on either side, and it was a mystery to the whole 'connection' when the girl at the age of fifteen began to write short stories. At school she confesses to having been no 'model' girl or having in any way distinguished herself; but she was a quick learner, and generally left her lessons to the last moment, and in play hours would gather a little knot of girls around her and keep them amused with thrilling tales. Her home up-bringing was singularly fortunate. Mr. Swan was a great agriculturist, a man of tender heart and refined mind; his sense of justice was so strong that it was proverbially said of him that he would 'divide a farthing between two people rather than that either should be wronged.' At first he was inclined to look on the story-writing somewhat as waste of time, but he soon recognised his daughter's natural bent, and thoroughly encouraged it. On looking back, Annie Swan acknowledges that she got her ideas—'very strong ideas'—of right and wrong from this beloved father's life and example—perhaps even more than from his precepts. To the happy, healthy out-of-door life in all weathers she owes a strong physique, for boys and girls alike indulged in all the country sports and amusements as the season might permit. 'Now I come to think of it, indeed,' says the young writer demurely, 'I believe that I was rather a harum-scarum, tom-boy sort of girl!'

Her mother combined with a refined and beautiful simplicity of character great wisdom and practical common sense, and, while always proud of her child's writings, she held the sensible doctrine prevalent in many of the old-fashioned Scottish families that, whatever lot in life her daughters should subsequently be called upon to fill, they would fill it none the less well for being thoroughly well trained in domestic duties. Accordingly a rule was made that in turn each girl should take a separate department in household work, one week at cooking, another at the dairy, a third at the napery press, and so on, until they all became adepts in every department and well qualified to carry on the entire management of a house, great or small, the while the intellectual bent, or musical bias, or a skilful pencil was by no means ignored or thrust out of sight.

To such a character as Annie Swan's—in which, under the youthful exuberance of high spirits and love of fun, there lay a touch of her country's reticence and reserve—no training could have been more judicious. Without crushing the bright, happy nature, the deeper responsibilities of life were gradually inculcated, and when the girl left home and kindred to become a wife, the knowledge that she had gained stood her in good stead; for, without drawing away the veil of sweet romance that hangs over those early days of married life, she makes no secret that in bygone years they 'began on small means and saved on them.' The systematic and thorough insight into domestic matters that she had gained, enabled her to order her little *ménage* with the maximum of comfort and the minimum of economy, as, hand in hand and in perfect sympathy, the young pair laughed over and surmounted little difficulties together until—the victory won—they sailed in smooth waters.

Bit by bit they collected each article of furniture with taste and judgment. Behind the glass doors of the old Chippendale bureau are many treasured pieces of Worcester, Crown Derby, and of Wedgwood. On the walls hang water-colour sketches and views of old Edinburgh. 'These are the Doctor's hobby,' says his wife. The author's literary work is carried on in an upstair room that is a veritable snuggery with its warm-tinted Turkey carpet, tapestry hangings, Louis Quinze clock, and other artistic surroundings, which indicate that, although Annie Swan cultivates her intellectual faculties to the uttermost, she has not omitted the study of art combined with comfort. The large Chippendale writing-table—so neatly arranged with MSS. and proofs—shows signs of a busy but methodical writer. Here her favourite photographs, books and reminiscences of girlhood are gathered together, while the great arm-chair opposite makes a luxurious lounge for the tired physician after a heavy day's work. In this pleasant room she works during the morning hours, 'not always wholly uninterrupted,' she remarks with a smile; 'but I am not easily disturbed, and I can go on again and take up the thread of thought without difficulty. I attribute this to being one of a large family where it was impossible to have a room entirely to oneself in which to write. My usual method is to have one central idea fixed on one central character; then the others seem to group themselves around it. Sometimes I have the whole plan worked out in my mind, and the people change places, as it were. After getting to a certain length the story seems to shape itself.'

Her first book took a long time to write, and was cut down over and over again. It was published by a company on the 'half profits' system, but came to an untimely end. 'There were no profits,' she says, laughing, 'but a considerable expenditure instead. I was one of the victims of the company's unfortunate speculation.' Her troubles in publishing may be said to have come to an end with this misadventure, as the long row of neatly bound volumes in the bookcase testify. Among them may be observed the titles of 'The Gates of Eden,' 'A Divided House,' 'Maitland of Laurieston,' 'Carlowrie,' 'Sheila,' 'A Bitter Debt,' 'Aldersyde,' and her latest work, 'A Victory Won.'

Bound just inside the cover of this work is a valued letter from Mr. Gladstone, written in the venerable statesman's own hand, in which he remarks, 'I think it is beautiful as a work of art, and it must be the fault of the reader if he does not profit by the perusal. Miss Nesbit and Marget will, I hope, long hold their places among the truly living sketches of Scottish character.' Another testimony to the merits of this charming story is a much-prized autograph letter from the late Lord Tennyson.

A propos of 'Sheila,' which is the author's own favourite, there is a pretty incident connected with the book. It first ran as a serial through the 'Glasgow Weekly Mail,' and whilst in course of publication a travelling basket woman wandered up on foot from Crieff to Amulree, where the scene of the story was laid, and called at a house to sell her wares. After a little talk with the woman of the house she drew a paper out of her basket, and asked to be directed to Dalmore (the abode of the heroine, Sheila McDonald), as she was quite sure that lady would buy up her whole stock-in-trade. She was very indignant when assured that Dalmore was a purely imaginary place, and again pointed to the copy of the 'Mail,' which contained a description of the house. 'When I heard the incident,' says Annie Swan, laughing, 'I felt that I had fallen in the estimation of my humble but sincere reader, and I wished I could have explained to her the mysteries and little necessary fictions of my craft.'

Her bright, sympathetic nature leads her in general to bring her stories to a happy conclusion. On one occasion, however, she deviated from this rule. 'St. Vera's' has a sad ending, and while it was running serially the young writer had so many letters imploring her to avert the heroine's impending fate, that she resolved never again to wind up in a minor key. Among these communications the most amusing and touching was expressed with more vigour than politeness on a post card, which ran as follows: 'Don't let Annie Erskine die! If you do, hanged if I read any more of your old stories!'

There is a purity and simplicity of style, withal a depth of thought and experience, that characterise all the writings of this talented and earnest young worker. They are homely and wholesome in tone, the thread of the story is always interesting, and compels the reader to follow the heroine to the end. With a keen insight into human nature, there is a strength and tenderness in her stories that appeal to all hearts. The brightness and utter absence of affectation in her own character are revealed in her works, as are also the strong religious principles that guide her life. These have, however, led her into no narrow groove, but have rather opened out and widened her sympathies, so that, like the branches of a great tree, they spread out far and wide.

In common with most well-known authors, Mrs. Burnett Smith has a large correspondence, and receives daily budgets from young aspirants after literary fame—chiefly women—and ofttimes she is sore oppressed thinking of the vast army of women who are seeking something to do. 'Many of them, alas! are so incompetent,' she remarks sadly, 'and show so little qualification for, or true appreciation of, the high calling they seek to pursue, that I sometimes feel it a hopeless task trying to convince them that there is no royal road to success in literature, but that it is synonymous with incessant anxiety and effort, which an increasing reputation only makes harder instead of easier.' It was owing to these innumerable letters from unknown writers, upon every conceivable subject, that her magazine was instituted. They poured in largely from housekeeping women of the middle class, and, as it became too much of a tax to answer them individually, it occurred to Mrs. Burnett Smith that it would be a good plan to start a journal, which would be a kind of medium between her and her readers. The idea has been fully carried out; many readers of the 'Woman at Home' regard 'Over the Teacups' as the tit-bit of the magazine, and she has received hundreds of letters of sympathy and congratulation on its success. Much the same reasons inspired Mrs. Burnett Smith to write a late book, called 'Courtship and Marriage' (Hutchinson & Co.), for so many young people wrote to her asking her for advice in these matters. This charming little book is written with mingled gravity and sweetness, and the most valuable 'advice' is tendered in simple, eloquent words. Published at the small price of one shilling, this modest little volume should be distributed in, not thousands, but tens of thousands among the young; indeed, there can be but few who would not feel the better for its perusal, and be inclined to follow the wise counsel so delicately suggested. 'It contains my views of life,' says the young author, 'and,' she adds reverently, in a soft tone, ' I try to live up to them.'

But Mrs. Burnett Smith has had wider experiences of life than Great Britain only can afford. From the early years of their married life she and her husband began to 'save up' to enjoy the luxury of a little annual holiday abroad, an experience which she considers to have been invaluable in her profession. In this way they have visited nearly every capital in Europe, and on one occasion made a trip to America, where she found herself already known through her books. It is possible that the latest and most welcome treasure in this home of love and sympathy may in the future somewhat interfere with these brief Continental wanderings. A most fascinating and dimpled infant lies contentedly smiling and cooing in her mother's arms, guarded by two handsome terriers, Jack and Paddy, who, having been first favourites for some time, are inclined to be extremely jealous of the baby, though they fix their great pathetic brown eyes upon her as if to promise their affection and fidelity in the future. 'Yes,' says the young mother in a tone of much pathos as she lays the bright, intelligent little one in your arms, 'she is indeed a treasure, and has filled our cup of happiness to the brim.'

TRISTRAM ELLIS

If a man's work be any index to his character, the collections of his paintings exhibited from time to time in the Bond Street galleries indicate that Mr. Tristram Ellis possesses a happy, sunny disposition, and an optimistic nature. While gazing at upwards of a hundred brilliant sea and land scapes here present, the outside world is temporarily forgotten, and the spectator is transported in a moment to the varied and smiling shores of the Mediterranean. The effects portrayed in these pictures are so varied that it is obvious it would have been impossible to have painted them otherwise than direct from Nature—that is, ever varying—even if the dexterous and rapid handling had not already shown it. This, then, is the key-note of the exhibition. It represents the Mediterranean as Mr. Ellis saw it, and the result is an absence of exaggeration and a freshness and vigour that should commend itself to all. The most important work in this delightful collection is 'The Courtyard of the Holy Sepulchre,' showing the forecourt of this celebrated church by early morning light. The dealers in rosaries, *crucifixes*, and other religious emblems have begun to assemble, and business is proceeding. The woman of Bethlehem, in handsome dress and peculiar headgear, is chaffering in the foreground with an old Bedouin, whose persuasive character one can read even in the pose of his back. The sunlight is unusually bright and glowing. Another, 'The Calvary at the Church of the Holy Sepulchre,' is a picture with admirable light and shade; the dark figures mounting the steps to the Calvary in the deep shade that is softly illuminated by the candles they carry, are well placed to give a feeling of religious mysticism to the scene.

It is a remarkable fact that, though Mr. Tristram Ellis was born a landscape painter, he was trained as an engineer. His father, the late Mr. Alexander J. Ellis, Lit.D., was made a Fellow of the Royal Society, chiefly in connection with his studies in the science of musical vibrations; but was better known through his standard works on the pronunciation of Shakespeare and Chaucer, which led to his being twice elected President of the Philological Society, though the Mathematical Society also claimed him, and in some circles he is best remembered in connection with stigmatics and baromic hypsometry. To his personal care Tristram Ellis owes his scientific education, for of art his father knew nothing. The painter was born at Great Malvern, and spent his early years at Bath, Clifton, and Edinburgh, whence he was sent to school in Hampshire. Here he studied chemistry under Professor Tyndall. Being a delicate lad, he was compelled to forego many of the athletic games so dear to boyhood, and devoted much time to mathematics, in which study he soon took a front place. Drawing was learned in a very perfunctory sort of manner. 'I hated it,' says Mr. Ellis, 'because I was made to copy things; often I would break out into originality and alter these copies, and it made the master mad and brought down his wrath on my head.'

At the age of eighteen he left school and went to King's College, where he made his mark by taking the highest distinction during his second year, in the Applied Sciences department, gained since the college opened. He was the first student who took all the scholarships consecutively, and in recognition of this unprecedented event he was admitted to the Associateship—contrary to the rules of the college—after only two years' attendance at lectures. He went through his pupilage as an engineer, under Sir John Fowler, at the time the District Railway was made. On the expiration of his articles Mr. Tristram Ellis joined a firm of engineers as partner, and worked steadily for some years at the business. Then, being in a position more or less of independence, and the claims of art asserting themselves too strongly to be resisted, he threw up the profession and took to painting in oils. Many of these pictures were exhibited in the Royal Academy, but after a time, feeling that it was impossible to obtain sufficient knowledge of technique in England, he went to Paris, and the art-student life, after which he had so long hankered, began. Resolutely eschewing all amusements and dissipations, he entered the *atelier* of M. Bonnât, and settled down to work for twelve hours a day.

'In right good earnest,' says the artist, thoughtfully, 'I was the only one of the one hundred and seventy students attending that studio who persevered in the practice; but my desire was to emulate my great master, of whom it was reported that he had worked twelve hours a day for two consecutive winters.' The hard-working young artist soon became a great favourite with M. Bonnât, who, admiring his steady resolution and recognising his genius, urged him to turn his attention entirely to historical paintings; but he was too fond of scenery and out-door life for this branch of art, and he determined to devote himself to his first love. '*A propos* of this portion of my student life,' remarks Mr. Ellis, smiling, 'I remember a curious incident that happened on the *fête* of the Republic. We decided to decorate the outside of our *atelier* with flags of all the nations represented by ourselves. We exhibited no less than forty-three flags in front, but, not satisfied with this, we desired that the studio should make a special one of its own. We utilised a large yellow sheet that was draped as a background for Negro, Arab, and other coloured models, and the design, a death's head and cross-bones, was boldly painted thereon by one of our number. While at work as usual sounds and steps were heard murmuring outside, which gradually became louder and louder until they developed into an angry roar. Half a dozen gendarmes rushed in and urged us to fly at once, as they were no longer able to keep back the mob, who had taken this flag as an insult to the Republic. Luckily all those who were present were got out through the rear of the building just before the crowd poured in and completely wrecked it.'

In 1878, Mr. Tristram Ellis went to Cyprus for six months to paint a series of sketches at the time of its occupation by the English. Notwithstanding repeated attacks of fever, he contrived to bring home some fifty or sixty water-colour drawings of land and sea. These were exhibited in Bond Street during the following April, and were all immediately taken off his hands by a dealer, an arrangement of transfer that proved perfectly satisfactory. His success with these pictures had brought him into public notice, and accordingly the next year he went to

Syria, Asia Minor, and Mesopotamia. On arrival at
Diarbekr, the capital of Khurdistan, he found the country
entirely disorganised by the terrible famine, and considerable caution had to be exercised in travelling, owing to the
large bands of marauders that infested the banks of the
river. The military English consul expressed much surprise at seeing him, and told him that all means of communication were cut off, and he had received no intimation
of his coming from the consul at Aleppo ; moreover, that
Mr. Ellis was the only traveller who had arrived without
being robbed. It was his intention to float down the
Tigris to Bagdad on a raft of inflated goat skins, but it
was seventeen days before the consul permitted him to
start, owing to the dangerous state of the river. Not one
of the many grain rafts that had been sent down to
Mossul had arrived for a month past. All were robbed
and sunk, and the navigators murdered. ' It was an exciting time,' says Mr. Ellis. ' My own raft only escaped by
being blown by a violent wind into a side bank, by which
I missed the largest band of these river thieves. Soldiers
were sent to clear the way to allow the starving popula-
tion to receive the stores in the depôts. I passed through
Hassen Kaiffe, one of the largest of the many troglodyte
towns of the upper Tigris. When it was cut, or by whom,
no one knows ; but some suppose that it belongs to the
time of the Hittites, who, without doubt, inhabited that
portion of Asia. At Mossul I found the bazaars full of
people dying like flies and professional beggars exposing
starving children to excite charity. There was no bread,
and the natives were literally living, like Nebuchadnezzar,
on the herbage which a chance rain had brought out
abundantly. I went on to Bagdad and Beyrout, returning
home through the desert *via* the Euphrates to Dan, then
by Palmyra to Damascus and Beyrout.'

This trip was productive of much good work, and the
artist brought home and exhibited in Bond Street about
ninety sketches, which were all immediately sold. The

year after the Euphrates and Tigris trip Mr. Tristram Ellis went to Egypt and stayed as late as May, just before the massacre at Alexandria that led to the war. He spent three weeks at the Pyramids, living in tombs with the well-known Egyptologist Professor Flinders Petrie. While there he was engaged in helping to survey the inner passages in the Great Pyramid, and spent two nights in its interior, the coolest place at that time, as the Khamaseen was blowing, and the thermometer standing over a hundred degrees after sundown.

Then came a gap of a few years before his next Continental wanderings took him to Athens. The King of Greece, hearing that there was a well-known English painter there, desired to see his portfolio of sketches. After inspecting them the King sent for Mr. Ellis, and, expressing his satisfaction, picked out three that he wished to keep. In the last two years he has thrice varied his Oriental experiences by visiting the land of the midnight sun and eternal snow, and pronounces it by no means an unpleasant part of the world in summer, and the climate soft and balmy; but his last trip to the Mediterranean was perhaps the most successful of all.

Many years of travelling in Eastern climes have given Mr. Tristram Ellis his strong love for bright effects and his profound insight into the powers of lights and shades. He maintains that he 'did not understand what brightness was until he went abroad.' You question him about the astonishing accuracy which underlies all his most rapid and most facile studies and pictures. To him it is the most simple thing in the world. The fact is that he has never thought it necessary to forget what he learnt as a man of science because he is now an artist. 'You see,' he says, without any assumption of giving forth a canon of art, 'I do these things knowing about them; how these rocks you notice came here and what made the troubled surface of the water there. I look on water as a reflecting surface, and compare carefully the reflections with the objects reflected, even when the water is ruffled and the comparison becomes difficult, for I have studied well the laws of reflection in all states of troubled surfaces. In fact, water is extremely fascinating in all its moods, and in pure landscape without figures its presence is almost necessary for producing an interesting picture. With the extraordinary variety of effect upon its surface, ever changing with the state of the air, the wind, and the weather, it is like a living thing.'

When out sketching, or at work in his own studio, Mr. Tristram Ellis likes to have a congenial friend with whom to converse. When quite alone he finds that he is sometimes liable to work too quickly while grasping floating effects, and the presence of some person is a check. His conversation is full of interest and of sparkling anecdote. Although entering occasionally with zest into amusements, now that he is married and has given hostages to fortune he confesses that, when in London, he chiefly prefers his own fireside, and is inclined to be somewhat lazy in respect to society. He is, however, happiest when in the open air and amidst lovely scenery, for to him the face of Nature is the face whose portrait he seeks and finds.

MRS. KENT SPENDER[1]

NOT only does a sense of reposeful dignity impress the visitor to the ancient and historic city of Bath, but also its air of smug respectability and well-to-do aspect. The streets are broad and scrupulously clean, the shop fronts might compare well with those in Regent Street, and the buildings are handsome and effective. Situated in a deep and picturesque valley with encircling hills and the river Avon winding through on two sides, the views around are

[1] Since the original production of this sketch, the death of the lamented writer has taken place.

of exceeding beauty, while the mineral baths, of great antiquity, draw thousands of visitors annually to their healing waters. The noble old Abbey—erstwhile a cathedral—stands on the spot once occupied by a Roman temple of Minerva, and the grand cruciform edifice casts a solemnity around with its great central tower and time-blackened walls, its flying buttresses and many beautiful windows. It is to one of the houses in the Circus, one of the finest specimens of Wood's architecture in the palmy days of the old stone-built city, that you bend your steps with a feeling of exhilaration in the pure air and exquisite surroundings, together with the assurance that a cordial reception awaits you. Broad, well-carpeted stairs, into which the foot sinks, lead to the great double drawing-rooms with parquet floors liberally strewn with skins of bear, leopard, and panther. The back room opens upon a large conservatory filled with fan palms and flowers, while from the front there is a view of the giant trees on the Circus lawn. The marqueterie cabinets are filled with valuable pieces of Royal Dresden, and candelabra of the same china are used to light the room. The 'Leda and the Swan' clock is a treasured relic, as are the specimens of jewelled Sèvres, with one large beautifully painted dish with Quentin's mark on it, said to have been in the Tuileries in the days of the Empire. A more modern article is the Yöst typewriter, whereat the author transmits, with much rapidity, her thoughts to paper. 'You must not think,' she says apologetically, 'that it always stands here. It is exiled when I am expecting visitors. But from long habit, formed during the years when writing was only an interlude in an active life, I feel that I can generally write better with brightness and even music in the room. The violin or the piano does not disturb me, while the gloom of a library rather depresses than helps me. When I was younger I used to write with my little children playing around me.'

Mrs. Kent Spender is the wife of Dr. John Kent

Spender, M.D., of Bath, and daughter of the late Dr. Headland, of Portland Place, London, a well-known medical man of his day, whom Thackeray, Dickens, Tennyson, &c. were wont to consult. If to do good in one generation be the primary object in life, she may be said to have fulfilled her mission excellently well. Enjoying from childhood the privilege of being much in the society of literary giants, she had also the advantage of the special form of training afforded by the classes held at Queen's and Bedford Colleges, the two schools which have been largely instrumental in the great movement of the age that has resulted in the working together of classes and sexes. It was the social atmosphere, so to speak, of these colleges that fired the young student with a desire to help in the world's work. Plumptre, Kingsley, and Frederick Denison Maurice, two of whom were her life-long friends, were among the masters. The higher education of her own sex was the subject near her heart, and with these views in her mind she was happy indeed when, in spite of her youth, she was selected to assist with a class at Mr. Maurice's working women's college. As may be supposed from her subsequent successful literary career, she began to write at a very early age; but it was after her marriage that she made her first mark in the world of letters as an essayist with a paper, written at the age of twenty, on 'Verbal Landscape Painting, Ancient and Modern.' This was at once accepted and handsomely paid for in a letter addressed to the Rev. L. Spender. 'I think,' says the writer, laughing, 'the mistake arose from two or three causes. I had learnt some Latin and Greek with the help of my brothers, and was rather fond of making classical allusions which I should certainly not do now, and my handwriting was said to be rather masculine. The delusion was the easier to keep up because my father-in-law was a metaphysician, and I read a good deal with him.' Various essays followed on 'Employments for Women,' 'The Non-Imprisonment of Children,' both subjects in which she was keenly interested; then, extending her themes, she became a contributor to several quarterlies, besides a reviewer of foreign literature—French, German, and Italian. During this time she held classes for mothers among the poor, and was shortly appointed to the post of local examiner and secretary to the Oxford Examinations, then for the first time introduced for girls at Bath, an important work that Mrs. Spender and her committee carried on for ten years. Always with the idea of promoting the higher training of women in her mind, her next desire was to co-operate in the establishment of a High School for Girls. At first the exclusiveness of the old city somewhat hindered the scheme, but gradually all prejudices were dispelled, and the High School was duly set on foot. She then took the secretaryship of a society for shopwomen, which entailed two more classes in addition to that which she had held for so many years, followed by the starting of Oxford Extension Lectures. In the midst of such a busy life it will be wondered when Mrs. Spender found time to write some twenty three-volume novels, of which the greater number passed previously through magazines and journals, and have constantly been republished. A few of their titles suggest themselves; as, 'Godwyn's Ordeal,' 'Brothers-in-Law,' 'Mark Eylmer's Revenge,' 'Jocelyn's Mistake,' 'Parted Lives,' 'Her Own Fault,' and 'Recollections of a Country Doctor.' Then came three called 'Mr. Nobody,' 'Kept Secret,' and 'Lady Hazelton's Confession,' that must not be omitted, and, later, 'A Waking,' 'A Strange Temptation,' 'A Modern Quixote,' and a new work entitled 'Thirteen Doctors,' a collection of clever and interesting tales. Most of her books were written during the children's holidays on the seashore, or at the Swiss mountains. It will be scarcely credited that nearly every picture in Dr. Spender's big house is his wife's work, chiefly of foreign landscape and lovely scenery. She compares her mode of writing with that of her painting, and observes, 'To paint pictures you must first make many sketches. The same rule applies to books, and in that sense I am always writing. I have note-books in which I jot down nearly all that I observe and think.' But once having thought out her subject thoroughly, Mrs. Spender is a rapid writer, and loves her work more and more as time goes on. She alters it but little, and, again choosing her simile from painting, she says that if she correct overmuch both outline and colour get blurred, and she loses her grip of the subject if she make any delay. She is all in favour of the one- or two-volume book, and declares that in this respect she has 'burnt her boats' and announced her intention of never again writing a three-volume novel. And although Mrs. Spender has been and still is of so much use in her day, husband, home, and children have ever been first in her mind, and nothing has been allowed to come in the way of domestic duties and pleasures. Two of her four sons — young University men — are well known in the social and journalistic world of London. Two daughters are at home, and combine philanthropic work with study, while a third has found her vocation in an early marriage.

In the course of a pleasant two days' visit you are taken all over the beautiful city, and your hostess does the honours and points out everything that is of note; the Guildhall, the Literary Institution, the Assembly Rooms, and the Great Pump Room, wherein stands a statue of Beau Nash, which at once conjures up a vision of powdered dames, sedan chairs, gallants with queues, running footmen, and all that there was of the most modish of those times. Returning past the Abbey, you step in and make an exhaustive inspection of the interesting interior with its wonderful fan roof, screen, oratory, and many fine monuments, the history of which is at the finger-tips of the author and her young daughter. Presently the bells announce that the service of evensong is about to begin. The great organ — one of the four largest in England — peals out in sonorous tones the voluntary, which resounds under the vaulted arches. Later, when the final benediction has been pronounced, you and the talented author part and go your respective ways. During the journey back to town you ponder at leisure over the immense amount of work so modestly and unassumingly carried on by the clever and highly cultivated woman whose early desire to be of use in her generation must indeed have been realised.

VIOLET VANBRUGH

(MRS. ARTHUR BOURCHIER)

A LARGE, cheerful house in a broad road, with a peep at some big gardens towards the left; opposite, tall, massive buildings—the whole constructed within the last few years over the site once occupied by a dingy lunatic asylum in old historic Kensington. Bright sunshine, just enough subdued by the art-blue curtains, floods the room and casts a radiant beam of light on a beautiful pastel portrait of the intellectual-looking young actress, Miss Violet Vanbrugh, a marriage gift from the painter, Mr. Charles Newton. The great, soft dark eyes are crowned with abundant masses of wavy brown hair, parted and sweeping low back from the brow. The pose is simple and graceful, yet not more graceful than the tall aristocratic-looking girl who glides in and welcomes you with such winning cordiality.

Brief as has yet been her stage career, she has had plenty of experience and very few occasions for 'resting.' A short account of her early struggles will be found of help and encouragement to those who are too soon cast down by non-success. Violet Vanbrugh is one of a family of six, and is the daughter of the late Rev. Reginald Barnes, of Heavitree rectory, and Prebendary of Exeter Cathedral. A much-beloved and respected parish priest, and a man of broad, liberal views, with a wonderful knowledge of life

and of strong common sense, he wisely decided that the
best of educations would enable each child to make his or
her own way in the world. Accordingly no expense was
spared in that direction, with the result that all four
daughters are highly cultivated. One has found her vocation in a happy marriage, and has made her home in
Kashmir with her husband, the Resident. Two younger
sisters are respectively an actress and a violinist, while
Violet Vanbrugh has already made her name before the
footlights, and has united her fortunes with those of the
well-known young actor Mr. Arthur Bourchier. Educated
by Mrs. Henry Hawtrey, a woman of high culture and
refinement, the girl soon became a hard-working student,
and carried off prizes in history and literature; but at the
age of sixteen she desired to strike out for herself with a
view to early independence. Fixing on the stage as a
career, she asked her father's sanction. As may be supposed, he, being altogether outside that profession, at first
demurred, and could not see how he could grant it; but
he wisely bade her judge for herself. 'I came up to
London,' says Miss Vanbrugh, smiling, ' with my old nurse,
took lodgings, and actually knew only one family in town,
to whom I used to go on Sundays. My first step was to
go to Mrs. Stirling and ask her advice. I begged for her
candid opinion, and meant to abide by it. If she said I
could do no good, I intended to go home. She gave me a
part to read, and on hearing it she said I ought to have
every chance, so I took some lessons in elocution from
her. My next step was to write to Miss Ellen Terry, but
it unluckily happened to be just at the time when ' Faust'
was to be produced at the Lyceum; and, as everyone
knows, during rehearsals a leading player has barely time
to eat and sleep, still less to answer letters from stranger
girls. Weeks went on, and I got absolutely hopeless. My
slender stock of money was nearly at an end, and I could
not bear to go home having done nothing. One day, when
things had come to their worst, a visitor was announced.

It was Ellen Terry herself! She seemed to me like an angel from Heaven! The queen of the stage to come to me in my little rooms! She took me to her rehearsal that day, and asked me to stay with her for a week. I went, and the week stretched out to a whole year!' To that year's visit Violet Vanbrugh owes much; for though the great artist, with wise and sound judgment, insisted that the girl, if she were to do well, must do it for herself, the life in that atmosphere of highest art and the opportunities she had of watching and learning from such a past master of her profession were invaluable. Meanwhile she was always studying and trying to get something to do. One day she wrote to Mr. Toole, which resulted in an invitation to walk on in Burnand's burlesque 'Faust and Loose,' to sing in the chorus, and to dance. In this art she was, fortunately, a proficient, having studied under Madame Rinaldi at Exeter. 'But the end of the season came,' says the young actress, ' and I was out, and had to begin all over again. I kept on writing to people, and was refused because I had no experience, and I was once more in despair. One broiling hot morning I took up the " Era," noticed that Miss Sarah Thorne's provincial tours were advertised, never waited to write, but then and there rushed down to Margate, and turned up at her luncheon hour. She was charming—delightful; but when the words came, " Have you any experience?" and I said " No," she shook her head. I was crestfallen—miserable, and wept. Then her kind heart spoke. " There is a vacancy," she said. " You look the part. Carry it home; and if you like to risk coming down next Saturday, and rehearse to my satisfaction, you shall go on tour with it." I returned to town and studied it till I knew every scratch on the paper. It was Rose Deane in " The Wages of Sin." I dodged up some old dresses of my mother's and went back to Margate. Miss Thorne met me at the station, and almost took my breath away by bidding me say my lines on the parade while walking home. It was a great ordeal. " I shall know," she remarked quietly. I said them, and she offered me a three years' engagement in her touring company.' But this was not to last long. In a few months a letter was forwarded to her by Miss Terry from Mr. George Loveday, asking : ' Where is that little girl who played at Toole's ? There is a part in Merivale's " The Butler " if she will come and rehearse on approval.' But the girl was happy with Miss Thorne, and did not at first wish to leave. Urged by Miss Terry, who knew well the good, unselfish heart of the kindly manageress, Violet Vanbrugh laid the letter before her. Miss Thorne reflected that the girl was now getting useful to her, but at once decided that she would not stand in her way, and cancelled the agreement. A passing tribute must be made to this excellent, large-hearted woman, to whom so many young players owe their present success under her able coaching and all-round goodness. ' She was kindness itself to me,' says the actress, ' and just to the core! Well, I left, and joined Mr. Toole's company first at Maidstone. I got into strange lodgings. I was sorrowful at parting from dear Miss Thorne, and felt sad and nervous.' At the first rehearsal a strange thing happened. Two gentlemen were standing on the stage. One of them looked hard at her, and when the morning's work was half over he addressed her. ' Who are you? Where do you live ? I know your face well.' The girl replied that she had never seen him, and had lived in Devonshire. ' But what is your real name?' he questioned. ' And what was your mother's maiden name ? ' Miss Vanbrugh informed him on both points. ' Ah ! ' remarked Mr. Herman Merivale, for it was he, ' then that accounts for it. I was a great admirer of hers and used to dance with her eighteen years ago, and you are the living image of her.' Rehearsals being satisfactory, Mr. Toole offered her an engagement for a year to play Lady Anne in ' The Butler,' a lucky part, for it required just the personality and the distinction that the young actress happily possesses. Again she has pleasant words to say, and pronounces the much-beloved comedian to be 'one of the dearest and best of men, and his personal kindness to have been great.' Her next move was to Mr. and Mrs. Kendal, when Mr. Pinero asked her to play Lady Gillingham in 'The Weaker Sex.' This piece ran through the season, and at its conclusion she accompanied them twice to America on tours, remaining with them in the interim. 'The line of business,' remarks Violet Vanbrugh, 'was really over my head, but Mrs. Kendal was indefatigable in coaching me. She is a wonderful actress to be under. She has so perfect a knowledge of her art, founded on the French school.' With such able teaching and example before her, the young girl was soon able to play successfully the part of the Baroness in 'The Iron Master,' Mrs. Macdonald in 'Impulse,' and a variety of other difficult *rôles*. All these experiences led her on to play, when invited by Mr. Irving, Anne Boleyn in 'Henry VIII.,' besides for two years understudying Miss Ellen Terry's Cordelia in 'King Lear,' and Fair Rosamund in 'Becket.' These were followed by a year's engagement at Daly's Theatre to take, among many impersonations, Countess Olivia in 'Twelfth Night' and Lady Sneerwell in 'The School for Scandal.' It will be remembered that this lady has to pretend that Charles Surface is in love with her, to effect his ruin; but it was no such thing in reality, for it so happened that Mr. Arthur Bourchier acted the character —and a very excellent Charles Surface he was—and there was no pretence needed. The two young actors played together in the piece for the first time, and very soon settled their own little private matters pleasantly and satisfactorily.

Their latest venture was to go into management, and at the Royalty Theatre they brought out a piece called 'The Chili Widow,' the success of which, it may confidently be predicted, will encourage them to introduce many more bright and original plays.

All around the study, which is the joint working room

of wife and husband, are evidences of their recent marriage,
for pretty wedding gifts are artistically arranged here and
there, while a great Chinese dog, Sphinx, a faithful friend,
nestles on his mistress's gown. 'I am trying,' says the
young wife prettily, 'to make him transfer half of his
allegiance to my husband.'

EVELYN MILLARD

AMONG the *débutantes* of the last three or four years not
one has come to the front more rapidly than Miss Evelyn
Millard. Together with a most attractive presence, a tall,
svelte figure, and a beautiful voice, she is gifted with a
strongly emotional and sympathetic nature, which enables
her to sink her own personality and so thoroughly to be
the character that she is impersonating that she carries
away the audience with her. She holds—so to speak—
the electric chain in her hand which communicates itself
to her hearers, and thus sways them at will, to enter heart
and soul into her mind, and to weep with genuine feeling
over her woes—and these are gifts that go far to make a
great actress. It might well be supposed that a career of
only five years would yield but little to record, and in
ordinary circumstances so it would be; but Evelyn Millard
is no ordinary girl, and from the date of her first performance in public she attracted considerable notice; while
great things in the future were freely predicted of her.
The prophecies are rapidly being fulfilled, as all who have
seen her charming Rosamund in Mr. Grundy's sweet and
pathetic play 'Sowing the Wind' will agree.

Evelyn Millard has been exceptionally happy in the
advantages of her surroundings. She was born in London,
and is one of three children of the late Mr. John Millard,
Professor of Elocution at the Royal Academy and the
Royal College of Music. Inheriting from both parents

cultivated artistic tastes, from her father comes her love of literature; but it was the system of education that was so judicious. That beloved and wise parent held the theory that all the gifts should not be sunk in one profession, and directed her reading into deeper channels than is usual. It was strange that, although most of the principal vocalists were under him, not only for singing, but for dramatic study, his three girls never attended his classes; nor did he give the young player regular lessons in her art, nor exactly teach her a part. 'But oh!' she says, in a low voice, the while the expressive grey-blue eyes kindle with emotion, 'how much I owe my father! There was the greatest sympathy between us. His idea was always to bring out the individuality of a person; he never believed in " parroting " a part, and I used from childhood to study Shakespeare and to talk over the poet with him. He would point out this and that, and explain it so clearly, and try to lead me, as it were, into the great heart of Shakespeare. He taught me to speak blank verse, and in all things was the most perfect instructor. His loss is irreparable.'

Thus it will be seen that Evelyn Millard has indeed been singularly fortunate in her home training. The studies in blank verse will bear rich fruit later, when, with an already intimate acquaintance with the immortal bard's works, she shall be called upon to play Juliet, Ophelia, and other Shakespearian characters. But to go back to her childhood and her first amateur performance at the age of twelve. With the delightful audacity of youth she had aspired to play Portia, with her younger sister, aged ten, as Bassanio, and had likewise undertaken the whole stage management, directing and coaching the others in their respective parts. Previous to its production her father had taken her to the Lyceum to see Madame Modjeska in 'Marie Stuart,' and at the conclusion of the play introduced her behind the scenes to Mr. Forbes-Robertson, to whom the child anxiously confided her inability to procure Bassanio's moustache. Mr. Robertson, who was playing the Earl of Essex, was much amused, took off his own, and presented it to her, the which hirsute adornment, after it had done duty for Bassanio, was for long preserved and cherished by the youthful Portia. Her next and only other effort as an amateur was in an open air performance—first at Fulham, and, later, at Copt Hall, Totteridge—in connection with the Shakespearian Reading Society, where she played Helena in 'The Midsummer Night's Dream.' Then she applied to Miss Sarah Thorne, who bade her do the balcony scene in her own room. This, Miss Millard played—with one of her father's pupils—so much to Miss Thorne's satisfaction that she at once engaged the young girl as leading lady in her stock company at Margate. 'I owe a deep debt of gratitude,' she says, 'to Miss Thorne. She was so kind and encouraging. Gordon Craig was there. Miss Ellen Terry came down, and was charming to me; she lent me the dagger that she herself had used in the part, which was very sweet of her.' After three months under Miss Thorne, where she gained much experience, Miss Millard passed on to Mr. Tom Thorne's company and played Miss Kate Rorke's part of Fanny in 'Joseph's Sweetheart,' and the title *rôles* of 'Miss Tomboy' and 'Sophia,' and Clara Douglas in 'Money.' A funny incident occurred when she was acting Fanny. In the scene where the girl is locked in the room in the villain's power she had to shake the door—which should have been invulnerable—and batter her hands against it, screaming, 'Let me out, let me out!' Unfortunately the door yielded only too readily, which was very disconcerting, and caused a laugh in front, but she went on with the act, and at its conclusion the audience—always kind when any little *contretemps* occurs and is successfully mastered—applauded her heartily. At the end of the tour Miss Millard went to the Grand Theatre, where she was seen by the Messrs. Gatti, and just nine months after her first start she found herself leading lady at the Adelphi, where she played Constance in 'The Trumpet Call,' and created the *rôle* of the heroine in 'The White Rose,' which she pronounces to be 'a very pretty part,' and the chief characters respectively in 'The Lights of Home' and 'The Black Domino.' These pieces ran for eighteen months, during which time she received eight offers of other engagements, including four from America and one from Australia. Feeling, however, that she had had enough of melodrama, she desired to break fresh ground. 'I longed for a part such as I had never yet had,' says Miss Millard earnestly, 'into which I could throw my whole soul.' The opportunity soon came. Mr. Comyns Carr was arranging, early in 1894, a tour with 'Sowing the Wind,' and Evelyn Millard was selected for Rosamund. Here her ambition and talent found full sway—'a beautiful part in a beautiful play,' she calls it. The play made an extraordinary success in Edinburgh, Glasgow, and Cambridge; and the undergraduates packed the house nightly. 'I persuaded the late Professor Blackie to go to see the piece,' she remarks. 'He was charmed with it, and wrote a long letter to the "Scotsman," saying he considered that it contained a moral lesson.' On her return to London she was engaged by Mr. George Alexander for a year—first to go on tour to play Dulcie in 'The Masqueraders' and the title *rôle* in 'The Second Mrs. Tanqueray,' and then to take up the part at the St. James's. A later part was the heroine in 'The Divided Way,' and in 'The Prisoner of Zenda' she plays the Princess Flavia.

The pretty house in which Miss Millard and her mother live stands in a broad and busy road, but, lying far back behind a long garden, nothing can be heard of the outside traffic. There is a quaint old-world look within that makes a suitable background for the graceful and picturesque beauty of the young Rosamund. The prevailing tints are sage-green; two deep recesses are cunningly arranged with white enamelled shelves for pictures. A comfortable saddle-back chair stands conveniently near a great bookcase filled with instructive literature and a little square table on which are scattered the current magazines and journals—notably the 'Saturday Review,' uppermost. Art-coloured bowls containing palms and ferns are arranged on a low shelf under the great mirror; the draped mantelpiece opposite holds many specimens of foreign bronzes, while pots of variegated poppies and yellow flowers dispersed here and there add brightness to the room. Three large photographs occupy a prominent position: one of Professor Blackie, a second of Mr. Comyns Carr— 'He is so kind and so charming to work for,' said Miss Millard. The third is of the veteran musician Mr. Charles Salaman, who quite lately went behind the scenes, and, with tears in his eyes, congratulated the young actress on her Rosamund, saying: 'I cannot tell you what I feel about it; I will write.' Among the books there is a little volume that she deeply values. It is a posthumous work of her father's—'Shakespeare for Recitation,' with an introduction by the Rev. E. A. Abbott, D.D., and edited by herself. It contains all the most dramatically effective scenes that could by judicious arrangement and cutting be made suitable for practice, together with the principal soliloquies —a work that is no less prized by his former pupils than valued by all dramatic students. Miss Millard recently had a very flattering offer from Mr. Irving to go to America, which she was unable to accept, as she has been re-engaged by Mr. George Alexander for another year. Modest and frank, she is very ambitious, and is 'never satisfied with herself, but always working for something higher.' She is a very quick study, especially under strong pressure, though she never exactly sits down to learn her lines separately. She thinks out the whole play first, and gets sure of its general meaning, walking up and down the room for hours together, and the words come at rehearsal and gradually soak in. 'The dearest wish of my heart,' she acknowledges, 'is to play Shakespeare and in poetical drama. There is a great field for women in that.'

FANNY BROUGH

THERE are few more desirable inheritances than a keen sense of humour and an appreciation of fun. Add to this powerful talents, a bright, happy nature, and a sweet disposition, which enables its fortunate possessor to see only the best side of people and of things. With these characteristics it will be at once seen why Miss Fanny Brough is so deservedly a favourite with the public, with all the members of her own profession, and with her innumerable friends.

At first sight there is a momentary gravity on the actress's face, but in an instant the soft dark grey eyes light up with an irresistible twinkle, and a merry smile beams over her whole countenance as she greets you with frank cordiality. The happy mixture—so to speak—of her inherited talents has resulted in a vivacious and sparkling originality of her own. From the one side of the house a gift for music and singing; from the other literary tendencies. Her father, Mr. Robert Brough, a well-known and brilliant *littérateur* of his day—poet, dramatic author, and novelist—died so early that his daughter was too young to remember him. Who does not know her uncle, Mr. Lionel Brough—so clever, versatile, and witty? He was the first of the talented family to come before the footlights. Of the young generation Fanny Brough was the first who elected to adopt a histrionic career at a very early age. Her cousin Sydney followed in her and in his father's steps, while her brother Robert is the popular manager of a theatre at Melbourne, and has their mother and a young sister in his company.

'On the whole,' says Fanny Brough demurely, ' I fancy I got more of my dramatic instincts from my mother's side than any musical lore. She is a most delightful singer, and a great favourite at Melbourne. She was the niece of the celebrated vocalist Miss Romer, of " Maritana," "The

Bohemian Girl," and "The Mountain Sylph" fame.'
But although Miss Brough speaks modestly of 'any
musical lore,' it is a fact very well known that she is a
brilliant pianist and a sweet singer. When you charge
her with this she laughs and says, ' There is so little time
to practise, and the singing has to slide somewhat, but the
playing never will; and one's voice suffers from non-practice
sooner than the fingers.'

The young player's first appearance was at the Prince's
Theatre at Manchester, when quite a child, as a fairy in
pantomime. She was terribly nervous, and the style of
dress rather troubled her; so that when some cousins in the
stalls afterwards informed her that they 'could not hear a
word she said,' she was inclined promptly to look on herself
as 'a failure.' 'It was Mr. Calvert's play,' she remarks.
' My kind, good friend; how much I owe him!' and she
sighs as she adds softly, after a pause, ' He died just as I
was beginning to feel my feet; but I have never forgotten the
good things he taught me, young as I was.' That these
' good things' bore good fruit was soon abundantly proved,
for only two years after this childish performance she found
herself at the same theatre playing Ophelia to Barry
Sullivan's Hamlet. Shortly after she made her *début* in
London at St. James's Theatre, under the management of
Mrs. John Wood, as Fernande in the play of that name.
Here a fierce difficulty had to be grappled with. It is probable that the very difficulty was of considerable service to
the young actress. The *rôle* was that of an *ingénue*, but
to such a very youthful *débutante* it appeared at first as if
she were heavily overweighted. However, here her ambition stepped in, and, concentrating all her powers and
energies, she soon vanquished the obstacles.

A little later, at the same theatre, she created the
heroine in ' War,' Mr. T. W. Robertson's last comedy.
The lamented author passed away while the piece was still
running. Her earlier parts are almost too numerous to
mention. For nearly a year she played a series of *ingénue*

rôles at the Gaiety with Mr. Toole and the late Mr. Charles Mathews. Then a provincial tour followed in the leading part of 'The Crisis,' with Mr. Wyndham's company, and a big success was scored in the original Ted Owen in 'The World.' Among many creations a special favourite was the Irish heroine Nora Fitzgerald in 'Harvest,' which, indeed, brought her prominently forward. She describes it as having been 'a delightful study.' None the less her masterly piece of character-sketching is Fuchsia Leech, the American heiress in 'Moths,' in which she 'revelled.' 'And you will remember how splendid Carlotta Addison was as Lady Dolly,' says the actress, eagerly, with that warm appreciation of a sister artist which is so attractive in her.

A succession of triumphs followed. In melodrama at Drury Lane she may be best remembered as Dorcas Gentle in Pettitt's 'Prodigal Daughter.' She declares at that time her ambition never vaulted higher than to play sentimental and weeping heroines, but the underlying spirit of mirth and humour could not long be suppressed, and, with considerable pathos likewise at her command, she has mounted to the foremost rank as a *comédienne*—wild farcical comedy occasionally, as in 'Mrs. Othello.' She has twice had tempting offers to go to America, but was unable at the time to accept them, as other engagements kept her in London, but she looks forward eagerly to 'a trip across some day,' and says it is only 'a pleasure deferred.'

A most finished and artistic performance of Fanny Brough's was Mrs. Egerton Bompas in Mr. Pinero's play of 'The Times' at Terry's Theatre. Her bright, sparkling nature found full vent in the impersonation of that character, which night after night evoked universal applause. Nor must another very big success be omitted. When Mr. George Alexander made his first start in management at the Avenue Theatre with the production of 'Dr. Bill'—a play which ran merrily through the whole season—it will long be remembered how delightfully she created the leading part of Mrs. Horton. At the end of that time she had to leave to join the Drury Lane company, being under a three years' engagement to Sir Augustus Harris, who used to 'lend' her to other managers while Drury Lane was closed. That enterprising manager and *impresario* has, however, lately recalled the loan, so to speak, and, as the heroine in the splendid spectacular melodrama 'Cheer, Boys, Cheer'—the finest, perhaps, that has ever been seen on the boards of Drury Lane—Fanny Brough won fresh laurels.

If, as will now and then happen, she gets a part where there is little comparatively to do, it is needless to say she does that little well. She is always contented, and when she has a *rôle* which at first sight looks as if it might not suit her, she studies to make herself suit the *rôle*, and this may be the secret of her unfailing success and popularity. In the matter of 'study' she is very quick, but she has no particular time for learning, and, indeed, not infrequently causes her people a little uneasiness on that score, for she is never seen to study; but presently some member of the family is asked to hear her go through her lines, as 'it is a help,' and then she is always found to be letter-perfect. 'As to being nervous,' she says, laughing, 'of course I am, but it is the nervousness that stimulates and exhilarates, and not the sort that paralyses.'

Now this charming actress has, among many versatile gifts, one that is all 'pure womanly.' She is nothing less than a genius with her needle; so is her mother, and so is her grandmother. For years she cut out and made every article that she wore on and off the stage. Nothing comes amiss to those nimble fingers. Of late, want of time prevents so much devotion to her needle and thimble. She is as fond of pretty clothes as anyone, but in that respect contents herself with her stage apparel, as she considers it 'a duty to the author, manager, and audience to be perfectly dressed there.'

Fond of the country and country pursuits, especially of driving, of which she 'can never have too much,' Fanny Brough finds her pretty home conveniently near London, while possessing many rural aspects. It is a large, old-fashioned house, within high walls, with some old trees in the still more old-fashioned garden. There is a great double hall opening out into several rooms. Her own special 'den' is simply but artistically furnished, and contains many little treasures. There is a picture standing on an easel, by which she sets great store. It was sent to her by the Spanish author of the play 'The Woman and the Law,' together with a letter of hearty congratulations and thanks on her brilliant creation of Petrella in that piece.

But, with all her excessive love of mirth, Fanny Brough can look as severe as a judge when occasion demands. In early days some juvenile actor would now and then mischievously declare, 'I'm going to make you laugh to-night,' but it was no use. The merriment springs from within, and her face would be set as immovably as the Sphinx; but she remarks, 'My sense of humour has served me in glorious stead throughout my whole life, and I should die if I could not laugh.'

OPINIONS OF THE PRESS

ON

"NOTABLE WOMEN AUTHORS OF THE DAY."

The Literary World.—" Readers of the *Lady's Pictorial* are already familiar with its bright and picturesque sketches of some of our well-known novelists, now republished under the title of 'Notable Women Authors of the Day.' The work is admirably done. . . . We feel that Mrs. Black's visits were somewhat different from those of the ordinary interviewer and that she possessed the tact and sympathy necessary to place herself thoroughly *en rapport* with the eminent women whom she visited. . . . Short as they are, they not only give a vivid impression of each author, but each is interspersed or introduced by some dainty bit of description or some historical reminiscence; while sketches of the home life, always characteristic but never impertinent, fill in the picture."

Saturday Review.—" The work is decidedly good work of the kind."

Court Journal.—" In her interesting and valuable volume, 'Notable Women Authors of the Day,' Mrs. Black has reprinted a number of interesting biographical and personal sketches of living authors. . . . Brightly and kindly written. . . ."

World.—" Mrs. Black writes with good feeling and good taste . . . the book will prove of very general interest. . . ."

Sunday Times.—" 'Notable Women Authors of the Day.' The reminiscences of well-known authors have been undertaken by Mrs. Helen C. Black. This lady has treated her task as a labour of love. . . . Mrs. Black has not given us a word too few or a word too many. . . . A biographical sketch of Jean Ingelow concludes Mrs. Black's delightful book."

Queen.—" It is as good as a novel with twenty-six heroines . . . the book is a lively and readable one, for Mrs. Black has collected her biographical and personal details with care and has handled them with literary skill."

Lady's Pictorial.—" The biographical sketches of 'Notable Women Authors of the Day,' which Mrs. Black was well advised to collect in this daintily got-up volume, originally appeared in the *Lady's Pictorial*. . . . A more acceptable gift-book for the gift season could not be found. . . . Mrs. Black's sketches are very bright and interesting, and there is in them just enough of those little personal details that readers love, but of vulgar and intrusive *personalities*, not a trace. . . . Mrs. Black has the happy knack of seizing upon the interesting episodes in the lives of the celebrities of whom she writes, and she sets them before us in simple and natural language."

Globe.—In " Notable Women Authors of the Day," Mrs. Helen C. Black supplies us with a series of biographical sketches and descriptive monographs. . . . These monographs are likely to have many well-pleased readers. The literary ladies dealt with are pictured in their habit as they live, while at the same time a succinct account of their career is given. . . . The public likes to read about the people who give it pleasure, and Mrs. Black's pleasant chit-chat will, we may expect, give great satisfaction to a large circle of readers."

Opinions of the Press—continued.

Overland Mail.—" Very few ladies resident abroad could fail to find an interest in Mrs. Black's 'Notable Women Authors of the Day,' a series of lively sketches of clever women who have by their writings impressed themselves on the age. Mrs. Black must be singularly sympathetic, for she has managed in these sketches to convey a really striking idea of each of the authors, and she is besides an intelligent critic of their work. . . . Mrs. Lynn Linton, Mrs. Riddell, Rhoda Broughton, John Strange Winter, Florence Marryat, Edna Lyall, Jessie Fothergill, with many others find a place in this gallery. Mrs. Black introduces them all round with grace and geniality."

Pioneer.—" Mrs. Black gives a cheerful, breezy, sympathetic portrait of her 'Notable Women Authors.' . . . The cleverness of Mrs. Black's style is brought out and illustrated by the effective touches and point she gives to the conversations, which place vividly before us their atmosphere and individuality. . . . There is a geniality and warmth about the description that is convincing and picturesque. Indeed, to read this bright, interesting and well-written book is to feel that whatever we may think of some of the novels, the writers thereof must, one and all, be charming."

Christian Leader.—" This fine volume is one which will be read by all with profit and interest. . . . Mrs. Black has much that is interesting to say, and she has said it gracefully and well. In her pen portraits she is especially happy, so much so that one feels as if one had been present at the visits and talked oneself with the various ladies in their homes. . . . As Mrs. Black has meted out impartial justice to all, no one will be disappointed on reading her most excellent volume."

Guardian.—" A book to reward patient reading . . . facts of real interest. . . . They are absolutely discreet."

Daily Chronicle.—"'Notable Women Authors of the Day.' Their portraits are here, in Mrs. Black's entertaining pages . . . this lively and well-written book."

Spectator.—" It could hardly have been more naturally or in better taste than in this volume by Mrs. Black . . . is thoroughly good natured. . . . She has got up her subjects with absolute conscientiousness. . . . She has a real command, also, of the style known as 'graphic,' and uses it to good purpose. . . . She supplies us with so much interesting information. . . . This book is almost all sunshine."

Manchester Examiner.—"'Notable Women Authors of the Day' is a book of permanent value and possesses great interest because of the insight it gives into the home-life of several of the female novelists. . . . Considerable tact is possessed by the author of these sketches. She has also a pleasant chatty style, and although we have here twenty-six lady novelists portrayed, there is no tedious uniformity of treatment. We see them as it were face to face."

Northern Weekly Whig.—" A delightful book for one's own perusal, and a most acceptable book to give as a present to some other woman, is Mrs. Black's 'Notable Women Authors of the Day,' a collection of articles written in a pleasant, chatty manner, and giving full and interesting details of all the authors dealt with. . . . The book is a capital one for reference, as well as entertainment."

Liverpool Mercury.—"'Notable Women Authors of the Day.' Mrs. Black's book is one of the most interesting volumes of literary history we have. It comes as womanly gossip, and this it is in the best sense, for it is sparkling and full of surprises. There is a dash of adventure, too, in connection with almost every paper, and the happy way in which the writer reaches her facts makes the story one of unmitigated enjoyment."

Nottingham Daily Guardian.—" Mrs. Black has made a charming addition to biographical literature in her 'Notable Women Authors of the Day.' . . . Most pleasantly described, and giving excellent pictures of the work, personality and surroundings of the subjects. . . . Full of interest. . . . The book is first rate as a work of reference, and Mrs. Black has a bright and graceful literary style."

Manchester Courier.—" In this volume we have presented in a permanent form a series of biographical and descriptive sketches of notable women authors. . . . The work is written in a genial, chatty, and entertaining form. . . . There is something entertaining on every page."

Eastbourne Chronicle.—"'Notable Women Authors.' A rapid sale of this readable work, which is from the facile pen of Mrs. Helen C. Black, has brought about another edition, which we are glad to welcome among the other cheery things of the season. The book contains a series of crisp biographical sketches of famous women authors of the day. . . . The papers contain in interesting and succinct form an abundance of biographical and literary details. . . . Mrs. Black is an ideal interviewer, a charming writer, and the perusal of her clever sketches cannot but afford sincere pleasure."

Oban Times.—" Carefully written biographical sketches of the more famous women authors of the day."

Scotsman.—" Brightly written and informative as it is, the volume answers well to the demand that always exists for a more intimate knowledge of an author's personal surroundings and history than her work gives."

Brechin Advertiser.—" All readers of the popular literature of the day will welcome this beautiful volume as giving, in a bright, lively, and gossipy way, an insight into the life of many authors whose writings afford them delight and instruction. . . . The author is well known as a graceful and effective writer, and she has evidently a wide knowledge and experience of life, literature, and character; and while depicting the talents and habits of her subjects, there is often a strong sense of the writer present. The volume is an important contribution to literary biography . . . it is sure to receive a warm welcome."

Bristol Mercury.—" Mrs. Black's articles give a pleasant account of the homes, tastes, and conversation of some of the principal novelists of the day . . . the volume makes an acceptable addition to the record of women's work."

Dumfries and Galloway Standard.—" This is a very handsome volume—a picture gallery of notable women authors, and much that is worth knowing of them communicated to the reader by a sympathetic biographer, who writes easily and never fails to interest. . . . The only regret one is apt to feel is that the number of the sketches is not greater."

Newcastle Daily Chronicle.—" Mrs. Black has a bright and sumptuous style. . . . Her agreeable book is embellished with reproductions of photographs."

Belfast News Letter.—" The volume deserves a good word to be said of it. . . . Many of Mrs. Black's sketches abound in interest. She is guilty of no error of taste. . . . Certainly many readers will welcome the little biographies of these writers."

Sheffield Independent.—" Those who wish to know something about the lives of the literary women of the day, cannot do better than purchase this chatty volume."

Southampton Times.—" 'Notable Women Authors of the Day,' by Mrs. Helen C. Black, is one of the most interesting and attractive gift books of the season. The talented author is well known to many of our readers, not only through her success in the world of literature, but also from the work of benevolence and mercy which for a long series of years she has carried on in our midst for the benefit of suffering humanity. . . . Her biographical sketches are replete with varied incident and personal reminiscence, which render them peculiarly interesting. Every one of us has his or her favourite authors, and it enhances our interest in their works to know something of them personally. Mrs. Black has afforded us an admirable opportunity of doing this. She brings us into pleasant and familiar acquaintance with the notable women sketched in this volume by her facile and discriminating pen, and wide circles of readers will be charmed and delighted with her life-like pictures."

Hampshire Independent.—" Mrs. Black is already well known far and wide beyond Southampton in connection with her Cottage Hospital, founded, established, and constantly visited by her. That she is a writer of no mean merit is probably not so well known. But the handsome volume before us reveals the fact. It seems that Mrs. Black was for some time a contributor of biographical and descriptive sketches to the *Lady's Pictorial*, and these have now been revised, enlarged, and brought up to date and reprinted in book form. . . . The style adopted by the writer is chatty and pleasant. . . . We cannot but enter into full sympathy with her mood. . . . Truly it requires a woman to properly describe a woman. Mrs. Black has performed her task in this respect with conspicuous success. . . . The subjects of the sketches stand before us distinctly, while the sketches themselves are altogether of exceeding interest, and form a most attractive volume of contemporary biography."

Kilmarnock Standard.—" 'Notable Women Authors of the Day.' This beautiful volume contains twenty-six sketches which originally appeared in the *Lady's Pictorial*. They are well worthy of permanent preservation in this handsome form. Exceedingly bright and readable in style, they are also full of valuable information with regard to the popular literature of the day. . . . Altogether the work is one of exceptional interest."

Glasgow Herald.—" 'Notable Women Authors of the Day,' by Helen C. Black. These sketches, which originally appeared as a series in the *Lady's Pictorial*, are no doubt already familiar to many readers. They are charmingly written, and as bright and attractive in point of style as they are interesting for the information which they convey, and few contributions to any of our periodicals are more deserving of republication. The volume which now contains them cannot fail to meet with a warm welcome from all who are not indifferent to contemporary literature."

PRACTICAL GASTRONOMY AND RECHERCHÉ COOKERY.

Containing up-to-date descriptions of the following branches:—Hors-d'Œuvres, Soups, Dressed Fish, Entrées, Removes, Sauces, Roasts, Second Course Dishes, Vegetables, Salads, Sweets, and Savouries, and much other information. By CHARLES H. SENN, Gold Medallist and Member of the Académie de Cuisine, Paris. THIRD EDITION. 1 vol. cloth, 926 pp. 10s. 6d.

JANE AUSTEN.

CHARADES, &c., written a hundred years ago. By JANE AUSTEN and her Family. With Introductory Note, Illustrations, and Portrait. Price 1s. 6d.; post-free, 1s. 8d.

CLUBS FOR 1896.

A List containing the Names and Addresses of 2,000 Social, Yacht, Golf, and other Clubs in London and the Counties of Great Britain and Ireland, in Foreign Countries and in the British Colonies. By E. C. AUSTEN LEIGH, M.A. Fcp. 8vo. Fourth Annual Edition. Price 1s.; post-free, 1s. 2d.

THE CHURCH QUARTERLY REVIEW.

Published in January, April, July, and October of each year. Price 6s.; or by Annual Subscription (received by the Publishers), £1.
Containing Articles on the following subjects—

Questions of the Day	Scepticism, Science, Philosophy, and Religion	Patristic Literature	Romanism
General Literature and History	Art and Archæology	Ecclesiastical Literature	Ritual
Biography	Biblical Criticism	The Anglican Position	Theology
		Dissent	Eschatology

Among the Contents for APRIL 1896, will be found the following Articles:—
Purcell's Life of Cardinal Manning.
The Denominational Tendency of State-Aided Education in Ireland.
Bishop Heber.
The French Pyrenees.
The New Poet Laureate.
Keble's Christian Year.

OFFICIAL PUBLICATIONS OF THE GENERAL MEDICAL COUNCIL.

THE BRITISH PHARMACOPŒIA. Price 7s. post-free.
THE MEDICAL REGISTER. Price 7s. 6d. post-free.
THE DENTISTS' REGISTER. Price 4s. post-free.
THE MEDICAL STUDENTS' REGISTER. Price 2s. 9d. post-free.
THE REGULATIONS FOR STUDENTS. Price 7d. post-free.

UNDER the SANCTION of the COMMITTEE of the STOCK EXCHANGE.

BURDETT'S OFFICIAL INTELLIGENCE FOR 1896.

Being a carefully revised précis of information regarding all classes of British, Colonial, American, and Foreign Securities. Contains particulars of some 8,000 undertakings—including Government, Corporation, Colonial, and Foreign Stocks; Railways, Banks, Canals, Docks, Electric Lighting, Financial, Gas, Insurance, Land, Mines, Shipping, Telegraphs, Tramways, Waterworks, and other Commercial and Industrial Companies, known to the London Market, and dealt in on the Principal Exchanges. 2,127 pp. price 42s. Carriage extra.

POOLE'S UNITED KINGDOM STOCK AND SHARE-BROKERS' DIRECTORY FOR 1896.

Containing information received direct from about 220 Principal Provincial Cities and Towns, including the various Stock Exchanges, with their Chairmen, Committees, Secretaries, Partnerships, &c., in Alphabetical Order; also Registered Telegraph Addresses and Telephone Numbers. Explanatory Introductions will be found at the head of each section. An Appendix is added which contains a selected list for London. Price 4s. 6d. net.

THE NAUTICAL MAGAZINE.

Published Monthly. Price 1s.
Contents of APRIL Number, 1896—
COWES AS A YACHTING CENTRE. By R. T. PRITCHETT. (Illustrated.)
THE NEW RULES FOR EXAMINATION OF MASTERS AND MATES. By Mr. J. BOLAM, of Leith.
THE DEVELOPMENT OF THE NAVAL PROGRAMME.
THE SEA TRIALS OF THE BELVILLE BOILERS. (Illustrated.)
THE DISPOSITION OF WEIGHTS AND THE TURNING POWER OF SHIPS.
AN ALTITUDE AZIMUTH DIAGRAM.
NOTES ON CURRENT EVENTS.

MARITIME NOTES AND QUERIES.

A Record of Shipping Law and Usage, and Book of Reference for Shipowners, Shipbrokers, Charterers, Consignees, Merchants, &c. Compiled, chiefly, from the *Shipping and Mercantile Gazette*. Vol. VIII. contains, among many general items of value and interest, specially treated cases of Bills of Lading, Brokerage and Commission, Charter Parties, Collision, Co-ownership, Demurrage and Lay-days, Freight, Insurance, Masters and Mates, Pilotage, Salvage, Seamen, Wages, &c., and the recent Merchant Shipping Acts.
Vols. I. to VII. are in stock. Price 7s. 6d. each; by post, 8s.

SPOTTISWOODE & CO., New-street Square, E.C., & 54 Gracechurch Street, E.C.

WALFORD'S
COUNTY FAMILIES OF THE UNITED KINGDOM.

"'Walford's County Families of the United Kingdom' is a compilation of such recognised utility, comprehensiveness and merit that it is not surprising that its popularity grows from year to year. It has reached its thirty-first issue, and has attained to the position of being *one of the most frequently consulted manuals of the aristocracy of the three kingdoms.* The plan adopted remains unaltered. A brief notice is given of the parentage, birth, marriage, and education of each person (with the name of his heir, apparent or presumptive), and also a record of the offices held by him, together with his town address and country residence. Such is its scope, and it may be seen that, apart from the changes rendered necessary by the efflux of time, the editor has to keep a watchful eye upon the other causes which lead to the gradual renewal of the titled classes. As heretofore, the volume is prepared with the greatest accuracy and attention to detail, and the high reputation of 'Walford' is well maintained."

Daily Telegraph.

Walford's County Families of the United Kingdom for 1896.
Price 50s. *Crown 8vo. Handsomely bound.*

LONDON:
CHATTO & WINDUS, 214 PICCADILLY, W.

www.ingramcontent.com/pod-product-compliance
Lightning Source LLC
Chambersburg PA
CBHW030424300426
44112CB00009B/846